Armed with Abundance

Armed with Abundance

Consumerism & Soldiering
in the Vietnam War

MEREDITH H. LAIR

The University of North Carolina Press
CHAPEL HILL

Set in Charis and Univers

Manufactured in the United
States of America

The paper in this book meets the
guidelines for permanence and
durability of the Committee on
Production Guidelines for Book
Longevity of the Council on
Library Resources.

The University of North Carolina
Press has been a member of the
Green Press Initiative since 2003.

Library of Congress Cataloging-in-Publication Data
Lair, Meredith H.
    Armed with abundance : consumerism and soldiering
in the Vietnam War / Meredith H. Lair. — 1st ed.
        p. cm.
    Includes bibliographical references and index.
    ISBN 978-0-8078-3481-7 (cloth : alk. paper)
    1. United States. Army—History—Vietnam War, 1961–
1975. 2. United States. Army—Military life—History—
20th century. 3. Soldiers—United States—Social life
and customs—20th century. 4. Lifestyles—United
States—History—20th century. 5. Consumption (Eco-
nomics)—Social aspects—United States—History—
20th century. 6. United States—Moral conditions—
History—20th century. 7. Vietnam War, 1961–1975—
Social aspects. I. Title. II. Title: Consumerism and
soldiering in the Vietnam War.
    DS558.2.L35 2011
    959.704'31—dc23   2011022140

15 14 13 12 11   5 4 3 2 1

To my father, who served,
and my mother, who waited

CONTENTS

ILLUSTRATIONS, TABLES, AND MAP

ILLUSTRATIONS

TABLES

MAP

One of the first Vietnam War stories I ever heard was about a Viet Cong prisoner. In fact, I heard the story several times as I talked to my father, a two-time Vietnam veteran, for school projects in middle school, high school, and college. My fascination with the Vietnam War stemmed from the emotion and mystery that pervaded its discussion when I was a kid in the 1980s and from a profound sense of pride I had—and still have—in my father's service. Now, as I am helping to write the history of the Vietnam War myself, I return to the story of the Viet Cong prisoner once more because every story needs a beginning, and my father's stories are how the Vietnam War began for me.

My dad was an adviser in Quang Ngai Province, on the central coast of South Vietnam, from September 1964 to September 1965. Life on the advisory compound was a bleak yet professionally satisfying existence, and it lacked most of the material abundance described later in this book. He was a young first lieutenant, just two years out of West Point, advising Regional Forces infantry officers, some of whom had been fighting communists for ten years. One day, on an operation in the countryside, they captured a Viet Cong insurgent who had been hiding in a canal. The prisoner had a wound on his hip but also a head wound that had gone undetected because he had been submerged in cold water and because he was standing up. When the Vietnamese medics laid him down to treat his hip, the head wound began spurting blood, and the man went into shock. Those on the scene did what they could to help, except for a man called Mr. Ba, who led a CIA-funded special intelligence platoon. "I was taking my poncho off to cover him up to try to get him warm," my dad explained in an interview I recorded in October 1993, "when Mr. Ba said something to the effect of 'I'll treat him for shock,' and . . . he just took his carbine and walked up and put two bullets in the back of the guy's head. I was just stunned."

When my dad later let me read his war diary, kept faithfully from September 1964 until May 1965, I learned some forgotten details of the killing. In an entry dated Sunday, 24 January 1965, he wrote, "By this time, the prisoner was bleeding profusely and having convulsions. Mr. Ba, of the spe-

cial platoons, ended the man's misery by firing two bullets into his head."
But the wounded prisoner was not alone. In the diary, my dad describes
seeing multiple prisoners being "given the usual rough treatment" by their
captors, and the sound of gunshots, away from prying American eyes, indicated that several were executed at the end of the operation. "This was the
first time I had seen this done," my dad wrote, "but by this time my senses
were numb to bloodletting." The diary also describes the aftermath of the
wounded prisoner's killing. "A senseless footnote to Ba's act of mercy (or
murder) was Dien, my interpreter, and a V.N. Lieutenant firing into the
dead body."

The story unfolded to me in fragments over a period of years as new
details emerged from the eddy of memory. But I was far more affected by it
than my dad, who, as a professional soldier, has always displayed a remarkable ability to compartmentalize his memories, to set them aside and place
them in context, as though the terrible things he witnessed were witnessed
by someone else. As I look back now, after years of research, teaching, and
writing about Vietnam, the story still fascinates me because it captures so
much of the grim essence of the war. First, the story's modest scale is far
more typical of Vietnam combat operations than epic engagements like the
Battle of the Ia Drang Valley, the siege of Khe Sanh, or the Sisyphean assault
on Hamburger Hill. But the little details—the wounded prisoner's convulsions, a stream of blood as thick as your finger—are potent reminders of
the intimate trauma involved in watching even one person die a violent
death. Second, the composition of the Regional Forces and their behavior
are instructive of the volatility and complexity of South Vietnam's politics.
As non-Vietnamese ethnic minorities, the Regional Forces soldiers relished
the opportunity to mishandle Viet Cong prisoners, who in this case were
ethnic Vietnamese, and they executed them in violation of international
standards. The Regional Forces troops' contemptuous approach to human
life raised ethical questions about U.S. support for the Saigon regime, while
their ethnically motivated hostility speaks to the anger and divisiveness
that plagued the fledgling nation of South Vietnam. But the Vietnamese
medics tried to treat the wounded Viet Cong prisoner, suggesting that any
narrative that universally vilifies the United States' ally as incompetent,
amoral, or unprofessional is overly simplistic.

Finally, there is the reaction of my father, whose shock and dismay capture the moment when a young officer realized the limitations of his training to manage the swift chaos of a real war. Nearly thirty years on, his
words to me were measured, but they still suggested an internal struggle

over just what was the right thing to do. "We had no hope of saving this guy . . . but my instinct—and the Vietnamese medics who were treating his hip wound when he went into shock—and this little CIA hireling went over and just put him out of his misery." He did not finish the sentence, but the thought was complete: "But my instinct was to try." For me, the spontaneous act of taking off a poncho to keep a dying man warm has come to represent all the good intentions American soldiers carried with them when they went to war in Vietnam. I kept that thought with me when I subsequently read and learned of the atrocities and degradations Americans also visited on the South Vietnamese. That this flash of compassion was extinguished so swiftly, with a cold-blooded execution, and that it was not even clear which option was more humane—well, that says everything about war, too.

There was also a practical consideration in the story of the wounded Viet Cong prisoner that relates directly to the material conditions of the Vietnam war zone addressed in this book. There was no way to evacuate him for treatment before he would surely die. The sophisticated logistical apparatus that would, just two or three years later, protect American soldiers from harm and insulate them from hardship had yet to reach the advisers who lived in Quang Ngai in early 1965. I know this from another story my dad told me, about an American sergeant who died of a shrapnel wound to the belly. No helicopter medical evacuation was available in the field, not even for an American soldier, at that point in the war. The other soldiers on hand commandeered a cot from a local villager's home, placed the dying sergeant upon it, and then ran the improvised litter, on foot, over a mile back to the airfield. They managed to put him on a flight to a base with a hospital, at Danang or Nha Trang, but it was too far, and he did not make it. The sergeant's death deeply affected me because it seemed just like how a war was supposed to be—dangerous, austere, and exquisitely tragic.

When my dad returned to South Vietnam for a second tour, in 1970, he found that the U.S. military had made a new world there, and it was like no war zone he could have imagined. When I was growing up, he told me those stories, too, about the "suffocating luxury" of Long Binh Post, where he was stationed for six months. He worked at U.S. Army Vietnam Headquarters as an "action officer" in the Non-appropriated Funds Branch of the office of the deputy chief of staff for personnel and administration. Being an action officer did not involve much action, just writing briefings and reports in an air-conditioned office, but he did hear outrageous stories about American corruption from colleagues charged with investigating the open mess system. It was a comfortable existence, but it hardly seemed worth the sacrifice of leaving his family for a year. He couldn't wait to move on, which he did in 1971, heading up-country to Bong Son and the 173rd Airborne Brigade, whose Sky Soldiers were still fighting a war the American people had already decided was over. As a kid, I struggled to reconcile the disparate parts of my father's Vietnam service with one another and to reconcile the war at Long Binh with popular treatments that framed the conflict solely in terms of spectacular violence and crushing deprivation. Decades later, this book is the product of that wondering. I know that the war zone abundance described in these pages will never supplant the image of wartime Vietnam as a violent wilderness nor will the experiences of support troops dislodge the idea of American soldiers as universal combat veterans. But perhaps the alternative view of war presented here will help readers rethink their assumptions about soldiering, wartime suffering, and American power and, in so doing, restore noncombat veterans and their sacrifices to the Vietnam War story.

Not many people can claim that their dad gave them the idea for their first book when they were twelve years old, but that is kind of what happened. When I conducted that very first research project, in seventh grade, my father was the first of dozens of people over the years to facilitate my work with an act of kindness: he let me cut up his Vietnam War photographs for a poster-sized collage. It was the first of many debts I would incur in my development as a scholar. In the years that followed, several public school teachers, especially Tom Pollock, Ginny Crowley, and Mark Ellwood, taught me to write and cultivated my interest in history; I find myself imparting lessons I learned from them to my own students day after day. At Penn State University, Daniel Beaver, Lori Ginzberg, Adam Rome, and Nan Woodruff taught me how to use the tools of the social and cultural historian, and Carol Reardon and William Duiker provided excellent training, from very different perspectives, on the Vietnam War. I owe a special thanks to Gary Cross, whose seminars on consumer culture later helped me to recognize the significance of all the *stuff* I kept noticing in the Vietnam war zone, and to Nan, who continues, in great friendship, to help me navigate the strange world of academia.

The blessings I enjoyed in my education have only been compounded in my professional life at George Mason University, where two semesters of leave and generous research travel grants were instrumental in preparing the manuscript for publication. My Mason colleagues in the Department of History and Art History, faculty and staff alike, have been exemplars of generosity and kindness. Cindy Kierner, Mike O'Malley, and Brian Platt were especially helpful as I picked my way through the publication and tenure mazes. My faculty mentor, Suzy Smith, deserves special thanks for knowing when to prod, when to back off, and when to call time out. I am so grateful to have her in my corner. Roy Rosenzweig and Larry Levine both played important roles in my hiring at Mason, and I am forever grateful for the interest and confidence they expressed in my work. I hope, wherever they are, that I have made them proud.

The research for this book was challenging because I was interested in facets of war—recreation, leisure, shopping—that nobody cared much about, which meant that the resources I needed were often obscure. I realized just how obscure when I peeled apart a Vietnam-era memo at the National Archives and found a Vietnamese mosquito still pressed between the pages. On my innumerable trips to that facility, archivist Richard Boylan and his staff worked tirelessly to find tons of weird stuff that no one had ever requested before. Mr. Boylan, especially, went above and beyond professional courtesy, at one point redacting documents for me on the spot. The staff at the Military History Institute at Carlisle Barracks was also endlessly courteous and helpful, especially John Slonaker. He was kind enough to grant me special dispensation from the institute's strict copying policies, which enabled me to read its collection of Vietnam-era military newspapers in its entirety. I can only repay Mr. Boylan and Mr. Slonaker by helping other scholars to overcome the barriers they confront in the research process.

Over the years, many colleagues in the profession at large have facilitated my research and weighed in on the manuscript and the ideas contained therein. Many thanks to David Brandt, for solving a vexing title problem, and to Jennifer Mittelstadt, who helped me think through the social and cultural meaning of the P.X. for American military personnel. As the formal readers for the manuscript, Christian Appy and Michael Foley provided daunting yet necessary feedback, and I am indebted to them for the time and care they invested in making this a better book. Michael Kramer, D. Michael Bottoms, and Christopher Hamner also read drafts of various parts, identifying problems in the text and, even better, proposing solutions to fix them. A special thanks to Mike Kramer for sharing my fascination with the ephemera of the Nam and for his generous spirit in sending all sorts of rare evidence my way.

I am also indebted to Stephen Krüger and Dennis Mansker, who graciously allowed me to use their Vietnam-era photos, and to M.Sgt. Steve

Opet, whose artistic talents are on display in the final chapter. The last people to handle this text were the good souls at the University of North Carolina Press, who have been exceedingly patient with this first-time author. Many thanks to my editor, Chuck Grench, and to all of the staff there for their hard work and thoughtful insights in bringing this project to fruition.

As every scholar knows, the line between the personal and the professional is gossamer thin, so much of the debt for this book is owed to people who provided advice, care, nourishing meals, distractions both wholesome and debauched, laughter, and love over the past few years. Many thanks to Anastasia Christman, Marcos De Leon, Christopher Hamner, Matt Isham, Sharon Leon, Liz Marshall, Erika Melman, Rachel Spector, Jen Werner, Sarah Richardson Whelan, and three dear Mikes—Bottoms, Kramer, and Smith—for their ongoing friendship. And finally, to my family, who have made all of my success possible: Mom, Dad, Dave, and Heather, the words "thank you" are so small, so inadequate to the task of describing my towering gratitude. The only thing greater than my appreciation is my love for all of you. Lydia and Wes, I have been writing this book your entire lives, and now it is done, on Lydia's birthday. I can't think of a better present to give you both.

ACRONYMS AND ABBREVIATIONS

AAFES	Army and Air Force Exchange Service
AFVN	American Forces Vietnam Network
AWOL	absent without leave (permission)
CIA	Central Intelligence Agency
CMTS	Command Military Touring Show
COLA	cost-of-living allowance
CONUS	continental United States
DEROS	date eligible for return from overseas
DFAC	dining facility
DMZ	Demilitarized Zone
G.I.	a member of the U.S. armed forces, especially a soldier in the U.S. Army; commonly taken to be an abbreviation for "government issue"
I.G.	inspector general
KBR	Kellogg, Brown, and Root
K.P.	kitchen police, or kitchen patrol
L.N.	local national, in reference to South Vietnamese civilian employees
L.Z.	landing zone
MACV	Military Assistance Command Vietnam
MOS	Military Occupational Specialty
MVA	Modern Volunteer Army
MWR	morale, welfare, and recreation
NCO	noncommissioned officer
NLF	National Liberation Front (Viet Cong)
PACEX	Pacific Exchange
P.X.	post exchange
R&R	rest and relaxation, or rest and recuperation
REMF	rear echelon motherfucker

RMK-BRJ	Raymond International, Morrison-Knudson, Brown and Root, and J. A. Jones Construction
TCN	third-country national
USAFI	United States Armed Forces Institute
USARV	U.S. Army Vietnam
USO	United Service Organizations
V.C.	Viet Cong (NLF)
VRE	Vietnam Regional Exchange
VVAW	Vietnam Veterans Against the War

Armed with Abundance

And no moves left for me at all but to write down
some few last words and make the dispersion,
Vietnam Vietnam Vietnam, we've all been there.
—Michael Herr, *Dispatches*

Vietnam and surrounding area

A War Refined

Reframing the Narrative of the Vietnam War

When Phil Kiver got out of the military in 2005, he published a diary about his experiences as a U.S. Army journalist who deployed in the global war on terror. His story emphasizes the danger, privation, and sacrifice endured by American troops, elements that are typical fare in memoirs of conflict. Where Kiver's book departs from the norm is with its glimpses into the banal details of daily life on an American base: shuffling papers around an office, sunbathing at the local pool, and chowing down at a typical military dining facility (DFAC). This last experience is depicted with a photograph of his base's DFAC, in particular its dessert bar, where an attendant clad in full chef's attire waits at the ready with a pastry server to dish up an array of sugary treats: slices of chocolate and vanilla sheet cake and wedges of torte and cheesecake, all piped high with frosting and whipped cream. Behind the dessert bar, soldiers in uniform eat at orderly tables beneath a ceiling of fluorescent lights festooned with colorful banners, the heraldry of a modern army. One can imagine the clatter of trays and cutlery punctuating the dull hum of conversation, as well as the thick aroma of American cafeteria fare. The scene is completely unremarkable, except for the body armor, weapons, and setting: Iraq circa 2004.[1]

It is difficult to reconcile Kiver's photograph, and the order and abundance it suggests, with traditional ideas about war. Compared with iconic images of modern conflict—Mathew Brady's gallery of corpses at Antietam, Robert Capa's grainy snapshots from Omaha Beach, Larry Burrows's unsparing portraits of American infantrymen in Vietnam, not to mention representations of noncombatants such as Margaret Bourke-White's stark photos of prisoners at Buchenwald, Nick Ut's napalm girl, or even the hooded prisoner at Abu Ghraib—the DFAC photograph is simultaneously comforting and unsettling. American troops abroad are well cared for, and rightfully so, but where is the danger and privation, war's faithful companions? And where is the suffering that comes of violence, or the hardship that sanctifies those who create it? These features existed, certainly, in other corners of the Iraq War, but not on the big bases where most Americans were stationed. And the elaborate DFAC itself was a cornerstone of daily life for American military personnel in the war zone, a banal fact of the occupation that complicates the public understanding of soldiering and veteranhood. Methodical and well provisioned, the armed force depicted in the photograph represents America at war.

The abundance Phil Kiver found so noteworthy in Iraq was not new to American warfare, for it first appeared in Vietnam some forty years before. But Kiver, like most Americans, was unaware of those antecedents, so complete is their erasure from public memory of the conflict. Reflecting on the DFAC photo, he compared his observations of the present with his impressions of the past, and he found his own service wanting. "To be honest, I never ate the dessert," he wrote. "I always thought of soldiers in wars past who never had it as good as this."[2] Kiver's assessment of the dessert bar was based on assumptions about what it was like to soldier in earlier wars: that a wartime deployment guaranteed danger and privation, that suffering was an integral part of historical military service, and that the urgency of life in the combat zones of yore rendered simple pleasures like fresh cake an impossibility. The U.S. military encouraged comparisons like this—hence the symbols, place-names, and rituals on every base that invoke past victories and losses. The flags floating over the DFAC's dessert bar connected the activities of Kiver's peers to the struggles and triumphs of their forebears, even as the desserts themselves complicated the narrative of shared sacrifice.

Soldiers' living conditions are not just the incidental details of setting, for they deeply influence a war story's plotting and interpretation in history. In the context of the Vietnam War, erroneous assumptions about soldiers' living conditions inform the public's ideas not just about what it was like to serve in that war but also about Vietnam veterans, who are presumed to have suffered material deprivations for the national interest. The imagined circumstances of a soldier's deployment also sustain the citizen-soldier ideal, which elevates veterans above ordinary citizens precisely because of their sacrifices on the nation's behalf. Ultimately, these assumptions inform ideas about the American way of war—in particular, that Americans go to war reluctantly and that austerity and deprivation are standard components of a brutal but necessary process. Because most American servicemen volunteered for duty—a majority during the Vietnam era, and all of them since 1973—whatever privations they endured were self-imposed, allowing the public to imagine each tour of duty as a purifying act of sacrifice that helps, in the story of a war, to clarify who deserves to win. Taken together, these misapprehensions form a powerful but deeply flawed narrative: American wars are fought by ascetic citizen-soldiers who willingly forgo the comforts of home to serve the homeland, and the nation is represented abroad by valorous warriors confronting mortal peril in an equal fight with a dastardly foe.

It is a good story, and for Americans, a comforting and affirming story, but it bears little resemblance to what actually happened in Southeast Asia in the 1960s. There, the U.S. military built an Americanized world for its soldiers to inhabit, while the high-tech nature of American warfare and a sophisticated logistics effort to care for the troops guaranteed that a majority of soldiers—perhaps 75 to 90 percent, depending on when they served[3]—labored in supporting roles, out of danger and in relative comfort. Material satisfaction displaced national interest as the animating war goal for many individuals because military authorities sought to encourage soldiers' compliant service with a high standard of living, relative to earlier wars, to Vietnamese poverty, and especially to the troops' expectations. Though unfamiliar in popular representations of the Vietnam War, this version of the conflict is well documented in military records, and it drew frequent comment from soldiers serving in Vietnam at the time. For example, when headquarters staff of the 34th General Support Group developed an orientation guide for personnel new to Vietnam, they chose three images to represent the American war experience there: a soldier in fatigues dancing with a big-haired blond in a striped minidress and knee-high boots; a belt of ammunition being fed into a machine gun; and an ice cream machine pumping fluffy soft-serve into a five-gallon canister. The caption read, "Beauty . . . Bullets, and . . . Ice Cream." The contrasts were deliberate, the irony palpable, and the images utterly representative of the American occupation of Vietnam.[4]

∽∘∾

War is cruelty, and you cannot refine it.
—William Tecumseh Sherman, 1864

The landscape of the Vietnam War has become familiar terrain. An author or filmmaker need only reference red earth, lush jungle, and the distant whir of helicopters, and we are there. We know the characters, too: impoverished Vietnamese peasants eking out a living, weary G.I.'s on combat patrol, and Viet Cong guerrillas waiting, watchful and silent. The violent encounters between these groups constitute some of the most searing moments of the twentieth century, and photographers, it seemed, were ever present to record the aftermath. For me, no single image better captures the combat world of the Vietnam War than Henri Huet's famous photograph of wounded medic Thomas Cole tending to an injured comrade, which graced the cover of *Life* magazine in February 1966. Cole's own bloody bandage covers most of his face, so that he must tip his head back to stare into the camera's lens, and his arm is extended toward us in an unfinished gesture of need. The medic's knee rests against the arm of a third figure, another soldier who lies just beyond the photo's edge. This man's upturned palm and gently bent fingers suggest a body at rest, forever or nearly so, and the close quarters of the trench imply a sheltered corner of the battle so small that life and death lay pressed against each other in a fierce embrace. The photograph depicts a world of mud and shadow, brutality and tenderness, privation and want; a world of limitless violence and endless horror; a world in which no other world exists beyond the frame.

In the following chapters, I will stretch that frame and reorient it toward another world of the Vietnam War, one that existed just miles away, where the mud was tamped into orderly streets, where ball caps replaced bandages, and where beauty and ice cream took precedence over the bullets. In Vietnam, the vast majority of American troops—at least 75 percent of them—did not serve in combat. Rather, they filled myriad supporting roles and lived on rearward bases far from the sufferings and deprivations of contested areas. And many of those who participated in combat, especially airmen, returned to comfortable, well-stocked base camps when an operation was over, lending the production of the war's violence a surreal, workaday quality. The U.S. military authorized these built environments in order to raise soldier morale, the better to keep up the fight and win the war, or at least to prevent the occupation's total collapse. It flooded the war zone with consumer goods to provide succor to soldiers' bodies as they worked and fought, but also to wrap the war's veterans in superficial affluence upon returning home. The U.S. occupation also had a profound impact on Vietnamese society, as American soldiers demonstrated the merits of capitalism through their extensive purchases, which often included Vietnamese labor and bodies as sources of gratification.

In the end, though, consumer goods and corporeal satisfaction were

Henri Huet's photograph of medic Thomas Cole treating other soldiers despite his own wounds graced the cover of *Life* magazine in February 1966. Huet's twelve-photo essay on Cole helped to establish the Vietnam War as a barren landscape of violence and deprivation in the American public's imagination. (Henri Huet/A.P. Photo)

poor substitutes for a just and winnable cause. Despite favorable material circumstances, soldiers still withheld their support for the Vietnam project in great numbers, and they struggled with the cultural meaning of the bounty they found in the war zone. Some soldiers lamented that their tours of duty failed to meet their own expectations of wartime military service, while others burnished their experiences with borrowed tales of heroism.

The lavish spending in the rear also created a caste system of well-fed, well-protected support personnel who were intensely resented by combat troops in forward areas. At the nexus of burgeoning self-interest, material plenty, and military occupation, soldiers found themselves inhabitants of "the Nam," a social and psychological construct in which contact with the war was mediated by distance, consumer goods, and media itself and where stateside checks on carnal appetites failed to reach. These comfortable, material circumstances equipped U.S. forces to generate violence, and, despite a conflict laden with futility, the war machine was always viciously effective. American soldiers were, quite literally, armed with abundance, making the project of war perhaps easier and certainly more palatable.

This alternative warscape offers a startling contrast to the bleak circumstances suggested by the Huet photograph and other iconic representations of the Vietnam War. Though the American way of war changed dramatically in Vietnam, when the U.S. military began to provide its soldiers with a degree of comfort unparalleled in military history, the public's understanding of the soldier's wartime experience still emphasizes danger and austerity. These perceptions have been formed and reinforced by thousands of histories and popular treatments of the war that established the Vietnam paradigm as a savage jungle in which violence is elemental and combat a way of life. In film and fiction, a Vietnam backstory is an easy way for a writer to establish a character's gravitas, and always, the fictional veteran's melancholy, bitterness, competence, or insanity is attributed to his time in combat. Virtually all movies about the war focus on combat, and even those that foreground the ironic absurdities of base camp life, such as *Full Metal Jacket* and *Apocalypse Now*, suggest that bases saturated with American popular culture were the quirky anomalies of the war's setting; violence still dominated its plot. Video games, in particular, have erased noncombat elements from the Vietnam story altogether, as they place the gamer in a world of war where all soldiers are warriors who can fight on endlessly. They have no need for food, rest, or comfort items, and no one has to clean out the latrines.

Even when noncombat experiences are acknowledged in treatments of the war, with a photograph in an edited collection or a few pages in a book, the proportions are misleading. For example, the photo-essay *Vietnam: Images from Combat Photographers* includes a snapshot of some soldiers playing basketball on a large American base. The caption explains, "Only a fifth of American soldiers spent the majority of their time on combat duty. For the rest, who staffed the military's massive logistical and clerical organization, supplies of American food, drink, music, and recreation made Vietnam a bit more familiar." The scale of the statistic one-fifth is lost, however, when nearly every other photograph in the collection depicts combat or its aftereffects.[5] Charts depicting the buildup of U.S. troops, a common device in histories of the war, yield a similarly misleading result. The numbers grow with every passing year, yet no distinction between combat and noncombat troops is made. Implicit in the statistics, then, is the message that the United States could not prevail in Vietnam despite a massive combat effort.[6]

Commemorative sites have hewed to this narrative, with the most influential example being the Vietnam Veterans Memorial in Washington, D.C. The endless rows of names are, in and of themselves, suggestive of death in combat, though over 10,000 of them—more than one-sixth the total—belong to men (and seven women)[7] who died of non-combat-related causes such as disease, suicide, homicide, drug overdose, motor vehicle and air accidents, base camp fires, drowning on recreational beaches, and other "misadventures," as the Department of Defense characterized them. Ironically, the Vietnam Women's Memorial adjacent to the Wall, which was installed to honor female Vietnam veterans, none of whom served in combat roles, also perpetuates battle as the war's dominant motif. The sculpture depicts a nurse shielded by sandbags cradling a wounded soldier in her arms—a staging more suggestive of a pietà than of an actual Vietnam War medical situation. Forgotten in all of these representations are the experiences of noncombat troops like Joe Dunn, an Army clerk in Vietnam, who served his year compliantly and without trauma. "I was not a hero; I was not a rebel," he recalled in his memoir, one of perhaps two dozen written by noncombat veterans about their service. "In many ways, I represented the norm of Vietnam veterans: I went, I bitched, I did my duty."[8]

Despite how it has been portrayed, the Vietnam War was, for most Americans who served in it, about making do, doing more with less, and making the best of it, but it was seldom about doing without. In that sense, the typical tour of duty in Vietnam reflected the essence of midcentury America, as the U.S. military flooded the war zone with consumer goods. In the 1950s, many Americans were able to leave behind the austere, work-centered days of the Depression and World War II to revel in the consumption-driven, leisure-oriented culture created by postwar prosperity. With wartime rationing programs lifted, Americans' pent-up desires to consume were unleashed just when wartime savings and G.I. Bill benefits were launching millions of working-class families into the ranks of the middle class. Cold War imperatives to demonstrate the economic and moral superiority of capitalism provided political and ideological justifications for indulgence, while television revolutionized advertising by beaming not just commercials but also programs replete with ideal homes and must-have products directly into American living rooms. It was a perfect storm of means, marketing, and desire that established a new minimum standard of living in the United States. The process also culturally entrenched two ideas about consumption: that material goods were the final measure of an individual's social worth, and that their frequent acquisition was the citizen's duty to the state.[9] When the children of the baby boom grew up and headed to Vietnam, they took with them expectations that the experience would be ugly and brutal, an understanding of war informed by collective memories of World War II and Korea. But they also brought with them high standards for what constituted comfort and satiety, standards that had been cultivated by the ethos of abundance in which so many of them were reared. Upon discovering that the Vietnam War would deliver relatively few opportunities for heroism and glory, American soldiers adjusted their John Wayne expectations to demand comfortable living conditions, time for leisure activities, abundant recreational facilities, and easy access to mass-produced consumer goods.

This new base camp culture in the midst of an active war zone was also the product of the U.S. military's own bureaucratization. During the same postwar period, the Pentagon borrowed administrative procedures from corporate America that rationalized the production of violence but that also undermined soldiers' faith in their leaders and the project of war itself. As Loren Baritz argues in *Backfire*, the Pentagon's adoption of corporate America's "up or out" promotional model recast officers as personnel managers and soldiers as workers. The resulting professional culture was inherently conservative, rewarding compliance rather than risk taking and penalizing those who questioned conventional wisdom. Under this system, officers fixated on "ticket-punching" to further their careers, rendering wartime deployment a necessary rung on the professional ladder. During the Vietnam War, the Pentagon further encouraged officers' self-interestedness by rotating them in and out of combat commands without regard for unit cohesion or leadership experience. Douglas Kinnard's post-Vietnam survey of the general officers who served there found that 87 percent regarded "careerism," defined as self-promotion at the expense of the mission, as a major impediment to victory. Short-term number crunching—bodies counted, weapons captured, hills taken—substituted for long-term strategy in Vietnam. As H. R. McMaster argues in *Dereliction of Duty*, military leaders at the highest level, the Joint Chiefs of Staff, had profound but unspoken doubts about whether the war could be won, causing them to focus on "means rather than ends"—that is, on managing the war rather than promoting a strategy likely to win it. These "five silent men" appeared to prize the institutional survival of the American military bureaucracy more than victory over communism, and their actions set the tone for how many of the men who served under them would approach their duties in Vietnam.[10]

Compounding the morale problems suggested by this necrotic institutional culture, political leaders failed to provide the American public with a convincing explanation for the war, leaving the men asked to fight it, in Baritz's words, with "no animating justification for combat or for risk."[11] Many soldiers, sensing the dangerous absurdity of their situation, questioned the necessity of their sacrifices, which for combat troops involved the potential loss of life or limb and for all soldiers was the loss of time, work, school, love, freedom, and the countless joys of family half a world away. Like industrial laborers in civilian life, the soldier-workers of the U.S. military found strength in their numbers, striking implicit bargains with their employers that exchanged compliant service for improved material conditions. To check this unsavory, unstable arrangement, Pentagon officials quietly backed President Nixon's 1968 campaign pledge to end the draft, planning for an all-volunteer force that was finally implemented in 1973. Instead of modern minutemen temporarily embracing their patriotic duty, the new model would consist of professional soldiers for hire selling their service to the state.[12]

Generous wartime spending on facilities for the troops in Vietnam was also an outgrowth of the ongoing privatization of American warfare, a process begun in the late nineteenth century. Instead of nationalizing shipbuilding and garrison construction in the 1880s, Congress elected to provide for an enhanced common defense by hiring private firms to build coastal fortifications and ships for the U.S. Navy. The precedent established then flourished in the twentieth century, with massive defense spending during the world wars and a sprawling Cold War that promised never ending conflict around the globe. Public reactions to the growing "military industrial complex" wavered. In 1934, accusations that "merchants of death" in the munitions industry had dragged the United States into the Great War resulted in a Senate investigation that documented a troubling relationship between arms dealers and American foreign policy, ratifying some Americans' support for neutrality in the impending world war. But just a few years later, government propaganda and corporate marketing campaigns jointly celebrated industry's commitment to defeating fascism and Japanese imperialism in World War II, cementing a partnership between the private sector and the federal government where warfare was concerned. The privatization of American war zones increased dramatically during the Vietnam War, diminished during the economically lean years of its immediate aftermath, and then exploded in its wake, culminating in Iraq, where private contract employees outnumbered American soldiers by 2005.

In the 1960s, hundreds of corporations received contracts worth billions of dollars to support the U.S. military's venture in Southeast Asia. Private construction and engineering firms built much of South Vietnam's new infrastructure at U.S. taxpayers' expense, and they supplied the U.S. military with the roads, runways, and cantonments required of a massive conventional force. Shipping concerns, food manufacturers, electronics dealers, and even carmakers provided the amenities and consumer goods that made military service in Vietnam so palatable for so many. Even if doing business with the U.S. military in Vietnam yielded only modest profits, as many contractors claimed, the potential for penetrating Asian markets with manufactured goods was ample incentive for private firms to go all in.

By hiring Vietnamese and third-country-national (TCN) employees to clean the barracks, peel the potatoes, and take out the trash, the contract system in Vietnam spared American soldiers a lot of manual labor, but it also challenged their faith in the legitimacy of the Vietnam project. Though G.I.'s serving in the war zone were not privy to the contracts, they saw American conglomerates' tankers, tractor-trailers, bulldozers, crates, cartons, and advertisements everywhere they looked. The presence of so many imported machines and products in Vietnam was a reassuring reminder of home, but the branding of the war also encouraged soldiers' cynicism and distrust. Accusations of war profiteering motivated the antiwar movement in general, but they animated the antimilitary G.I. Movement in particular. Underground newspapers published for American soldiers on or near U.S. military bases were rife with cartoon editorials depicting Wall Street fat cats, bloodthirsty industrialists, and insatiable machines like the "Profiteer 35000," a grotesque contraption that relied on dollars to fuel its lethal operation.[13] In Vietnam, the nagging feeling that corporations were making money off soldiers' sweat and tears sullied the experience, rendering wartime service less patriotic and more transactional. For many G.I.'s, "getting over"—doing the least for the most—became a way of life.

War profiteering, self-interest, the arbitrary assignment of discomfort and danger—casting military service in this light is uncomfortable, accounting for the public's desire to think of the Vietnam War in more heroic terms. Vietnam's image as a cruel, tragic, unnecessary war began rehabilitation in the 1980s, when Hollywood took note of the marketability of the Vietnam brand and political operatives recognized the voting strength of Vietnam veterans and their families. Candidate Ronald Reagan reframed the conflict as a necessary struggle in his 1980 stump speech, and as president he symbolically welcomed all Vietnam veterans into the fold of national heroes. In Reagan's first inaugural address, he situated Vietnam in the pantheon of epic American struggles when he paid tribute to the nation's war dead: "Each one of those markers [in Arlington National Cemetery] is a monument to the kind of heroes I spoke of earlier. Their lives ended in places called Belleau Wood, the Argonne, Omaha Beach, Salerno, and halfway around the world on Guadalcanal, Tarawa, Pork Chop Hill, the Chosin Reservoir, and in a hundred rice paddies and jungles of a place called Vietnam." As historian Christian Appy writes, "Reagan's battlefield litany seeks to incorporate Vietnam into a vision of American history as an unsullied continuum of virtue, heroism, and national unity."[14] Through its references to Arlington and some of the most scorching battlefields in military history, the speech also posited combat as the dominant experience of the Vietnam War. The elision of everything else made good rhetorical sense because the values associated with combat—courage, persistence, teamwork—reaffirmed Americans' perceptions of their national character as hardworking, beneficent, selfless, and just. If Vietnam was not an aggrandizing victory, the argument went, then at least it was a noble struggle. The presumed suffering of American soldiers, rather than the war's outcome, earned Vietnam a place on the rolls of heroic, nation-defining conflicts that runs, in the collective imagination, from the snowcapped battlements of Valley Forge to the windswept deserts of the Middle East.

Of course, not all Americans embraced the noble-struggle interpretation of the Vietnam War. Antiwar activists challenged the war's necessity and nobility throughout the conflict, and their objections intensified after the My Lai massacre. The savagery of the incident, once it became public in 1969, could not be denied: American troops had raped several women and girls and murdered 300–500 unarmed civilians during a four-hour rampage in March 1968. Given the confessed guilt of the perpetrators, public debate centered around their culpability and whether My Lai was an aberration or business-as-usual for American forces in Vietnam, where routine use of "free-fire zones" authorized soldiers to fire at will on civilians remaining in a particular area. Similar charges lay at the heart of testimony by antiwar veterans in the 1971 Winter Soldier hearings and other protests. Sponsored by Vietnam Veterans Against the War, this three-day event placed American brutality in Vietnam center stage, prompting outrage from supporters of the war and investigations by military authorities. Though poor media coverage of the hearings undermined organizers' hopes of reinvigorating the antiwar movement, the veterans' disturbing, self-incriminating testimony nonetheless affirmed critics' views of the war, that it was senseless and corrupt, that it made killers of otherwise decent men.[15]

In confronting the charges leveled by antiwar activists, Americans who supported—and still support—the anticommunist cause in Vietnam placed patriotism at the center of their war narrative. In their version of the story, the particulars of who got killed and why were less important than the fact that citizen-soldiers struggled against impossible odds to fulfill their service to the state.[16] The composition of those odds varies dramatically, depending on who is telling the story, but they generally include some combination of Vietnam's landscape and climate; tenacious South Vietnamese insurgents and deadly North Vietnamese regulars; the callousness and/or incompetence of American political and/or military authorities, who squandered young lives by fighting too aggressively, or not aggressively enough; the media, which "turned" the American public against the war by documenting its violent excesses; and the collective indifference of the folks at home, often represented by young women who abandoned their men with cruelly timed Dear John letters. By focusing solely on how they overcame the physical and emotional challenges of warfare, Vietnam veterans could lay claim to valor while ignoring the political complexities of U.S. intervention and rejecting accusations that they committed atrocities—or at least rejecting the idea that atrocities matter.

Critics on the left argued that American soldiers were exploited in a neo-imperial misadventure that required them to kill innocent people. Critics on the right argued that American soldiers ably performed their duty but were betrayed by their leaders, politicians, and the media. What they had in common were shared assumptions about how those soldiers lived and worked in Vietnam: that every day was a struggle, that every night was cut with fear. Placing combat at the center of the story has long served interests at both ends of the political spectrum. But how might hawks' defense of the war, then and in years since, be different if they took into account living conditions for most soldiers in Vietnam, that the violence meted out by American forces was not attended by universal deprivation, nor was it matched by the physical strength of the enemy? And how would doves' critiques resonate with the public if, instead of foxholes and fire-fights, antiwar soldiers invoked softball and soft-serve ice cream when they testified and marched? Defenders of the war used the myth of universal deprivation to lionize soldiers' actions on the battlefield, while critics of the war accepted the myth of universal combat duty in order to show that, while they opposed U.S. policy, they still "supported the troops." Both sides united in a shared understanding that the Vietnam War really was about making war for the majority of its American participants, but the reality of the occupation was far more complex.

Interpreting collective experience, especially one shared by millions of people, is a vexing historical problem, one made more difficult in the Vietnam context by vast differences in soldiers' tours of duty. Some have argued that the Vietnam War was so dynamic that it is best understood as many separate wars, with American escalation or North Vietnamese and Viet Cong offensives demarcating each new phase of the conflict. As John Paul Vann, the American adviser who inspired Neil Sheehan's *A Bright Shining Lie*, liked to put it, "America doesn't have ten years' experience in Vietnam—we have one year's experience ten times."[17] Individual soldiers' experiences were likewise differentiated by time, but also by several other factors, such as where they were stationed, their branch of service, and their military occupational specialty, further complicating efforts to under-stand what it was like to serve in Vietnam. There probably is no dominant soldier experience for the Vietnam War, but even if there were, the num-bers confirm that it would not be the infantryman humping the boonies on ambush patrol that *Platoon* and other popular treatments have enshrined in public memory.

The most important factor determining what a year in Vietnam was like is time, for when a soldier arrived in-country determined the contours of the war he found there, though no generalization is absolute. The advi-sory phase (1961–65) was the most austere of the war, such that American military personnel could not count on timely medical evacuation in the event of serious injury. When the first official combat troops were sent to Vietnam in 1965, the support system available to them remained minimal, though greater numbers of Americans in-country did translate into more reliable transportation, resupply and reinforcement, and medical care. As the war dragged on, with its attendant effects on public support and sol-dier morale, military authorities provided the troops with more and more services to keep their spirits up, skewing the ratio of combat to noncombat personnel even more. When the drawdown began in 1969, wounded combat troops were usually only thirty minutes by helicopter from a surgical hospital, so vast and sophisticated was the logistical apparatus supporting them. As the withdrawal of combat troops progressed, that logistical apparatus remained intact. By 1972, over 90 percent of Americans stationed in Vietnam were noncombat personnel serving in supporting roles.[18]

Location also profoundly influenced a soldier's tour of duty in Vietnam. The American military presence was strongest on the coast, where big bases—Danang, Qui Nhon, Nha Trang, Cam Ranh, and Vung Tau among them—and their satellites housed troops in relative comfort and safety. The area around Saigon, home to huge installations at Tan Son Nhut, Bien Hoa, and Long Binh as well as to tens of thousands of American military personnel living in Saigon-Cholon itself, was also relatively safe. In terms of comfort, these assignments were among the most choice because American troops stationed in the Saigon area were free to enjoy the sensual pleasures of the Asian market. There were also large, relatively secure bases up-country, especially Pleiku in the Central Highlands, but amenities there were slower to come, and danger was a more frequent visitor. Troops stationed near the Demilitarized Zone, in the Mekong Delta, and all the little places in between the big bases had it the worst, for their war was mostly about preparing for war, with few interruptions from entertainment tours, P.X. grand openings, or new swimming pool dedications.

Service branch was another important factor influencing a soldier's brand of war because it determined where military personnel were stationed and in what capacity. The Military Assistance Command Vietnam (MACV) divided South Vietnam into four regions, numbered I to IV north to south. The Marine Corps controlled I Corps in the north, where it prosecuted the war aggressively and its troops lived more ascetically than soldiers farther south. Though bases in the Danang area featured many of the amenities discussed in this study, the marines generally did not engage in the same kind of logistical cushioning authorized by other service branches. With their focus more squarely on military objectives, marines in Vietnam endured the most austere tours of duty and suffered the highest casualty rates of the five service branches. In contrast, most Navy, Air Force, and Coast Guard personnel served in supporting roles that kept them aboard ships or on large, rearward bases—in either case, mostly out of harm's way. As a result, these branches had the lowest casualty rates in Vietnam. The U.S. Army suffered the *most* casualties because it committed over 60 percent of the total force, but it did not suffer the highest casualty *rate*, because so many of its soldiers served in noncombat capacities. MACV charged U.S. Army Vietnam (USARV) with providing logistical support not only for itself but also for the other service branches, enabling infantrymen, airmen, and sailors to enjoy a war zone standard of living unparalleled in military history.

Within each service branch, personnel were assigned a specific occupation, a designation that determined how a soldier would spend his workday. The military generally divided its forces into three groups: combat, combat support, and combat service support. The first group was specifically charged with taking the war to the enemy on foot, by helicopter or plane, or through some types of artillery. The second, and somewhat larger, group provided immediate combat support as engineers, signal operators, artillerymen, pilots, supply drivers, and forward medical personnel, sometimes placing them in harm's way. The third group was the largest and provided support to the other two in the form of mail, food, housing, laundry, electricity, running water, equipment maintenance, entertainment, and medical care. The paperwork involved in this effort was overwhelming, so there were probably as many clerks as infantrymen in Vietnam. Combat service support troops never engaged in combat, unless the enemy directly attacked an American convoy or compound.

The factors of time, place, branch of service, and occupational specialty conspired to shape each and every tour of duty served by the United States' 2.5 million Vietnam veterans. These factors have also profoundly influenced the scope of this study. Because the American logistical apparatus in Vietnam did not come fully into its own until 1968, and because the extant paperwork of the war survives from its most sedentary period, the focus here rests mostly on 1968 to 1973, though American impulses toward physical comfort and material satisfaction were present throughout the conflict. Because rearward installations were the most well developed, and because the extant paperwork from these places addresses noncombat concerns that did not receive as much written attention in combat zones, this study also focuses mostly on the big bases. However, the warscape of consumption, recreation, and leisure drawn here is not discrete, for these impulses were present, in their own way, even in remote, contested areas of South Vietnam. And finally, because the U.S. Army provided so much of the manpower in Vietnam, and because its troops were engaged in the logistical effort more so than any other service branch, this study relies largely on USARV records, though MACV materials, which address the war effort as a whole, are also used to a considerable extent. The discussions of living conditions, G.I. consumerism, and recreation and leisure, as well as the complex relationship between rearward personnel and combat troops, may rely on Army sources, but they do not address only Army personnel. U.S. Air Force, Navy, Coast Guard, and even Marine Corps personnel stationed at well-developed bases enjoyed the same benefits as their U.S. Army counterparts, they struggled for similar improvements to their quality of life, and they wrestled with the same conflicted emotions over serving in a war that did not meet their expectations.

The usual factors for consideration in social and cultural history—the troika of gender, class, and race—are also represented here. American women served in large numbers in the Vietnam War, though exact figures are difficult to come by. An estimated 7,500 to 11,000 military women deployed to Vietnam, the majority of them as nurses and medical specialists who tried to mend the damage wrought by combat. Thousands more served as civilian employees in military headquarters, U.S. government agencies, charitable and relief organizations, and private corporations administering military contracts. Among them, Red Cross and United Service Organization (USO) volunteers provided compassionate care to American soldiers, disrupting their own lives to bring comfort to others.[19]

Studies of American women in the Vietnam War have tended to emphasize the ways in which they endured danger and made sacrifices comparable to those of men. This project is in concurrence, not because of women's proximity to danger but rather because of their distance from it. Female military personnel tended to be stationed in the very places that inspired this study, where they and the majority of their male counterparts shared a relatively comfortable standard of living, though social deference to women often afforded low-ranking women quarters usually reserved for high-ranking men. Despite the contributions of women to the war effort, the focus of this study falls almost exclusively on men because the war story I am seeking to reframe belongs to them. However, gender does provide a useful analytical perspective, since the fulfillment of masculine ideals is a key feature of military service, especially in wartime. It is axiomatic that boys go to war to become men, but what happens when military service fails to provide appropriate circumstances in which to prove one's self?

Class and race also factor into this study in subtle ways. As in most American wars, working-class people disproportionately did the fighting and dying in Vietnam. Less able or willing to exploit loopholes in the draft system, the economically disadvantaged, especially black and Latino Americans, found themselves headed to Vietnam in disproportionately large numbers.[20] At issue, then, is how that fact influenced their tours of duty and how these men approached their service. The post–World War II, middle-class ethos of abundance was a powerful force in Vietnam, yet college-educated, middle-class, and wealthy men were underrepresented in the ranks of Vietnam recruits. The discrepancy is explained by the fact that, though postwar abundance belonged to the middle and privileged classes in the United States, the *desire* to relax and consume belonged to everyone. Working-class young men, whether black or white, saw service in Vietnam as a potential springboard to affluence, an impression cultivated by military authorities who promoted consumption at military-run retail outlets in order to encourage enlistment and quiescent service. Once in Vietnam, American military personnel found that class inequities in the United States were reflected in the distribution of danger and privation in the war zone. Soldiers with special technical, administrative, or verbal skills were routinely assigned to jobs on rearward bases that made use of their expertise, while soldiers lacking in these were deemed suited for the infantry. Hence, education, a principal signifier of class, was a primary factor in whether a soldier was sent into combat. Years later, Americans found comfort in Ronald Reagan's description of Vietnam as "a noble cause" during his 1980 run for president. But while the war was still raging, many soldiers found the nobility of the experience wanting because something so mundane as the ability to type could literally save your life.

Maintaining the war machine's costly cogs and ghastly gears required hundreds of thousands of young soldiers, sailors, and airmen who served in an array of supporting roles. They ably performed their duties far from danger and, for the most part, hidden from memory. Their service is examined here. Chapter 1, "Same Side, Different Wars," highlights the myriad duties American military personnel performed in Vietnam, most of which did not involve combat or even danger. Though Vietnam veterans are understood to be a homogeneous group, divided only by branch of service and their political opinions about the war, the relationship between infantrymen and rearward personnel was actually fraught with conflict. Efforts to close ranks in pursuit of federal benefits and public recognition after the war contributed to the erasure of noncombat soldiers from the war's collective memory. Chapter 2, "This Place Just Isn't John Wayne," describes the elaborate bases that resulted from subtle negotiation over living conditions between soldier-workers and their military employers, who eventually called for a force composed solely of professionals. When soldiers realized that their war experiences in Vietnam would never measure up to the heroic stories of World War II they had heard as kids, they felt alienated and betrayed because comfortable living conditions were no substitute for a war they were proud to fight and likely to win. Chapter 3, "Total War on Boredom," outlines the massive recreation program established to maintain troop morale and prevent soldiers from engaging in illicit activities. The war on boredom was the only facet of American strategy in Vietnam in which the U.S. military went all out, and the resources directed toward it were staggering, especially compared with the spare morale programs conducted by the enemy. Chapter 4, "The Things They Bought," focuses on the retail war, an all-out effort to maintain troop morale by providing easy access to consumer goods, even in contested areas. In military publications, authorities framed Vietnam as an economic opportunity for American soldiers who could be transformed, at least superficially, into men of means by acquiring consumer goods at military-run retail outlets. Finally, Chapter 5, "War Zone Wonderland," considers the war's festive yet disturbing possibilities for its American participants. In the carnival of "the Nam," young men raised at economic and social disadvantage in the United States suddenly found themselves empowered by American guns and dollars, yet without the behavioral restraints imposed by family, religion, and law. Isolated from combat and insulated from danger, rearward soldiers sought ways to authenticate their war experiences by taking photographs and hunting souvenirs as they came to terms with their new status. They were veterans, yes, but veterans of what? The Epilogue finds the comfort-for-morale equation still at work during the Iraq War, suggesting a need to reconsider American warfare in light of the strange, overbuilt worlds the United States creates to sustain its service members in the field.

This is not the usual way war is understood, for Americans take pride in the humility and self-sacrifice of their soldiers serving abroad. The collective memory of American infantrymen sharing their rations with European refugees in the uncertain summer days of 1944 remains, through the films and memoirs of that war, a source of national pride. And more recently, Americans took satisfaction from reports that units at the forefront of both the 1991 and 2003 invasions of Iraq provided succor to surrendering soldiers and civilians alike, sharing their rations despite tenuous logistical situations. It is at the intersection of violence and compassion that Americans tend to locate their heroes, who are understood to be people capable of inflicting great injury one moment and exercising tender restraint the next. Soldiers' mercy and self-denial, especially when they benefit the enemy, serve to legitimize the political project of a war, but also to affirm the good intentions of the American people. The offering of food or aid would not be nearly so impressive, so affirming, if it did not take place in the context of combat, where life is stripped to the bare essentials. But when abundance is understood to permeate a war zone—enough food, ammunition, and creature comforts to stay in the fight forever—the violence suddenly appears less restrained, the charity seems less ennobling, and the men who mete out both appear, somehow, less heroic. It is no surprise, then, that the abundance accompanying American soldiers to war, for the first time in Vietnam and in every major deployment since, is often ignored or forgotten. Despite their infrequency, combat and deprivation continue to dominate the war stories Americans like to tell.

Some veterans may object to the reframing of the Vietnam War narrative proposed here. They may read in my work not just an analysis of American policy and culture in Vietnam but also a critique of their service as individuals and, perhaps, a diminishment of their sacrifices for the nation. That is not my intent. This book brings to light a wealth of documentation about material conditions for Americans in the Vietnam war zone, not for every U.S. soldier in every place at every moment, but for enough soldiers, often enough, that these noncombat experiences surely belong in any telling of the conflict. This is not to say that American soldiers in Vietnam "had it good" or did not suffer; the dead and wounded testify to the war's desolation. Rather, it is my hope that this book will recalibrate the concept of wartime sacrifice to encompass more than just the actions of infantrymen who spent their year on patrol, waiting for hell to break loose, or the heroics of pilots flying into hostile fire—brave men, but men who are few and far between in modern American warfare. Combat veterans' service in particular is made more special by this study, with its reminder that a slim minority of soldiers shed most of the American blood in Vietnam. For the rest, the veterans whose memories and diary pages are bereft of moments the market deems worth sharing, these pages are one of the few places in public life where their stories and struggles are acknowledged.

Since World War II, Americans have excelled at making war, becoming so good at it that fewer and fewer of them are needed to serve in combat. The violence U.S. forces can rain down on their enemies defies comprehension, and the military bases from which they generate it contain so many aspects of civilian life that the appellation "war" hardly seems adequate to describe their efforts. In Vietnam, some 2 million Vietnamese people were killed (including about 250,000 South Vietnamese troops who fought alongside the United States), compared with 58,000 Americans, with a majority of the massive civilian casualties attributed to American bombing and artillery. In the Persian Gulf War, American forces suffered 382 dead, while Iraqi soldiers and civilians suffered losses in the tens of thousands. In the Iraq War that began on 20 March 2003, American forces suffered 139 dead during "major combat operations," which ended on 30 April of that year. During that period, between 10,000 and 45,000 Iraqi civilians and combatants were killed. The obvious conclusion to draw from the United States' ability to create so much devastation at so little cost is that it is a superpower the likes of which history has never seen before. Yet Americans nonetheless cling to the notion that their soldiers are plucky underdogs just barely making it through.

War is cruelty, General Sherman wrote the town fathers of Atlanta when he ordered evacuation of the city in 1864, but as it turns out, it *can* be refined. With enough money, power, and motivation, amenities can decorate a combat zone like the buttercream rosettes on an Iraq War dessert. War zone abundance protects American soldiers from discomfort, in part because military authorities want, like benevolent parents, to shield their charges from harm. Abundance also helps to maintain morale, which is, in turn, necessary for extracting compliant and efficient service from a workforce under tremendous stress. At the same time, base camp amenities insulate the American public from one of war's usual hardships, the pain and frustration of families bearing witness to their loved ones' deprivation far from home. Finally, abundance works to ensure a continuous supply of new recruits and faithful public support for subsequent military endeavors. What is at stake, then, is nothing less than a war's success. To that end, the U.S. military now takes such good care of its soldiers that Phil Kiver had to impose his own hardship in Iraq by denying himself a piece of cake and, apparently, chiding other soldiers who he felt "were abusing the privilege and hadn't done much to deserve such a treat."[21] Kiver wanted his own, twenty-first-century war to live up to his perceptions of the past. He needn't have tried so hard. Abundance has long accompanied American soldiers to war, and in Vietnam, sheet cake was only the beginning.

CHAPTER ONE

Same Side, Different Wars

Grunts and REMFs in Vietnam

Somewhere outside Saigon, a large black-and-white sign stood by the side of the road: "WARNING: You Are About to Enter One of the Most Dangerous Combat Areas in Viet-Nam / A Public Highway / Please Drive Carefully."[1] This sign, and others like it, used the war as a metaphor to make a clever comment on local traffic, that a Vietnamese public highway represented a battlefield all its own, where military convoys and civilian vehicles fought for position along the road. Separated from its context of reckless drivers and heavy traffic, the sign would seem to demarcate safety and danger, as though the war's sprawling expanse could be confined to a specific area and labeled accordingly. But the lines between safety and danger were not drawn so clearly in Vietnam.

In theory, hostilities could break out anywhere because the enemy was everywhere. The military wing of the National Liberation Front, also known as the Viet Cong, relied on unconventional tactics to achieve its twin objectives of destabilizing the Saigon regime and forcing an American withdrawal. Prior to the American buildup, acts of terror like car bombings and grenade attacks pressed the war into unusual places: the bleachers of a softball game attended by American military families in 1964, or the sidewalk outside the American Embassy in 1965.[2] Later, any place where American G.I.'s congregated was a potential target for guerrilla attack; tourist markets, restaurants, bars, and brothels across South Vietnam all saw their share of violence. Viet Cong rockets and mortars also ensured that no American base, no matter how large or how close to Saigon, was ever totally safe, a fact made plain by the 1968 Tet Offensive. In that watershed event, Viet Cong and North Vietnamese units attacked five of six major South Vietnamese cities and thirty-six of forty-four provincial capitals. American bases from the Demilitarized Zone in the north to the

Ca Mau peninsula in the south came under fire. So fluid was the nature of combat in South Vietnam, and so complete was the Viet Cong's hold over the countryside, that one G.I. described life on an American base as living "on an island in a country controlled by the V.C."[3] While life on the island could be quite good, the calculus of terror ensured that soldiers on rearward bases still lived with the gnawing fear that the world might explode at any moment.

And yet, the location of a soldier's tour and the duties he performed clearly demarcated the borders of the war. The lines between combat and noncombat areas might be difficult to draw in Vietnam, but they were still easily understood by the Americans who served there. "Safety" was a relative phenomenon, and "the rear" was anything behind you. To the infantryman walking point, the rear was the back of the column. To the guys on ambush patrol, the rear was their remote base camp. To the guys whose duties confined them to that raggedy little outpost, the rear was brigade or division headquarters. To headquarters personnel stationed up-country, the rear was Long Binh, Tan Son Nhut, or Danang. And to personnel stationed at those massive installations, the rear was American bases elsewhere in Asia or even the United States itself. Still, the difference between a Saigon street and a trail in the Central Highlands was measurable and real to the soldiers who traversed them. Out in the boonies, fear—the chest-pounding, heart-stopping kind—was a constant companion, and death seemed to lurk in every shadow. In the cities, the threats were more diverse—thieves on motorcycles, fatal traffic accidents, the occasional fragmentation grenade—and violence was less a certainty. Because of this discrepancy, the location of a soldier's tour of duty profoundly influenced his Vietnam War experience.

A soldier's occupational assignment also shaped his tour of duty in Vietnam, sometimes more so than the location of that tour. Infantrymen were sent into contested areas, while support personnel generally did their work in more secure places. Uncertainty abounded, except when it came to combat versus noncombat roles. It was hard to know a safe path from one planted with mines, and it was often impossible to distinguish a Viet Cong guerrilla from a Vietnamese peasant. But every American who served in Vietnam could tell a grunt from a cook, a ground pounder from a pencil pusher, and the airborne from the chairborne. They enjoyed vastly different living and working conditions and endured divergent levels of danger and suffering. These differentials created a profound schism between American soldiers ostensibly serving on the same side in two very different wars. And soldiers' reactions to these inequities demonstrate how the American way of war failed to provide new recruits with the life-altering experience they expected, hoped, or dreaded Vietnam would be.

༺○༻

All Gave Some, and Some Gave All.
—popular post-9/11 slogan

Approximately 2.5 million Americans served in the Vietnam War. Though the number of American troops who served in combat is not precisely known, military historians generally accept 10 to 25 percent as an appropriate estimate, recognizing that the proportions changed over time. Several factors make determining an exact figure extremely difficult. First, soldiers assigned to combat units might never see combat, while soldiers assigned to support units might find themselves under enemy rocket attack while walking to the P.X. Second, the definition of "combat" itself is elastic, ranging from daily encounters with the enemy to random acts of terror or sabotage. Third, the ratio of combat to noncombat troops varied by branch of service, preventing the division of military personnel into neat categories. Most Navy and Air Force personnel supported pilots and their crews from the ground, and the Coast Guard focused on surveillance and port security that kept its sailors from confronting the enemy directly. The Marine Corps had the highest percentage of its Vietnam forces engaged in combat, and statistics for the Army fall in between. While some Army units took the war to the enemy, the majority of its personnel provided logistical support for the Army as well as the other service branches. Finally, the percentage of American troops engaged in combat operations varied throughout the war; as more troops and equipment were sent to Vietnam, the number of personnel required to support them grew exponentially.

The ratio of combat to noncombat troops drew criticism from the media and some members of Congress. In 1967, reports out of Saigon indicated that only 70,000 of the 464,000 American soldiers in Vietnam at that time were combat troops, raising questions about the efficiency of the American war machine. The following year, Congress debated whether the Pentagon's budget was too fat, with critics citing Vietnam force structure as evidence. Of 525,000 troops stationed in Vietnam in early 1968, only 40,000 were riflemen, whose numbers were regarded as the primary measure of combat strength for counterinsurgency operations. Critiques of the Vietnam tooth-to-tail ratio were rooted in traditional ideas about war, specifically that combat was its normative experience, though support troops had increasingly outnumbered combat troops since the Civil War. The Pentagon refuted the charge of inefficiency embedded in reports about the ratio, arguing that the figures were based on an oversimplification of military force structure.[4]

Within the military, Pentagon officials explained, troops were divided into three categories, not two: combat units engaged the enemy directly; combat support units provided immediate support to combat troops; and combat service support units provided logistical support to ensure that enough of whatever was needed reached those on the front lines. Even if only 70,000 personnel in 1967 were assigned to combat units (the Pentagon refuted this figure without providing an alternative), tens of thousands of soldiers in combat support units were frequently placed in harm's way. And yet, Secretary of Defense McNamara seemed to legitimize concerns over American military efficiency when he commented that the situation in Vietnam could be improved by "reducing the ratio of support to combat forces."[5] Just the opposite occurred. As troop strength rose until its peak in mid-1968, so too did the percentage of noncombat forces. Then, as troop strength began its decline in late 1968, the proportion of noncombat personnel increased. By 1972, 90 percent of American servicemen in Vietnam were in noncombat roles, and only 2,400 of the 49,000 troops still stationed there were allocated to fight the enemy on the ground.[6]

The complexity suggested by the Pentagon's three-tiered force structure and historians' inability to settle on a uniform set of statistics ignores the simplicity of the war's map, as soldiers understood it at the time. There were contested areas, and then there was every place else. In combat zones, war zones, "the boonies," or even "Indian Country," infantrymen, or grunts, probed the countryside looking for North Vietnamese regulars and Viet Cong insurgents, suffering injuries from snipers, booby traps, mines, and all the non-combat-related mishaps that occur on heavily armed hikes through untamed wilderness. Combat itself drew even more blood, and remote outposts dealt with the constant threat of mortars, rockets, and direct enemy attack. In contrast, rear echelon personnel in noncombat areas held down the fort and provided the arms and amenities combat soldiers needed to stay in the fight. At some unknown time and place, the acronym REMF entered the Vietnam vernacular to describe these men. The dearth of affection and respect implied by the term, which stood for "rear echelon motherfucker," only begins to suggest the tensions evident between factions of the United States armed forces.

Identifying REMFs was easy, especially compared with infantrymen. Their fatigues might be green and crisp, their boots retained a shine, and they often sported paunches resulting from rich mess hall fare and sedentary duty. When infantrymen returned from the field, they presented a marked contrast to the permanent residents of rearward bases. The grunts were lean and grizzled, the dirt of the trail resided in every crevice of their bodies, and their uniforms and boots were bleached white from scuffs and sun. A soldier's appearance demonstrated his tenure in Vietnam, veteran Joe Dunn explained, so "an infantry private with months in the field felt quite justified in looking down on any newly arrived officer of any rank clad in the tell-tale greenish fatigues." Airman Tom Yarborough confessed in his memoir to tuning out his first in-country briefing because he was thinking about how to modify his uniform. "I may not have been a combat veteran," he recalled, "but I sure wanted to look like one."[7] Because of their access to laundry and new fatigues, and because of commanders' greater scrutiny of rearward troops' appearance, REMFs might always look freshly minted, no matter how long they had been in-country. Some newly arrived soldiers felt so self-conscious of looking like REMFs that they tried to distress their uniforms, especially the boots, to blend in with battle-hardened troops. Combat veterans were also aware of how their appearance transmitted experience; veteran George Watson recalled one infantryman who refused to replace his bleached fatigues during a second tour as a REMF because, he claimed, "he had a reputation to uphold."[8]

Grunts may have felt superior to support personnel, but they were certainly outnumbered by them. The modern American war machine is a sophisticated affair, requiring enormous resources not only to subdue the enemy but also to sustain the troops. There was so much war work to be done in Vietnam, as the list of Military Occupational Specialties (MOS) attests. Supply personnel drove trucks into contested areas to bring ammunition to combat troops. Armaments personnel repaired the rifles, machine guns, and grenade launchers used by the infantry. Communications specialists relayed the messages that "kept the shooters talking," and construction engineers paved a literal road to victory, or at least to stalemate, building ports and airfields along the way. Data processors compiled the information used to determine how the war was going, and staffers for the command historian conducted interviews and logged details that would one day become the Pentagon's official record of the war. In the meantime, reporters and editors for unit newspapers with circulations ranging from 95 to 95,000 published informative articles about local units, helpful reminders about military policies, and breathtaking pinups of budding starlets. Feeding the troops required a legion of butchers, bakers, and ice cream makers, and keeping them entertained required legions more. Librarians shelved the books in base libraries, American Forces Vietnam Network (AFVN) television and radio technicians kept the airwaves filled with programming, entertainment specialists planned morale-boosting field trips and talent shows, specially trained escorts shuttled celebrities around the war zone, craft shop attendants minded the kilns and darkrooms, and lifeguards kept watch at the pools and beaches. Military-run retail outlets and bars employed even more personnel to stock the shelves, pour the drinks, book the bands, and count the slugs in the slot machines. Every occupation imaginable was represented in the ranks of the U.S. armed forces somewhere in Vietnam.

Because many American bases were comparable to cities in the United States, they required similar services. Military maintenance personnel worked to ensure that everything ran smoothly; an army of plumbers, electricians, and refrigerator repairmen kept the water running, the lights on, and the drinks ice cold. Military policemen guarded the gates, set speed traps on the highways, and even ran a central prison for American servicemen who violated civil or military laws. Air traffic controllers monitored thousands of fixed-wing flights each day at jet-capable airfields throughout Vietnam, which were some of the busiest airports in the world. At inprocessing centers, military personnel welcomed new arrivals, and at outprocessing centers they searched the bags and processed the forms that allowed short-timers to return home. In between, soldiers could serve in a variety of helping professions, including social workers who assisted Vietnamese civilians with self-help projects, medical and dental assistants who provided inoculations and checkups to Vietnamese civilians and American soldiers alike, and veterinary technicians who maintained the teeth and coats of sentry dogs, scout dogs, mascots, and soldiers' personal pets. The U.S. Army even employed specially trained canvasmen who reupholstered the seats and soft tops of military vehicles. Working in this capacity, one lucky private got to spend part of his 1969 tour of duty restoring the ragtop on a Russian scout car that was being refurbished by his unit as a gift for South Vietnamese president Thieu.[9] Regardless of how they served, all of these military personnel and thousands more stationed offshore on naval vessels, many of whom never went ashore in Southeast Asia, are called by the same name: "Vietnam veterans."

Of all support troops in Vietnam, clerks were archetypal because their sedentary living and working conditions were usually furthest removed from conventional notions of war. Military clerks came in several varieties: stenographers, court clerks, postal clerks, personnel and administration clerks, supply clerks, finance clerks, chaplain's assistants, and medical records specialists, among others. The MOS 71B, or clerk-typist, was found in every Army office in Vietnam. According to the Army's handbook of Military Occupational Specialties, the clerk-typist had to have high verbal and reading abilities and the ability to type. His duties included organizing and typing reports based on verbal and written instructions, filing regulations and correspondence, and operating office equipment like mimeographs, copiers, and adding machines.[10] Depending on the security situation and the amenities on his base, the clerk's war work might be indistinguishable from a stateside deployment.

Clerks were so ubiquitous because the U.S. military modeled its occupation force on the modern corporation. Uniformed and civilian bureaucrats directed the war from air-conditioned offices in and around Saigon, and legions of clerks stationed throughout the war zone did their bidding. Managing what went where generated thousands of pages of documentation, and assessing the success of combat operations—through body counts, kill ratios, and weapons captured, among other metrics—required thousands more. So massive was this cumbersome bureaucracy that, by the late 1960s, the American military presence in Vietnam constituted the third-largest command economy in the world, behind the centralized bureaucracies of the People's Republic of China and the Soviet Union.

Despite their number, clerks received very little attention from journalists covering the war because their duties did not make for good copy or compelling photographs when compared with the exploits of infantrymen or pilots. Mark Jury was one of the few photographers who bothered to capture what he termed "the paper-clip war." In his photo essay *The Vietnam Photo Book*, Jury assumes a wry but belligerent antiwar posture when describing the strange world of the war as he encountered it in 1969 and 1970. A series of captions and pictures depicts "a typical day at Army headquarters: a draftee with a college degree listens to Simon and Garfunkel as he types the endless stream of paperwork. The colonel's driver grapples with his latest hot rod model. And the sergeant major, who's earning over $10,000 a year from the U.S. taxpayers, pushes on with his all-consuming project—reading through the Encyclopedia Britannica." Jury did not deny that many Americans experienced deprivation and danger in Vietnam. Rather, by focusing on the paper-clip war, he paid subtle but bitter tribute to them: "For [support personnel] the killing and dying war is just something to read about in *Stars and Stripes*." To underscore the disconnect between the two wars, Jury included a photograph of the Posthumous Awards office at U.S. Army Vietnam Headquarters, where staff determined appropriate commendations for the fallen. Fluorescent lights, file cabinets, and mounds of paper belie the somber nature of the work performed there, as does a festive banner with Charlie Brown, Snoopy, and the rest of the Peanuts gang wishing visitors a "Merry Christmas from All of Us."[11]

As Jury's photographs attest, working conditions for soldiers in many supporting roles were comparable to those of civilian employees toiling in stateside office complexes. Many clerks labored in rotting shacks or suffocating Quonset huts, but at the big bases, American military offices were often air-conditioned with acoustic tile ceilings, tiled floors, and the usual metal desks, file cabinets, and caster chairs. The presence of electricity and the availability of batteries and consumer goods at the P.X. meant that G.I.'s could improve their working conditions by bringing portable radios, tape players, electric fans, and coffee makers into the office. Even if conditions were lousy, clerking still had its advantages; these workplaces shielded clerks from both the elements and the line of fire. Monotony and frustration were often the greatest occupational hazards.

Labor in the rear, however, could also be grueling. With so many tasks performed at different kinds of bases and at different points in the war, it is difficult to make generalizations about the workday. But for soldiers who had the worst of it, short of participating in combat, work might begin before dawn and extend past dusk, with only a break or two in between; eighteen-hour days were not unheard of. Support operations required some soldiers to work year-round on docks, in warehouses and hangars, or on the tarmacs of helipads and airfields, as well as in a variety of wood-frame or prefabricated metal buildings that may or may not have had windows, let alone air-conditioning. Blazing sun, stifling heat, and high humidity increased the physical challenges associated with providing manual labor in support of the war. Adding to their exhaustion, soldiers could also expect to help with security for their bases, especially at smaller installations. After their regular duties ended, they dug trenches and bunkers, filled sandbags, and ran drills in preparation for enemy attack. Guard duty, performed on a regular basis, added hours more to the day, as soldiers peered into the darkness, struggling to stay awake.

Some soldiers had to work until exhaustion, and they crashed on their bunks at the earliest opportunity. But others, especially those stationed in rearward areas in the later years of the war, found that there was not enough work to go around. The long hours between shifts became a time to replenish body and soul, to make friends and memories, and to stave off boredom and loneliness. To the extent that they had them, support troops' off-duty hours might be well removed from the dangers and deprivations of war. They could upgrade their barracks décor with homey touches, eat their fill of hot chow in the mess hall, get an ice cream cone at the snack bar, and participate in a variety of leisure activities: drinks and live entertainment at the open mess club (a military-sanctioned bar), free outdoor movies, pickup basketball or intramural softball, or the pleasant slide into inebriation on one's own bunk. Veteran Joe Dunn, who later went on to earn a doctorate, remembered life in the rear for the rich food and ample supply of beer. He felt that the Army took such good care of him that "ironic as it may sound, my life in Vietnam in many ways was more relaxed and less stressful than graduate school." One medical unit's newspaper cheerfully summed up life in the rear by detailing a soldier's going-away party at which twenty cases of beer were consumed, a jeep trailer was converted into a dunking tank, and two men were treated for injuries sustained during a softball game: "War can really be rough, can't it?"[12]

Soldiers' living and working conditions on large, rearward bases are only a starting point for understanding what life was like in these places. An examination of one of them, Long Binh Post, helps to fill in the details. At first glance, Long Binh seems exceptional among American bases in Vietnam because it was the largest in terms of area and population, and it was among the most well developed. Since so many detachments were headquartered at Long Binh and so many troops passed through there, a great deal of documentation about it survives, providing the most complete portrait of life on any large base in Vietnam. But it is important to remember that, given a military force structure that required so many support troops, the barracks and amenities of Long Binh Post are closer to the norm for soldiering in Vietnam than a barren hilltop firebase or a bullet-streaked rice paddy, especially late in the war. Not every base had every amenity Long Binh could boast, but soldiers and commanders stationed elsewhere aspired to have them, and they might have if the war had gone on long enough. For the ironies it imposed on traditional notions of war, then, Long Binh Post was exceptionally weird, but its culture was not exceptional.

Construction of Long Binh Post began twenty miles north of Saigon in the mid-1960s as part of Project MOOSE, which stood for "Move Out of Saigon Expeditiously." As of 1966, some 10,000 American military personnel were quartered in over eighty billets sprinkled throughout civilian Saigon. There were also several military installations in the area that housed thousands more troops, creating a sizable American presence in South Vietnam's capital city. This led to several problems for military authorities. First, the U.S. military was spending hundreds of thousands of dollars each year to lease hotels and apartment buildings to house American soldiers. Second, rearward personnel required entertainment and services in their off-duty hours, leading to inflation of the local economy, prostitution, and a surge in bars, bathhouses, and massage parlors. The proliferation of tawdry establishments concerned South Vietnamese officials, and roving bands of drunk G.I.'s had a deleterious affect on civil-military relations in the area. American soldiers were also vulnerable to terrorist attack or, more likely, street crime as they ventured out after work. To alleviate these concerns, MACV elected to relocate as many American units as possible away from Saigon. Project MOOSE and Long Binh Post were the result.[13]

At its inception, Long Binh cost around $130 million to build and was slated to house 35,000 American military personnel. Construction costs eventually exceeded that sum, and up to 60,000 Americans at once were stationed there in the late 1960s. Size estimates of the base itself vary from 27 square miles to 80 square miles to 145 square miles. The discrepancy is accounted for by the expanding nature of the base and by different definitions of its perimeter, which included fenced-in, densely populated compounds, an enormous supply depot, an ammunition dump, airstrips and helipads, firing ranges, and a lot of wide-open space. From the air, Long Binh was a massive but orderly city composed of 3,500 buildings connected by 180 miles of roads. The base was so big—by the Army's estimate, comparable in area to Cleveland, Ohio—that one colonel joked, "If we ever really got attacked, the V.C. would have to use the scheduled bus service to get around the base." Indeed, Long Binh had its own local transportation system. Sixteen buses ran on three routes, servicing the primary residential areas, work areas, and recreational facilities every fifteen minutes.[14]

Home to U.S. Army Vietnam Headquarters, which included the 1st Logistical Command, the Army Corps of Engineers, the Army Chaplaincy, the Judge Advocate General's Office, the Finance Office, and a host of other detachments, Long Binh Post was, in the words of one resident-employee, "a virtual REMF citadel."[15] The war at Long Binh Post was mostly sedentary and routine, leaving plenty of downtime for the base's inhabitants. From the earliest construction, the Army placed particular emphasis on recreational facilities, even if it meant delaying construction of permanent

The manicured lawns and permanent structures of U.S. Army Vietnam Headquarters at Long Binh Post, photographed in 1971, belied the war in the countryside and suggested a long-term U.S. occupation. (Courtesy of Stephen Krüger)

billets. Because "a great majority of the disciplinary problems occur on off-duty time," a 1967 Operational Report suggested, "suitable outlets such as dayrooms, libraries, craft shops, and clubs" had to be provided "in spite of the fact that the troops would remain housed in tents longer."[16]

To keep Long Binh's residents busy after hours, military authorities allowed recreational facilities to mushroom. As of July 1971, Long Binh Post boasted the following amenities: eighty-one basketball courts, sixty-four volleyball courts, twelve swimming pools, eight softball fields, eight multipurpose courts, six tennis courts, five craft shops, three football fields, three weight rooms, three libraries, three service clubs, two miniature golf courses, two handball court complexes, one running track, one archery range, one golf driving range, one skeet range, one party area, and one amphitheater for movies and live shows, in addition to barbecue pits sprinkled all over the base.[17] By 1972, Long Binh Post even had a go-cart track. Built by the 79th Maintenance Battalion, it was five-eighths of a mile long and included several hairpin turns, a starting stand, a public address system, and a pit for on-the-spot repairs. The go-carts could reach speeds up to fifty miles per hour, so, in the interest of safety, the 24th Evacuation Hospital dispatched an ambulance to the track for every Sunday race.[18]

Open mess clubs, which served food and alcohol, often with live entertainment, also abounded on Long Binh Post. At its peak in 1969, Long Binh's club system consisted of forty annexes (separate clubs) with a net worth of $1.2 million, including $270,000 in cash on hand. If soldiers preferred to stay in at night, Long Binh's impressive post exchanges (military-run retail stores) stocked all the food and alcohol required to host private parties in the pools, barracks, or barbecue pits.[19] An unofficial brothel, a "male beauty bar" with salon services, and outdoor movies—by one account, up to one hundred each night—rounded out Long Binh's recreational offerings.[20]

Construction of new recreational facilities on Long Binh Post continued until the end of the war. As of 1970, over a year into troop withdrawals from Vietnam, the U.S. Army was still planning to build two 474-seat movie theaters at a cost of $117,000 each; additional handball courts at a total cost of $69,000; two in-ground swimming pools with bathhouses, at a total cost of $650,000; and a recreational lake. This ambitious $110,000 project demonstrates just how far from expediency Long Binh's construction priorities had strayed. The project involved building a 1,900-foot earthworks dam west of the post to create a 1,690-acre lake for "swimming, fishing, water-skiing, and picnic activities" to be enjoyed by individual troops in their off-duty hours or by entire units on stand-down.[21] Plans for one of the theaters, one of the pools, and the recreational lake were eventually scrapped, in part because of media scrutiny of the military's spending habits. Though most of these projects were not funded with taxpayer dollars but rather with nonappropriated funds generated by soldiers' spending at P.X.'s and open mess clubs, the American public in the early 1970s was still in no mood to watch more money disappear into the Vietnam sinkhole. Military authorities making these decisions clearly monitored the public's mood, as evidenced by the presence of civilian news clippings in their files. One article cited "official Navy documents" (the Navy was technically in charge of major construction contracts) allocating $1.4 million "for new playthings," figures and information that the Army hotly disputed. Whether for political or military reasons, authorities scrapped most of the pricier projects, but one movie theater, one in-ground swimming pool, one multipurpose craft shop, one squash court, and one miniature golf course remained under construction in July 1971.[22]

Over time, Long Binh Post became one of Vietnam's most elaborate bases and perhaps its most secure; by 1970, few occupants of the base were issued weapons. But the war did occasionally intrude. The post's ammunition dump, located away from populated areas, was an occasional target of Viet Cong rocket attacks, and the base itself was attacked during the 1968 Tet

Offensive. On a more regular basis, however, a post facility known as the Nature of the War Museum served as a reminder to personnel that there was indeed a war going on somewhere nearby. Erected in 1967 in a courtyard at U.S. Army Vietnam Headquarters, this odd facility was designed "to accurately portray the ever changing face of the war." Its official mandate was to demonstrate the "enemy environment" by displaying weapons and booby traps associated with a typical Viet Cong–controlled village. The museum consisted of a full-scale hut, a Buddhist temple, and a water buffalo pen (though no water buffalo), each connected to the other by an underground tunnel. In the middle sat a bamboo and dirt bunker and a hollow haystack hideout with an entrance cut into the side. This simulated village was protected by mock-ups of various booby traps: a punji pit (a hole or depression filled with sharpened bamboo stakes), pressure-detonated 105mm rounds, rusty metal spikes hidden beneath vegetation, and a claymore mine. Each feature was labeled with a little wooden sign stenciled with an explanation like "Booby Trap," "Tunnel Entrance," or "Hiding Place in Haystack."[23]

A replica of a Viet Cong–controlled village was designed to educate Americans who were unfamiliar with such a place—VIP guests of the military, civilian personnel, and soldiers who had not experienced the killing and dying war. Though the Nature of the War Museum attempted to portray the tenacity of the enemy and pay homage to the bravery of infantrymen who encountered these dangers every day, hazardous features labeled with neatly stenciled signs failed to evoke the fear and apprehension grunts had to suppress as they entered village after village searching for the enemy. The museum intended to depict the war but trivialized it instead, with exhibits reminiscent of dioramas at Disneyland. By 1971, the displays had fallen into disrepair, an issue addressed by memos from the commander of the 16th Military History Detachment about maintenance of the facility. He reported to his superiors that the grass was not getting cut and that vegetation had grown over the mock booby traps, ironically rendering them authentically dangerous. But the facility was getting use. Folding chairs, Pepsi cans, and other litter had been found in the hut and haystack, which were ideal places for a headquarters clerk to hide from the work of the war for an afternoon.[24]

As the Nature of the War Museum and Long Binh Post's construction priorities attest, this base and others like it were far removed from combat and even from the country of Vietnam. Writing about Danang, military policeman Charles Anderson reflected on this sense of isolation. "All of

An off-duty G.I. plays tourist for a day, posing in front of a mock temple in the Nature of the War Museum at USARV Headquarters in 1970. The exhibit's structures and weapons displays were the closest many of Long Binh Post's residents came to experiencing Vietnamese culture and the war in the countryside. (Courtesy of Dennis Mansker, author of *A Bad Attitude: A Novel from the Vietnam War*)

these comforts and services made the world of the rear a warm, insulated, womb-capsule into which the sweaty, grimy, screaming, bleeding, writhing-in-the-hot-dust thing that was the war rarely intruded." William Upton, who served at the R&R center at Vung Tau, told his mother upon returning home, "It wasn't all that bad. . . . Most of the time you didn't know you were in a war." Arthur Wiknik described the "fine trimmed lawns, hedges, and flower gardens" of Tan Son Nhut airbase near Saigon as "a tiny piece of transplanted Middle America. . . . Even the buildings were reminiscent of a stateside military post. It was hard to believe I was still in Vietnam." And Tom Fitzharris, stationed at Long Binh Post, wrote a friend in the United States, "I have not lived in Vietnam for ten months. I have had a shit existence on a bad army post in a deserted area. . . . At the moment, it doesn't seem too absurd to say that if the Army wanted to go to the trouble, this might all be a charade. I might be on an island in the Pacific being fed news, radio and television reports about what is supposedly happening around me."[25]

Whatever war news Fitzharris did get, it was not coming from the *Long Binh Post*, the base's weekly newsletter. Whereas combat units' newsletters reported tales of violence and bloodshed, a typical issue of the *Post* makes plain Long Binh's isolation from the war. Employing the breezy tone of a stateside newssheet, the *Post* ignored war news completely to focus on the perils of drug addiction, reviews of new fiction, sports highlights from various unit leagues, classified ads for soldiers wishing to buy and sell their belongings, puzzles and trivia quizzes, and listings for upcoming events like movies, religious services, radio and television programs, and live entertainment at the clubs. There was bad news in the *Post*, just not the killing and dying kind. An August 1971 issue warned of a rash of property thefts and a dangerous conjunctivitis (pink eye) "epidemic" ravaging Military Regions III and IV, which resulted in a ban on the afflicted from mess hall kitchens and swimming pools. Two months later, the *Post* warned of a rabies outbreak among the local animal population, resulting in the eventual extermination of the monkeys that resided in a wild area of the base near the aptly named Monkey Creek.[26]

Rabid monkeys aside, Long Binh Post was very much like a stateside base, a fact that did not escape the attention of soldiers stationed there. One G.I. diarist described his accommodations in 1966, consisting of a locker, cot, and mattress in a cement-floor barracks with an aluminum roof, as "the best I've ever had in the Army." Another remarked that aside from the "more primitive conditions and separation from families, life at

Long Binh wasn't that different from any large Stateside base." The G.I. editor of *Guardians & Enforcers* went a step further in a September 1969 issue, arguing, "Someone should declare Long Binh a State Side Post."[27] Like a fortress wall, Long Binh's material abundance had managed to shut the war out altogether.

The Army brass concurred that rearward areas in Vietnam were closer to home-front life, adopting a decidedly stateside posture toward appearance and military tradition for soldiers stationed there. In the late 1960s, MACV introduced "Courtesy Patrols" to the Vietnam war zone to cruise the streets of stateside bases looking for unmilitary behavior or appearance. The Courtesy Patrols' mission was to "deter incidents, uncover AWOLS and deserters, protect lives and property, identify potential problems and elevate standards of behavior and performance." They roamed rearward bases' many streets, paying special attention to public areas like clubs, snack bars, recreational facilities, and P.X.'s, where they identified inappropriate behavior such as vandalism, insubordination, public drunkenness, and brawling, infractions the patrols then reported to commanding officers or the military police. Soldiers did not regard the Courtesy Patrols well, for most of their time was spent making "on-the-spot corrections" related to the presence of facial hair, the lack of nametags, and the wearing of "ragged, torn, or excessively dirty clothes."[28] Rearward personnel seeking to exert their individual identities with long sideburns and graffitied fatigues bristled at the extra scrutiny.

Photojournalist Mark Jury saw the Courtesy Patrols as part of another war altogether. Writing in 1970, he alleged, "The enemy at the Rear is the petty harassment of an organization with little to do and too many people to do it. Military haircuts, daily shave, starched fatigues, and shined boots are a must." It wasn't all bad, however. "[F]or those who play the game, the time passes quickly at the swimming pool, clubs, sports events, movies, and endless parties."[29] Out in the countryside, where the Viet Cong and North Vietnamese Army were still the enemy, time slowed to a crawl, and niceties like starched fatigues and a clean shave were usually forgotten. For combat troops who passed through bases like Long Binh Post, Courtesy Patrols became emblematic of the rear, a place where regulations could supersede the imperatives of war, where neatness counted for more than bravery.

For its weird blend of military and recreational facilities, its dioramic homage to the "nature of the war," and its stateside-like emphasis on neatness, Long Binh Post was surreal—not quite home, but not quite the war either. It occupied space in between, a place born of the necessity of the war but not beholden to it. Like a sprawling suburb, it grew over time, becoming ever more elaborate even as the war itself was grinding to a halt. For over six years, combat troops encountered Long Binh Post and other bases like it as places of transition on their way to and from the States, on their way to and from R&R, and on their way to and from the hospital. Through these encounters, they came to understand the difference between their war experience and that of rearward personnel, creating an uneasy and complicated relationship between the two groups.

Grunts' encounters with support personnel were sometimes documented in unit newspapers, making the gulf between their separate worlds all the more apparent. For example, the American Division's newspaper *Southern Cross* reported in September 1969 about the training of a professional reserve company composed of rearward personnel "to act as an 'Ace-in-the-hole' if any emergency should arise." The article went on to describe the company's potential missions: to relieve a rifle company from firebase security so that it could be deployed elsewhere; to secure a landing zone in the field so that a besieged company could be extracted; and to relieve those "in serious jeopardy" if all other elements of the battalion were engaged in combat. Underscoring the message that this was a force of last resort, the article described how the support troops "traded in their trucks, cooking ladles, and typewriters for rucksacks, M-16s, ammo, and rations for an overnight mission in the jungle." It is not difficult to imagine the incredulity with which the full-time infantrymen of the American Division viewed such a haphazard assemblage of soldiers.[30]

Likewise, in January 1971, U.S. Army Vietnam's official newspaper, *Army Reporter*, described an encounter between residents of Long Binh Post and the 1st Cavalry Division's Fire Support Base Silver. Through a morale initiative that allowed military musical acts to tour in contested areas, the band 8-Foot Clearance, composed of five soldiers and a nurse, was airlifted to the remote outpost to play at the base's Christmas party. Under the headline "Grunts, Remfs Give Each Other Some Joy," *Army Reporter* acknowledged the tensions that usually existed between the two groups. The article described "the dichotomy of the war in Vietnam" not in terms of communism versus capitalism or democracy versus totalitarianism but rather as "remfs vs. grunts, chairborne, air-conditioned soldiers vs. blood, sweat, and tears." Yet on this day, for a few hours, "smiles, laughs and tears flowed and no one remembered or cared that the entertainers and the entertained lived in two separate worlds while fighting the same war."[31] In emphasizing the reconciliation of grunts and REMFs, the article also highlighted the tensions that existed between them, that their disparate living and working conditions laid bare the unfairness of modern military service.

On even more rare occasions, a REMF would inadvertently stumble into combat, exposing his inexperience as a warrior. After months of desk duty, Joe Dunn got sent into the field as part of a program to deposit intelligence-gathering sensors in remote areas. As he and his host unit set out on a night mission, one of the squad leaders warned him not to fire his weapon if they walked into an ambush. "He explained that we were not infantry and did not know what we were doing. We would be more likely to shoot one of our own than the enemy." Though chastened, Dunn recalls that he "concurred with his analysis totally."[32] Dunn's self-effacement long after the war is admirable because it acknowledges the hierarchy of soldiery that post-war celebrations of veterans tend to leave out: some soldiers utilized their training to become effective warriors, while others served mostly as laborers and technicians, their fighting skills atrophied or forgotten in Vietnam's secure areas.

The drama and irony of these fish-out-of-water stories were perfect for retelling as human-interest stories in military newspapers. In August 1971, the *Observer* printed the tale of SP4 Lyle Roush, a clerk in the 25th Infantry Division's Finance Office. "Clerk Wanders Right into Action" describes how Roush was sent to check the 1st Battalion's leave records, but when he arrived, he saw all the men boarding helicopters. Roush assumed they were returning to a base camp, so he hopped on. Instead, he found himself dumped into a combat assault. Though he was sporting a flak jacket, Roush was armed with only a .45 and some leave records. During a heavy firefight, he spotted an officer and shouted to him, "Sir, I'm not supposed to be here!" The officer quickly outfitted Roush with some grenades and ammunition, and "for the next four hours the finance clerk fought alongside the infantry-men." How must they have regarded one another? Was Roush awed by their courage and professionalism under fire? Were the grizzled combat veterans amused and protective of their misplaced charge? In this encounter, as in others, the disparity in war experiences of grunts and REMFs was laid bare, giving each side a comfortable sense of belonging among their own but, at the same time, mapping the chasm that lay between their worlds.[33]

When SP4 Roush returned home from the war, he undoubtedly had a good story to tell his friends and family, but it is unlikely he parlayed his inadvertent brush with combat into a book. Memoirs of the Vietnam experience are helpful for understanding the sacrifices and contributions of so many Americans to the cause of containing communism. Yet although hundreds of thousands of soldiers were stationed at Long Binh Post and "REMF citadels" elsewhere in Vietnam, few ever bothered to publish their stories. Combat memoirs of the Vietnam War abound, however, and their titles often highlight the duties performed by the veteran-authors: *Cleared Hot! A Marine Combat Pilot's Vietnam Diary*; *Marine Sniper: 93 Confirmed Kills*; *When Thunder Rolled: An F-105 Pilot over North Vietnam*; *Pathfinder: First In, Last Out*; *LRRP Team Leader*; *Doc: Platoon Medic*; *Death in the Jungle: Diary of a Navy Seal*; and *Blood on the Risers: An Airborne Soldier's Thirty-five Months in Vietnam*, just to name a few. These books and dozens of others like them constitute an action-oriented subgenre of Vietnam War literature, which at its best is represented by W. D. Ehrhart (*Vietnam Perkasie*), Tobias Wolff (*In Pharaoh's Army*), and the masterful Tim O'Brien (*If I Die in a Combat Zone*). While some of these authors used their Vietnam experiences to make a mark on American literature in general, most set out merely to tell a good story. A typical back cover, from Jack Leninger's *Time Heals No Wounds*, promises readers "the living nightmares behind the headlines and TV news . . . the tragic mistakes, the selfless courage, the precious young lives lost."[34]

With taglines like these, it is difficult for a memoir about riding a desk to compete on the shelves at the local bookstore. Only a handful of support troops made the attempt with memoirs about their Vietnam tours, though several were self-published and only one, Tracey Kidder's *My Detachment: A Memoir*, was widely distributed. Charles Anderson's *Vietnam: The Other War* depicts life "in the rear with a beer" during the author's six-month stint with the 3rd M.P.'s (military police) at Danang. David Willson's *REMF Diary: A Novel of the Vietnam War Zone* and its sequel *The REMF Returns* maintain the pretense of literary fiction, yet both books contain only the mind-numbing minutiae of an obsessively kept diary, suggesting that they are, in fact, the published versions of Willson's own Vietnam War diary. Willson attempts to dress up his memoir with an improbable helicopter accident, but no amount of literary license can conceal the banality of his thirteen months as a headquarters clerk. As mentioned previously, Dunn's *Desk Warrior* also tries to bridge the divide between combat and clerking, but his brush with death in a firefight bears the ring of truth: it was chaotic and brief, Dunn did not discharge his weapon, and when it was over, he authenticated his presence in combat by snapping pictures of the Vietnamese dead with his Kodak Instamatic.

The quotation marks in the title of Dean Muehlberg's *REMF "War Stories"* are deliberate because the author's 1969 tour as a clerk-typist was so far removed from combat that his rifle actually grew mold while it sat idle in its rack. His typical workweek in coastal Nha Trang involved ten- to twelve-hour shifts, six and a half days a week, followed by heavy partying in his off-duty hours. "A good afternoon was drinking for a few hours until a mild high came on, and then making a trip to our local steam bath or one of the others downtown. After this pause we continued drinking in the bars until a couple of hours before curfew, when we went to a brothel to finish off the day." In *Pizza and Mortars*, William Upton describes a similarly predictable routine as a crew chief on a Caribou transport plane based at Vung Tau. Each morning, Upton prepared the plane for takeoff. "A half hour later, in Saigon, we unloaded passengers, loaded cargo for Hue and Quang Tri up north, with a stop at Qui Nhon on the central coast scheduled for our return trip. That, or something similar, was my general day-to-day routine—every day, all day long." Upton did once encounter small-arms fire during a drop-off at Quang Tri, but otherwise, he recalled, "crewing a Caribou in a war zone was much like working a regular job in the states." George Watson's tour as an administrative clerk for the 101st Airborne Division at Bien Hoa, detailed in *Voices from the Rear*, was even further removed from the war. The tedium of office work was sometimes broken up by lunch breaks at the local pool. "The water was refreshingly warm. We could sit up on the sides, swim, do laps, or whatever. There weren't any girls lolling around, but I had no complaints. I had pulled one lucky assignment."[35]

Since none of these books delivers much in the way of bloodshed, suspense, or drama, they tend to rely on humor and irony to keep the reader's attention. Juxtapositions between conventional notions of war and the banality of rearward service abound, particularly in Willson's work. "19 July 1967, Wednesday Morning: It's 6:10. Just ate breakfast, had formation, and here I am ready to go to the office to do battle." On another day, he described being "wounded" when he tucked into some mashed potatoes and found a stray piece of bone. Upton's memoir offers the contrast of "pizza and mortars" in the title, a phrase that refers to an episode the author dubbed "the pizza wars," when he ate too many hot-pepper pizzas in a service club. Later in his tour, Upton suffered another injury, a cut to the arm made by a razor-wielding drunk as he left a bar girl's apartment. "So, I was wounded in Vietnam," he writes, "but not in battle." Pete Whalon, author of *The Saigon Zoo: Vietnam's Other War*, actually emerged from the war in better shape than he went in. During his stint at Long Binh Post, he underwent elective surgery for a deviated septum, which had prevented him since childhood from breathing through his nose during physical exertion.[36]

While infantrymen had to contend with mud and leeches, not to mention the enemy, support troops struggled under their own adverse working conditions. Soldiers and airmen in a variety of roles cleared land, erected buildings and bunkers, and maintained equipment, all day, every day, in the stifling heat. Some of them worked indoors, though, in environments far removed from combat. In *The REMF Returns*, Willson started an entry for Tuesday, 25 July 1967, as any grunt might: "I feel very grimy and dirty." But he goes on to explain the problem: "Coffee grounds stuck to my Adam's apple, carbon black on my ears, orange peel residue under my nails along with cigarette ashes and other detritus of the great midden into which I delve every other day, it seems."[37] The most serious occupational hazard many support troops faced was boredom. In *Vietnam: The Other War*, Anderson describes getting coffee at work as an elaborate, thirty-minute ritual that, performed several times each day, was designed solely to kill time. He explains, "Victory to the rear-echelon unit member was not measured in terms of dead bodies or captured weapons and rice or secured villages. Victory was measured in terms of completeness of isolation from the war."[38]

If that is how victory was measured, then Pete Whalon's two-year deployment was fought to unconditional surrender. At his first duty station, a warehouse near Saigon, Whalon and his G.I. co-workers conducted a "lazy-ass competition" to see how long they could go without doing any work, as in "nothing, not lift, move or place one piece of material on a shelf, not help anybody else do any work or give assistance in any way." To pass the time, they constructed a hidden clubhouse in a loft of the warehouse and conducted forklift races in an empty building. Overall, "with zero motivation and ambition, our work pace was slightly slower than grass growing." Later, Whalon was transferred to Long Binh Post, where he worked at a communications center. There, the corporal in charge instructed his soldier employees that if they showed up promptly at 8:00 A.M. and looked busy for a few hours, they could leave at eleven and spend the rest of the day at a nearby swimming pool. They could not show their faces in the company's barracks until after 4:00 P.M., lest they draw the notice of officers and lifers (career soldiers). Whalon eventually parlayed his work avoidance into the ultimate Vietnam gig, lifeguarding at one of Long Binh Post's many swimming pools. In this capacity, Whalon's duties included maintenance of the pool, rescuing imperiled swimmers (by yelling "Stand up, stupid!" because the pool was only four feet deep), and presiding over a nightly party with music, beer, water football, and drug-fueled Monopoly marathons. Since there were seldom any women present, Whalon "often felt like [he] was hosting a perpetual, out-of-control bachelor party—seven nights a week." The greatest hazard he faced was burnout, causing him to eschew marijuana before noon on Sundays in order to have "a clear head for at least six hours a week."[39]

Some support troops were so isolated from the war that it ceased to have any meaning as a dangerous enterprise or any historic connection to American wars past. In *REMF Diary*, clerk David Willson describes hearing the song "John Brown," written by Bob Dylan in 1963, on the radio while at work. The song is a classic tale of disillusionment: a young man filled with hope goes off to war for honor and country. He is gravely wounded and returns home cruelly disfigured, embittered at his mother for encouraging him to serve and at his country for sending him to kill other young men like himself. The song is rich with allusions to the American Civil War— trains, cannon, and the title character, "John Brown"—enabling Dylan to condemn war generally without making specific reference to the growing militarism of the Cold War. Yet by alluding to a war most Americans viewed as just, Dylan challenges the notion that war offers any solution at all to the problems of mankind. Hearing the song in Vietnam in 1966, an American soldier might connect his own experiences with those of the title character, and the Vietnam War with other American conflicts. But in the context of a rearward headquarters, isolated from violence and death, the song raised no such probing questions. Rather, it seemed out of step with the kind of war being waged there. Willson's REMF listened intently to "John Brown" and offered this critique of Dylan: "[It's] a good song, but I think it is an obvious effort of someone who hadn't been to war. Most of war is office work."[40]

This offhanded remark raises important questions about the meaning of military service: what was the dominant experience of the Vietnam War, and to whom does the memory of the war belong? One answer is found on the front cover of Jack Leninger's memoir *Time Heals No Wounds*, where the publisher eagerly promises "the agony of the real war in Vietnam—the grunt's war—told by a soldier who lived through it." Soldiers serving in ground combat operations would have agreed; the "real" war was their war. The U.S. Army also tended to endorse this point of view. In 1970, the

Army Reporter—with a peak circulation of 95,000 copies weekly, it was the Army's mouthpiece in Vietnam—published a multipage photo essay entitled "The Grunt—It Was His War." The accompanying text compared the grunt of Vietnam to the doughboy of World War I and the G.I. of World War II, situating his sacrifice for the nation on the same historical continuum. The photographs accompanying the article offer archetypal images of the Vietnam experience that also hearken back to World War II's Pacific theater: foot soldiers taking cover in tall grass, crossing a waist-deep river holding their weapons overhead, and shooting during a firefight. The essay concludes with a photograph of a heroic-looking G.I. wearing a helmet, rifle in hand, standing in silhouette alone atop a hill. The images are so focused on the infantry that a clerk would have struggled to locate himself in the Vietnam story they purported to tell.[41]

The *Army Reporter* images portrayed the grunt as a noble figure, separate from other soldiers but ready to die for them, and as an ideal man. The nobility of the grunt was also addressed in *The Professional*, the semimonthly newsletter for the 5th Battalion, 46th Infantry. In an essay entitled "G-R-U-N-T Spells HELL" for his regular column, the battalion's chaplain connected service in the infantry with manhood, endowing grunts with a particularly potent form of masculinity. "G-R-U-N-T spells 'HELL' for the 11-B [infantryman] whose pad for the year is a jungle floor. But it also spells 'man' because he becomes a man as he humps through 'HELL.' Because the name of the game is survival and it takes the qualities of a man to make it." The body of the essay is an acrostic that explains the qualities of the grunt: G for genuine, R for ready, U for united, N for noble, and T for thoughtful. Each passage reflects back on the theme of masculinity by concluding with the tagline "And that's a man." The import of the essay is clear: the real war was being fought by the grunts. For their efforts, they earned and displayed a manhood that exceeded that of soldiers serving in other capacities, and they took on a kind of noble martyrdom specific to those who sacrifice without proper recognition. The essay closes with a prayer in all caps, at once a call to arms for would-be grunts, an ego boost for existing grunts, and a divine sanction for their conduct: "GOD GIVE HIM THE GUTS TO BE A GRUNT."[42]

Soldiers did not necessarily enjoy serving in the infantry, but grunts did embrace their suffering as a right of passage and as the primary element that distinguished their service from that of other military personnel, including combat aviators. A letter from marine David Westphall to his brother demonstrates grunts' sense of pride, as well as their desire for recognition of the hardships they endured. After weeks of patrolling in the monsoon rains,

> [w]e were all in sad shape now. I know that at one point, my feet about to crack open, my stomach knotted by hunger and diarrhea, my back feeling like a mirror made of nerves shattered in a million pieces by my flak jacket, pack, and extra mortars and machine-gun ammo, my hands a mass of hamburger from thorn cuts, and my face a mass of welts from mosquitoes, I desired greatly to throw down everything, slump into the water of the paddy, and sob.

Immediately following this description, the young marine concluded his letter with the following anecdote: "I remember a captain, an aviator, who, observing a group of grunts toasting the infantry in a bar, said, 'You damned infantry think you're the only people who exist.' You're damned right we do." An ambush ended Westphall's life not long after.[43]

Some support troops regarded grunts admiringly, as Westphall felt they should. On his way to an overseas R&R, clerk-typist Dean Muehlberg encountered a company of infantrymen on stand-down at the Danang out-processing center. "We were in awe of the marines," he gushed. "We didn't speak to them or get in their way. We didn't know their language. You sensed that after the constant threat of death, of terrible harm, nothing else scared them (at least earthly things), and that they wouldn't or couldn't tolerate any real or imagined harassment." Years later, when he wrote his memoir about the war, Muehlberg's admiration was still intact as he described the marines he saw that day. They were the "direct descendents of the men in Caputo's *Rumor of War* . . . the men that went into the pages of Herr's *Dispatches*."[44] That is, they transcended ordinary soldiers; they had become icons, a transformation that was possible only because there were so few of them.

Grunts' service is further distinguished when compared with the wartime experiences of the majority of Vietnam veterans, who served in supporting roles, often safely in the rear. And yet, in one of its own histories of the Vietnam War, the U.S. Army denied any friction between combat and support troops. In particular, the *Vietnam Studies* volume *Logistic Support* cites the "close and wonderful relationship between the man doing the fighting and the man providing support." The Army attributed this relationship "to the fact that both were exposed to the same dangers" in Vietnam and cited as proof the story of an Army truck driver who was posthumously awarded the Medal of Honor for using his supply convoy to break up an ambush.[45] To be sure, rearward personnel did on occasion have to demonstrate their valor, but such cases were rare. Infantrymen were a slim minority of U.S. forces in Vietnam, but they did most of the dying. This uneven distribution of danger, privation, and suffering led to grunts' resentment of support troops, who risked far less and endured fewer hardships.

The Army's history of the war was too generous toward internal conflicts between combat troops and support personnel because expressions of grunts' resentment during the war are not hard to find. Sometimes G.I. journalists made fun of support troops in their unit newspapers, such as the humorous advice column "Dear Nguyen," printed in *Octagon* in June 1969.

> Dear Nguyen: Is it true that Saigon warriors have more rank than us out here in the boonies? —Field Grade
>
> Dear Field: Yes, they are ranker, but that's only because their air conditioners are usually broken.[46]

Grunts also pleaded their case to higher authorities, such as this seething letter to President Nixon from thirty members of a combat infantry company written in April 1969:

> In order to clarify the matter, I think it is necessary to explain to you that basically there are two different wars here in Vietnam. While we are out in the field living like animals, putting our lives on the line twenty-four hours a day, seven days a week, the guy in the rear's biggest problem is that he can receive only one television station. There is no comparison between the two. . . . The man in the rear doesn't know what it is like to burn a leech off his body with a cigarette, to go unbathed for months at a time; to walk all day on feet raw from immersion foot; or to wake up to the sound of incoming mortar rounds and the cry of your buddy screaming "Medic!" In short, he does not realize the tremendous emotional and physical strain that the men in the field are forced to endure.[47]

Although the letter complains that support troops failed to appreciate the hardships of combat, its real targets were public and civilian authorities. It was they who did not understand the discrepancies between the front and the rear, as they afforded Vietnam soldiers of all kinds equal measures of deference and respect.

On occasion, combat soldiers pleaded their case directly to the American people. In December 1970, retired officer John H. Funston wrote a letter to the editor of the *New York Times* criticizing military pay structure that failed to compensate riflemen commensurate with the risks they took in the field. According to Funston, riflemen constituted 7 percent of U.S. forces in Vietnam, but they took 50 percent of the total casualties. In return, however, riflemen received only base pay and combat pay, and not the hazardous duty pay that would have set their paychecks apart from those of rearward personnel. The significance of combat pay had been trivialized, Funston argued, because every soldier received it, "regardless of his rank and whether he is a rifleman being shot at or a lifeguard at a rest area swimming pool."[48] Funston accurately described military policy at the time, which afforded infantrymen like David Westphall, who died in combat, the same pay as support troops like stoner lifeguard Pete Whalon. Even if Funston's statistics on the distribution of casualties were wrong altogether, his letter is still important as an indicator of combat soldiers' perceptions: that they were risking their lives and suffering disproportionately, and they were not even being compensated for it.

Published in 1970, Funston's critique of pay inequities was actually old news. In 1967, the *New York Times* reported on budget cuts in the cost-of-living allowance (COLA) paid to 31,200 military personnel in Vietnam. Unlike combat pay and hazardous duty pay, the COLA was a more obvious target for cost savings because it affected fewer servicemen. Military authorities chose to eliminate the COLA, instead of cutting support troops' combat pay, because drawing such clear lines between types of military personnel would have rewarded the bravery of the few while incurring the wrath of the many. Ranging from $27 per month for privates to $84 per month for generals, the COLA was ostensibly designed to offset "excessive living costs in Vietnam" for personnel in the Saigon area who had to arrange their own housing. But, the *Times* reported, an *Air Force Times* study found that 60 percent of personnel drawing the COLA were actually living for free in air-conditioned hotels acquired as military housing, allowing them to pocket the extra money. In addition to a savings of $21 million each year, the *Air Force Times*—like the *Army Times* and the *Navy Times*, a quasi-official publication of the U.S. military—cited fairness among the Pentagon's reasons for canceling the COLA. "It is difficult for men in the field to understand why those in the air-conditioned hotels should draw more money than those in the dugouts and bunkers."[49] Compared with the total cost of the war, the savings was as symbolic as the gesture, which acknowledged that rearward troops already benefiting from a stable tactical environment ought not to get doubly compensated for their good fortune.

Unequal living conditions and an unfair pay structure were not the only issues chafing combat personnel in Vietnam. Rearward personnel enjoyed greater freedom of movement and easier access to recreational facilities, whereas combat troops stationed in contested areas had to follow strict regulations formulated in the interest of safety. And because grunts tended to serve in unstable, less accessible areas, the construction boom in recreational facilities was also slow to reach them. In a 1971 discussion of morale problems, military authorities addressed the inequity:

> Compounding this problem is the soldier's knowledge that although
> he, as a member of a combat unit[,] is thus restricted, rear echelon
> personnel stationed in the metropolitan and resort areas are often
> free to enjoy the available recreational facilities. Many soldiers will
> not accept the idea that U.S. Army personnel, who by virtue of luck
> or the possession of a certain skill, and who are not often called
> upon to risk their lives, should be able to avail themselves of recreational privileges, while those who are assigned to combat units are,
> in their own words, "kept in jail."

The memo concluded that regulations restricting combat troops to their base camps ought to be eased, enabling soldiers to get "some freedom from the Green Machine." With ominous reference to "incidents . . . indicative of increased troop discontent," its author warned of "even greater problems unless some sort of local safety valve is provided."[50]

Grunts' resentment over the material conditions of life in the rear—the standard of living, pay, freedom of movement, and access to recreational facilities—masked concern about a less tangible disparity, that of class. Despite military publications' attempts to frame combat as an ennobling experience, grunts were not buying it. Writing in the 1980s, former marine lieutenant William Broyles recalled bitterly that, within the culture of the war, "it was not a privilege to be able to fight; it was instead evidence that one had failed to understand how to manipulate the system, as if anyone not smart enough to get a deferment or at least to get a job in the rear was too dumb to do anything but carry a rifle."[51] A 1980 Veterans Administration study supported what Vietnam veterans already knew, that "high school dropouts [serving in Vietnam] were three times more likely to experience heavy combat than were college graduates."[52] Further exacerbating tensions between grunts and REMFs, rumors described a "watch list" for the sons of the wealthy and well connected. Whether a verbal warning or an actual document, the watch list circulated among the various U.S. headquarters in Vietnam, ensuring that local commanders were aware of the presence of a particular VIP soldier in their unit. These fortunate sons might then be given favorable duty to keep them out of harm's way, shielding both the soldier's body and his commanding officer's career.[53] The unfairness of it all, especially in a war ostensibly for democracy, undermined morale because combat troops resented the opportunities and amenities their role denied them, and rear echelon troops labored with a gnawing awareness that someone else was fighting in their place.

U.S. military authorities throughout the world addressed the morale crisis of the late 1960s and early 1970s in many ways. In Vietnam, they eased regulations governing appearance, alcohol consumption, and female companionship; they eased pass restrictions and work schedules; and they increased soldiers' access to recreational facilities and consumer goods. Military authorities also waged the war for morale by trying to ease tensions between grunts and REMFs. In 1971, *Army Reporter* began running a column entitled "MOS Close-up" focusing on noncombat Military Occupational Specialties. These articles implicitly acknowledged that rearward personnel were underappreciated by asking readers to remember the contributions support troops made to the war. The descriptions of their tasks and trials also gave support personnel permission to forgive themselves for not serving more rigorous tours of duty.

For example, "Dog's No Problem in 'Nam" reminded G.I. readers about the role Army postal clerks played in raising their spirits. "If you are in a good mood today, it could be because you got a great letter from home, and without the help of the postal clerks, you might never have received the letter." In a second-person appeal, the article asked soldiers to be kind to postal clerks, suggesting that resentment and hostility may have leeched into interactions between the two. "Take the time to smile and be pleasant with these men whenever possible, for you have them to thank for keeping those cards and letters coming in." Likewise, the MOS Close-up "All the World's a Stage" explained the presence of uniformed artists and actors in Vietnam. After highlighting the Special Services Entertainment Specialist's function—planning and producing concerts and plays—*Army Reporter* asked soldiers to appreciate this contribution to the war effort. "They are members of the Green Machine, but more than that they are actors, and more than that they are concerned human beings who try to bring a lot of joy and entertainment into your life. How about a round of applause?" And an MOS Close-up on clerk-typists laid that article's intentions bare: "No matter how often you put down those 'chairborne' clerks, they're an absolute necessity for your existence."[54]

Other unit newspapers, some published earlier in the war, shared the defensive tone of the MOS Close-up articles in reminding grunts that REMFs suffered too. *Delta Advisor*, for example, covered the Can Tho Special Services branch in September 1968. "On the surface an assignment with special services appears to be a soft job. But a look at what it takes to provide the things expected reveals it as a job full of headaches, last minute changes, and plenty of work." The Marine Corps publication *Sea Tiger* addressed hardships faced by a data-processing platoon operating in an air-conditioned office around the clock. "Although the labor is not physically taxing, remaining mentally alert throughout a 12-hour shift can be challenging." Some rearward personnel did function in physically demanding jobs, such as troops in the quartermaster corps, who lifted heavy crates all day long. "While the rifleman on the front is cutting his slow way through wait-a-minute vines, men in supply—like the 15th's Redhat riggers—can match him drop for drop in sweat and strain, even though they work in the rear area."[55]

As these articles point out, support troops' hardships often consisted of boredom and chafing against military authority. "They may call him a rear echelon warrior, a man that 'gets over,' one that 'has the good life,'" a 1969 *First Team* exposé on clerks explained, but clerks also had to perform K.P. duty, guard duty, and other menial tasks. In quoting an administrative officer, the article offered clerks praise for their wartime sacrifices that must have seemed superficial to the combat veterans of the 1st Air Cavalry Division. "Clerks have got to be frustrated at times. They deal with such large numbers, complex problems, different regulations, all kinds of forms. The job isn't physically tough, but it causes mental anguish . . . call it the burden of boredom." On the subject of rearward personnel "getting over," the American Division's *Southern Cross* was even more blunt, in case anybody wondered: "Lifeguard's Job, Not an Easy One."[56]

The U.S. military's attempt to moderate differences between combat soldiers and rearward personnel was obviously guided by concern over morale for both groups. If grunts felt that the burden of the war was unshared, military authorities feared they might prove less effective at their work, refuse to take risks or follow orders, and succumb to the lure of drugs. And if support troops felt that their contributions to the war were trivial, they might slack off, go AWOL, participate in black market activities, or spend their off-duty hours getting high. According to the U.S. military, everyone, from the Special Services clerk to the Special Forces sniper, contributed to the mission and shared its risks. But instead of moderating differences between the two groups, articles like the MOS Close-ups tended to highlight them. No reasonable person serving in Vietnam could possibly equate the challenges of typing reports, processing mail, or unloading shipping containers with the misery of long-range patrols, the cruelty of combat, and the omnipresent fear of death. William Broyles, whose tour of duty in Vietnam was a mix of combat duty and work in secure areas, recalled the informational campaign with cynicism. "We were constantly told that Vietnam was a war without front lines, that the enemy could strike anywhere. It was a lie." Despite military authorities' best efforts to bridge the divide, the fact remained that grunts and REMFs may have served on the same side, but they did not serve in the same war.[57]

For their part, rearward personnel were also aware of disparities between their wars. If grunts were hostile, REMFs in turn reacted with defensiveness, humor, gratitude, and a measure of guilt for their relative good fortune. Like combat troops, support personnel articulated their version of the war in unit newspapers published for general consumption. The MOS Close-up articles are actually a prime example. The G.I. journalists who wrote them, especially those assigned to Command Information offices who reported the news as part of their official duties, usually had more in common with the clerks and cooks they profiled than they did with the grunts actually fighting the war. In this sense, the defensive tone of the MOS Close-ups can be seen as personal in nature, with G.I. journalists asking consideration for themselves through profiles of their REMF peers.

At other times, rearward personnel dialogued among themselves about their contributions to the war. In 1970, the quarterly magazine *Kysu*, published for U.S. Army Engineers, included what can only be described as a pep talk on its inside back cover. It listed several engineering feats in South Vietnam: miles of road paved, acres of forest cleared, tonnage of rock crushed, and so on. The engineers' accomplishments are not the instructive element, however. The title of the piece is "What Did You Do in the War, Daddy?," an obvious reference to the memorable World War I British recruitment poster and the persistent, vaguely accusing query it spawned. In the original poster, a cherub-faced child asks her tweedy father about his contribution to the Great War, shaming him and other middle-class family men into enlistment.[58] In the context of the *Kysu* piece, the question resonates with similar concerns—that in the modern world, wars are won or lost on the basis of industrial capacity and, by extension, organized bureaucracy. Because the American effort in Vietnam was contingent on the free flow of weapons and supplies around the war zone, the argument went, support personnel shared the burden of war and the pride of victory equally with their combat peers. Unfortunately for the Army engineers in need of a morale boost, the editors of *Kysu* chose a profoundly unheroic photograph to represent their feats in Vietnam: a guy riding a squat cart down the center of a vacant asphalt highway, painting a long white stripe on the pavement as he goes.[59]

A G.I. editorialist in the MACV Traffic Management Agency in Saigon also mused about his peers' sacrifices. He framed the REMF experience in contrast to combat yet also as something to be genuinely proud of. His essay "And the Rockets Red Glare" described recent enemy rocket attacks in the Saigon area and the hysteria that accompanied them. The author then pointed out the war's banal but necessary patterns on rearward bases.

> No, the war as we know it in TMA is a quieter thing, more tedious, more drawn out than it is fearsome, a war that calls more on our reserves of patience and self-denial than on flash demands of battle- field courage and heroism. We must be here, for twelve long months, away from family, friends, campus and coffee-shop and our favorite "fishing holes" back home. We're not griping about it. We're simply doing our bit. Taking our turn at freedom's watch. Our "thing" is to move men and supplies through this country. Our burden is to stand on guard through the long hours. Putting in days at the airline coun- ter or in the port TCMD counter or behind some steel desk.

The remainder of the piece characterized the American occupation force in Vietnam as a massive "demonstration" in support of freedom, a clear dig at the antiwar movement agitating for troop withdrawals back home. As a whole, the essay seems designed to provide soldiers with arguments in support of their noncombat brand of service, perhaps to assuage the doubts that might emerge in idle moments.[60]

Other examples of REMF self-awareness include the cartoon series "PFC Remf," printed in *Hi-Lite Magazine*, a slick quarterly published for the men of the U.S. Army Support Command in Saigon. One cartoon depicts a clerk at his desk sharing a laugh with two buxom Vietnamese co-workers. In his typewriter sits an unfinished letter to his sweetheart that reads, "Dearest Margaret, I'm writing you from the battlefield of Vietnam to tell you how very much I love you and miss you. Things are very dull around here, what with no beautiful girls around here." Another cartoon depicts an angry G.I. truck driver at the wheel shaking his fist at a small Vietnamese person on a bicycle, whom he has just run over. The caption, stating the thoughts of both the driver and the reader, exclaims, "Whattsa matta you? Think you're in New York City or somethin'?" A third "PFC Remf" cartoon depicts an off-duty G.I. sitting in a lawn chair nursing an iced drink and listening to his stereo. He fiddles with a knob on the tuner, indicating that it is on the fritz. The caption relates his thoughts: "Accursed generator power is fading out again."[61] The cartoons have an inside-joke quality about them as they illustrate the unflattering excesses of life in the rear.

Some clerks of the 25th Infantry Division were profiled by *Army Reporter* in August 1970 for their ability to poke fun at themselves. They knew they would never earn a legitimate valor award, so they created one of their own: the Silver Paper Clip. These clerk comedians fashioned the award, wrote up a citation, and held a ceremony in which the Silver Paper Clip was bestowed on the shortest man (i.e., the one with the least amount of time left on his tour) in the unit. His citation read as follows:

> Specialist Howard distinguished himself with conspicuous gal-
> lantry and intrepidity at the risk of his life when he single-handedly
> answered over 200 telephone calls and processed in fifteen new
> men, exposing himself to a hail of questions. He moved from the
> relative safety of his desk to the P.X. where he repeatedly bought
> cases of soda. He organized and led his section as they swept out
> their hootch. Ignoring the personnel NCO, he cleaned his typewriter,
> picked up the mail, petted four dogs, ran off three stencils and took
> his malaria pill. Specialist Howard's profound courage and devo-
> tion to duty were in keeping with the highest traditions of military
> service and reflected great credit upon himself, his unit, the 25th
> Infantry Division, and the United States Army.[62]

Embedded in the parody is a wealth of information about the typical clerk's daily life. He spent his days answering phones, answering questions, running errands, following regulations, keeping house, and keeping up spirits. But the citation also contains a generous dose of rueful self-reflection.

Created by and for rearward personnel, the jokes behind the "PFC Remf" cartoons and the Silver Paper Clip award are instructive of how rearward personnel regarded their role in the war. With the fake award, the joke is obvious: the clerk's war was so banal, so devoid of bravery, that it invited ridicule. The award's creators seemed to understand their place in the war story and, instead of trying to make their contribution something more than it was, they accepted and celebrated their status by poking fun at themselves and the monotonous tasks they performed each day. The humor behind the "PFC Remf" cartoons is darker and more complex. The images likewise relate the reality of a very unwarlike war, but they depict support personnel in a consistently unfavorable light: that they held little respect for Vietnamese civilians; that they were sedentary and spoiled; and that they tended to amplify their hardships to the folks at home. Because they were drawn by a soldier stationed in the rear, the cartoons suggest an element of self-loathing in their accusations that support personnel were most concerned with their own material comfort and that their sacrifices were merely illusion calculated to extract sympathy from loved ones at home who did not know any better. Unlike the creators of the Silver Paper Clip, who implicitly referenced the sacrifices of soldiers who earn real awards for valor, the "PFC Remf" cartoonist did not acknowledge the perils of combat for other, less fortunate Americans. To do so might hint at support troops' complicity in the deaths of the soldiers who took their places on the front lines, draining the jokes of their fun.

In their memoirs, former support personnel have acknowledged, directly and indirectly, the complex feelings evoked by serving in safety while others risked their lives. As a clerk in Nha Trang, Dean Muehlberg worked in the Awards and Decorations section, where he processed recommendations for medals. He had to read each petition and decide what type of commendation was appropriate. "For the first month it seemed a dirty job. I did not feel worthy! I was sitting in relative security reading grizzly, awe inspiring accounts of the courage of my not so fortunate brothers who were out in the thick of it. And then sitting in judgment on the 'degree' of their courage, their deed." Looking back in *Desk Warrior*, Joe Dunn seemed accepting of his place in history and grateful for the kind of war he fought in Vietnam. "If I could replay the Vietnam year, I probably wouldn't live it much differently. Fortunately, by the grace of God, I didn't experience that many traumas and I didn't carry back with me ghosts with which to struggle for the rest of my life. I don't have that many regrets." It could have been worse, he seemed to say, much, much worse.[63]

For Dunn, who became a history instructor at a small South Carolina college, the Vietnam War continued to play a role in his personal and professional life long after he returned home. Likewise, a veteran-turned-archivist at the National Archives and Records Administration in College

Park, Maryland, kept a reminder of his time in Vietnam close at hand. Sitting on his desk for inquiring researchers to see was a framed black-and-white Department of the Army poster titled "The Soldier in Vietnam." Beneath the title were four wartime contributions bulleted by stars. The companion drawing depicted a standard-issue grunt charging over debris in ankle-deep water. His fatigues are torn at the knee with a wound that appears to be spurting blood. But judging by the determined look on the soldier's grizzled face, he is undeterred by pain or fear. He is in a ready stance, and his muscles flex as he grips his rifle.

By itself, the original image is unironic and tends to obscure the knotty realities of military service in Vietnam. The complexity of the image and its interpretive value come from the modifications the veteran made to the poster when it sat on his desk decades earlier, when he was an Army clerk stationed at Nha Trang. Back then, he doctored the poster to make the idealized soldier look more like himself. He added a dark mustache, glasses, and his own name over the G.I.'s nametag.[64] The result is an odd discourse between the military and one of its soldiers. On the one hand, the poster depicts an ideal soldier in Vietnam and cites compelling reasons for his service that would make any grunt's chest swell with pride. On the other, a clerk serving in that same war examined the image and found it wanting because the soldier depicted was so far removed from his own experience. By making the soldier on the poster look more like himself, he bridged the divide, but the result is an intended absurdity that raises difficult questions for all soldiers who serve in less-than-glorious capacities: What is my contribution? How is it valued? Where do I fit in the story of the war?

Writing home to his father in June 1969, Rob Riggan, a clerk in a medical battalion near Lai Khe, wondered the same thing. Riggan's letter suggests an emotional war within, where his desire to serve and demonstrate bravery, to prove his manhood and be a hero, battled with his instincts for self-preservation. "I wonder, [if] I really needed to fight, would I, and at the same time hope to God the situation never arises. [Yet I] still wish the comfort [of knowing] I am brave. Am I a fool?"[65] Riggan's questions about combat resonated with other soldiers as well. A rocket attack caused the introspective Muehlberg to wonder how he would respond if he "ever really got into some shit." Writing in REMF "War Stories," he explained: "It was that old harping thing about war and guts and stuff, that thing way deep down that was always there, not so far down at a time like this when you felt humiliated. . . . I could see how it would make men do crazy things at the wrong time, fearing the question mark in their own soul more

than death. I felt cheated again, but not enough to volunteer for combat."
George Watson's reaction to a rocket attack on the airfield at Bien Hoa was
less reflective and understandably more self-serving. As the rockets fell farther and farther from his hiding place, he thought, "Good, the 'gooks' are
finally zeroing in on the airport."[66]

This scenario—rockets falling on otherwise safe bases—was somewhat
common. It was not so common that Pete Whalon ever describes experiencing it during his two years at Saigon and Long Binh, but it was common
enough that rearward personnel had to wonder about it. In 1969, a G.I.
journalist writing for *The Professionals* asked, "What is it to be a veteran
of combat?" He provided an answer from a combat soldier's point of view.
Referencing the "omnipresent bunkers, wire and enemy mortars" at bases
large and small throughout South Vietnam, the writer suggested that some
may equate service in a war zone with combat. "But is this combat? No,"
he concluded, "to run at the blast of a siren or to hit the dirt as a mortar
round detonates into a ball of flame is instinct." Actual combat required the
individual to suppress fear in order to fight, not just to survive a dangerous
situation. The remainder of the piece focused on an archetypal Vietnam
combat mission, a helicopter assault on a Viet Cong–controlled village, in
which soldiers advanced toward danger instead of cowering from it.[67]

Curiosity about what they were missing occasionally got the better of
support troops. When soldiers went on R&R, most chose one of two options:
a sojourn at an in-country resort run by the military, or an out-of-country
vacation in one of several Pacific Rim destinations. Very rarely, they availed
themselves of a third option, which involved experimenting with another
form of duty in Vietnam. For example, the *Castle Courier* article "R&R Spent
'Eating Jungle'" told the story of a legal clerk with an engineering brigade
headquartered at Long Binh who "yearned to go where the action was."
For three days during his R&R, he joined a land-clearing company known
as the "Jungle Eaters" operating in a remote area east of Saigon. There,
he learned to operate a Rome plow, an enormous bulldozer that shredded
whatever lay in its path. Because of their size and power, Rome plows were
often used to clear old-growth jungle, placing their operators in contested
territory. The sense of adventure, the danger, and the thrill of operating a
machine larger than a mimeograph probably motivated the legal clerk to
spend his R&R this way.[68]

Soldiers who participated in dangerous missions knew exactly who and
what they were, combat veterans, but other soldiers spent their tours in
Vietnam questioning their role, their contributions, their very identity. In

his letter to his father, Rob Riggan wrestled with these issues. A friend of his had volunteered for five months of service in the field, an option open to rearward personnel but one that Riggan and most other support troops did not take. This friend returned from the front to tell Riggan about his experiences in combat, creating still more confusion. "Donny can go back home and tell what it is that he has done and seen, but never why. And I can go back feeling that I've both seen a war, and not been in one, so maybe I'd best keep my mouth shut, not even trying to answer why." The remainder of the letter consists of Riggan struggling to come to terms with the contradictions that had come to define the war for him. "Everything else that has happened to me here [is] only eruptions of this basic thing, little poutings both good and bad." He concluded, with sadness, "It is not nice to find out that you can't always be a hero."[69]

You *can't* always be a hero, and grunts serving in contested areas would have thought a soldier crazy for trying. Though the antagonisms between grunts and REMFs ran deep, the contempt grunts had for REMFs did not override their desire to save their own lives by getting a job in a secure area. As one veteran who served in both capacities recalled, "I promise you that every man who has taken fire, who has heard bullets coming his way, if he has any sense at all, wishes he were somewhere else."[70] In these moments, grunts wanted to *become* REMFs, and many endeavored to do so by requesting alternate assignments, making the relationship between the two groups even more complex. For example, the soldiers of the Americal Division, who wrote to President Nixon in April 1969 to complain about the disparity between their war and the REMFs' war, did not merely offer a list of grievances. They also requested a change in policy mandating that soldiers who had survived eight or nine months of combat be allowed to cycle into rearward jobs. As evidence, they cited a heartbreaking fact of the twelve-month tour of duty: "You cannot imagine how disturbing it is to have a friend with just days left before he goes home lose his life." They also argued that a man becomes "tense and nervous" as he "gets short," causing him to hesitate "in situations where he once would have acted instinctively."[71] They imagined that an end-of-tour stint in the rear might enhance combat effectiveness, but it probably just would have shifted the unease of getting short to earlier in a soldier's tour. What they really wanted was to even out the unequal distribution of danger and discomfort, to make the war more fair.

The wartime research of military sociologist Charles Moskos validated their concerns about getting wounded or killed shortly before going home.

Moskos's research on the "Vietnam Combat Cycle" determined that combat troops new to Vietnam were excited about being there and looked forward to their first combat experience. Thereafter, they lost their enthusiasm but gained a yeomanlike attitude toward fighting. During the eighth and ninth months of their tour, Moskos found, troops regarded themselves as "old soldiers" and performed at the peak of their abilities. Then, toward the end of the year—defined by the DEROS, or the date expected to return from overseas—soldiers became cautious and less efficient.[72]

Some commanders made a point of rotating combat troops out of harm's way for the last few months of their tour, and the U.S. Army itself offered such rotation as incentive for reenlistment. As one staff sergeant's column put it, "You don't have to be in RVN very long to know that two of the choicest duty stations for the U.S. soldier are located at Cam Ranh Bay and Qui Nhon. And it's not difficult to get to these former resort areas." If soldiers re-upped, they could finish their current tour at either place and be able to change their MOS to "just about anything except the Infantry."[73] Making such a choice was a potentially lifesaving maneuver. But because soldiers made that choice under duress, they entered life in the rear with a host of resentments. They hated the Army for its coercive tactics; they hated the grating, stateside militarism of secure bases with their "strict attention to detail, as in grass detail, concrete detail, paint detail, garbage detail"; and they especially hated support personnel, who did not have to serve in combat to earn the relative safety and comfort they enjoyed in rear areas.[74]

The grunts who survived to become REMFs straddled two worlds within the same war, and in a sense they experienced the best of both. As combat veterans, they could be certain of their bravery and their masculinity, and they knew that their contribution to the war really mattered. Then, once safely ensconced in the rear, they could take full advantage of the amenities of rearward life and enjoy the balance of their tour. Support personnel, however, always had to wonder about their place in the war, about the meaning of their service. And yet, upon returning home, a transformation took place, one that solidified combat as the dominant public memory of what was an often banal war. The REMFs *became* grunts, in the collective imagination at least, as both groups merged into one undifferentiated mass: Vietnam veterans.

Some G.I.'s were aware of this transformation even before they returned home from Vietnam. Just as newly minted soldiers arrived in Vietnam with combat-oriented expectations of wartime military service, the American public also held preconceived notions of what a war should be. Stocking shelves in a P.X. or baking bread in a field bakery, though important to the morale and logistical efforts, was not what came to mind. To restore the luster on their tours of duty, some veterans embellished the hardships they endured in Vietnam. As one G.I. editor asked the readers of *The Professional* in 1969, "Why is it that over here no one wants the job the infantry soldier performs, but when they return to the United States, everyone was an infantry soldier or wishes they had been?" Dripping with sarcasm, his attack continued, "You can hear the best adventure stories involving the infantry soldier from any support unit. They have a rough tour."[75]

Media representations of the "typical" Vietnam veteran also tended to ignore noncombat service, compounding the false impressions spawned by individual embellishments. The image of the Vietnam vet has evolved over time, though no new version has ever fully managed to supplant previous iterations. In the early 1970s, veteran antiwar demonstrations—embodied most famously by Vietnam Veterans Against the War's (VVAW) Operation Dewey Canyon III, in which veterans flung their medals onto the steps of the U.S. Capitol—made an indelible impression and created some of the most enduring images of the antiwar movement as a whole. In the 1980s, the shaggy vet in faded fatigues competed for prominence with the capable and charismatic "Magnum P.I." and the noble, if overmuscled, "John Rambo." While cultural critics sifted through the semiotics of these disparate representations, some veterans chafed at the prominence that they felt disheveled, homeless, drug-addicted, or otherwise damaged veterans received in the press. A backlash developed, leading to studies in the 1990s that sought to unravel or dispel "the enduring myths of the Vietnam War." B. G. Burkett and Glenna Whitley's 1998 polemic *Stolen Valor* launched a movement to expose phony Vietnam veterans at all echelons of society, especially those who used their borrowed veteran credentials to elicit pity, excuse bad behavior, or condemn American foreign policy. *Stolen Valor* eventually spawned a Web site dedicated to outing phony veterans of Vietnam and other wars, and it inspired the Stolen Valor Act of 2005, which sought to criminalize "medal fraud," or the wearing of unearned commendations.[76]

In recent years, the most recognizable Vietnam veterans have not been television or movie heroes but esteemed politicians, especially John Kerry and John McCain. In the 2004 presidential campaign, Kerry used his exploits as a swift boat captain to legitimize campaign claims that he was "the real deal," while McCain ran on his reputation as a kind of super-veteran for his years of incarceration in the infamous Hanoi Hilton. The POWs' sacrifices in the war were unmatched, except by those who died or lost limbs, giving McCain unusual credibility to comment publicly on a host of issues, from the 9/11 attacks to the use of torture on detainees at Abu Ghraib, Guantanamo Bay, and elsewhere. The public stature of McCain, Kerry, and others like them had a cumulative effect, yielding a dominant impression of the Vietnam veteran as strong, stoic, and accomplished, a person whose claim to citizenship surpassed that of ordinary Americans.

Whether a bedraggled panhandler using a Vietnam past to elicit sympathy or a powerful senator in custom-made suits, all of these iterations of the Vietnam veteran share the assumption that service in Vietnam equaled service in combat. Activist veterans aided the conflation of Vietnam with combat, during the war and after, as they demonstrated en masse against the war, against the military's treatment of the individual soldier, and in favor of increased federal benefits. As Gerald Nicosia writes in *Home to War*, veterans recognized that "the public would listen to them about Vietnam *because they had been there*."[77] The credibility accrued by their military service is rooted in the physical suffering, whether real or imagined, that they endured on behalf of the nation. Historian Eric Leed has termed this relationship an "economy of social guilt" that entitles the soldier to "demand restitution in the form of honor, prestige, or financial rewards."[78] That is, by virtue of their service, veterans were entitled to special consideration in many public forums, such as financial assistance to acquire a university education, priority hiring in the civil service, or dispensation from prosecutors or juries in criminal matters. For veteran activists seeking to fulfill this social contract, dividing their ranks or creating combat/ noncombat hierarchies among them made no tactical or political sense. Doing so would have undermined the strength of their numbers and the legitimacy of their cause.

In the Vietnam era, the unpopularity of the war and a general decline in Americans' respect for military service conspired to deny many veterans the social recognition traditionally associated with military service. Beginning in the late 1960s, soldiers home from the war issued outspoken critiques of Veterans Administration policies, military service, and the war itself. They objected to the indiscriminate violence produced by search-and-destroy tactics used in Vietnam, to the authoritarian strictures of military life, to the appalling conditions in many Veterans Administration hospitals, and to the paltry sums they received (less than World War II veterans, even before adjusting for inflation) courtesy of their own G.I.

Bill. After the war, they agitated for recognition of and compensation for service-related illnesses like post-traumatic stress disorder and the host of maladies since linked to Agent Orange exposure.[79]

Some activist veterans were still on active duty when they began to voice their concerns through underground newspapers, individual or small-group acts of rebellion against military authority, and the formation of organizations like the Movement for a Democratic Military, founded in 1969. Others, like the founding members of VVAW, hoped to use their credibility as veterans to lend legitimacy to the antiwar movement. Still others did not become activists until they began to suffer social, economic, psychological, or medical effects attributed to service in Vietnam that the federal government was unable or unwilling to address. Regardless of when or why they joined the "G.I. Movement," these activists were, during the war and for years after, the most visible Vietnam veterans in the United States. They therefore played a significant role in shaping the American public's early perception of vets.[80]

Facing an indifferent public and a miserly government, Vietnam veterans relied on the strength of their numbers to establish their credibility and emphasize their unity. Former grunts and REMFs did not necessarily forget the resentments and antagonisms that divided them in Vietnam. Rather, they chose to close ranks to face a common enemy in the United States. So complete was the erasure of fissures between them that organizations within the G.I. Movement scarcely acknowledged that the divisions ever existed. The Movement for a Democratic Military, for example, called for a number of quixotic reforms, such as an end to military censorship, racism, and the glorification of war. Only its desire to "abolish the class structure of the military" suggested antagonism between soldiers, though this demand is more easily read as antipathy for the officer corps on the part of enlisted personnel.[81]

Likewise, Vietnam Veterans Against the War, whose membership peaked at 30,000 to 40,000 in the early 1970s, avoided hierarchy within its ranks and "insisted that all members be treated equally." In his history of the G.I. Movement, author Nicosia relies on interviews with over one hundred participants, including key figures in the founding of VVAW. Based on their telling, Nicosia describes the antipathy of the "average fighting man" for the "so-called REMF (rear-echelon motherfucker) officers at MACV." But he characterizes the "REMFs" solely as officers "who devised missions for [combat soldiers] that had little connection to the exigencies of guerrilla warfare, and which might lead to their being wounded or killed unnecessarily."[82] Gone are all the enlisted support personnel, who, by virtue of luck, family connections, or skill, were spared service in combat. Though he acknowledges the existence of rearward life, Nicosia obscures its prominence in Vietnam by describing the war experience of Carl Rogers, one of the earliest members of VVAW, as "totally atypical" compared with the bullets-and-battlefields tours of his peers. Rogers had been a chaplain's assistant stationed at Cam Ranh Bay, where he spent his off-duty hours sightseeing and snorkeling in the balmy coastal waters.[83]

Rogers marched alongside other VVAW members in the early days of the G.I. Movement, their postwar unity trumping any service-related antagonisms that festered back in Vietnam. Through their visibility at antiwar demonstrations, veterans implicitly asserted that their trials in combat entitled them to protest a war they had experienced firsthand, savagely and intimately. Other antiwar activists welcomed the G.I.'s because they lent an air of legitimacy to their shared cause. To the public, they were simply "Vietnam veterans." Only the vets knew that they had served on the same side in different wars, that Carl Rogers's sedentary tour and off-duty excursions set him apart from combat veterans but *made* him part of the norm.

Despite the efforts of the G.I. Movement to unite veterans behind their shared need for recognition and recompense, the tensions between grunts and REMFs that divided them during the war still persist, but more so in personal discourse than in public demonstration. In his 2005 memoir *Nam Sense*, Arthur Wiknik's bitterness toward support troops was palpable and seemed not to have abated after thirty-five years. Explaining his "low opinion" of REMFs, he seethed,

> A REMF tour was easy compared to that of a Grunt, yet REMFs often complained about how rough and dangerous it was to be in Vietnam, going so far as to retell overheard war stories to raise a level of self-importance to those around him. As near as I could tell, the only danger a REMF faced was from catching gonorrhea or being run down by a drunken truck driver. And the biggest hardship a REMF contended with was when a generator broke down and their beer got warm or there was no movie that night.[84]

Writing in the early 1990s, veteran George "Sonny" Hoffman also fumed about support personnel. "Grunts hated REMFs and with good cause," he wrote. "If you lived behind wire, you were in the rear echelon. If you slept in a bed, ate hot food, took hot showers, used a flush toilet, and got laid regularly, you were a Mother Fucker." At some point, Hoffman posted his Vietnam writings on the Web site VietVet.org, which hosts a collection of veteran remembrances, where his anger can resonate in perpetuity.[85]

Elsewhere on the Web, Bob Wheatley created the "Viet-REMF Home Page" in 2002 to honor "those of us who served 'in the rear with the gear'" and to educate visitors to his site about support personnel in Vietnam. Wheatley's Vietnam tour of duty, like those of many Vietnam-era veterans, did not even take place in Vietnam; he served as an Air Force interpreter in Thailand. His use of the term REMF, a pejorative, was deliberate, if a little naïve. "In so naming [the Web site], I hope to blunt the effect of the term. Today I would propose a 'kinder, gentler' interpretation of the acronym REMF. I would turn it around into something more respectable and worthy of honor, and redefine it to mean simply: 'Rear Echelon Military Forces.'" Wheatley issued a gentle corrective to the "Hollywood stereotype image" of Vietnam veterans as combat-hardened grunts, but he also fell back reflexively on the trope that all Vietnam veterans shared a stake in the suffering, and hence a stake in the nation's goodwill, because "there were no truly safe rearward positions." He concluded his explanation for the Web site, just a little defensively, with a plea. "To the oft quoted line, 'All gave some; some gave all' I would add the reminder . . . 'But ALL gave. . . .'"[86]

It is impossible to argue with Wheatley's logic or take issue with his claim that Vietnam "has left its mark on every one of us." And yet life in the rear with a beer, or the gear, or any number of amenities and labor-saving devices, is not what the "oft quoted line" evokes. The line is actually a lyric from the 1992 Billy Ray Cyrus song "Some Gave All," a treacly ballad tailor-made for swaying in a crowd with lighters blazing.

> All gave some and some gave all
> And some stood through for the red, white and blue
> And some had to fall
> And if you ever think of me
> Think of all your liberties and recall
> Some gave all[87]

The vague story told in the song references a "hero" named Sandy Kane who "left a boy, came back a man." A veteran of an unnamed war, Sandy Kane is the one who issues the call to remembrance: "Love your country and live with pride / And don't forget those who died." The last line of the chorus, "some gave all," has surpassed the popularity of the song itself, becoming a motto for veterans groups, an inscription for war memorials and online tributes, and, in the aftermath of 9/11, a popular tattoo, bumper sticker, and T-shirt slogan to remember the sacrifices of first responders who perished in the attacks and servicemen and -women who died in the ensuing wars.

All gave some, and some gave all. It is a catchy bifurcation that implies, with sentimental logic, an ahistorical America of unified purpose and singular devotion. How comforting, how stirring, to imagine a people mobilized in concert for the greater good, each individual working toward a common goal and each contribution equally valued and rewarded by the state. The appeal of this vaguely socialist ideal is understandable, but its distance from reality is evident in the way Americans actually remember the Vietnam War and celebrate the citizens who fought it: as warriors and veterans of combat. In public commemorative activities, little else seems worth acknowledging because the American narrative tradition tends not to cast its wartime protagonists as being laden with abundance and blessed with overwhelming military strength. As a result, the experiences and contributions of drivers, technicians, and clerks are largely forgotten. Eliding the daily life of noncombat soldiers is politically expedient because it enables Americans to ignore the wealth and power they have invested in their armed forces and, instead, to regard them as perpetual underdogs. The Vietnam War was often brutal, exacting a terrible toll on 150,000 Americans who were seriously wounded and another 58,000 who perished, and on millions of families, who waited in quiet agony for their loved ones to return. But the wages of war for most Vietnam veterans were not the injury, trauma, or death evoked by the song but rather the loneliness, boredom, exhaustion, and doubt of an occupation army far from home. And then, for their troubles, noncombat troops found themselves erased from the story altogether.

CHAPTER TWO

This Place Just Isn't John Wayne

U.S. Military Bases in Vietnam

In 1998, the New Jersey Vietnam Veterans Memorial Foundation opened its Vietnam Era Educational Center in Holmdel, New Jersey, the first permanent museum dedicated to the Vietnam War in the United States. The ribbon-cutting ceremony followed months of controversy in which local veterans condemned the content of the museum's exhibit script as having an antiveteran bias. Because controversy had marred the National Air and Space Museum's *Enola Gay* exhibit in 1995, the foundation's content committee had taken pains to include veterans in the script's development process so that their feedback might be incorporated before the museum opened. So how did the public kerfuffle in New Jersey get started? It all began with the following paragraph:

> For the individuals who served there, Vietnam was many wars, each
> delineated by time, region, and branch of service. Air Force pilots
> stationed in South Vietnam, Thailand, or even Guam might enjoy
> cold beer and clean sheets upon safe return from a bombing run,
> while Navy personnel and Marines stationed aboard ships lived
> in close quarters out of direct contact with the South Vietnamese.
> Ground troops in the field lived out of their packs or in sand-bagged
> bunkers at firebases, where weeks of boredom were punctuated by
> moments of sheer terror.[1]

Entitled "Tour of Duty," these sentences were part of a 160-word panel I wrote to describe what it was like to serve in Vietnam. (Space is at a premium when an entire era must be covered in just a few hundred linear feet of wall space.) In late 1997, at a meeting about the exhibit script, one of the Vietnam veterans on the project's content committee stated forcefully that the panel offended him, though he conceded that it was technically accurate. After a lengthy and frustrating discussion, we finally identified the offending phrase: "cold beer and clean sheets." Initially, I agreed to remove it, but later I reconsidered on the grounds that it was true and that the image helped to establish the inconsistent living conditions endured or enjoyed by American soldiers in Vietnam. I left the phrase in the final draft I submitted. Sometime later, calls, faxes, and press inquiries started pouring into the foundation. A veteran involved in the project had shared the draft with local veterans' groups, and they were angry.[2]

New Jersey Vietnam veterans were not just concerned about the "Tour of Duty" panel; once the exhibit script became public, they also objected to its coverage of the antiwar movement and Vietnamese civilian casualties. But it was the phrase "cold beer and clean sheets" that led to a public debate in the first place. These simple words convey a powerful image, one appreciated by anyone who has labored in the heat or slept on the ground. In the developed world, cold beer and clean sheets are a standard reward for a difficult task or an uncomfortable journey once it is over. In the context of Vietnam, they suggest a respite from warfare in the midst of ongoing struggle.

For aviators, as the "Tour of Duty" panel suggests, the Vietnam War acquired a workaday flavor because aircraft need frequent maintenance and refueling. Though they might enjoy the luxuries of cold beer and clean sheets in their off-duty hours, the airmen's sense of sacrifice remained intact because some of them did fly into danger and because the machines, rather than the airmen themselves, mandated the pause. So it was not solely the idea of *airmen* enjoying cold beer and clean sheets at the close of the day that bothered the New Jersey veteran who protested the "Tour of Duty" panel so strenuously. Rather, his objections suggested that *any* acknowledgment of cold beer and clean sheets in the Vietnam combat zone was unwelcome in the museum's exhibit script because the inclusion of such luxuries is incongruous with traditional ideas about war. If aviators enjoyed cold beer and clean sheets, others must have too. What's more, cold beer and clean sheets cast American soldiers as favored contenders in the war, rather than beleaguered underdogs, because the United States was rich enough, powerful enough, to wage war in Vietnam while ensuring that the sheets were clean and the beer stayed cold.

Ultimately, the inclusion of cold beer and clean sheets in a description of a typical Vietnam tour of duty is uncomfortable because these simple items hint at a forgotten element of the Vietnam War: a potential war zone standard of living so comfortable that the war itself was merely the abstraction that had drawn Americans to Vietnam in the first place. Restoring a sense of that standard of living to the Vietnam narrative undermines conventional depictions of the war as unrelenting and all-consuming. Moreover, it casts doubt on the American way of war in general as efficient, violent, dangerous, or even particularly warlike for the vast majority of American combatants, some of whom expressed dismay, bewilderment, and even disappointment that the war did not live up to their expectations. By voicing their dissent and engaging in activities that military authorities interpreted as evidence of low morale, soldiers subtly negotiated better terms of employment. In the process, they helped to transform the U.S. military into a force reliant not on citizen-soldiers fighting for a cause but on professional fighters soldiering for a wage.

∽o∾

No one builds bases like Americans.
—Michael Herr, *Dispatches*

Wars always pose a logistical challenge for the nations fighting them. In the case of the United States, the story of how that challenge was met is essential to the nation's foundation myth. Popular mythology holds that the Continental Army's encampment at Valley Forge in the winter of 1777–78 was a turning point in the Revolutionary War because General Washington's soldiers emerged from the experience as a tougher, more disciplined fighting force. They lacked food, fuel, and clothing, leaving bloody footprints in the snow, or so the old yarn goes, but they did not want for patriotism and divine inspiration. Meanwhile, the British army was enjoying a decadent sojourn in Philadelphia, availing itself of feasts and fêtes as its commanders waited for spring. The contrasts are overdetermined, of course, but in the discourse of the times and in national histories since, those contrasts helped to establish an American identity separate from the English, one predicated on humility, fortitude, and thrift. Americans in uniform have demonstrated these qualities in other defining moments, such as the 101st Airborne Division's defiance of German encirclement at the Battle of the Bulge during World War II. For the suffering endured there, sites like Valley Forge and the Ardennes Forest are revered as shrines, places to visit or contemplate as key moments in the creation and defense of the nation, and as key examples of the American spirit.[3]

To suffer and endure—this was the seminal experience of American soldiers in wars throughout the nation's history, at least until Vietnam. There,

American soldiers seldom experienced serious want due to a confluence of forces. First, post–World War II economic prosperity enabled the U.S. government to direct unprecedented resources toward its citizens in uniform. Second, the bloom of American consumer culture had a vast reach, raising standards of living throughout the United States or, through mass media, cultivating desires in ghettos and hollows where prosperity failed to reach. Military authorities worked hard to replicate a stateside standard of living for as many troops as possible in Vietnam. Third, a unique logistical situation, at least compared with earlier wars, enabled American policymakers to pour vast resources into South Vietnam, creating a new nation where none had existed before.

"South Vietnam" was a political fiction established in 1954 as part of American containment policy in Southeast Asia. In practical terms, the United States' nation-building effort in South Vietnam consisted of massive aid infusions and technical advice to improve the fledgling state's agriculture and industry; to create viable institutions like a government bureaucracy, a national police force, and a military capable of defending against internal and external threats; and to improve the average Vietnamese citizen's quality of life, thereby cultivating a sense of national identity and loyalty to the state. As James M. Carter argues in *Inventing Vietnam*, American policymakers had committed to "building something that did not exist" in Vietnam. Ten years into the process, "U.S. military policy [had] evolved slowly into a military defense of a piece of real estate in Southeast Asia," a place governed by a hollow client state to which only a fraction of its inhabitants were loyal. In 1964, the Johnson administration planned for military escalation, but the scale of the intervention had "outstripped the capacity of southern Vietnam to receive it. Infrastructure was insecure, inadequate, or nonexistent."[4] A nation would have to be built before American troops could amass to liberate it.

It would have taken U.S. Army engineers and the Navy's construction battalions an eternity to create that infrastructure, necessitating an even greater expansion of the armed forces than that which was planned to contain communism in Southeast Asia. Instead, the Johnson administration turned to private firms for about 90 percent of the construction, with the remainder provided by military engineers. The U.S. Naval Facilities Engineering Command arranged the no-bid contracts, which were cost plus fixed fee. The arrangement yielded the construction companies profits of 1.7 to 3 percent, a modest sum when compared with an industry average of 6 percent for overseas construction. What made the contracts profitable was their volume—project costs ran into the billions—but also the lack of oversight, which led to inflated costs and, hence, profits. For example, a 1971 General Accounting Office study found that at least $18 million worth of construction materials could not be accounted for in South Vietnam, and cost overruns on a variety of projects were reported widely in the press. By 1972, construction leviathan Raymond International, Morrison-Knudson, Brown and Root, and J. A. Jones Construction (RMK-BRJ) had provided $1.9 billion in projects to help the war effort, yielding profits of $40 million to $50 million. More important, the success of the Vietnam venture ensured RMK-BRJ's component firms' partnerships with the U.S. government ever after.[5]

The massive buildup, completed in just four years, was aided by the tactical peculiarities of the Vietnam War. Unlike in World War II, sea and air supply lines from the United States to the military theater of operations were unchallenged by the enemy; the U.S. Navy and Merchant Marine had no enemy submarines to contend with. Logistics operations within the Vietnam combat zone were also unthreatened by attack from the air, as they had been in World War II, because the United States maintained 100 percent air superiority over all of South Vietnam. Only two factors really imperiled the logistics effort, and both were remedied through the aggressive application of resources. First, the lack of deep-draft ports early in the war slowed the offloading of supplies, sometimes leaving cargo ships waiting five deep at South Vietnam's few ports. Second, because of the material needs of the insurgency, as well as the related issues of Vietnamese poverty and government corruption, no port was entirely secure, resulting in high rates of theft and pilferage. American authorities addressed these problems by accelerating the development of port facilities and by adopting a "push" method of supply. Essentially, the U.S. military ordered more than enough of everything so that shortages would be nonexistent, flooding Vietnam with war matériel that piled up in depots or remained unloaded on cargo ships—so much stuff that the Viet Cong and enterprising South Vietnamese civilians could never steal or destroy it all.[6]

The profusion of supplies in the Vietnam war zone was also part of a deliberate attempt to maintain support for the war, not just from U.S. soldiers but also from Americans on the home front. The U.S. military pursued a "dollars for lives" policy in Vietnam, a phrase coined by Secretary of Defense Robert McNamara, which placed a premium on deploying material resources to prevent American casualties. Fewer American casualties, the reasoning went, would forestall the collapse of public support and allow for a longer occupation of South Vietnam, buying time to stabilize the country before an American withdrawal. As a matter of policy, according to the Army's official history of the logistics effort in Vietnam, there would be no rationing of essentials like ammunition and oil, only "inventory control" to monitor where supplies went. This "policy of plenty" also applied to matériel allocated for soldiers' comfort. President Johnson elected to wage war on the cheap in terms of manpower by declining to call up the National Guard and Reserves for fear of igniting a divisive debate about the war. But his subordinates at the Pentagon relied on abundance to ensure continued support from within the ranks and from the American people.[7]

Though American military construction in Vietnam was not as extensive as in World War II,[8] it made up in quality what it lacked in quantity. And the quantity was nonetheless staggering. By July 1972, when the last private construction contracts were closed out, the United States had built the following in South Vietnam: over 100 airfields, including 15 that could accommodate jets; 7 deep-draft ports and thousands of feet of small-craft wharfing facilities to receive shipments from overseas; 3 billion barrels of storage for oil and other petroleum products to fuel the war machine, as well as miles of pipeline to deliver it; permanent billets for over 350,000 troops; new hospitals with over 8,000 beds; 56 million square feet of covered and open storage areas; 2.5 million cubic feet of cold storage; over 600 miles of improved streets, roads, and highways; new bridges spanning over 5 miles if laid end to end; and some 50 miles of railroad track. In pursuit of these objectives, contractors moved 91 million cubic yards of dirt; utilized 3.7 million cubic yards of concrete and 10.8 million tons of asphalt; produced 48 million tons of crushed rock at local quarries; and dredged 97 million cubic yards of earth at 40 different sites along South Vietnam's many rivers.[9] In addition to building the bases, civilian firms fulfilled repair and utilities contracts on behalf of the U.S. military. By 1969, these activities included treating 4 billion gallons of water annually; producing 25 million kilowatt-hours of electric power per month; servicing 37 million square feet of government buildings and 4 million square feet of leased facilities; maintaining over 700 miles of road; collecting and disposing of 350,000 cubic yards of garbage each month; and providing fire protection to American installations all over South Vietnam.[10]

The scale of these accomplishments is difficult to comprehend. MACV commander General William Westmoreland once compared American base development in South Vietnam to "constructing the basic facilities for the population of a city the size of Toledo, Ohio."[11] The buildup proceeded so

This photograph of Bien Hoa Air Base, taken in 1964, shows the massive scope of American military installations even early in the war. Bien Hoa and other large bases continued to expand as the war went on, eventually incorporating all the comforts and hassles of life on a stateside post. (Horst Faas/A.P. Photo)

quickly in the mid-1960s that construction materials constituted 40 percent of the total U.S. military tonnage arriving in South Vietnam, with the remainder composed of actual war matériel. So much plywood was directed toward dunnage and the military construction boom that, despite low housing starts at home, a plywood shortage developed in the United States because of the war. And the civilian engineers' presence in Vietnam was so enormous that, at one point, the Army estimated that as many bulldozers as armored personnel carriers were operating in the war zone.[12]

In practical terms, the buildup meant that U.S. military engineers and private American firms could quickly transform wilds into built environments dedicated to sustaining warfare. The story of Camp Enari, home to the 4th Infantry Division near Pleiku, is typical of base development in Vietnam. When vanguard units of the division arrived in-country in July 1966, they found that the road from Qui Nhon on the coast to their future home in the Central Highlands was just "a trail in the wilderness." Living in tents and drinking from a nearby stream, the division's construction engineers immediately began clearing land to make way for the base, a process that included removing enormous mahogany trees with heavy explosives.

Next came a road network, then concrete foundations for important buildings. Once these were complete, construction began on mess halls, orderly rooms, and 400 billets housing 10,000 men. Four years later, Camp Enari was so large and well developed that it was impossible to imagine that it had not always been there. The landscape had been transformed from fields and old-growth forest into a small, militarized city, complete with an airstrip, helipads, an aircraft hangar, and dozens of recreational facilities. Over the course of the war, tens of thousands of American soldiers called its orderly streets and buildings home.[13]

Far to the south, the American base at Dong Tam also materialized from nothing, in this case emerging from the mucky bottoms of a Mekong River tributary. The base was designed to support military operations in the region, but its presence in such an inhospitable place also sent a strong message to Viet Cong insurgents: there is nowhere we cannot reach you. In September 1966, Dong Tam consisted of a small group of tents huddled on an island of high ground in a sea of wet rice. Within a few months, engineers of the 9th Infantry Division had pumped in 2 million cubic feet of fill to raise the level of the ground 10 feet and reclaim over 90 acres of land from the ancient river. Over the next two years, the base continued to expand, becoming ever more sophisticated in the process; two-story barracks for the entire division, paved roads, and a tactical airfield were added. Basewide running water, sewage treatment, and a power plant completed the base in early 1969, by then the largest combat heliport in the world. Like Camp Enari, Dong Tam was a small American city, home to over 10,000 military personnel and a permanent feature grafted onto a transient, riparian landscape. Then, faster than it had appeared, Dong Tam became a ghost town: the 9th Infantry Division withdrew from Vietnam in late summer 1969, leaving empty buildings and deserted streets.[14]

Though the military transformed dozens of large bases from wilderness into protocities, there were always troops living poorly somewhere in Vietnam, and most treatments of the war tend to foreground their difficult circumstances. Foot soldiers got the worst of it. When on patrol, for days or weeks at a time, they lived out of their packs and at the mercy of the elements. As one soldier put it in a letter home, "Mud, I never knew how much mud I could hate. We live in mud and rain. I'm so sick of rain that it is sometimes unbearable. At night the mosquitos plague me while I'm lying on the ground with my poncho wrapped around me. The rain drips on me until I go to sleep from exhaustion." By the time these men loaded their packs and belts with the accoutrements of war—rations, water, outerwear, extra socks, flak vest, weapons, smoke grenades, ammunition, and other equipment—they were too laden down to carry much else. As another wrote home, "There are absolutely no comforts in our job. I carry nothing but a razor and a bar of soap for comfort, [and we] wear the only clothes we have and wash them in rivers and streams as we cross them."[15] Luxury was a hot meal, which grunts sometimes made for themselves by heating C rations with explosives compounds or an improvised fuel mixture of insect repellent and peanut butter. Otherwise, they had to wait until their units were placed on stand-down to get warmed up, cleaned up, and rested.

For military personnel stationed on fire support bases (artillery bases strategically located on high ground to cover entire valleys) or radio relay stations perched on narrow mountaintops, the living conditions at their work sites also remained bleak throughout the war. For example, the soldiers and Special Forces troops manning the radio relay station on Nui Ba Den literally had nowhere to go and nothing to do in their off-duty hours. They lived in rude structures adjacent to their workstations and had to haul their own water for outdoor showers.[16] Like infantrymen in the field, military personnel stationed atop these lonely outposts seldom remained there indefinitely. Usually they rotated in and out, in the case of Nui Ba Den, every thirty days. When these units returned to their base camps, they found living conditions that were considerably better, and it did not escape their attention that some soldiers lived that way all the time. In fact, because troops in Vietnam always passed through one of the large bases on their way to and from combat areas, hospitals, or Vietnam itself, everyone knew that somewhere, someone else was living better than he was, and even living well.

Examining the ways that basic needs like food and shelter were met on a daily basis exposes how much typical versions of the Vietnam war story leave out. Napoleon's observation that "an Army marches on its stomach" was just as true in Vietnam as it ever was, but with less marching and fuller stomachs. American military authorities endeavored to provide the best food they could to the troops, an effort that cost about $220 million each year. When weather and the tactical situation permitted, soldiers received A rations, which by definition consisted of "fresh foods as often as possible [or] frozen, canned and occasionally dehydrated foods . . . when fresh items are not available." In laymen's terms, according to military publications, the A ration involved "fresh meat, potatoes and other items normally associated with 'mom's' home cooking." C rations and other ready-to-eat foods were consumed by troops on long-range patrols or stationed at remote bases, or whenever enemy activity threatened the usual lines of supply. When order was restored, delivery of A rations would resume. In this well-supported, routinized way of war, food nourished soldiers' bodies and served to remind them, with its lavish availability, of the power and resources at the U.S. military's disposal.[17]

To maximize efficiency, the military codified soldiers' food consumption, an effort that speaks to the static routines most soldiers followed day in and day out. Policy dictated that every soldier should enjoy at least one hot meal each day, and each meal, regardless of where it was served, was supposed to be part of a preplanned, twenty-eight-day cyclic menu. U.S. Army dieticians designed meals "to meet the dietetic requirements of the men serving in the hot, humid climate of Vietnam under the strenuous combat conditions."[18] The resulting product was laden with salt and fat, guaranteeing soldiers about 4,500 calories each day. The menus, which were often printed in base or unit newsletters circulated locally, looked remarkably like stateside cafeteria fare:

- Grilled hamburgers with catsup and mustard, French-fried potatoes, buttered corn, sliced onions and tomatoes, salad and ripe olives, hamburger rolls, and ice cream and vanilla pudding.
- Roast beef with gravy and mashed potatoes, Harvard beets, garden salad, marinated green bean and onion salad, and cherry pie.
- Grilled beef patties, buttered noodles, buttered asparagus, stuffed celery sticks, hot biscuits, yellow cake with mocha butter cream frosting.[19]

These all-American platters delivered comfort foods in the most literal sense of the term, in that they provided something warm and familiar in a foreign and sometimes hostile environment. The menus also worked to maintain soldier morale by invoking American settings and rituals, suggesting the reach and superiority of American culture—there was very little command emphasis on U.S. forces engaging local traditions in Vietnam—and serving as deliberate, tasty reminders of home.

The technical mastery involved in creating these meals in a largely undeveloped, war-torn nation was an incredible testament to American wealth, innovation, and stubbornness. Even in the middle of a war zone, "quality" meant "fresh": fresh vegetables traveled thousands of miles to soldiers' trays, fresh dairy products poured into refrigerated cartons at local, American-run dairy plants, and fresh bread baked up golden brown in the ovens of enormous military field bakeries. By 1968, the Army's 1st Logistical Command ("First with the Most") had deployed twelve "bakery platoons" throughout Vietnam to areas with troop concentrations of 15,000 or more. Run by American soldiers and Vietnamese employees, these field bakeries operated up to twenty hours per day, seven days a week, to provide a variety of fresh baked goods for the troops. Smaller field bakeries, serving up to 40,000 troops, could produce over 67,000 pounds per week, while Long Binh Post's bakery—the largest field bakery in the world—could bake 180,000 loaves per day to serve military personnel in III and IV Corps and the 1st Air Cavalry Division.[20]

The U.S. military's commitment to fresh baked goods went well beyond the basic loaf. Cooks in local unit mess halls were expected to be able to bake bread but also to have facility in rolling out pies, rolls, cookies, cakes, and other pastries. Most mess cooks had no prior training or had been trained stateside under ideal conditions, so they were often unprepared for the vagaries of equipment and supply in a war zone. After years of burned crusts and dry biscuits, the U.S. Marines applied their elite brand of service to the kitchen, developing an in-country baking school for cooks from all military branches. Located at Camp Jay K. Books in northern South Vietnam, the school's two-week training program emphasized baking from scratch under primitive conditions but also addressed the finer points of garnishes, icings, and glazes.[21]

The U.S. military spent enormous resources to ensure that fresh fruits and vegetables were also staples of the troop diet. About 30 percent of the produce served to American soldiers came from within Vietnam itself. In a photo montage captioned "Fresh from Dalat," the 1st Logistical Command explained the process with copy that could have been lifted from the pages of *Better Homes and Gardens*: "The Vegetable Fields of Dalat . . . Tended with Skill and Care . . . Chosen Only after Careful Inspection . . . Puts Only the Finest on the Line."[22] The remainder of the perishable food arrived in-country via refrigerated cargo ships from the United States, Japan, and Australia. The availability of fresh fruits, vegetables, meats, and dairy products in mess halls across South Vietnam represented an engineering and logistical feat because temperatures often soared over one hundred degrees. To prevent spoilage, the U.S. military erected dozens of ice plants, each one cranking out between three and fifteen tons of ice per day.[23] In addition, the military constructed several cold-storage facilities throughout the country. For example, the warehouse at Long Binh Depot covered three football fields and held, on average, $3 million in frozen and chilled food. As huge as this facility was, it was not the largest. In 1969, U.S. Army Engineers completed a cold-storage warehouse at Qui Nhon that was twice that size—so large, in fact, that it proved to be the largest American-built structure in all of Vietnam.[24] There was so much food stashed in these warehouses that, as of April 1968, the U.S. military had enough on hand to feed every soldier, all 540,000 of them, three meals each day for several weeks. And food stocks were sufficient to continue to feed American armed forces for several months in the unlikely event that "all supply lines from the states [were] cut off by the enemy." These cavernous facilities required enormous quantities of electricity, spare parts, and manpower to keep them stocked and operational, effectively rendering the U.S. Army a giant, international grocery chain.[25]

Through its extensive food program, the U.S. military sought to close the gap between stateside cuisine and war zone fare, even when it meant ferrying heads of lettuce across the Pacific to garnish hamburger patties sent from Australia that sat atop buns baked by the U.S. Army in the middle of a war. All that remained was the slice of cheese to melt on top and a milkshake to wash it down. If the U.S. military was undeterred by the challenges associated with suppressing an insurgency in an undeveloped protonation, then launching dairy production in an unbearably hot country devoid of cows or grassland was just another challenge to be met; milk and cheese would be on the menu.

American ingenuity prevailed, with private firms stepping in to manufacture dairy products where none had been made before. In 1964, the U.S. military signed a $7 million contract with International Dairies of Asia, a subsidiary of the American giant Foremost Corporation ("The Longest Milk Route in the World"), to operate a dairy plant in Saigon. The plant did not rely on battalions of Holsteins to supply it with milk. Rather, this "cowless dairy" produced "filled milk" by mixing imported ingredients (dehydrated, nonfat milk crystals, coconut oil, and flavorings and colorings) with heated water. The Saigon plant was just the first of four: Foremost opened a second plant to support military operations in the northernmost part of South Vietnam in 1967, and Meadow Gold Dairies, a subsidiary of Chicago-based Beatrice Foods, fulfilled a $5.75 million contract to open plants in Cam Ranh Bay and Qui Nhon. The plants were prolific, producing 17 million gallons of milk and 2 million gallons of cottage cheese for American troops in 1968, as well as healthy profits for Foremost and Meadow Gold.[26] More important, for the dairies at least, the military contracts helped American firms to penetrate the lucrative Asian market with their products, especially the sweetened condensed milk that was a staple in Vietnamese coffee drinks. Foremost alone had sold hundreds of millions of tins to South Vietnamese civilians by 1971.[27]

Given the cold-storage warehouses, the ice plants, and the cowless dairies, serving ice cream to the troops was a logical next step. Military newspapers published in Vietnam often marveled at the irony of finding such an "unbelievable treat in the tropics," but ice cream was quite common on American bases, especially after 1967. The big dairy plants responsible for producing milk and cheese also made ice cream, up to 550,000 gallons per plant each month, and the military erected over forty smaller plants run by American soldiers and Vietnamese employees solely to produce ice cream. They relied on a dehydrated ice cream mix that could be flavored a dozen different ways, and military publications boasted about the variety. Military dieticians attempted to serve ice cream at every sixth meal on the cyclic menu, and many bases had snack bars or parlors where it was available all the time. To ensure even distribution, refrigerated trucks delivered it by the ton to nearby installations, and helicopters hauled it by the gallon to remote firebases. An ice cream plant was even set up on a refrigerated barge that floated up and down a tributary in the Mekong River delta, delivering perishable food and frozen treats to American and Free World troops stationed along the way.[28]

The food effort paid off; by April 1968, over 90 percent of American military personnel in South Vietnam were eating at least one hot meal each day, and most enjoyed two or more. On smaller bases, troops could dine for free at a single mess hall, but bigger bases provided hot chow from a variety of sources. Free meals could be had in a unit's own mess or a basewide consolidated mess, and meals for purchase were available at a variety of retail outlets. Snack bars and P.X. dining rooms specialized in burgers, fries, and ice cream, and some of these establishments remained open twenty-four hours a day. Some bases had their own ice cream parlors, and in 1971, doughnut production ramped up at several bases just as the war was winding down. For example, Uncle Jimmie's Donut Shop at Marble Mountain Airfield near Danang cranked out 7,000 doughnuts each day, and plans were in the works to add cinnamon rolls to the menu when the 1973 Paris Accords abruptly ended the war.[29]

It is tempting to think that rearward bases would enjoy better food than those up-country, but in fact, as the statistics attest, hot chow was available everywhere. In fact, the food at smaller bases was sometimes better than at the big messes because a single cook could better control the quality of a smaller-scale preparation. Military authorities even tried to extend hot chow to combat troops serving in the field. If conditions permitted, cooks at support bases prepared hot meals and packed them in insulated food containers for truck or helicopter delivery to soldiers on patrol. The men would put down their packs and enjoy a hot picnic lunch. Then, when they were finished, they tossed their trash and resumed the war.[30]

American soldiers did not necessarily expect the culinary bounty they found in Vietnam, but they certainly appreciated it. John Adams, an officer stationed at Tan Son Nhut, fondly recalled, "The mess halls in Vietnam served the best food I have eaten anywhere in the military." In from the field, William Broyles spent a week enjoying the especially luxe mess hall of 1st Marine Division Headquarters at Freedom Hill near Danang. "The food was excellent—steaks, shrimp cocktail, fresh strawberries, and ice cream: nothing was too good for our fighting men!"[31] And in his Vietnam memoir, enlisted man George Watson seemed downright nostalgic for the extensive buffet:

> Army chow in Vietnam was a surprise. . . . Food was overly plenti-
> ful and, for me, always better than acceptable. Breakfast eggs came
> in standard American, scrambled, fried, and poached, with huge
> mounds of sausage or bacon. Hot cereals, grits, toast, juice, milk,
> and coffee accommodated every soldier's taste. . . . In the evening,
> the Army cooks put out a proliferation of assorted meats, chicken,
> potatoes, vegetables, and dessert day after day. The wholesome,
> planned diet never offset demands among the troops for junk food,
> hamburgers and pizza.

Even if American soldiers in Vietnam did not quite enjoy a stateside standard of living, it far exceeded that of the typical Vietnamese peasant. Watson noticed this contrast at the end of the meal, when he would deliver his tray to the Vietnamese employees who did the dishes. "The abundance always made the grim and silent local women the more poignant as they collected from a single troop's discarded tray enough to live on for a week in the Vietnamese scheme of things. We got spoiled."[32]

With so much good stuff on the menu, weight gain eventually became a problem for troops who did not have the rigors of combat to keep them fit. The military communicated as much to soldiers through unit newspapers. For example, the flight surgeon for a combat aviation battalion stationed at Qui Nhon reminded soldiers of their obligation to stay physically fit: "Sure, you say, 'I eat three squares a day, get eight hours of sleep a night and so I am fit as a fiddle.' Are you now? What about those muscles you sit on all day if you work in an office? Or those you don't use if you have a job requiring light physical work?" To help soldiers maintain their weight, the mess halls on the base posted a suggested diet with a calorie count for each food to help soldiers keep track of their consumption. A month later, the same columnist warned of more authoritarian measures to help soldiers slim down: mandatory weigh-ins when soldiers picked up their pay.[33]

Like food, shelter is also critical to keeping an army in the field, and soldiers' living quarters could be as varied as the mess hall menus. On patrols, grunts struggled to find some measure of comfort on the cold, damp ground. Units stationed at new installations resided in tents until permanent barracks could be built. And on rearward bases, high-ranking officers might reside in air-conditioned trailers. Because most American military personnel in Vietnam did not serve in combat, they tended to sleep in the same bunks night after night, and even combat troops eventually returned to barracks or bunkers they called "home." Vague military standards also contributed to the disparity in living quarters. Early in the war, soldiers' quarters were supposed to be "minimum and austere," but the definition of that phrase proved elastic over time. According to an official Army study, the vagueness of the policy allowed local commanders to requisition equipment and supplies "from supply catalogs as if they were Sears and Roebuck catalogs" in an effort to improve their units' quality of life. In general, Air Force and Navy personnel were better able to take advantage of the trend than their Army and Marine counterparts because their bases remained fixed, with fewer troop relocations. Yet the Army admitted that even its base development got out of hand.[34] One general lamented that American forces suffered from "Okinawa Syndrome," an analogy signifying that "we had resigned ourselves to immobility and impermanence, as if the war would last forever and if we could not win at least we could be comfortable."[35]

Comfort is relative, of course, and American military construction standards had changed dramatically since World War II. Then, pre-engineered metal or painted wooden buildings with modern utilities were, by definition, considered "permanent" structures, and thousands were still in use on American military installations all over the world decades later. By the 1960s, however, the military's concept of "permanent" had shifted to mean multistory, concrete structures, and "temporary" was used to denote the same types of structures that had once been considered permanent.[36] The robust postwar economy and Cold War defense spending are no doubt partly responsible for this shift. But these designations are also an example of the semantic sleight of hand that helped to obscure the reality of the American occupation in Vietnam. In the military's lexicon, "neutralize" meant kill, "sanitizing operations" were assassination campaigns, and "restructuring" was the forcible relocation of Vietnamese civilians. By describing permanent dwellings as "temporary structures," the military vaguely asserted that the American presence in Vietnam would soon end, despite the erection of a massive infrastructure suggestive of long-term occupation.

When a new base was under construction in Vietnam, local engineering units would struggle to keep up with the demand for housing. As the transition from tents to barracks unfolded, overcrowding and inequities in living quarters sometimes caused disgruntlement and safety concerns. In an attempt to standardize sleeping quarters across the board, MACV issued a billeting policy in 1970 that covered all U.S. military installations in South Vietnam. Soldiers were allotted personal space based on rank, and each was given a "billeting precedence date" that made length of Vietnam service a factor when assigning quarters (rank still had its privileges, however). Ultimately, the policy stated that "minimum space criteria per individual shall be 110 square feet per officer and seventy square feet per enlisted man," not including bathroom facilities. Enlisted personnel at the rank of sergeant or below could expect to live in a barracks with rows of bunks and a shower and toilet for every six people. The number of roommates and persons per bathroom declined further up the chain of command, such that colonels and generals usually lived alone.[37]

The typical barracks in Vietnam was not luxurious, but it was a far cry from the foxholes and bunkers most soldiers expected. Squat buildings with wooden siding and open eaves for ventilation were the norm. Screens were usually provided, but the heat and insects still crept in. Some barracks were open rooms with rows of bunks, and others were divided by plywood partitions erected under official direction or unofficially by the troops themselves. George Watson, stationed at Camp Ray near Bien Hoa Air Base, recalled the first time he saw his new home. "To my initial surprise, we each had separate areas containing a bed, a footlocker, and a wall locker. Thin as they were, the walls gave a great illusion of privacy. Each cubicle door consisted of a curtain of beads. . . . At the far end of the hooch was an open space the size of four cubicles with a plywood bar, a couple of small tables, and some chairs. 'This is fuckin' Vietnam?' was my first impression." Dean Muehlberg, stationed near Nha Trang in 1969, found his quarters exceptional compared with the rest of his military career. "I had never had this much privacy in the army nor would I have later for my few months in Germany." The newness of Vietnam construction and the morale imperative to constantly improve housing meant that soldiers in the combat zone sometimes slept more comfortably than garrison troops elsewhere in the world.[38]

Soldiering can be a dirty business, and iconic images of grunts from throughout America's wars show men with stubbled faces, torn or faded uniforms, and bodies creased with grime and sweat. In Vietnam, however, many bases functioned more like stateside posts, and the majority of the occupants never had to leave the wire. Regulations required soldiers to keep their quarters clean and to maintain a tidy appearance, a process that devoured resources like water and electricity. Like everything else, the military codified bath and shower policies to guarantee soldiers a minimum degree of care. In the case of showers, the policy dictated a minimum of five per man per month, a woefully inadequate figure given the hot, dirty environs of Vietnam. In the early days of the American occupation, eighteen mobile military bath teams roamed the countryside with portable showers, providing 126,000 showers per week to some 184,000 men. Over time, permanent shower facilities replaced the bath teams, and the need for field showers decreased to just 20,000 per week by 1969. As was the case with other amenities, soldiers stationed in contested areas who performed the most hazardous duties were the ones who had to wait days or weeks for a bath team to show up before they could feel human again. Everyone else was at liberty to shower as often as he liked, and some veterans recall taking two a day.[39]

A shower was only half the battle against sweat and grunge in the military's effort to keep its soldiers squared away. Laundry was key to maintaining a kempt appearance, and the U.S. military planned for it as thoroughly as any combat mission. Though U.S. Army technical manuals suggested that twenty-two pounds of laundry per man per month should be sufficient, soldiers in Vietnam sweated through their uniforms at a much faster rate than anticipated, so the actual figure ended up being fifty to sixty-eight pounds per man per month. The extra grime strained the military's own field laundries, so it also distributed laundry to Vietnamese contractors at a cost of $10 million per year. This sum covered only the washing of uniforms and did not include soldiers' personal expenditures for dry cleaning or linen service, which accounted for millions more.[40]

Soldiers also had to keep their quarters clean, but the U.S. military did not require them to perform this duty themselves. In previous American wars, only officers had living spaces that warranted hired domestic help, and only officers had the wherewithal to pay for it. But in Vietnam, the unusually stable tactical situation meant that more units stayed put, and the high ratio of support personnel to combat troops meant that an unprecedented proportion of American soldiers actually had living space to call their own. At rearward bases, local Vietnamese women, called "hooch maids" or "mamasans," did the housework, a service for which soldiers paid out of their own pockets. At Long Binh Post, for example, the going rate was $5 to $8 per month, depending on the size of the billeting area and, hence, rank. Official regulations dictated that, Monday through Saturday, the maids clean the rooms and mop the floors; empty the trash and ashtrays; wash bed linens and light laundry (underwear, socks, and towels; uniforms were done by a service); make the beds; shine the boots; and clean out personal refrigerators.[41] The war provided the labor supply, as millions of Vietnamese refugees fled their rural homes in fear for their lives or because American relocation policies forced them to. A third of South Vietnam's population became homeless in the process, causing refugee camps and city slums to brim with despair. One survival strategy was to camp outside American bases in search of employment because American contractors and soldiers were the only people with money to spend. Vietnamese civilians lived in crushing poverty that, coupled with the strength of the dollar in the Vietnamese marketplace, put domestic service financially within reach of American enlisted men, many of whom had mothers and sisters similarly employed in the United States. In essence, the availability and affordability of this labor, coupled with the erection of permanent bases and the stable tactical situation, made Vietnam the first American war to come with maid service, such that even the poorest-paid private did not have to shine his own boots.

Soldiers worked long hours, but many of them still had ample free time, which they used to pursue recreational activities that will be discussed in the next chapter. They also applied their free time to making home improvements, just like middle-class nesters in the United States. Instead of visiting the local hardware store, however, they scavenged their workplaces for items that might be adapted to home décor or purchased housewares and decorations at the local P.X. These G.I. bricoleurs plastered the walls of their bunkers and barracks with pinups and posters sold on base or sent from home. Black lights, for sale in some P.X.'s, enhanced the wall hangings, creating a psychedelic mood. Camouflage poncho liners served as privacy curtains hung between bunks, and parachute silk or nylon field blankets created billowy "ceilings" when hung from the rafters. Soldiers installed scavenged wood and linoleum floors to warm up the usual concrete slabs. And they painted cheerful, hand-lettered signs naming their hooches and listing the occupants. As an extra decorative touch in large barracks, where the rows of exposed cots had been "paneled" for privacy, soldiers would scorch the plywood partitions with a blowtorch to darken the grain lines, creating a groovy, striped effect.[42]

The efforts of G.I. decorators were occasionally profiled in unit newspapers that praised their creativity. For example, a group of officers stationed near the Demilitarized Zone spent five months making additions to their shared hooch. Despite minimal carpentry skills, they erected a game room, a sun deck, and a bar adjacent to their private sleeping areas. When they were profiled in *The Eliminators* base newsletter in August 1969, plans were under way to build handmade desks and to install one-by-ones to give the rooms a "paneling effect."[43] An enlisted man stationed at Pump Station 8 near Qui Nhon surpassed these officers by remodeling the interior of the sandbagged bunker he called home. With a shovel, plywood, and paint, he created "an attractive foyer, sunken living room and soundproof bedroom" that featured "cool green interiors, beamed ceilings, wall-to-wall oriental mats, and hand-crafted furniture." Soft, colored lights enhanced the photographs and Vietnamese souvenirs that hung on the walls, and a stereo system added acoustic ambience. Future plans included a six-foot addition for a bar with running water. The bunker's resident-designer summarized his achievements by saying, "If I had my wife and kids here I could call this place home."[44]

These home makeovers did not result in stateside-quality digs, for they still festered in the heat and could be overrun by insects and lizards. What is noteworthy is the effort involved, which tells us something about how soldiers experienced the war. The extensive digging and carpentry suggest time to spare and energy to burn after soldiers fulfilled their daily duties. Also, the planning—talk of adding extra rooms, of enhancing the appearance of improvements already made—suggests that these soldiers expected to remain in one place for an extended period of time. Their war was more about staying put than moving out, allowing them to invest a great deal of themselves in their homes away from home.

At first glance, the elaborate modifications American soldiers made to their living quarters in Vietnam seem to hearken back to earlier wars. In World War I, the German defensive posture enabled construction of deeper, more permanent trenches, compared with those erected by French and

British units on the attack. These heavily fortified bunkers featured telephone lines and a thin current of electricity for lighting, enabling some occupants—usually German officers—to operate comfort items like phonographs. The availability of electricity, however weak and erratic, contributed to rumors in the Allied trenches that all German soldiers lived in the lap of luxury. And in World War II, correspondent Ernie Pyle observed American infantrymen digging bunkers in the North African soil, making ever more elaborate modifications the longer they stayed. "The American soldier is a born housewife," he reported in 1943. Like their Vietnam counterparts, these men were immobile for an extended period of time, as they awaited orders to launch the invasions of Sicily and Italy. Pyle's dispatch went on to describe "two- and three-room apartments underground" with fireplaces, wall safes, and decorative Arab mats, but no electricity. "The accessories inside provided one of the greatest shows on earth. Wandering among [the makeshift dwellings] was better than going to a state fair. The variations were infinite." So it seems that the desire to improve one's living conditions has long accompanied soldiers to war.[45]

The similarities between the soldiers' decorative efforts are acute, but two key elements set the Vietnam experience apart: widespread consumer goods, and a steady supply of power to run them. Electricity's robust availability in military living quarters meant a degree of comfort previously unknown among soldiers stationed in a combat zone. Whereas the average electricity consumption per American soldier per day was just one-half kilowatt hour (kWh) in World War II, the U.S. Army estimated that it had quadrupled to two kWh per soldier per day in Vietnam.[46] The increase was, of course, due to the technological sophistication and relatively static nature of the Vietnam War: more office complexes, modern kitchens, cold-storage depots, and hospitals than ever before. However, individual use also accounted for a significant (though unknown) proportion of electricity consumption in Vietnam. Consider: the average American household used 20.5 kWh per day in 1970, up dramatically from 13.69 kWh per day just five years before, and from just 5.05 kWh per day in 1950. These statistics reflect trends in household purchases: in 1965, over 90 percent of American households owned an electric iron, refrigerator, radio, and television; 70 percent owned a refrigerator/freezer; 22 percent had some air-conditioning (only 8 percent actually had central air); 83 percent owned a toaster; and 70 percent owned an electric coffeemaker. Having been raised in environments with hot coffee, cold drinks, cold air, crisp toast, crisply pressed clothing, and entertainment on demand, Americans' understanding of "comfort" had expanded to include these items. When they came to Vietnam and realized the possibilities afforded by the stable tactical situation and the amenities on well-developed bases, American soldiers sought to emulate home-front standards of living as best they could.[47]

Acquiring the appliances was one thing; consumer goods were available almost everywhere in Vietnam, a phenomenon that will be addressed in a later chapter. Generating the electricity to run them was quite another. In the mid-1960s, the U.S. military contracted with private firms to erect power plants across South Vietnam, but in the interim, stopgap measures were taken. In 1967, the military converted eleven petroleum tankers into floating power stations moored at military-run piers on the coast.[48] Still, power outages were frequent, resulting in investigations into use. At the headquarters of the 101st Airborne Division, one 1968 inquiry revealed that privately owned refrigerators and unauthorized air conditioners in offices and barracks were draining power and overtaxing the system, a situation repeated elsewhere.[49] Overuse of this kind also led to fire hazards, particularly when coupled with the plywood partitions that were so common in barracks. A 1972 USARV report found that U.S. military electricity consumption had quadrupled in five years, despite troop withdrawals begun in 1969, while the capacity of wiring had not increased. A walk-through inspection of enlisted and officer billets at USARV headquarters on Long Binh Post found a crazy assortment of dangerous electrical modifications: "octopus plugs" being used with up to twelve appliances plugged into a single outlet; spliced cords secured with Scotch tape; extension cords run under mats, around rafters, between mattresses, and through walls; and electrical cords with plugs removed and wires jammed into the holes. All of these modifications were made to accommodate personal appliances— fans, coffeemakers, refrigerators, stereos, and the like—that made life in Vietnam more bearable for Americans seeking the comforts of home. Ultimately, the report shouted in all capital letters, the drain on resources and lack of concern for safety was so acute that "MORE FIRES START FROM ELECTRICAL MIS-USE THAN FROM ANY OTHER KNOWN CAUSE"—more than enemy rocket attacks, more than Viet Cong sabotage, more than the war itself.[50]

American military bases in Vietnam were ostensibly built for a variety of tactical and strategic purposes that directly served the war effort. The way these bases were staffed and stocked far exceeded the imperatives of war, however, because the U.S. military had to do more than just keep its soldiers alive and in the fight; it also had to keep them happy. As time passed and amenities proliferated, the bases became semipermanent homes away from home for some 2.5 million servicemen and -women. In retrospect, these Americanized worlds influenced a host of related social and political struggles between soldiers and commanders over living conditions and morale, between soldiers of different classes who recognized the fundamental unfairness of the way manpower needs were met in Vietnam, and between G.I.'s who objected to the war and the command that held sway over their lives. Military authorities knew they had a problem on their hands, and how they chose to address it is illuminating of both post–World War II American culture and the intractability of the Vietnam quagmire. In the end, the U.S. military sought to raise morale not by resolving soldiers' doubts about the war but by improving their material circumstances.

Morale has for centuries been understood as an essential component of any military endeavor, particularly in democracies where soldiers may opt out of military service or unsupportive publics may sabotage the continued prosecution of a war. In Vietnam, morale's tenuousness made it a command obsession. To be sure, military authorities relied on the martial culture of hierarchy and team building to achieve soldiers' compliance, as well as on policies that prescribed soldiers' decorum and productivity, enforcing their orders with punitive measures that included confinement to quarters, extra duties, threat of transfer to hostile areas, and even incarceration. But as infractions piled up and jail populations swelled, commanders looked for ways to curtail or prevent negative troop behaviors in the first place. By relying on material abundance to maintain morale, military authorities effectively tried to purchase soldiers' compliance and productivity with tasty food, homey barracks, and readily available consumer goods.

The U.S. Army field manual codified the Army's definition of morale, providing insight into military authorities' approach to the vexing personnel problems that confronted them in Vietnam. The 1955 manual framed the Vietnam-era leadership's concept of the problem:

> Morale is the state of mind of an individual as indicated by his willingness to do his duty and to participate as a member of a team for the accomplishment of the team objective. Good morale is indicated by a positive drive on the part of the individual, a push beyond that which is expected, and an eagerness and enthusiasm, almost an intuition, concerning the leader's desires. Poor morale is displayed by dissatisfaction, indifference, lack of discipline, and lethargy.

Military authorities in Vietnam were looking for "eagerness and enthusiasm" in their charges, regardless of occupational specialty. The Army also recognized a causal relationship between effective leadership and good morale: "[Morale] is the subordinate's expression of obedience, confidence, respect, and loyal cooperation elicited by command influence and direction. . . . With proper leadership good morale will exist despite physical fatigue, hardship, privation, and self-sacrifice."[51] This vision of morale is greatly informed by the social, strategic, and political realities of World War II. In that war, Americans enthusiastically agreed to serve in large numbers, the soldiery endured tremendous hardships in an open-ended campaign, the occupation of territory signaled progress on the battlefield, and belief in the mission—whether organic or cultivated by government propaganda—ensured continued public support. Vietnam could not have been more different.

Maintaining troop morale in any war is challenging, but for several reasons Vietnam proved a special case. From the conflict's inception, the necessity of the United States' war goal—preserving an independent, noncommunist South Vietnam—was poorly articulated by successive presidential administrations. And even when that message did come through, it was a tough sell. Some Americans preferred to "fight to stop communism in South Vietnam [instead of] Kansas City,"[52] but others questioned the validity of the so-called domino theory and the logic of monolithic communism. Painting all communists with the same red brush and drawing a thick, black line around them may have made sense in the abstract, but many soldiers who encountered Vietnamese people on a daily basis came to understand this particular Cold War battlefield differently. What they saw were impoverished people who were indifferent to the political dimensions of the conflict but who were inspired to fight the United States by love of country, hostility toward invaders, and the basic will to survive. Compounding the U.S. government's failure to sell the war to the American public, combat in Vietnam was a nonlinear process composed of constant but isolated battles to take one minor objective after another, only to abandon them when an operation was over. Evidence of progress, defined by the enemy's attrition, was almost impossible to discern. The media's unfettered access to the battlefield provided stunning images of wounded American boys and devastated Vietnamese civilians, a gallery of horror that seemed to suggest a morally bankrupt misadventure. And G.I.'s themselves became agents against the war, intentionally or not, as they cycled back to the United States with troubling stories and disturbing wounds. For all of these reasons, the American public's doubts became questions, and the whispers of dissent grew into an angry chorus. By 1968, the resulting antiwar movement was an unwieldy coalition of leftists, pacifists, and others who questioned the morality of American methods in Vietnam; cold warriors who questioned the urgency of the Vietnam sideshow; and true believers left disappointed by military and civilian leaders' refusal to unleash the dogs of war on North Vietnam. Against this impossibly complex backdrop, American commanders had to keep their soldiers' spirits up.

Concerns about the efficacy, urgency, and morality of the Vietnam War deeply affected the generation asked to serve. In the 1960s and early 1970s, hundreds of thousands of young men expressed their doubts by refusing, fleeing, or manipulating the Selective Service system. Though a majority of Americans who fulfilled military service in the Vietnam era volunteered, their motives often involved some subtle form of coercion, rather than support for U.S. policy. Of the 2.5 million Americans who did go to Vietnam, about one-third were drafted and another third enlisted when conscription appeared imminent, embracing "choice not chance," in the words of military recruiters. The proportion of draftees and draft-motivated volunteers increased over time, and by 1971, draftees and draft-motivated volunteers accounted for about half of the Army's overall strength. Others enlisted for the economic opportunities, vocational training, and chance to see the world that military service afforded, opportunities that might otherwise be denied them. Though it is impossible to know each man's state of mind, it is fair to say that a majority of troops arrived in Vietnam less than enthusiastic about their circumstances.[53]

Compounding their sense of disgruntlement, the draft system itself was riddled with inequalities. Between 1964 and 1973, fewer than half of the 27 million draft-eligible men in the United States served in the military, and of those, only one in five went to Vietnam. Educational deferments tended to favor men who were well-off, and the local nature of draft boards tended to advantage those who were well connected in their communities, further heightening the likelihood that working-class men and men of color would be sent to war. As a young marine officer, William Broyles took an inventory of his rifle platoon that told the story in microcosm: of fifty-eight men, only twenty-one had high school diplomas, only ten were over twenty-one years old, most had no fathers, and they reported premilitary occupations like "laborer, pecan sheller, gas station attendant, Job Corps." They were, he recalled, "[k]ids with no place to go. No place but here." The public knew it too. As early as 1966, two years before troop levels would peak in

Vietnam, only 43 percent of Americans surveyed considered the draft system fair.[54]

Once in uniform, soldiers projected their enmity for the draft and the war onto the military, an institution that demanded obedience and conformity in a cultural moment that, for many, was defined by their rejection. A 1971 study found that more than half of servicemen polled at five stateside bases had engaged in some form of resistance to military authority, including activities like reading underground G.I. newspapers (not to be confused with officially sanctioned unit or base newspapers), attending antiwar events or coffeehouses, or refusing orders, especially orders governing personal appearance and behavior. Of those soldiers who engaged in resistance, the study found that 58 percent did so because of their opposition to the war, followed by 38 percent who cited "the way the army treats the individual."[55] For thousands of soldiers, opposition to the war coalesced with objections to military culture, yielding a broad G.I. Movement composed of soldier-activists who had returned from Vietnam or were opposed to going. The movement's underground press was rife with editorials that framed constitutional protections of speech and assembly as "void for servicemen," and military service itself as a dead-end existence. In one cartoon, military service was characterized as a human being's slow transformation into a pig and, in another, as "eating shit" for the duration of one's enlistment.[56]

In Vietnam, soldiers could not help but notice that inequities in the draft were compounded by inequities in duty assignments, as the military held men with education, technical expertise, or even just good test scores in the rear to exploit their abilities. (The proportion of noncombat personnel was so great, however, that working-class men also served in the rear in large numbers.) Class issues aside, danger and discomfort were not evenly distributed in Vietnam, and the military's efforts to ameliorate physical discomfort tended to exacerbate the inequalities. Morale-building initiatives like indoor plumbing, air-conditioning, hot food, big P.X.'s, and recreational facilities were easier to provide in uncontested areas, favoring noncombat troops. In short, the most was given to those who risked the least, and combat troops knew that they were getting the short end of the stick. William Broyles recalled his radioman, tired of living exposed to the elements, exploding in anger over this very issue. "We're here to save the asses of those REMFs!" he raged. "They hog all the fucking socks! They hang the fucking nylon blankets from the ceilings of their hootches! They carry all the new fucking M-16s! They eat hot fucking chow! They eat cold fucking ice cream!" His tirade included an unimpeachable irony: "*They're supposed to be supporting us!*"[57]

All these social and political factors, coupled with Southeast Asia's challenging climate, the sometimes difficult living conditions, the loneliness of being far from home, not to mention the fear of injury or death, created a morale situation in Vietnam that was tenuous at best. The Morale and Welfare Branch of the Army's Military Personnel Policy Division carefully measured in-country soldier morale through a series of "indicators," behavioral patterns that were tracked by compiling data from local commanders. The indicators prescribed in the 1955 field manual included men absent without leave and deserters; courts-martial and other punishments; requests for transfer; the sick call rate; the venereal disease rate; self-inflicted wounds; use of rations; and chaplains' monthly reports. The list is almost charming for the benign quality of the negative behaviors it suggests: disappearing without authorization, requesting a new assignment, calling in sick, having unprotected sex, eating too much or too little, or talking to the chaplain about these and other concerns.[58] In Vietnam, where drugs were cheap and plentiful, where alcohol ran like water, and where lots of men were heavily armed, soldiers found more acute ways to express their discontent. Drug use was widespread, though perhaps not as common as previously thought,[59] alcoholism was rampant, occasional mutinies emboldened others to resist, and fragging—the attempted assassination of a superior with a fragmentation grenade or other weapon—was a menacing new reality.[60]

On the surface, the Army appeared to understand the importance for morale of abstract factors like leadership and ideology, but it relied on material fixes for soldier dissatisfaction that seemed to contradict the lofty ideals set forth in official pronouncements. The Army produced scores of pamphlets, posters, unit newspaper editorials, and orientation guides for soldiers that explained the mission in heroic, Manichaean terms. Documents like "The Truth about Our Economic System," "The Soldier on Freedom's Frontier," and "Our Mission in Vietnam" established clear and compelling reasons for the American occupation, but they did not necessarily reflect the reality soldiers witnessed around their bases day in and day out. And these ideologically driven pronouncements competed with other messages from military authorities that emphasized the acquisition of goods and services as the primary way to assuage a soldier's dissatisfaction. The same orientation guides and newspapers that explained the necessity of the mission also contained scores of ads and announcements outlining the amenities the U.S. military provided for its soldiers in Vietnam. Military authorities may have tried to instruct the troops about "why we fight," but their efforts to stir soldiers' patriotism were muted by ongoing attempts to ease the burden of "how we fight," by improving material conditions on American bases. The U.S. military could not provide convincing guarantees that the war would be won, that the ends would justify the terrible means, so it tried to make its unhappy charges as comfortable as possible.

Low morale in Vietnam led to a greater problem of general force readiness throughout the world, and this, too, military authorities addressed by trying to improve soldiers' quality of life. In democracies, the problem of troop morale is particularly acute because unhappy soldiers do not have to mutiny to register their collective dissatisfaction. Rather, they only have to survive the conflict and communicate their objections to the folks at home, thereby poisoning the well of potential new recruits. In the Vietnam era, military service was, for a time, culturally discredited, resulting in problems with recruitment and retention. The draft was extremely unpopular, so increased draft calls proved a political liability for both the Johnson and Nixon administrations. Faced with a critical manpower shortage, Johnson administration officials looked for creative ways to swell the ranks, in particular by lowering entrance requirements to admit previously ineligible men to military service.[61] Though this initiative did increase the number of new recruits, the military still faced problems with low retention. The reenlistment rate for volunteers fell from 25 percent in 1960 to 20 percent in 1971, while draftee reenlistments fell by half during the same period. Soldiers' low opinion of military service proved contagious, causing even potential officers to reconsider. Enrollment in Reserve Officers Training Corps programs on college campuses dropped precipitously from 165,000 in 1961 to just 74,000 ten years later. As the *New York Times* reported ominously in a 1971 front-page story, "The bitter Vietnam experience has left the United States Army with a crisis in morale and discipline as serious as any its oldest and toughest soldiers can remember."[62]

In the midst of this crisis, the Pentagon began to study the merits of shifting to an all-volunteer force composed entirely of professionals who would be willing to accept danger and discomfort as a matter of course. Morale problems in Vietnam were only partly responsible for the Pentagon's study of the issue, however. Two weeks prior to the 1968 presidential election, Richard Nixon promised American voters that, if elected, he would end the draft. According to historian Beth Bailey, once Nixon was in office, libertarian economists who had the president's ear provided intellectual justification for a policy originally rooted in political opportunism. They argued that individual liberty surpassed civic obligation as a core American value and that an all-volunteer force reliant on the free market for recruits would preserve individual liberty while improving on the draft's efficiency. The all-volunteer force, finally implemented in 1973, relegated the citizen-soldier to the National Guard and filled the ranks of the regular forces with men and women who signed up not to support a particular cause but to work and perhaps fight as part of a military career.[63]

For the Pentagon, Nixon's election-year promise to end the draft signaled the beginning of the end for conscription and all the public scrutiny it entailed. Each service branch began to plan for the shift, paying careful attention to how manpower needs would be met. Getting Americans to join was the tricky part. In remarks to a panel charged with creating the Modern Volunteer Army (MVA), General Westmoreland, now the Army's chief of staff, outlined the complicated task at hand: to create a force that maintained "those immutable principles of dedicated professionalism, loyalty, integrity of character, and sacrifice" enshrined in Army tradition but that people would freely elect to join. Since the shift to voluntarism would result in a kind of public referendum on military service, Westmoreland suggested eliminating "unnecessary irritants and unattractive features of Army life where they exist," the better to attract mass support and new recruits.[64] That is, the military should ease some of the very restrictions that set military life apart from civilian life, in the hope that more Americans would enlist.

Westmoreland wanted a list of those "irritants," and no place was more irritating to American soldiers than Vietnam. In response to Westmoreland's request, the USARV deputy chief of staff for personnel and administration asked unit commanders at Cam Ranh Bay in early 1971 for suggestions about policies to eliminate. The responses represent an oddly unmilitary approach to service in a war zone, and they are instructive of the tensions between unhappy servicemen and military authorities. In terms of appearance, the commanders recommended easing policies governing haircuts and facial hair, compulsory hat requirements, and the wearing of civilian clothing during off-duty hours, measures that would result in soldiers who looked more like civilians. Easing other policy restrictions would result in soldiers who lived and acted more like civilians. In terms of living conditions, the commanders advocated limited inspections of barracks, installation of more toilets and hot showers, more privacy for enlisted personnel, free reign for soldiers in decorating their billets, bus service between important buildings, more recreational opportunities, and the paving of all roads in the cantonment area. At Cam Ranh Bay, the war was usually remote, and work patterns were similar to those on stateside bases. The unit commanders suggested formally regimenting the schedule by adopting a Monday-through-Friday workweek "unless really required" and formally shortening the workday to nine hours with thirty minutes for lunch. They also advocated the complete elimination of K.P. and other menial duties by replacing G.I. labor entirely with civilian hires or machinery. Other suggestions included extending curfews, "less shouting, more talking" to resolve conflicts between officers and enlisted men, and providing day trips outside the base to "eliminate the feeling of being 'caged in'" and to give personnel the opportunity to play tourist in the Vietnamese countryside. Last, the commanders' suggestions for promoting the MVA included relaxed rules on female companionship. Some commanders in Vietnam looked the other way when women made their way into soldiers' sleeping quarters, rationalizing that easy access to sex ameliorated soldiers' tendency to go absent without leave. The Cam Ranh Bay report sought to codify the wink-wink approach, with one officer arguing, "Sex is natural and personal. If an individual desires to have a woman he should be allowed to and even to have her in the barracks without interference from others."[65] Take away the hats, extend the sideburns, shorten the workday, eliminate menial labor, spruce up the base's amenities, and let the ladies in — except for the actual war, military service might not seem so bad.

Of course, Westmoreland's request for data described *unnecessary* irritants, but that concern never came up in the discussions of the MVA at Cam Ranh Bay. It seems that at least some commanders, and probably most of the troops, regarded *all* the irritants there as unnecessary. And why not? Soldiers surely looked around and saw what American economic and military might could accomplish: build bases the size of small cities from nothing in a matter of months or throw down airstrips in a matter of days, to say nothing of its ability to destroy. Under these circumstances, why couldn't the military put in more flush toilets or get the mashed potatoes right? And what did it matter if your mustache crept beyond the corners of your mouth? The commanders at Cam Ranh Bay did not have to imagine the irritants they compiled in their report to Westmoreland. They merely cataloged the infractions they had observed and the complaints that they had received from soldiers reluctant to submit to their authority.

As the U.S. military transitioned from a citizen-soldier force to an all-volunteer, professional force in the early 1970s, the Joint Chiefs of Staff issued a series of servicewide directives designed to broaden the military's appeal, a process that dovetailed nicely with efforts to improve morale in Vietnam. For stateside Army personnel, Westmoreland ended reveille formations, sign-out policies, bed checks, and travel restrictions, and he approved, on a trial basis, beer in mess halls and the installation of beer vending machines in barracks. (These last two measures were unnecessary in Vietnam, where beer was readily available to all troops, regardless of their age.) Under the direction of Admiral Elmo Zumwalt, the Navy preceded the Army with relaxed regulations, including alcohol in barracks, casual dress in off-duty hours, and Zumwalt's personal guarantee that no sailor would have to wait in line for more than fifteen minutes. According to *Newsweek*, one stateside base commander told his staff, "If the soldiers want go-go girls, we'll give them go-go girls!"[66] Satisfying corporeal desires and granting soldiers more individual freedom were welcome changes in the military—the G.I. Movement had demanded as much for years—but in terms of troop morale, the policies beg the question: Did they work? Did the abundance permeating the Vietnam war zone actually raise troop morale?

Despite the changes, recruiting the all-volunteer force proved difficult, and the military languished in the mid-1970s; budgets were slashed, morale was low, reenlistment rates were low, and readiness was poor. The quality of the American armed forces did not improve until the Reagan years, when massive defense spending rehabilitated the physical strength of the military and a conservative political resurgence restored its stature in the eyes of the American people. In terms of morale among U.S. forces in Vietnam, the answer is a peculiar sort of "no." During House Armed Services Committee hearings on military morale in 1972, Congressman Les Aspin framed the issue perfectly: "I don't see how the hell painting the barracks is going to make a guy feel good if he thinks he's fighting in an immoral war."[67] Indeed, the evidence suggests that painted barracks—and all the other amenities available on American bases in Vietnam—did not assuage soldiers' objections to being there. Instead, the material satisfaction only seemed to make things worse.

By the military's own measures, soldier morale in Vietnam was lower in the rear, where the living was easiest. Rates of criminal activity, absenteeism, and drug use were higher there because absent the urgency of combat, rearward soldiers had time to think and make mischief. They went on excursions off post and forgot to come back, they dabbled in black market activities to make a quick buck, and they experimented with drugs to self-medicate, escape, and have fun. (The military regarded drug use as indicative of low morale, but alcohol abuse, which was far more prevalent, was considered just a part of life.) These behaviors do not so much indicate misery as they suggest a general rejection of military life and ambivalence toward the mission; indeed, no one would accuse marijuana-fogged revelers at Woodstock guilty of having low morale. Fragging, on the other hand, communicated unmistakable rage toward officers and NCOs, but despite its shocking frequency—perhaps 1,000 incidents (mostly nonfatal) over the course of the war—it was still a fringe response, given the massive size of the occupation force. Likewise, mutiny suggested both immediate dissent—refusal to go on patrol, for example—and contempt for military authority. Historian Loren Baritz frames behaviors like these in terms of labor relations, that soldiers withheld their compliance and productivity to negotiate more favorable terms of employment. Casting soldiers as employees is not merely an interpretive conceit, however, for Baritz locates their transition from warriors to workers in the military's bureaucratization following World War II. With officers functioning more as risk-averse personnel managers than battlefield leaders, Baritz argues, soldiers questioned why they should risk their lives if the "bosses" did not have to.[68]

Fragging and mutiny have received a fair amount of attention because they are spectacular examples of discontent. A more nuanced index of morale is the lodging of complaints, formal and otherwise, that provide concrete examples of how ordinary soldiers in Vietnam regarded their living conditions. When disgruntled troops put pen to paper, they sometimes addressed their complaints to the division, USARV, or MACV inspector general (I.G.), but soldiers' letters to family, elected officials, and military officials back in the United States could also prompt an I.G. investigation. The resulting case files yield a fascinating portrait of the convoluted dynamics between expectation and reality in the Vietnam war zone. Complaints are dual articulations of experience, in this case expressing both the way things were and the way they should have been, according to the author of the complaint. What emerges from the records is a sense that, as a group, soldiers were deeply ambivalent, not just about the war but also about the amenities they enjoyed while fighting it. Some of the troops welcomed them, to be sure, because they eased the discomforts of deployment, but others felt a little cheated.

Some soldiers complained about how bad conditions were, and they really were. I.G. investigative reports confirmed that the war could place steep demands on soldiers, particularly those serving in the infantry or on fire support bases. Armand Heroux wrote the following letter to President Nixon in August 1969:

> I am a PFC in the U.S. Army, I have been in Viet Nam for five months now and have encountered a problem which I believe only you can solve. . . . When I came to Viet Nam I was issued only the barest of necessities, I didn't even get any type of cover or blanket to protect me from the elements at night. I don't live in a barracks, I live in a bunker but most of the time I live & sleep under the sky because I am ussually [sic] out on an Ambush Patrol in some wet rice paddy. . . . Also food is a serious problem. We get two hot meals a day. The food is of poor qaulity [sic] and we recieve [sic] barely enough to keep a child healthy.[69]

William Edelburg leveled similar complaints in a 1971 letter to President Nixon. He alleged that at one hundred pounds, his rucksack was too heavy, that his unit had gone three days without food and two days without water, and that personnel had to wear the same clothes for two to three weeks at a time. In both cases, the investigators concluded that these men had the food and equipment they were supposed to have and that the hardships they endured were the "occupational hazards" of being infantrymen.[70]

Sometimes soldiers complained about how bad conditions were, relatively speaking. The USARV I.G. solicited soldiers' complaints at Cam Ranh Bay in December 1969, and the resulting list sounds like it came from a completely different war than the one Heroux and Edelburg were fighting. Thirty-six men made eighty-three complaints, alleging generally "bad" food, dirty or missing mess hall utensils, a lack of fresh fruit, unkempt cooks, a single occasion when sour milk was served, clogged shower drains, a lack of privacy in the barracks, "poorly operated" nightly movies, insufficient recreational facilities, and "unfair" policies regarding visits to a nearby Vietnamese village. The soldiers also filed "requests for assistance" on this I.G. visit. These included heart-wrenching family concerns that spoke to the universal sacrifice made by soldiers deployed far from home: a request for help with marital problems between a soldier and his stateside wife, and a request to return to the United States to visit a sick baby. But the requests also included self-serving plaints that lacked urgency. One soldier filed paperwork requesting the return of female Red Cross volunteers to the base, and another filed paperwork requesting the construction of a bowling alley, an amenity available on other big bases.[71]

The most obtuse complaint in the USARV I.G. files concerned allegations of an unfair distribution of meat in the 9th Infantry Division's mess halls. "We have had grilled steak only once in several months," pleaded an unnamed soldier to the Department of the Army's Food Service Department. "That was when the Div. Com. Gen. was visiting. There are bar-be-que grills at every club and nearly every officers['] and NCO's [sic] quarters in Viet Nam, and they have Sirloin and fresh chicken to cook. Why are we always issued roasts, hamburger, or swiss steak in leiu [sic] of grill meats?" The case of the missing meat spawned an investigation that took an astonishing seven months, but no filched fillets were ever found, only a faulty refrigerator and some bookkeeping errors.[72] This soldier was so concerned that grill meats were going astray in Vietnam that he failed to appreciate how extraordinary it was to find Swiss steak in Southeast Asia, or how fortunate he was compared with other soldiers in Vietnam, who had only prepackaged meals to eat; with millions of Americans living on the margins of poverty; and with most Vietnamese, who grappled daily with the threat of hunger. All he knew was that some officers and NCOs seemed to be eating better than he was.

Sometimes soldiers complained that conditions were *too* good. In the rear, stateside standards of living were desired by some but resented by others. Several soldiers complained in a letter to President Nixon that "while the unit is striving to improve the available facilities and to maintain a high state of readiness . . . command emphasis is placed on painting everything that doesn't move and making everything else shine. We are in a supposed war zone, [but] we are building and beautifying continually. And we are training. The situation is one of bewilderment, badgering, and bungling."[73] Another soldier was so disappointed at the comforts of the rear that he wrote to his congressman requesting more war in his war: "This duty here is too stateside: a G.I. party once a week, inspection in ranks, keeping your buckle polished, Command Information [briefings] once a week. This, Mr. Zion, I don't feel should be put on a soldier." Camp life was not what he had signed up for.[74]

Some soldiers complained that conditions were worse than they really were, exaggerating their circumstances in order to impress the folks at home. Douglas Robertson wrote to his mom that he had gone a day and a half without food and that his unit had to pick through the trash at a firebase in search of discarded C rations. Mrs. Robertson then wrote to the secretary of the army that her boy was not getting enough to eat in Vietnam, and the secretary of the army initiated an investigation. George

Anderson, a sergeant serving with an advisory team, wrote home to his wife that he had to buy liquor in Saigon to trade for food at his base. She, in turn, assailed her senator, whose office then started making inquiries with the Army. She seethed, "The United States Government takes my husband away from me to do an impossible job, does not provide him with the resources and tools he needs to do so, and worst of all, cannot even feed him!"[75]

In both cases, the resulting I.G. investigations found that the soldiers had embellished their plight in letters home. After interviewing Pfc. Robertson, the I.G. investigator determined that Mrs. Robertson's letter, "in all probability, was prompted by her son's portrayal of a combat mission [and not normal circumstances] and he, like most soldiers writing back home, tended to add that little hardship touch to let the folks back home know that he's fighting a war." Sergeant George Anderson also admitted as much, offering I.G. investigators a "quite disavowal" of his wife's letter-writing campaign. He explained, "Frequently chow gets quite slim up here . . . but it definitely does not warrant a congressional inquiry. It has its place in a G.I.'s grumblings, but no further, when you consider how many people over here eat C-rations all the time. My dear wife's intentions are indeed good and honest, but everything over here is relative, and she doesn't understand this."[76] In his memoir, veteran William Broyles recalled seeing this economy of guilt in action when his radioman wrote a laughably dire portrait of life in Vietnam to the parishioners of his church back in the States. Anticipating the church ladies' response, the radioman explained, "It's worth three or four dozen chocolate chip cookies."[77]

Sometimes soldiers openly mocked the pettiness of their complaints, relative to the stakes involved in combat or even to conditions in other wars. For example, the advice column "Dear Hugh," printed in the G.I. monthly newsletter *Fireball Express* in May 1970, fielded a letter from four enlisted men who wrote to complain of a lack of electric fans in their barracks and places of work. Columnist "Hugh" responded, "Ah, yes gentlemen, I am aware of your plight and horrible loss of weight [from sweating]. Your condition and subsequent suffering reminds me of the famed Bataan Death March, but let us not dwell on the past, let's look ahead to a new and cooler future, one with circulating air for all to breathe, yes, a restoration if you will, of normal body weight."[78] The Bataan Death March was one of the most notorious atrocities of World War II: 7,000 American and other Allied prisoners of war died at the hands of the Japanese on a fifty-five-mile forced march. By referencing it, the editor was directing his G.I.

readers' attention to a "real" war, one in which soldiers' suffering was more common and acute. Though some facets of the Vietnam experience fit this description, the war fought by most American soldiers, especially by 1970, could not compare.

Ironically, those who had it the best in Vietnam usually complained the most. In general, soldiers serving in "combat service support units"—that is, rear echelon personnel—had higher rates of complaints than combat units, whose struggles to survive provided a shared sense of purpose. Overall, formal complaints rose throughout the war but increased dramatically starting in 1969, after troop withdrawals began, when the war was being prosecuted less aggressively and the troops had more down time.[79] Clearly, the comfort and amenities of the rear were not enough to inspire the loyalty and dedication military authorities hoped for. Once soldiers arrived in Vietnam and adapted to the strange environment they found there, comfort seemed to have an ever-expanding definition. The more insulated soldiers were from the war, the more accommodations they expected. Soldiers who slept in beds wanted maids to make them; soldiers who ate hot dinners each night wanted ice cream for dessert; soldiers who worked in offices wanted fans or central air; and soldiers who worked nine-hour shifts wanted entertainment for the rest of the evening.[80] There was no point at which group satisfaction was achieved because, just as in civilian life, there was always some new amenity being enjoyed by some other unit somewhere else: a bowling alley, a pizza oven, American Red Cross girls, or a bowling alley where American Red Cross girls served pizza. There was always something.

As the world of the rear became more insulated from the exigencies of the war, soldiers questioned why they needed to be in Vietnam in the first place. Indeed, some soldiers at the big bases seemed to wonder whether there was a war going on at all. When I.G. investigators solicited complaints at Cam Ranh Bay in 1969, at least four soldiers alleged that officers were using alerts to harass enlisted men. This accusation, which the I.G. declared "unsubstantiated," suggests a feeling of safety such that sirens and calls to arms were unnecessary, except for maintaining the illusion of danger to rally and motivate the troops.[81] By 1970, life on the big bases was so distorted from what soldiers had expected to find in Vietnam that they referred to both the conflict and the pettiness of rearward life as "the Mickey Mouse war." The icon many of them used to characterize their year at war was a cartoon mouse. What they wanted was John Wayne.

In the present, John Wayne remains an American icon, but even by the 1960s, his public understood him not just as an actor but as the embodi-

Purchased in Vietnam in 1970, this souvenir shield mocked Long Binh's absurd isolation from the shooting war by superimposing Mickey Mouse ears on USARV's iconic sword. (Personal files of the author)

ment of a set of ideas. Transcending the roles he played, Wayne was a model of patriotism, strength, and stoicism in the face of danger—everything Americans at war felt they should be. His filmography included so many World War II pictures that it was like he fought the war all by himself, and the soldiers, sailors, and airmen he played collectively suggest an idealized American fighting man. One film, *The Sands of Iwo Jima* (1949), stands out because veterans and public figures—Newt Gingrich, Oliver North, and Ron Kovic, among them—have so frequently invoked it as the inspiration for their concepts of leadership, patriotism, and war itself.[82] As Sgt. Stryker, Wayne was grizzled and stern, doling out tough love to his young recruits so that they might survive the punishment of an island campaign. On the Iwo Jima beachhead, Wayne's Stryker was the archetypal leader (strong, confident, authoritarian yet selfless), and the beach was the archetypal battlefield (unforgiving, chaotic, and uphill all the way). During the Vietnam War, when green recruits were anticipating beachheads of their own in Vietnam, "John Wayne in *The Sands of Iwo Jima*" was a constant refrain, as though the film had become a shorthand for warfare in the twentieth century.[83]

Hollywood's depictions of World War II worked nicely with anticommunist government propaganda in the 1950s to socialize young Americans into accepting the harsh realities and inevitability of military service. By the 1960s, new recruits headed for Vietnam were deeply concerned about the violence they expected to encounter on arrival. Contemporary mass-media representations of the Vietnam War privileged combat because the shooting war provided the most compelling images, and it drove the foreign policy and antiwar movement narratives forward. Soldiers' training also emphasized facility with weapons and preparation for harsh conditions. But even without the bloody leads on the nightly news or the boot-camp training scenarios, soldiers still had particular ideas about what a war should be because of the stories they had absorbed as kids growing up in the wake of World War II. As a result, troops bound for Vietnam formulated their expectations based in part on the beachheads of Normandy and the South Pacific, as well as on what they had heard firsthand. Emotionally and physically, they steeled themselves for the worst.

In World War II, most American fighting men arrived at the war by train or boat, quiescently getting on and off when ordered, stretching their legs, toting their duffels, and taking in the new, unfamiliar surroundings. These peaceful arrivals were punctuated by the violent, chaotic, sometimes desperate, oftentimes heroic arrivals that have been seared in private and public memory. Most potent is the memory of American infantrymen landing at Omaha Beach. Until Steven Spielberg's *Saving Private Ryan* offered shaky, sepia-toned moving pictures to American movie audiences in 1998, Robert Capa's D-Day photographs for *Life* stood alone in shaping the public's memory of that day. Capa rode ashore in a landing craft, documenting the soldiers' exit from the vehicle with a crisp photograph of the men, backs turned, wading in formation toward the beach. Moments later, Capa too was in the water. His remaining film was damaged, compromising the clarity of subsequent images but also capturing, through their blear, the chaos of the battlefield. A grainy photograph of soldiers taking cover behind obstacles immortalizes the grim confusion of the landing: water meeting sky in seamless gray, a foamy wave approaching, dark shapes—bodies?—floating nearby, black steel obstacles jutting from the gray morass, another landing craft about to disgorge its cargo in the distance. We understand from the photographs that war has a transformative effect. On exiting the landing craft, the soldiers left behind some former version of themselves that could never be reclaimed. Moving through the water toward the land, they became veterans of war, men who have seen and know the blackened edges of human experience.

Vietnam was not like that for most Americans who served there, but the young men headed to its shores did not know it. They thought it would be like the movies, a belief reinforced by combat scenes on the six o'clock news. One marine who arrived in Vietnam by ship, as some combat troops did, remembered jitters rising as rumors circulated about Viet Cong human wave attacks, so that "by the time these stories got around it was Tarawa all over again."[84] It was most common for American soldiers to arrive in Vietnam via chartered commercial airliner, but concern about what awaited them on the tarmac still festered in their stomachs. One brand-new lieutenant remembered, "Looking down on the lights of the base below us, I wondered if incoming planes were shot at? Did we have to run for cover when we landed? Or was the airfield safe?"[85] The fear on the planes was common and palpable. A U.S. Army greeter at the Bien Hoa air terminal told the *New York Times,* "Ninety-nine and two-thirds of the time these guys are scared to death and don't know what's going on." Another added, "Most of them expect to jump off the plane and into a foxhole with bullets flying."[86]

For hardened veterans in Vietnam, the new arrivals' fear was a source of humor and irony. "Remember when you flew into this country?" one G.I. newspaper editor asked his soldier-readers. From the plane, "every mud hole is a bomb crater, every fire is due to artillery, and every shiny piece of metal is a V.C. position with 50 calibers. Then you start looking for emergency exits. As you land, you are forming personal reaction plans to ground attacks or incoming rounds." Another newspaper asked members of the 1st Cavalry to think back to their first day in Vietnam. "Were you surprised you did not have to low crawl down the ramp from that big Pan Am 707?" Even civilian airline pilots could not resist taking advantage of the new arrivals' naïveté. One veteran recalled the plane's captain reporting the weather as they prepared to land at Cam Ranh Bay. "The ground conditions consisted of 'light to scattered automatic weapons fire' and a few other things I don't remember but designed to scare the crap out of you." These jokes worked because anyone who had spent time in Vietnam knew just how absurd the foxhole-under-fire expectations were. In fact, the military calmly loaded new replacements onto buses and drove them down civilian streets to a military processing center. "Coming from Tan Son Nhut [air base] there were all these traffic lights, and a four lane highway," said one bewildered newcomer. "This place just isn't John Wayne."[87]

There is a palpable sense of irony in his remark; expectations of war based on John Wayne's performance on Iwo Jima were not met by the Vietnam experience. There is a sense of disappointment, too. John Wayne was and remains an archetype of American masculinity, the very embodiment of American manhood at war: strong, silent, and self-sacrificing. He often died in the movies, and even if he didn't, he almost never got the girl because such a tangible reward would undermine the selflessness of his actions. His were huge boots to fill, and soldiers who survived days or months of combat earned the right to walk in them. Those who served on rearward bases, however, never got the chance to try. The very duty that spared them a year of discomfort and possible death also thwarted any hope of making a sacrifice for brotherhood, for the mission, or for the nation. By saying "This place just isn't John Wayne," that new recruit did not just acknowledge the fundamental weirdness of Vietnam. He was recognizing the war's refusal to make him a hero and its inability to make him a man.

As historian George Mosse observed, "War is an invitation to manliness."[88] Though he was writing about Europeans on the eve of World War I, Mosse's thesis holds true for other wars as well. Societies have, for centuries, relied on a traditional set of enticements to draw civilians into military service. These include appeals to patriotism, promises of camaraderie and a satisfying barracks life, and opportunities for travel and adventure. In the twentieth century, education and job training offered additional incentives. But, sociologist Bruce Watson notes, "all of these enticements paled before another that was consistently offered by armies, especially in the western world: joining the army was and remains a way to be a man." In the United States, twentieth-century recruitment posters and films depicted idealized warriors who were strong and fit, who worked together as a team, and who, despite their suffering, were "uncomplaining, toughing it out, denying pain — 'walking it off' — [to be] 'one of the guys.'"[89]

An American soldier's desire to prove his masculinity may have been more acute during the Vietnam War. Traditional patriarchy, in particular white male authority, was under assault in the mid-twentieth century. The growing emancipation of women, the extension of civic and social equality to African Americans, and the explosion of youth culture challenged the privileges white, American men had come to expect. African American men looked at military service as a means of seizing economic control of their lives and as a way to publicly express their manhood, through military symbols of authority like weapons and uniforms, in a way that white society had long denied them. The racial dynamics of the war itself were also gendered, as American soldiers feminized their Vietnamese enemies for refusing to fight in the open and their Vietnamese allies for not being able to defend themselves. In so many ways, the gender stakes were high.

Raw American recruits psyching themselves up for deployment expected an opportunity to fulfill their country's masculine ideals against a feminized Asian other and to claim the privileges of manhood they felt their history and culture had promised them. They soon figured out the war's limitations.[90]

The Vietnam War, for most Americans who served in it, was not the war their nation's recent past had prepared them to fight. The South Vietnamese seemed inscrutable, not like the smiling Europeans their fathers had liberated a generation before. The enemy was elusive, hiding among the peasants and not easily identified by uniforms, equipment, and insignia. Danger, for those who experienced it, came without warning, creating a contagion of fear. And the sacrifice, in blood and bone, seemed to accomplish little, just the seizure of squares on a map that would be abandoned when an operation was over. For rearward personnel witnessing the spectacle from afar, the war was abstract and remote, making their own intimate sacrifices—the irritants of camp life, the loneliness of being far from home—seem unnecessary. As a result, individual aspirations supplanted the patriotic ideals that had been proffered by the nation. If the war would not make them heroes, soldiers reasoned, they might as well be comfortable. To that end, better food, better sleeping quarters, more free time, and more entertainment became the "war goals" of American military personnel who recognized that their service would not stop communism or preserve freedom or protect the American way of life. In consolation, they retrieved that way of life—comfort, leisure, satiety—from their memories and looked for ways to make it live in Vietnam.

"Nobody builds bases like Americans," journalist Michael Herr wryly observed in *Dispatches*. At first glance, Herr's comment seems to describe the abundance that prevailed on American military installations and that encouraged the demands of disgruntled soldier-workers. In fact, he was writing about an elaborate base that wasn't: Khe Sanh. Herr observed that despite its strategic importance sitting astride a major communist infiltration route, Khe Sanh was for years only a tiny outpost and home to a few hundred troops. Then, in late 1967, General Westmoreland poured 6,000 combat troops into Khe Sanh to address the threat posed by North Vietnamese regulars amassing in the area. The base became legend in early 1968, when its occupants endured a seventy-seven-day siege with no ground resupply. Knee deep in mud and rats, sometimes eating only two C ration meals each day, living in fear of enemy human-wave assaults, and struggling to rest amid constant shelling by both sides, survivors of Khe

Sanh endured one of the bona fide hell holes of the Vietnam War. As one young marine wrote home to his parents just eight days into the battle, "I think with all the death and destruction I have seen in the past week I have aged greatly. I feel like an old man now."[91] In his speedy maturation, the war's promise had been fulfilled. He was a man, but broken too.

For Herr, author Tim O'Brien, and other postmodernists writing about Vietnam, the randomness of the violence obliterated whatever romantic notions of war John Wayne and the American imagination had conjured. There is no symmetry in their written works, no justice, and no glory. In *The Things They Carried*, O'Brien goes so far as to suggest that any meaning teased out of a war story ought to make the audience suspicious of its veracity. "In the end," he writes, "really, there's nothing much to say about a true war story, except maybe 'Oh.'"[92] In the true war story of Khe Sanh, 250 American soldiers died defending the base, which was largely abandoned a few months later. By then, the survivors of the siege had come to know the blight of war, and they emerged from the conflict in full concurrence that Vietnam "just isn't John Wayne." Khe Sanh veterans learned firsthand that war is not like the movies because it is unimaginably worse.

For soldiers who never experienced combat—the vast majority of Vietnam veterans—their John Wayne expectations also went unmet. They, too, learned that war is not like the movies because it can be so much better. For them, the Vietnam War was defined by hot chow, private bunks, doughnuts and ice cream, hard work, office work, leisure time and laundry day, forms, formations, digging holes and filling sandbags, guard duty, and all the petty harassments of military life—everything but combat. It was what they wanted, the best they could hope for under the circumstances, but not what they had prepared for. They reveled in the abundance, and they hated it, too, because it stole their best chance to prove themselves as men. It also insulated them from the war so well that there scarcely seemed any point in being there. They endured loneliness and boredom, their freedom was curtailed, the distance strained their relationships, and they watched helplessly as stateside life went on without them. And for what? Not for leaders who inspired them, not for a cause they believed in, or—if they did believe in it—not for one they expected to prevail. In answer to their grievances, military authorities softened the war experience but failed to infuse it with meaning. Despite staggering efforts to replicate the comforts of American life, soldiers still suffered low morale because, in the end, most of them did not want home-front living in Vietnam. They wanted to go home.

CHAPTER THREE

Total War on Boredom

The U.S. Military's Recreation Program in Vietnam

The North Vietnamese and their southern allies, the National Liberation Front (Viet Cong), often had little to sustain them in their war with the United States and its ally, South Vietnam. As Ho Chi Minh put it when facing similar odds against the French in 1946, "I have no army. I have no finance. I have no diplomacy. I have no public schools. I have just hatred, and I will not disarm it until you give me confidence in you."[1] Yet in 1954 his forces prevailed against an army with what seemed to be superior technology and logistical capabilities. The so-called American War repeated this dynamic. U.S. soldiers patrolled contested areas with up to a hundred pounds of gear on their backs and heavy firepower just a distress call away, but North Vietnamese and Viet Cong fighters usually traveled light and fought with only the bare essentials. American intelligence conducted in the mid-1960s determined that North Vietnamese troops carried little on the march: uniform, poncho, tent, hammock, mosquito netting, canteen, mess kit, first aid kit, weapon, and ammunition. The typical Viet Cong guerrilla carried even less: mosquito netting, hammock, weapon, and ammunition. Without logistical support in the field, soldiers with both forces carried their food with them, a meager ration of rice that might be augmented by cassava or, rarely, a little meat. Alternatively, American soldiers' packs were so laden with weapons, rations, and supplies that an internal report on the Vietnam logistics situation determined, "There is considerable evidence that the [U.S.] soldier is overly equipped and discards items on the march."[2]

Despite their lean circumstances, North Vietnamese and Viet Cong military authorities did seek to improve their troops' morale, but they relied primarily on censorship and propaganda to do so. Their material efforts were spare. Photographs of North Vietnamese and Viet Cong soldiers at rest depict their limited recreational options: hammocks hung in the shade a few hundred yards off-trail, or a performance by an acting troupe sporting tattered hand puppets in a makeshift jungle theater. Not surprisingly, their R&R facilities were also limited. A 1970 *Ivy Leaf* article described the destruction of a "company-sized V.C. R&R camp" by elements of the 4th Infantry Division. The after-action reports from the operation described the confiscation of 725 pounds of polished rice, two 20-volt batteries, 20 disposable gas masks, some personal effects like diaries and photographs, and an M-16 ammunition can full of plastic explosives. The only items that even hinted at the recreational nature of the facility were covered sleeping quarters and a few picnic tables made of logs and branches. Indeed, the North Vietnamese and Viet Cong waged war and took their rest with equal measures of austerity.[3]

In contrast, the United States waged war in Vietnam with almost unlimited resources, providing American military personnel with a degree of comfort that was unparalleled in military history. As previous chapters have described, American soldiers who went to war in Vietnam did so in heady anticipation of danger and deprivation. But once the beaches were taken and the foxholes dug, American soldiers adjusted their expectations to account for the strange tactical situation that prevailed in most of South Vietnam. From relatively safe rearward bases to eerily calm forward positions, the war could take on a monotonous, workaday pattern. In a 1968 *Los Angeles Times* story on soldiers' readjustment issues, one Vietnam veteran commented, "For all except the marines who get locked into position or some men who volunteer for hazardous duty, Vietnam is a nine-to-five kind of war. We'd see the grunts . . . go out on patrol in the morning and by five they'd be back for hot showers, good food, and 'Star Trek' on the tube."[4] Soldiers' idle moments concerned their superiors, for that was when they might contemplate their circumstances and question the necessity of their sacrifices. As one commanding general described the problem in 1971, "They are not only resentful, they are also bored."[5] The widespread availability of sex, gambling, alcohol, illegal narcotics, and weapons proved a potent recipe for mischief, eventually leading to disturbingly high levels of venereal disease, substance abuse, petty crime, and violent assaults within the American occupation force. To combat these social ills, military authorities provided a staggering array of recreational opportunities to the troops in Vietnam, diverting resources the North Vietnamese and Viet Cong could only dream of to a total war on boredom.

Charlie don't get too much USO.
— *Apocalypse Now*

Unlike their American counterparts in previous wars, or their Vietnamese counterparts in Indochina, G.I.'s knew with some degree of certainty the day the war would end for them. Most of them rotated in and out of Vietnam as individuals, rather than as members of a unit, each with his own twelve- or thirteen-month tour of duty to endure. Excepting serious injury or death, the DEROS—date eligible for return from overseas—marked the end of that long expanse of time, and it preoccupied American soldiers from the moment they arrived in-country. Having more than 300 days left on a tour was a source of derision and pity, while being "short" was a mark of distinction. The term spawned innumerable, envious jokes, as well as the tradition of requiring the shortest man in a unit to carry a "short timer's stick." Usually a walking stick or crop, the sticks had carvings at the top, often of a hand with an upended middle finger, suggesting the sentiments of the departing soldier toward the experience of serving in Vietnam. If a soldier entrusted with the stick was caught without it, local custom dictated his punishment, usually buying drinks for his unit. This meant that the sticks went everywhere, even into battle, like protective talismans designed to guarantee a safe ride home. In a sense, time worked backward for American G.I.'s as they ticked off the days until they could go home. DEROS calendars—usually tear-away monthlies marked with an X for every day gone—were everywhere. Soldiers could buy custom calendars that featured their own date, or desktop tear-aways that featured a joke on every page, or novelty calendars modeled on advent calendars that exposed a new piece of a pinup's flesh every time a section was removed. If there was nowhere to hang a calendar, soldiers drew them on their bodies, marking off the days on the helmets, packs, and flak vests that accompanied them into battle. These rituals expose American soldiers' priorities, which were ordered not around victory but around departure. For them, leaving Vietnam was only a matter of time.

In this culture of collective yet individualized longing, military authorities recognized the importance of breaking up the year, of creating an interim experience that made the time yet to be endured seem shorter. The R&R program (rest and recuperation, or recreation, or relaxation) afforded that break, with a five-night overseas excursion guaranteed to every soldier sent to Vietnam for one year. According to the MACV directive that governed the program, its official purpose was to "remove the individual from his normal duty environment in order to provide a respite from the rigors of a combat tour in Vietnam."[6] But since so few Americans actually participated in combat, the program more often relieved the monotony of rearward jobs and served as a bonus for a year of compliant service to the state. R&R was also used as incentive for reenlistment because soldiers who extended their tours in Vietnam were eligible for a second excursion after ninety days. Last, R&R gave soldiers who were trapped on American bases, because of the tactical situation or by military regulations designed to prevent fraternization with the locals, the opportunity to behave as tourists in Asia, stockpiling souvenirs and memories of a once-in-a-lifetime adventure.

Initially, the R&R program offered only a few destinations—Bangkok and Taipei among them—to troops in Vietnam. Then, as the war expanded, so too did the R&R options, the better to absorb tens of thousands of American G.I.'s streaming into Asian cities each month. At its peak in 1969, soldiers could choose from Hawaii, Hong Kong, Kuala Lumpur, Manila, Penang, Singapore, Sydney, Taipei, or Tokyo, depending on a number of variables. Procedures varied by branch of service, but in general each battalion-sized unit was granted a certain number of R&R slots per month. Local commanders then allocated them to individual soldiers based on seniority, merit, and whether they could be replaced during their absence. Further complicating the process, the military allocated only a certain number of R&R slots to each official R&R destination.[7] Fewer R&R destinations were available as the war wound down, and with a couple of exceptions, Bangkok, Taipei, and Hawaii were the only choices left by 1972.[8]

Soldiers had to pay for most of the trip themselves, making R&R the ultimate Vietnam consumer experience. Often they could fly for free, space available, on military flights, especially to Thailand or Japan, but they also flew commercial airlines to their destinations. To give a sense of the expense involved, in 1970, roundtrip tickets from Vietnam to Bangkok were about $72, Hong Kong was $130, Taipei $218, Sydney $627, and Oahu $558. While abroad, soldiers had to cover their own room and board, but expenses at Asian R&R sites were mitigated by the strength of the U.S. dollar on the local economy. Even so, there were problems with American soldiers arriving in foreign cities with insufficient funds, so the military required them to leave for R&R with a minimum of $250 in cash. Unit newspapers published guidelines for how much a soldier could expect to spend at various destinations, the better to help him budget his paychecks. In 1970, for example, the military estimated the average expense of five days in Sydney to be $325, $320 in Hawaii, $300 in Bangkok and Manila, $285 in Taipei and Hong Kong, and $200 in Tokyo. If soldiers wanted to get out of Vietnam—and the raging popularity of The Animals' song "We Gotta Get Out of This Place" strongly suggests that they did—there was another low-cost alternative. The U.S. military ran an R&R center at Camp Zama in Tokyo that cost only $11.30 a week. Soldiers still had to get there, but the military required them to have only $50 in cash when they left for Japan.[9]

Departing for R&R could be an adventure in itself because soldiers had to find their own transportation to the nearest out-processing facility. In the mid-1960s, troops departing from Saigon or Cam Ranh Bay stayed in billets specifically designated for R&R travelers, but men leaving from Pleiku or Danang had to find their own housing while they waited for paperwork to clear. They crashed with friends or new acquaintances, they slept in transient barracks, or they hung out in a local club, drinking the time away. The processing time in Vietnam did not cut into the time abroad; rather, it kept soldiers away from their responsibilities. Eventually, the military addressed their itinerancy by building Camp Alpha, an R&R out-processing center on Tan Son Nhut Airbase outside Saigon. The Army poured $7.5 million into the facility—originally a tent city—to increase R&R traffic and improve soldiers' comfort while they waited to depart. Newly remodeled, Camp Alpha featured "one of the most elaborate clubs in the USARV open mess system," plus "a mass of shops and services." The facility included billets for over 1,400 men, baggage storage areas, a laundry, a custom-tailor shop, a shoeshine stand, a Bank of America branch, and basketball and volleyball courts for recreation. By adding these amenities, military authorities ensured that a G.I.'s transformation from soldier to tourist began even before he got on the plane.[10]

Despite the effort involved in taking an out-of-country R&R, hundreds of thousands of American soldiers traveled abroad in the midst of their Vietnam tours. The traffic through Camp Alpha in the early 1970s gives some indication of how many G.I.'s took advantage of the program, for the facility went from housing 300 men per day in 1969 to 1,200 men per day by 1971. Military authorities also tracked overall R&R usage because it was an indicator of troop morale, though countrywide statistics are hard to come by. In the latter half of 1970, nearly 17,000 soldiers went on R&R each month. As the war slowed and troops were withdrawn from Vietnam, the R&R program was scaled back and usage declined, but the numbers remained strong. In the first four months of 1971, usage averaged 11,800 men per month, but then fell to 6,500 soldiers per month by the end of the year.[11]

Soldiers were eligible for R&R after ninety days in-country, but most delayed their trip until a few months before the end of their tours. In the meantime, the days stretched out before them. To further divide the time, the U.S. military created two "in-country R&R centers" in South Vietnam to provide lucky soldiers with a quick respite from duty that was in addition to the out-of-country R&R experience. Taking advantage of Vietnam's vast coastline and natural beauty, the military located these centers at Vung Tau, a short flight from Saigon, and at China Beach near Danang. Because travel time and the duration of stay—three days as opposed to five—were considerably shorter than out-of-country R&R, soldiers found it easier to get commanding officers to agree to the time off. On request, soldiers could also stay at an in-country R&R facility for six days in lieu of taking an out-of-country R&R. A soldier could enjoy as many three-day visits to these centers as his commanding officer would allow, assuming his unit had the necessary allocations, which made this option even more appealing.[12] The in-country R&R program was not as popular as the out-of-country program because it did not offer as clean a break from the environment of the war and especially from the military itself. Even so, thousands of soldiers took advantage of the sun and surf so close at hand, with 29,000 American servicemen visiting Vung Tau in 1968.[13]

Soldiers vacationing at these facilities could expect comfortable accommodations, especially late in the war, after multiple renovations had taken place. China Beach was a complex of one-story buildings and white picket fences close to the water. The facility could house 200 enlisted men and 24 officers in "hut-type rooms with clean sheets daily."[14] Vung Tau's original center was more elaborate, located in a former resort rented by MACV for $93,000 a year. It could accommodate 260 guests at once, with soldiers sleeping four to a room in air-conditioned suites. The three-hotel complex surrounded a large, tiled patio that was shaded by tropical plants and cooled by a crisp, blue pool. Both centers offered a lot of activities. Vacationing soldiers could work out at a variety of athletic facilities, sign up for bus tours to local cultural attractions, take a shuttle to the nearest P.X., watch movies, play games at a service club, or try the slots and catch a floorshow at the local open mess.

The centers' primary draws were Vietnam's scenery and the restful, civilian-minded setting. Southern Vietnam's coastline is among the most spectacular in the world, with 500 miles of silky, white sand and gentle waves ideal for surfing. The U.S. military made the most of these features, maintaining a half mile of beach at Vung Tau and nearly a mile at China Beach. Both facilities provided equipment for outdoor activities and water sports, including football, volleyball, and horseshoes for fun on the sand, and surfboards, sailboats, ski boats, snorkeling gear, and water skis for fun in the surf. Efforts to improve facilities at both China Beach and Vung Tau continued throughout the war, but the most coveted amenity the centers provided was policy related. In 1971, new rules permitted female guests inside the gates. Though local women were not permitted in the billet areas, they were allowed on the beach, in the bars, and in any other nooks and crannies creative G.I.'s could find.[15] Unit newspapers that promoted the availability of these facilities to the troops highlighted the incongruity of finding such peaceful settings in a war zone. As U.S. Army Support Command Saigon's *Hi-Lite Magazine* put it, "The scene could be the California coast, the French Riviera, the Caribbean—or Vung Tau, Republic of Vietnam."[16]

In-country R&R folded the tourist experience directly into the war's milieu, for soldiers fresh from combat did not have to travel far to exit the war and enter a tropical playground. Another program, known as "Stand-down R&R," brought these disparate worlds even closer together. Because granting multiple three- or five-day R&Rs to every soldier in Vietnam was so logistically complex, the military provided an interim experience to combat units as a whole. After a maximum ninety days in the field, most units on stand-down simply returned to their base camps, where they rotated in and out of barracks shared with other units. The lucky ones reported to "stand-down R&R centers." These facilities could not compete with the adventure and exoticism of out-of-country R&R, but they still offered experiences of simple luxury that felt extraordinary to soldiers used to life in the boonies. Some reveled in the mattresses and clean sheets, sleeping for most of their stays. Others partied the entire time, gorging themselves on beer and fast food as if there were no tomorrow. A *Cavalair* story on the morale-boosting benefits of the centers reported that one guest ate twenty-two pizzas in three days, and his friends were busted for drunken skinny-dipping in the pool at one in the morning. A return to service in the field was inevitable, but understanding commanders tried to ease the transition. "We'll take it easy for a day or so," their captain told *Cavalair*, "until they can sweat off the beer and soda."[17]

Some stand-down R&R centers served the needs of a particular brigade or division, with individual units rotating in and out. Their names reflected either the sponsoring unit's nickname or the cynical humor that pervades military life. The 5th Infantry Division's Wunder Beach, the 101st Airborne Division's Eagle Beach, the 173rd Airborne Brigade's Sky Soldier Beach, and the 1st Logistical Command's Logmen's Beach were all located on the coast. Other stand-down facilities were located inland and were open to several units: Freedom Hill Recreation Center near Danang, Waikiki East near Cu Chi, the Tay Ninh Holiday Inn near Tay Ninh, and the VIP Center at Bien Hoa near Saigon. Although combat units on stand-down had priority, soldiers stationed permanently in the immediate vicinity of all of these centers were eligible to use the facilities in their off-duty hours.

Accommodations and amenities varied greatly from center to center. The Tay Ninh Holiday Inn, which was in a dangerous enough area to be hardened with sandbags, was the least removed from life in the field. Its barracks could sleep two squads at a time in open rooms, and the amenities consisted of hot food, cold beer, athletic equipment, and an aboveground swimming pool—facilities that were luxurious compared with life on ambush patrol but that were standard on most midsize posts. The nearby P.X. was also a big draw, "like Saturday night after payday in the States."[18] Another inland center, Waikiki East at the Cu Chi Base Camp, was a bit more elaborate. Its swimming pool was an in-ground affair complete with sundeck, patio furniture, and snack bar. Evening meals of steak and beer were served in a covered picnic area, and every bunkroom was equipped with a television. The center also featured a basketball court with floodlights for nighttime play, an evening movie, and frequent live entertainment.[19] Though Freedom Hill Recreation Center did not have a pool, it did have everything else: an on-site P.X. with concessions and a snack bar; a library; a variety of clubs; indoor and outdoor movie theaters; athletic facilities; a miniature golf course; a twenty-lane bowling alley; and a patio bar known as the "beer garden" that provided floorshows every night and alcohol all day long. Freedom Hill was an extremely popular destination for units and individuals stationed in the Danang area, averaging 2,500 visitors per day in 1971.[20]

The stand-down R&R centers on the coast also varied in their accommodations, but they had the advantage of sun and surf. Eagle Beach, located on an island across from the city of Hue, was known for its "exceptionally clean beach" for swimming and sunbathing. Living quarters consisted of one-story barracks right on the beach, and "modern clubs" served alcoholic beverages almost around the clock. The center also offered a shaded

American military personnel use an amphibious landing craft to ferry supplies for a barbecue on one of South Vietnam's many recreational beaches in 1970. Philip Jones Griffiths, one of a few journalists who documented the excesses of life in the rear, reported in the photo's original caption that "vast quantities of meat and beer were consumed while local Vietnamese looked on. Such activities were prompted to engender morale among the troops and to expose the Vietnamese to what was considered the superior American way of life." (Philip Jones Griffiths/Magnum Photos)

picnic area, barbecue pits, a miniature golf course, a basketball court, a gift shop and P.X., and a massage parlor, which almost certainly catered to soldiers' neglected libidos. Sky Soldier Beach had similar accoutrements, but it also offered watercraft like surfboards, sailboats, and motorboats for waterskiing.[21] Logmen's Beach was the most elaborate. On the beach, soldiers could enjoy boating, inner tubes, waterskiing, surfing, and scuba diving classes. Just inland, a miniature golf course, driving range, horse-shoe pits, badminton, volleyball, basketball, a craft shop, and a music room with instruments for checkout were available for soldiers to pass the time. A snack bar convenient to the beach served fast food, unit cookouts were held at barbecue pits around the installation, and there was live music each weekend in an open-air theater.[22]

These festive spaces helped soldiers enduring the rigors of combat or the irritants of base camp life imagine that they were safe and free. They did not have to sleep with one eye open, in anticipation of enemy attack, or set the alarm to report for work at the crack of dawn. R&R was like a reunion between soldiers and the civilian versions of themselves, but the transformation was only fleeting. Eventually, the return flight to Vietnam beckoned, or the captain told the company to pack their duffels for the trip back into the boonies. All R&R, whether in-country, out of country, or stand-down, was a bounded experience designed to give soldiers a pause from their normal duty environments and break up the monotonous trek toward the DEROS. R&R might be a goal for a soldier to focus on, but beyond the anticipation beforehand and the memories after, it did little to distract him from the war on a regular basis. For that, the U.S. military integrated relaxation into soldiers' daily lives by establishing recreational facilities and programs on virtually every American base.

The U.S. military's day-to-day war on boredom was fought on several fronts: athletics, including fitness-oriented activities like running and weightlifting, but also more elaborate pastimes like swimming, bowling, and golf; craft shops, libraries, and education centers that facilitated whole-some self-improvement; entertainment centers that allowed local troops to dabble in the performing arts; myriad touring productions of plays and musical acts sent into forward areas; and a slew of places to hang out and watch TV, play games, listen to music, drink alcohol, and look at scantily clad women. All of these programs emphasized the consumption of mate-rial resources, not for the good of the war but for the good of the indi-vidual fighting it, in the hope that the national interest would, by exten-sion, be served. But, just as with the living accommodations the military provided for its troops in Vietnam, there was no point at which success was reached or soldiers' expectations met, no moment when "high morale" was finally achieved. Instead, what emerges from the official record of the U.S. military's recreation program in Vietnam is a portrait of an open-ended campaign to defeat boredom, with statistics that describe the program's expansion but not its victory, rather like the troop concentrations and body counts of the war itself.

The day-to-day war on boredom began modestly as an improvised guerrilla effort to cobble together athletic facilities for the troops. Like their World War II predecessors who carved basketball courts out of the jungles of Bougainville or scratched football fields into the sands of North Africa, G.I.'s in Vietnam initially made do with the basics.[23] A ball, a bat, some open space, a net or a rim—these were all that was needed for baseball, football, basketball, or volleyball. This do-it-yourself approach to recreation continued in undeveloped areas throughout the war, where soldiers improvised with whatever materials they could get their hands on. For example, troops near Danang joined 100- and 500-mile running clubs to maintain physical fitness, earning certificates of completion if they ran 100 miles in ninety days or 500 miles in a year. Elsewhere, soldiers made their own athletic equipment, pouring cement into molds for makeshift weights and using scrap metal and tie-down webbing to make gymnastics equipment like rings and parallel bars. In the newest, roughest camps in Vietnam, improvised athletics were all the recreation soldiers had.[24]

Elsewhere in Vietnam, in the permanent bases that grew into small cities, recreation was formalized under the aegis of "Special Services," a U.S. Army agency that conducted morale programs on behalf of all five service branches. Since its advent in World War II, Special Services provided "military personnel with the best morale, welfare, and recreational programs possible under existing circumstances."[25] In Vietnam, the tactical circumstances in the rear were quite good, leading to an amazing array of boredom-fighting programs. As the combat war escalated from 1966 to 1968, Special Services enjoyed "an almost unlimited budget" for procuring supplies and entertainment, a period of tremendous growth that one staff member fondly recalled as "empire-building together."[26] Even after troop withdrawals began in 1969, Special Services remained a vital part of the war on boredom, but with greater emphasis on flexibility and mobility to adapt existing recreation programs to the changing tactical situation. Budget reports underscore the degree to which the agency remained a military priority, with Congress allocating over $9 million in appropriated funds (taxpayer dollars) on average per year to Special Services in Vietnam during the peak years of the war, 1966–70. These moneys were supplemented by more than $10 million in nonappropriated funds, which were generated by the soldiers themselves through Vietnam P.X. and club profits, during the same period.[27] Even though funds for Special Services declined late in the war, the programs themselves were still a vital part of the morale effort. By the early 1970s, hundreds of permanent recreational facilities had already been built, substantially reducing the need for new construction and freeing up funds for operating costs.

These figures only begin to suggest the resources directed toward Special Services morale-building programs. Vietnamese workers, who were paid substantially less than their American counterparts, provided much of the labor required to build, maintain, and staff Special Services facilities. Also, a great deal of construction for Special Services was done through "assistance-in-kind" programs in which idle troops were ordered to erect facilities like swimming pools, athletic courts, or social clubs. Hence, the actual dollar figure for construction costs would be substantially higher if Special Services had to pay for this labor outright. Compared with the billions spent prosecuting the war against the enemy, the tens of millions spent fighting boredom are a paltry sum. But considering how much was built, how fast it went up, and how inhospitable the surroundings, Special Services got a lot of bang for its buck.

Athletics were the heart of the Special Services program because not only did they fill soldiers' free time, but they also enhanced esprit de corps and emphasized physical fitness in an often sedentary war. In 1968, MACV formalized its policy on athletics, advising commanders that "competitive sports activities should be organized on the intramural level. Pickup games and competitions between small units are encouraged where mission requirements and available facilities permit."[28] These recommendations resulted in an explosion in the number of athletic fields, courts, and gymnasiums built on American bases around Vietnam. The most prolific of these was the "multi-use court," an asphalt pad with accessories to play basketball, volleyball, and tennis that cost around $7,000 to install. Baseball diamonds, football fields, and handball courts were also common, and some were extremely well developed. The main athletic fields at large bases like Cam Ranh Bay and Long Binh Post eventually included bleachers for spectators and exterior lighting for nighttime play.

By June 1971, Special Services had built 1,339 athletic facilities in Vietnam, mostly fields and outdoor courts but also gymnasiums and other indoor facilities, concentrated in areas with large troop populations. As of mid-1967, there were fifty-seven fields and courts in the Saigon area alone, with sixty-one more under construction. But less well-developed bases still provided soldiers with ample athletic opportunities. In early 1971, Pleiku in the Central Highlands was home to 5,400 personnel, who shared two baseball fields, two football fields, nine volleyball courts, seven basketball courts, one tennis court, one badminton court, seven multiuse courts, and a weight room.[29]

As a land-clearing operation alone, the construction of athletic fields and courts in Vietnam was impressive. But Special Services did not stop there; its athletic program also included swimming pools, bowling allies, and golf courses. In the north, the U.S. Marines took over Danang's French-built course in the mid-1960s. Special Services managed it, lending out free balls and clubs to the troops. In the south, the residents of Long Binh Post enjoyed an on-post driving range seven days a week, while lucky soldiers with passes into Saigon could visit the Saigon Country Club, a lovely remnant of French colonialism. The club had just 700 members, mostly American and European civilians and prominent Vietnamese, but it was open to all U.S. military personnel, up to forty-five each day. To facilitate its use, Special Services provided soldiers with free transportation from nearby bases. In both cases, Special Services operated pro shops to serve the consumption needs of serious enthusiasts wishing to invest in their golf hobby. Troops could buy "top-name equipment, including clubs, balls, bags, and jaunty golf hats" at steep discounts. Even if a soldier got to use them only once or twice in Vietnam, a new set of pricey clubs was an odd but worthy souvenir of the war.[30]

Special Services also erected a few bowling alleys to entertain the troops. Camp Eagle, home to the 101st Airborne Division, and the Freedom Hill Recreation Center near Danang were perhaps the only up-country installations with bowling alleys, but soldiers stationed in the Saigon area had ready access. Before Long Binh Post got its own bowling alley in 1972,[31] Special Services bused soldiers into Saigon to use the U.S. Army Headquarters Area Command Bowling Center. This facility was open seven days a week from 9:00 A.M. to 11:30 P.M. to all American military personnel. Fees were 20¢ per frame and 10¢ for shoe rentals, but bowlers who wanted to purchase their own gear could do so at the center's pro shop. It stocked $3,000 worth of bowling accessories—balls, shoes, gloves, and bags—at 60 percent off the stateside price. Soldiers who did not want to lug their gear back to base could rent a locker at the center for 50¢ per month, suggesting that some soldiers held a real dedication for the sport.[32]

With temperatures frequently topping one hundred degrees and life-sucking humidity throughout the year, a tour of duty in Vietnam was a thing to endure, even if combat was not part of the experience. Seeking relief from the heat and a respite from war work, American soldiers stationed all over the country did what they had done as kids growing up in the States—venture to the local swimming hole. In less-developed areas of Vietnam, the local swimming hole really was a hole—a creek or river designated safe enough for G.I.'s to clean up and cool off. Other swimming holes were more formally developed, such as the Armed Forces Recreation Area on the Saigon River. The river's muddy consistency and dubious sanitation rendered the shoreline off-limits to swimmers, but Special Services provided equipment for waterskiing and fishing. On the coast, sand and surf were the norm for off-duty personnel. For example, the Cam Ranh Bay Sub-area Command, home to some 8,500 troops in 1971, provided swimming and boating at three separate beaches. Likewise, Chu Lai Special Services lent out fins, snorkels, and fishing gear to off-duty soldiers stationed near its seaside recreation area.[33] For these amenities and their security, relative to forward areas, coastal installations were among the most coveted postings in all of South Vietnam.

Over the course of the war, Special Services sought to extend the benefits of coastal living to soldiers stationed in South Vietnam's interior by making swimming pools a lynchpin of local morale-building initiatives. Special Services requisitioned the equipment, but installation and maintenance were often contingent on "self-help" programs that used the labor and expertise of local troops. Military-issue swimming pools in Vietnam were typically aboveground affairs that came in standard sizes—forty by sixty feet or fifty by one hundred feet—with a graduated depth of four to eight feet, though there were other variations.[34] Depending on the interest and resources of the host unit, these pools might be surrounded by elaborate decking complete with patio furniture and changing rooms. Given the lumber required for decking and supports, the motor for pumps and filtration systems, and the electrical wiring and plumbing involved in pumping and treating 100,000 gallons of water, the installation of each swimming pool was an expensive and labor-intensive production. And yet, they were everywhere in South Vietnam.[35]

By July 1970, Special Services was operating forty-eight swimming pools in twenty-two locations, including small compounds like the 43rd Signal Command compound at Pleiku, population 412.[36] (There were even more pools on U.S. bases in South Vietnam that were run not by Special Services but by local units themselves.) Most of these pools were aboveground, but some were considerably more elaborate. At the MACV Annex compound in Saigon, American military and civilian personnel could enjoy an Olympic-size pool built by the civilian construction consortium RMK-BRJ at a cost of $181,000. This facility included a fifty-meter pool with eight lanes and a graduated depth of four to eighteen feet, three diving boards, a sundeck with patio furniture, restrooms, showers, and a snack bar. Operating 10:00 A.M. to 10:00 P.M., the pool could accommodate over 200 people at once. When this facility originally opened in November 1969, the general who cut the ribbon commented that the pool was "proof that the United States Government provides the best for the members of its military, no matter where they are located in the world."[37] The swimming pools, so common and yet so dear, were the ultimate replication of stateside living. They represented American prosperity to soldiers far from home, but also technological mastery, over the enemy as well as the elements.

While the athletics program tended to soldiers' bodies, other initiatives in the war on boredom tended to soldiers' minds. The U.S. military had long posited itself as an instrument of self-improvement through which the rigors of training, a disciplined barracks life, and even the hardships of combat could make civilians into soldiers who would one day return home as empowered, educated, and well-rounded citizens. To that end, Special Services and other military agencies sponsored a series of programs to formalize soldiers' acquisition of education and new skills. They could work on projects at their base's local craft shop, check out a book from the base library, take courses for college credit, and even participate in the performing arts — in essence, improving the self while serving the state.

The first of these initiatives was the Army Crafts Program, a kind of occupational therapy program that enabled soldiers to explore their creativity and develop new vocational skills. Founded by the War Department in 1942, the Army Crafts Program was initially designed to use troop labor and creativity to enhance the appearance of military installations. It was redesigned in 1944 to "provide [soldiers with] opportunities for self-expression, serve old skills, and develop new ones." According to a 1965 Army publication, arts and crafts could assist soldiers in their work: the clay, minerals, and stone necessary for ceramics and sculpture could contribute to a better understanding of terrain; painting and drawing could aid the observation and coordination required for marksmanship; handicrafts like lapidary and leatherwork could teach soldiers how to manipulate a variety of materials, the better to improvise on the battlefield; and so on. Of course, these tortured, MacGyver-like justifications for the Army Crafts Program were pure pretense. In practical terms, Special Services administered the crafts program in Vietnam strictly as a morale builder, catering to the needs and tastes of G.I. artisans as they became identified.[38]

The craft shops varied in size and scope, but at the bare minimum all craft shops in Vietnam provided worktables and basic tools for hand-built pottery, drawing, painting, and model construction. More sophisticated facilities offered a full complement of power tools for woodworking, stone cutters and polishers for lapidary, and darkrooms and enlargers for budding photographers. Soldiers with professional experience in the industrials arts and art usually managed the craft shops, offering instruction in various media to interested patrons. Both appropriated (taxpayer) and nonappropriated moneys funded the Army Crafts Program, such that soldiers had to pay only nominal fees for their supplies. To encourage use, craft shops typically stayed open nine to twelve hours per day, and many were air-conditioned, adding to their appeal. Frequent mention in G.I. newspapers helped make new arrivals aware of local facilities, and arts and crafts contests sponsored by Special Services rewarded soldiers for their participation.[39]

The Army Crafts Program in Vietnam was so popular that it expanded from one shop in 1967 to fifteen full-service craft shops and twenty photo labs a year later. By June 1969, Special Services operated forty-six fixed craft shops and two mobile units, with plans for dozens more. Most were located in heavily populated areas, such that, by June 1970, seven large installations enjoyed thirty craft shops, while twenty smaller bases shared thirty-one. Yet even installations too small to support a craft shop of any size were not entirely bereft, for Special Services issued tens of thousands of model kits to units serving in remote areas.[40] Toward the end of the war, small, mobile facilities became the norm, enabling soldier-crafters to pick up and move their projects, along with the craft shop itself, as the tactical situation required.[41]

Like the Army Crafts Program, the Army's library service was a wholesome way to keep the troops in Vietnam occupied during their off-duty hours. The Library Branch of Special Services erected several types of facilities to encourage reading and private study. The most sophisticated of these were fixed libraries established in permanent buildings on large bases, where the tactical situation and large troop concentrations warranted a long-term facility. Professional military or civilian librarians maintained collections of 4,000 to 8,000 volumes, most of them hardback, plus reference guides and periodicals. The larger the library and the longer it was in operation, the nicer its accommodations. Most fixed libraries were air-conditioned with comfortable reading areas and well-lit writing tables where soldiers could draft letters home. Some even offered tape rooms where soldiers could listen to music on headsets, dub the library's collection, or record messages to loved ones. About thirty-seven fixed libraries were in operation throughout South Vietnam at the peak of the library program in 1970. An interlibrary loan program enhanced local collections by allowing soldiers to request a specific item from the USARV Command Reference Library's 13,000 volumes.[42] Soldiers stationed far from a fixed library could also borrow "Books By Mail," a program in which an individual's written request for a book was directed to the Saigon Library Center. There, the librarians would procure the book and mail it to a soldier in the field along with a self-addressed label for the book's return.[43]

Since the Library Branch's primary goal was to provide "reading matter to men in faraway places," it also managed field libraries that could be set up, dismantled, and moved as the tactical situation required. Field libraries consisted of 2,000 books, mostly paperbacks, that required only 120 linear feet of shelving. These facilities could be established almost anywhere: a supply shed, a unit's dayroom, or a corner in a Special Services club. Some field libraries in Vietnam were even set up in abandoned shipping crates.[44] The library program's emphasis on flexibility increased late in the war, when budgets were shrinking and troop populations shifted more often. The Library Branch relied more and more on bookmobiles to serve the troops, since they could pick up and drive away on a moment's notice. These mobile libraries circulated among several units, much like stateside bookmobiles that travel between underserved communities.[45]

Whether stocking bookmobiles or fixed libraries, the Library Branch coordinated the distribution of massive quantities of reading material throughout the war. For example, in 1969, the 113 libraries in III and IV Corps circulated an annual average of 130,000 items to about as many patrons. The Saigon Library Center also issued library kits consisting of 25 paperback books and an assortment of magazines directly to individual units. By 1970, the Library Branch was distributing 14,000 of these book kits and over 300,000 magazines each month to some 4,700 units stationed in South Vietnam. This material was stored in designated library facilities, if they were available, or in dayrooms, offices, or bunkers if they were not.[46] By the summer of 1971, 427 Army library facilities remained in Vietnam, most of them consisting of several hundred volumes carefully shelved in the back of a truck.[47]

The war on boredom also encompassed efforts to formalize the learning process beyond pleasure reading. After World War II, the G.I. Bill enabled millions of veterans to attend college, helping to transform a generation of blue-collar sons into white-collar workers. During the Vietnam War, war zone military service enabled soldiers to get a jump on their education. The U.S. Army managed up to twenty-two education centers at one time in Vietnam, providing evening classes for remedial education, special military training, and even college credit. For soldiers stationed in remote areas without immediate access to a center, the Army's educational program provided correspondence courses with on-site study groups and field testing for credit. The education center facilities varied from a single desk to complexes of several buildings, depending on the size of the base and its tactical situation. The U.S. Army provided qualified military or civilian instructors, course materials, and even textbooks, which were special-ordered from a book dealer in Madison, Wisconsin.[48]

Though American soldiers in Vietnam were on average the best-educated armed force the United States had ever sent to war, hundreds of thousands of them nonetheless were educationally deficient. For soldiers completely lacking an education, the education centers offered courses and testing to certify passage of primary school. In the first half of 1971, for example, 741 American soldiers in Vietnam took Eighth Grade Completion tests. The education centers' General Educational Development (GED) tests were also extremely popular, with 2,347 administered during the same period.[49] Data from earlier in the war is spotty, but in 1967 the Long Binh Subarea Command reported that its education center was administering forty GED tests each day. And in 1969, when the Americal Division Education Center sent a staff member to administer GED tests to soldiers at a remote firebase, the overwhelmed private found that 120 soldiers had signed up to participate.[50]

Most American soldiers in Vietnam had at least a high school diploma, motivating them to set their educational aspirations higher than the GED. To accommodate and encourage them, the military's education centers offered a series of post-secondary educational opportunities. The United States Armed Forces Institute (USAFI) offered two different types of correspondence courses to American military personnel stationed around the world, including Vietnam. USAFI's own courses ranged from standard high school fare—English composition, American government, algebra, and typewriting—to college-level courses in a range of disciplines: math, social sciences, history, accounting, business law, and dozens of language courses, including "Colloquial Dutch" and "Melanesian Pidgin English." USAFI also offered correspondence courses to help a soldier return to the States with a trade, such as auto mechanics, carpentry, plumbing, electrical work, and the repair of radios, televisions, and refrigerators. USAFI's second program consisted of some 6,000 college-credit correspondence courses administered by the extension departments of forty-five American colleges and universities. Each course cost a soldier between $10 and $30 and resulted in credits that could be transferred, with the military's assistance, to any stateside school. Among the participating institutions were the military's own training facilities, which offered correspondence courses to help military personnel develop skills within their existing Military Occupational Specialties. If he chose, a soldier serving in Vietnam could spend his leisure time studying up on how to be a better rifleman or signal operator.[51]

The U.S. military also contracted with the University of Maryland to provide college courses directly to the troops at most education centers. The instructors were military or civilian personnel, each with a Master's Degree or higher in the requisite field. A three-credit course cost $66, $49.50 of which was subsidized by the military. Enrollments in University of Maryland courses were much lower than those for USAFI correspondence courses, because of the time involved—four hours of class per week plus study time. Soldiers stationed furthest in the rear were best able to participate, because their jobs created stable routines. Over the years, thousands of soldiers took classes. This estimate is based on a countrywide audit of the Army's educational program conducted in the fall of 1970, when over 1,000 soldiers were enrolled in University of Maryland courses offered at the twenty-two education centers then in South Vietnam.[52]

As prevalent as Special Services' athletic facilities, craft shops, libraries, and education centers were, the best-remembered weapon of the war on boredom is entertainment. During the Vietnam era, military authorities still held great stock in the power of crooners and comedians to distract and uplift, just as they had in World War II. Even today, the most recognizable form of recreation for American soldiers serving overseas is the USO show—live entertainment and celebrity visits courtesy of the United Service Organizations. Though footage of Bob Hope telling jokes and Ann Margaret stalking the stage in go-go boots may dominate memories of entertainment in Vietnam, USO shows were but one part of a massive effort to entertain American troops stationed there. According to the Army, its international entertainment program was "the largest, most inclusive combine of musical and theatrical activity in the world; it is the largest single producer of legitimate plays, musical shows, concerts, choral and instrumental groups, music and theatre festivals, thematic productions, and touring shows, as well as many other types of theatrical enterprise."[53] In essence, the U.S. Army was a massive production company that opened a new front in the war on boredom every time a performer took the stage.

Part of this effort involved putting the tools for music and theater in the hands of soldiers themselves. From 1966 onward, the Entertainment Branch of Special Services coordinated this program, establishing some thirty-seven Entertainment Centers throughout South Vietnam. These facilities varied in size from 1,000 to 4,000 square feet and were designated not just for performances but also for practice and experimentation. Each center included rehearsal and performance space, office and storage space, basic musical instruments and supplies, sound and lighting equipment, and tools and materials for set construction. A Special Services Entertainment Director, and perhaps an assistant or two, staffed the centers and provided programming in accordance with military guidelines. Jam sessions, private practice sessions, music appreciation lessons, choral societies, and talent shows flourished on many rearward bases.[54]

Some centers also formed repertory companies and mounted plays. These efforts could be hampered by the unavailability of either all-male material or women. As one Special Services report put it, "The chances of finding a qualified actress in a combat zone are practically non-existent." And yet, plays were performed by American soldiers stationed in Vietnam, and none of the productions described in surviving records were of *Twelve Angry Men*. Bases with hospital facilities and, hence, nurses, or that were staffed by Department of the Army civilians, were able to support co-ed theater programs.[55] The most successful community theater company in Vietnam was the Long Binh Post Players, founded in early 1967 by a drama-major-turned-soldier who eventually extended his tour of duty by two years to run the company. The Players produced several plays and musicals during the war (*The Odd Couple, Barefoot in the Park, Come Blow Your Horn, The Fantasticks*, and *The Rainmaker* among them), drawing their talent from as far away as the DMZ. In addition to talented grunts given temporary duty at Long Binh Post, company members included a Brigadier General's civilian secretary, a chaplain's assistant, a Central Finance clerk, and a member of the 266th Army Band. Commanding officers were generally supportive, but one performance was jeopardized when an "unsympathetic sergeant" put an actor on guard duty.[56] Starting in 1969, Long Binh Post was also host to Armed Forces Theatre Vietnam, a military-run touring company that sponsored auditions for soldier-actors countrywide. The casts spent three weeks rehearsing at Long Binh, then another four weeks touring to other military installations. Productions included *You're a Good Man, Charlie Brown* and *Guys and Dolls*, which was described in *Triumvirate* as "the largest military theatrical production ever to be staged in Vietnam."[57]

The heart and soul of the military's entertainment program was the live musical touring show. In the early years of the war, just two to four professional touring shows made the rounds in Vietnam each month, but the program quickly grew to incorporate hundreds of performance groups and thousands of entertainers from all over the world.[58] Of these tours, the USO shows were the largest and most sophisticated. They came in two forms, the mounted show and the handshake tour. The former consisted of music, dance, and comedy acts, famously headlined by stars like Wayne Newton, Connie Francis, Martha Raye, and, of course, Bob Hope. More often, though, mounted shows consisted of unknown bands and entertainers still hoping to make it big in the entertainment industry. These acts were recruited by the USO, which then made arrangements for the tour with the Entertainment Branch of Special Services. The USO paid these performers a $10 per diem and a salary of $150 per week out of USO funds, while the military provided transportation, housing, and security. In return, USO performers did ten to fifteen shows per week on grueling four- to six-week tours.[59]

According to military publications, the USO handshake tours consisted of celebrity visits to "small advisory components or hospital wards or just [to] out-posts in places where you wouldn't want to live." The celebrities were expected to make six to ten stops each day, where they signed autographs, posed for pictures, and discussed "military duties, work, and future career interests" with the troops. VIPs who made the handshake circuit in Vietnam include Raymond Burr, Jimmy Stewart, Ron Ely (TV's "Tarzan"), college football coaches, professional athletes, beauty queens, and even Sgt. Stryker himself, John Wayne.[60] The manager of the USARV Special Services Entertainment Branch explained the handshake tours' appeal: "It can be a big contribution to a soldier's morale to have a famous person or a pretty American girl visit him at his job."[61] Through some kind of celebrity magic, they imagined, the golden glow of fame cast its spell over

Twelve thousand marines watch Bob Hope's USO Christmas Show at Danang in 1967. Though scenes like this one have come to represent the entertainment effort during the war, the majority of shows for American military personnel in Vietnam were put on by talented G.I.'s and thousands of other unknown entertainers. (A.P. Photo)

American G.I.'s, making them better soldiers and making a year in Vietnam a little more tolerable. In reality, though, the effect of a handshake tour was somewhat less glamorous. For example, when Troy Donahue, who had made teenage girls' hearts go pitty-pat in the 1950s, made the rounds in early 1969, Special Service's documentation of the tour was enthusiastic but open to interpretation: "The troops at the fire bases were completely unbelieving of the fact that someone like Mr. Donahue would come out to them and be interested in how they felt about the war."[62]

Despite its tremendous presence in public memories of American wars, the USO did not provide most of the live entertainment enjoyed by American soldiers in Vietnam. Special Services also contracted directly with hundreds of entertainers to perform on the Vietnam circuit. These "Commercial Entertainment Units" consisted of floorshows and bands, which were governed by military regulations prescribing membership, instrumentation, and the length of each gig. The pay was quite good; floorshows received $275 to $425 per performance, and bands received up to $325 per show. As a result, entertainment troupes clamored to be put on the payroll, forcing Special Services to hold auditions every Monday and Thursday at the Saigon USO. By 1970, an average of 3,200 performers in 250 groups from 26 countries were playing the Vietnam circuit at any given time.[63]

After auditions, Special Services compiled a "Roster of Approved Commercial Entertainment" from which local entertainment directors could choose acts for booking. Though a few groups hailed from Australia or the United States, most were Vietnamese, Filipino, or South Korean. Their names suggest some vague understanding of the young, American audience to whom they tried to appeal: the Chop Chop Tempo Band, the Christian Lords Band, the Flunkies Floor Show, the Proud Mary Floor Show, the Uptight Band (by turns, a reference to Stevie Wonder's hit "Uptight (Everything's Alright)," or G.I. slang for something good), the Teen Angels Band, the Freedom Birds Band (a reference to the plane that would one day take a soldier home), and the Joe McCoy Cocktail Act, which consisted of two Vietnamese men. Virtually every musical act, regardless of its name or style, featured female dancers who, depending on the venue, might go topless. "A night at the club may not be like a letter from home," wrote one G.I. newsman, "but don't tell that to a weary soldier who, with a beer in his hand, is intently watching four gorgeous go-go girls. He may just give you a good argument."[64]

The military carefully tracked the progress of the entertainment effort in Vietnam, assigning each touring company an escort officer who wrote an "After-Action Report" about the tour when it ended. These reports make for some interesting reading, quite in contrast to traditional after-action reports that document combat situations. The reports identified problems with the entertainment program or a particular group, including the reception the entertainers received at each stop. For example, when the band "Axe" played aboard the USS *Sphinx* in March 1971, the after-action report documented only fourteen people in attendance. The notes describe the audience's "reaction [as] good, except for the ship's [canine] mascots who hate women—they barked continuously." Other programs had trouble finding the right audience, such as the "Mr. Daniel and Friends Show," which consisted of Mr. Daniel, who cut hair for "entertainment purposes," and several models who demonstrated various fashions. The intended audience for the show was young men, but that fact was consistently lost on local entertainment directors who mistakenly advertised the show to female personnel. As a result, the audiences were very small, consisting of "entirely uninterested" military and civilian women, though Mr. Daniel did give at least a dozen haircuts at every stop.[65]

The commercial entertainment tours spread a lot of cheer, but they also had their share of problems. It is noteworthy that Mr. Daniel received the reviews he did, for Special Services reported in 1971 that many local units were reluctant to give performers bad evaluations. The hosting units feared they might be denied future entertainment if they appeared ungrateful; in addition, the performers got to read the reports, sometimes while they were still on base. The hosting units did not want to hurt the performers' feelings, a touching concern that expressed appreciation for their efforts but also a desire to avoid awkward moments in the chow line at the company mess hall. Another persistent problem with the entertainment program involved celebrity handshake tours with unknown "celebrities." Participation in a Vietnam tour was a star's expression of patriotic duty, but for unknown performers or those whose careers had faltered, a tour of Vietnam meant a steady paycheck and perhaps some press coverage to raise one's public profile. Because of the uncertain tactical situation in forward areas, professional entertainment tours tended to focus on secure, rearward bases. As a result, soldiers stationed there were so saturated with live entertainment and handshake tours that the presence of minor celebrities on post was sometimes met with a yawn.[66]

Though G.I. audiences might be jaded, the performers were not. Touring Vietnam could be an overwhelming experience, so the Entertainment Branch instructed them about what to pack and what to expect, leaving a concise record of American entertainment venues. Flexibility was a key virtue, for staging facilities varied radically from place to place. Some locations had elaborate amphitheaters with covered seats, concealed wings, and sophisticated lighting and sound systems. Other sites offered a Quonset hut with a stage at one end, or even a flatbed truck parked in front of some improvised benches.[67] To better serve troops in contested areas, Special Services began in 1969 to prioritize small, mobile entertainment troupes "which require minimum logistical support and can perform with little or no equipment in remote areas." Eventually, Special Services asked the USO to ensure that half of its acts destined for Vietnam be limited to four people and 300 pounds of equipment. The effort to streamline the process was especially ironic because the qualities Special Services stressed for its entertainers—efficiency and mobility—were more in line with Viet Cong operational values than with the American way of war.[68]

Despite efforts to streamline touring shows, there were still places too dangerous or remote to send civilian performers. Special Services was determined to bring the war on boredom into contested areas, however, so the Entertainment Branch increasingly relied on musical acts composed of American servicemen. As one Special Services officer explained, "Sometimes these men perform from the back of a two-and-one-half ton truck right out in a night defensive position. They go where the pros can't."[69] Some tours, known as "Area Military Shows," consisted of performers who made a circuit within a corps area. Others, known as "Command Military Touring Shows" (CMTS), traveled throughout Vietnam. Once selected for a tour, the soldier-entertainers were placed on temporary duty for sixty days, including ten days for rehearsal. They received about $280 to cover costumes and equipment, and they continued to draw their regular military pay. The pace of the tour was exhausting, with a performance every day, six days a week, somewhere in Vietnam.[70]

All in all, performing on a military entertainment tour was a good gig, one that beat most other kinds of duty in Vietnam. Groups like The Holy Buckers, Happy Our, Communications, The Sinister Soul Set, The Tailgate Chowder Marching Society, The Downbeats, and Something Special all made the tour in 1968. Getting selected, however, was not easy. Talented soldiers came to the attention of Special Services through a variety of channels. Sometimes their talent was apparent to a commanding officer, who recommended the soldier for an audition in Saigon. Regional Special Services branches also held local talent shows to entertain the troops and let them compete for a chance to join a command tour. At one point, the 1st Logistical Command and AFVN-TV sponsored "Operation StarSearch," a countrywide talent competition to find personnel for CMTS tours. The desire to join a CMTS tour was so strong that sometimes the bookings preceded formation of the band. A 1971 classified ad in the *Long Binh Post* sought the following: "Bass player and/or drummer for country/western band. Also need female vocalist. Must have at least six months left on tour. Plenty of bookings already lined up, all needed now is talent. Contact 'Lefty' Howard, manager, 'The Country Boys.'"[71]

The military's self-improvement and entertainment programs were surely much appreciated by soldiers who desired to use their time in Vietnam to better themselves or create lasting memories of a brush with celebrity. But the draft sent many reluctant warriors off to war, men who did not want to serve their country and who perhaps did not want to do anything anywhere at all. The Sixties were defined by a new cultural appreciation for just hanging out and doing nothing, and Americans increasingly saw recreation as a passive activity centered around the absorption of broadcast media. When soldiers in Vietnam did "go out" in their off-duty hours, it often was not to the local gym or craft shop but rather to the local bar or brothel, as evidenced by the proliferation of such establishments, usually with Americanized names and English-speaking staff, adjacent to U.S. bases. Soldiers' desire to go off-post in pursuit of alcohol and prostitutes led to a host of disciplinary and security problems: getting drunk, getting mugged, brawling, committing crimes against local Vietnamese, falling victim to Viet Cong terrorist attacks, returning to duty with incapacitating venereal diseases, or not returning to duty at all. To prevent these outcomes, military authorities tried to channel soldiers' need for entertainment and relaxation into on-post venues, where their behavior could be monitored and their dollars captured. To that end, the U.S. military built or sanctioned hundreds of places on its bases for troops to just hang out.

The most basic of these facilities was the standard dayroom, a lounge area the military authorized for every company- or battalion-sized unit stationed at a permanent base. Dayrooms were often air-conditioned, providing a comfortable place for soldiers to read, write letters home, or play board games. In terms of amenities, they varied from unit to unit, depending on the tactical situation, the sympathy of commanding officers, and the initiative of local soldiers looking for an off-duty project. Some were spare rooms sparely furnished. Others, like the dayroom for Central Finance on Long Binh Post, were quite elaborate, with "several writing tables, a TV and viewing area, two fancy bookshelves, a regulation pool table, and a bumper pool table." Dayrooms on small installations often had to serve multiple functions. "Hog Heaven," a hangout for a battalion of the 196th Infantry Brigade at Landing Zone (L.Z.) Ross, doubled as a nightclub. It included a red-topped bar, twelve multicolored tables, and psychedelic paintings enhanced by infrared lights. American bases often lay at the surreal intersection between comfort and combat, as units conducted war work in and among facilities designed to replicate stateside living. At Hog Heaven, the decorative infrared lights were occasionally flicked off while the red-topped bar was used to conduct mortar classes for the battalion's mortar crews.[72]

One of the main enticements of the dayrooms was that each was supposed to contain a television set, though later in the war many soldiers owned their own or bought them in groups for shared use. Just as in civilian life, TV viewing in Vietnam was an easy way for soldiers to disconnect from reality, and the U.S. military obliged this impulse by saturating

Vietnam with broadcast media. The development of in-country radio and television programming unfolded quickly over the course of the occupation. In August 1962, Armed Forces Radio began official AM broadcasts of "information, education, and entertainment" eighteen hours per day from the Rex Hotel, a bachelor officers quarters in Saigon. Three years later, radio programming was expanded to twenty-four hours per day, including FM broadcasts during afternoon and evening hours. The military installed twenty-two repeating transmitters throughout the country, but pockets of poor reception remained. To address the problem, in 1966 MACV authorized construction of a permanent studio in Saigon to provide AM and FM master control for the budding network, as well as a newsroom, three radio production studios, and a record library. Five large radio transmitters near Saigon, Pleiku, Cam Ranh Bay, Danang, and Qui Nhon filled in gaps in reception.[73] Renamed American Forces Vietnam Network, or AFVN, the nationwide network enjoyed extremely large audiences, such that over 99 percent of all U.S. military personnel in Vietnam owned or had access to a radio by 1970.[74]

Television programming in Vietnam was a natural spin-off of the AFVN radio network, providing military authorities with another venue to entertain and educate the soldiery. The first American television broadcasts in Vietnam were made in 1965 from C-121 Super Constellation aircraft, known as Blue Eagles, that were outfitted with $3 million worth of equipment, including in-flight studios from which announcers delivered news and information for forty hours each week.[75] The Blue Eagle broadcasts were a novel, if imperfect, solution to the difficulty of providing television in a hostile environment. Sometimes the war intruded on broadcasts, like when the aircraft would have to be diverted because of air strikes conducted on terrain below. As one pilot explained, "That's when the announcer back there goes on camera and tells the audience, 'Due to atmospheric conditions, we are shifting our flight pattern five miles to the west.' Then viewers get up and swivel their antennas a bit."[76] The Viet Cong also attacked some aircraft when they were parked on the tarmac, temporarily disrupting broadcasts and demonstrating the need for permanent ground facilities. Finally, in October 1966, AFVN-TV moved into a permanent ground facility under the same roof as AFVN radio. The new space included master control for the network, a television film library, and a large television studio that produced original programming. Ground facilities were also developed upcountry, as AFVN-TV slowly became a network, with six affiliates at Nha Trang, Tuy Hoa, Qui Nhon, Danang, Quang Tri, and Pleiku.[77] By October

1967, AFVN claimed that its television signal could reach 85 percent of American personnel in Vietnam.[78]

Like TV viewers everywhere, American soldiers in Vietnam sought entertainment and anesthesia in the gentle flicker of the small screen. Starting in March 1966, an underwater cable link between Saigon and the Armed Forces Radio/Television Service–Los Angeles allowed AFVN-TV to receive West Coast programming twenty-four hours per day. This technology facilitated the broadcast of major news and sporting events live or on tape-delay. (Prior to the underwater cable, coverage of news and sporting events was put on 16mm film and flown to Vietnam for broadcast.) Presidential addresses, election returns, NASA launches and landings, and big-time sporting events kept the troops informed and up to date, tempering the feeling that they had fallen off the edge of the world.[79] AFVN-TV also broadcast a range of popular commercial programs, eventually providing forty-two discrete hours of recent shows each week.[80] Soldiers relaxing in a dayroom or even on their own bunks could escape the monotony and authoritarianism of military life by watching an hour of *Laugh-In* or *My Favorite Martian*. But some soldiers also desired an escape *into* war, or at least into a fantasy depiction of it. In 1967, a *TV Guide* reporter conducted an informal survey and found that the most popular show among American G.I.'s in Vietnam was the World War II drama *Combat*.[81]

Still, many soldiers wanted to go *out*, to escape military life physically as well as mentally, and to roam beyond the confines of their little barbed-wire enclosures. To absorb this impulse, the military created what it hoped was an appealing destination: the on-post service club, which offered programmed activities, live entertainment, and American fast food, courtesy of Special Services. (The USO and the Red Cross ran their own clubs for American soldiers, and most of them were also located on U.S. bases.) Army regulations standardized the amenities at Special Services clubs to manage expectations and guarantee patrons a good time. Each club was supposed to provide easy chairs and settees, tables and chairs, and equipment to facilitate public programs like slideshows, movie nights, and bingo tournaments. Furnishing a club to these specifications cost around $13,000, not including construction and maintenance of the building itself.[82] The first service club in Vietnam opened in January 1967, and two dozen more of varying sophistication followed in the next three years, most of them on large, rearward bases.[83]

With no alcohol on the menu, what was the draw at these service clubs? Their staffers were usually young American women, who waged war on boredom by "fighting to get more Americans to visit" their establishments. When resources permitted, service clubs sponsored elaborate parties for local troops. Saigon Special Services offered a regular boat cruise on the Saigon River using a specially equipped landing craft unit that could comfortably seat between forty and eighty guests for dinner, movies, and fishing. And at Long Binh Post, Special Services once treated 550 people to a Hawaiian luau complete with 150 pounds of poi sent airmail from Hawaii and 650 pounds of pork that had been slow-roasted in a specially dug pit.[84] On a regular basis, however, service clubs offered nightly activities reminiscent of the programming in a stateside college dormitory. The calendar for the Copter Corner Service Club at Soc Trang, for example, offered members of the 13th Aviation Battalion the following activities in March 1969: a pinochle tournament, a "Discotheque Jam Session," "Trivia-delia," a "Whup It On Me Weenie Roast," "Sgt. Pepper Jazz Night," chess lessons and tournament, a moderated group discussion called "It's Your Bag," a slideshow called "Trip Out on R&R," and weekly card nights, movie nights, pool tournaments, bingo tournaments, and Sunday-morning coffee hours.[85] Service club programming was wholesome and cute, in stark contrast to the sleazy entertainments G.I.'s sought in Vietnamese bars, brothels, and steam baths. As historian Heather Stur suggests in her work on Vietnam-era Red Cross workers, the service club attendants—earnest, young American women—were a deliberate symbol of home, a physical manifestation of American womanhood that reminded war-weary troops of what, ostensibly, they were fighting for.[86] But the clubs' look-but-don't-touch ethos was surely frustrating to lustful soldiers, explaining the appeal of open messes with nudie floorshows that burned off some of the troops' sexual energy and of brothels that extinguished the rest.

In the war on boredom, the service clubs were supposed to provide soldiers with a wholesome alternative to alcohol and drug consumption. The effort was well intentioned but also laughably ineffective because the most popular on-post venues in Vietnam (besides steam baths and massage parlors that emerged on bases with commanders willing to look the other way) were open mess clubs, where soldiers could drink as much as they could hold. In these officially sanctioned bars, the U.S. military waged war on boredom with civilian décor, American food, slot machines, live entertainment (often including go-go dancers), and a tsunami of alcohol. More than any other endeavor, the open mess clubs speak to the desires and tastes of American servicemen in Vietnam: to get drunk, eat hamburgers, listen to Western music, and ogle half-naked women.

The peculiar operation of the open messes, which lacked strict oversight for years, explains both their ubiquity and their profitability. Open messes often emerged from the ether; all that was required was a spare room, some start-up cash, and a commander's permission, though the prevalence of unauthorized open messes suggests this last requirement was unnecessary. To blunt public criticism of what were often unseemly operations—some clubs basically devolved into strip joints—the open messes were not supported with taxpayer dollars but rather with funds generated by the soldiers themselves. Start-up costs were covered by loans, usually $10–25 from individual unit members who were repaid from club proceeds within a few weeks or months. The clubs were usually segregated by rank, and patronage was limited to personnel from the sponsoring unit. Base commanders and local boards of governors elected by club members were charged with overseeing operations, but specially trained military personnel were supposed to manage the clubs on a day-to-day basis. The open messes were officially barred from turning a significant profit, and proceeds were supposed to be handed back to the military to support other, more wholesome morale-building initiatives.[87]

Despite the mandate to surrender excess club profits, most boards of governors used the money to upgrade or renovate existing open mess facilities. Though some clubs struggled to maintain basic amenities like running water and electricity, many became elaborate as the war dragged on, including some in contested areas. For example, the 39th Combat Engineers (motto: "Fight, Build, Destroy") planned to renovate their enlisted men's club at Chu Lai with a psychedelic Wild West motif: new tables and chairs, strobe lighting on the walls and ceilings, and "western-style gates in the doorway." Not surprisingly, clubs safely in the rear were especially fancy, with those in the Saigon area sporting combinations of the following: black "leatherette" swivel chairs, faux gas lanterns, mural scenes from the Old West, mirrored walls, upholstered swinging doors, deep-shag carpeting, and gurgling indoor fountains.[88]

The scope of the open mess system was staggering, with new clubs opening all the time in Vietnam. By 1969, roughly the height of the Army's open mess system, 7,200 part-time and 1,320 full-time U.S. military personnel staffed over 2,000 clubs sprinkled around the country. The open messes also employed tens of thousands of Vietnamese workers as wait staff, bartenders, cooks, dishwashers, and custodians. As soldiers drafted into the American war on boredom, they worked for wages that the U.S. military set intentionally low to reduce inflation plus a daily ration of rice.[89]

Meanwhile, the lure of the clubs for bored, lonely, or resentful G.I.'s was so strong that hefty profits quickly resulted. In 1969, the Army's open mess system generated $177,454,000 in annual gross income and realized a staggering profit of $22,276,000; Navy and Air Force clubs presumably generated millions more. That year, the Army finally wised up to the potential malfeasance involved in such a haphazard assemblage of highly profitable, cash-based businesses. The newly created Vietnam Open Mess Agency, under the aegis of the deputy chief of staff for personnel and administration, was charged with overseeing the open mess system as a whole and bringing much needed accountability to its finances. The agency's audit of open messes eventually confiscated enough cash from local slot machines and safes to build a multi-million-dollar high-rise hotel complex for military personnel on R&R at Fort DeRussey in Hawaii.[90]

While the prevalence of open mess clubs encouraged soldiers to toast their successes, drown their sorrows, and build esprit de corps through alcohol consumption, the military simultaneously discouraged drug use that served the same purpose. Drug use was prevalent among G.I.'s in Vietnam, especially late in the war, especially at secure, rearward bases where soldiers enjoyed their free time unconcerned about enemy attack. Marijuana was most common, but painkillers, amphetamines, and heroin were readily available and extremely pure and cheap. High-ranking officers had little experience with drugs—one commander posted a warning to his troops of dire consequences if they were caught "injecting" marijuana[91]—but, like civilian law enforcement in the States, they regarded all drugs as universally bad. Military authorities interpreted drug use solely as evidence of low morale, as opposed to a recreational indulgence akin to drinking that facilitated relaxation and enhanced leisure activities. To discourage drug use, the military incarcerated, hospitalized, or discharged thousands of servicemen for their indulgence. The military also encouraged drug abuse prevention and voluntary compliance with information campaigns and amnesty programs that invited soldiers to turn in their illicit stashes. Some bases even developed "Coffee Houses," lounge areas that were specifically designated for recovering addicts. Initiated by chaplains as an "answer to the drug problem," the coffeehouses looked a lot like dayrooms or service clubs. They had lounge furniture, small libraries, and civilian décor, and some ironically sported psychedelic paint jobs lit by black lights, accoutrements usually associated with psychedelic drug culture. Despite their casual feel, these facilities were not just for hanging out. Chaplains used them to provide individual counseling and conduct group "rap sessions" to transition former users back into military life. These efforts enjoyed only passing success, as soldiers repeated in Vietnam behaviors that were common among young people back in the United States.[92]

Drug use and low morale in general also prompted the U.S. Army chaplaincy to create the Religious Retreat Center on the beach at Cam Ranh Bay. The initial 1970 proposal requested $200,000 to build a new compound, but only a pared-down request for $76,921 to renovate existing structures was subsequently approved. The resulting facility opened in early 1971 and could accommodate up to one hundred participants at a time with housing, meals, and spiritual guidance. Chaplains at the center conducted two three-day retreats each week consisting of "seminars, worship services, private meditations, fellowship, and recreation."[93] The Religious Retreat Center was developed late in the war and thus engaged relatively few soldiers in its activities. But its very existence is telling of the war's routinization and the military's fixation on tending to the needs of the individual. As a 1971 article in *Army Reporter* put it, the program "reflects current Army emphasis upon personnel: their environment, working conditions, leisure time activities, and personal growth and development. One might compare it to preventative maintenance." Some soldiers embraced the concept in good faith, but others saw it in more practical terms. "I came with sham time in mind," said one soldier, "but I became involved and enjoyed it. I think anyone could gain from being here; it's just like being back in civilian life."[94]

As this remark suggests, the various programs of the war on boredom all worked together to ease distinctions between civilian and military life, to loosen the authoritarian bonds of military service, and to allow soldiers to feel free, if only temporarily. By demilitarizing war zone life, military authorities sought to create a content, productive force, the better to wage war against North Vietnam and the Viet Cong. In measuring the effort's effectiveness, military authorities placed the same emphasis on statistics as they did for combat operations, in which success was defined not by territory held nor by cities conquered but by weapons captured, bodies counted, and kill ratios calculated. For the war on boredom, authorities carefully tracked participation in athletic programs, man-hours logged in craft shops, library patrons and book circulations, enrollments in educational programs, attendance at service clubs and entertainment shows, and profits in open mess clubs. The surviving data is incomplete, but it suggests that the military's recreation programs directly engaged hundreds of thousands of soldiers, who spent perhaps millions of man-hours in pursuit of fun and relaxation each year.[95]

Though statistics on participation were dutifully logged, they have to be taken with a grain of salt. In his memoir about life on Long Binh Post, lifeguard Pete Whalon describes the care with which he recorded attendance at his pool. "Attendance was a snap; make up a number at the end of the day between seventy-five and 250 (depending on how hot it was) and write it in the book. If you forgot to enter attendance for a day or two, or three, no problem; just make up numbers and add them the next time you remembered to take attendance."[96] There was nothing particularly self-serving about Whalon's hazy record-keeping, for his pool was likely always full. But the same cannot necessarily be said of every baseball diamond, photo lab, and library in Vietnam. The same career pressures that compelled combat arms officers to inflate body counts in order to portray an image of success on the battlefield may also have prevailed in the war on boredom. Failure to demonstrate usage of facilities might affect an officer's performance evaluations or result in the slashing of budgets. For the lower ranks, poor usage rates could cause an enlisted man to lose his prized, noncombat gig if the craft shop closed or the education center shut down. Still, the war on boredom was a massive campaign, and even if the numbers documenting usage were inflated, the facilities were real. The money, equipment, and staff required to maintain them were too, so at the very least, some significant number of Vietnam veterans were front-line soldiers in the war on boredom, even more so than in the war on communism.

It is important to remember, too, that resources spent directly on morale programs were only a fraction of the effort's total cost. Because the National Liberation Front was waging a guerrilla war in South Vietnam, every entertainer, vehicle, volleyball net, can of beer, or gallon of gas that the U.S. military brought into the war zone was a legitimate military target for enemy attack. Indeed, the entire rationale behind the introduction of combat troops to Vietnam in March 1965 was base security for American personnel and aircraft in the wake of a deadly insurgent attack at Pleiku. As the war progressed, escalation followed a circular logic: more war matériel in Vietnam required more American military personnel to provide security, which antagonized Vietnamese locals and presented more targets for enemy attack. This, in turn, prompted the need for more American personnel, more supplies, and more military hardware to protect them.[97]

The war on boredom only taxed the system further, necessitating the secure transport of swimming pool liners, balls and bats, books, art supplies, alcohol, and entertainers all over the war zone. Touring entertainment shows were a particular drain, for local commanders had to develop security plans to ensure the safety of both the performers and the unarmed G.I.'s who amassed to watch them. A 1971 USO show starring Miss America offers a prime example of the war on boredom in all its excess. When the tour visited the 101st Airborne Division near Phu Bai, the base commander launched "Project Denton Beauty" to protect the base and encourage maximum attendance at the show. Named for Miss America Phyllis George, who hailed from Denton, Texas, the security plan involved three on-post measures to fill and protect the venue where she would perform. First, all competing entertainment options like local service clubs, the post exchanges, and other recreational facilities in the area were closed for the afternoon. Miss America would be literally the only show in town, suggesting that at least some of the audience was ambivalent about being there. Second, spot checks were initiated to prevent soldiers from smuggling weapons or explosives into the Eagle Bowl, the giant amphitheater where the show was held. Finally, military policemen were out in force to direct traffic and control the crowd, estimated at 8,300.

These on-post security measures paled in comparison with the steps taken to ward off external threats. Project Denton Beauty authorized "necessary additional external security . . . by directing efforts against the probable enemy action (standoff indirect fire attack) and protecting the enemy objective (VIP party)." In other words, measures had to be in place to prevent the Viet Cong from lobbing rockets at the Eagle Bowl in an attempt to kill Miss America. The external security plan consisted of aerial reconnaissance to detect enemy activity; aerial rocket artillery fire to suppress enemy forces in the area; ground patrols throughout the Hue–Phu Bai area before and during the show; a chase team of two helicopter gun ships and a Huey with a medic on standby to evacuate the VIP party in the event of an attack; and a reaction force consisting of one rifle platoon on five-minute standby alert and a full company on thirty-minute alert, plus the requisite air power to carry them into battle. All the soldiers assigned to these tasks knew they were risking their lives not to defeat the insurgency but to protect Miss America and the talents she brought to the stage. Providing security for the show, to say nothing of mounting the show itself, was an incredible logistical feat, one that demonstrates the staggering resources the U.S. military was willing to direct toward soldiers' off-duty amusement, whether they wanted it or not. And Miss America's visit to the Eagle Bowl was just one of some 5,500 USO performances given during the war.[98]

In the end, the Viet Cong did not kill Phyllis George. Their attacks and acts of sabotage did create significant consternation for U.S. military authorities and ultimately contributed to the hostile deaths of some 48,000 American soldiers, sailors, and airmen. But the war on boredom was largely unaffected by their efforts, for it continued in earnest long after the shooting war began to falter. Whether it was effective is another matter. Certainly, morale initiatives like comfortable quarters, the widespread availability of consumer goods, R&R excursions, and frequent entertainments made military service in Vietnam more comfortable and less boring for the majority who got to enjoy them. But they could not compensate for the miseries of camp life and combat duty or for soldiers' moral and political objections to the war itself.

The U.S. military spent lavishly on these programs, providing an unparalleled degree of comfort on American bases, subsidizing soldiers' acquisition of consumer goods, and funding a massive recreation program that encouraged soldiers to ask not what they could do for their country but what their country could do for them. And yet the troops' appetite for comfort and recreation seemed to increase as more facilities became available. Military authorities continued to propose construction of ever more elaborate amenities—such as the dammed recreational lake near Long Binh Post—even as the war was winding down. No matter how much was built, it was never enough.[99]

The American ethos that more is better also pervades one of the enduring myths of the Vietnam War, namely, that the United States might have won the war if its military assets had been deployed more aggressively—that American soldiers, sailors, and airmen were compelled by civilian leaders to fight with the proverbial one hand tied behind the back. Ronald Reagan helped solidify this narrative in the public's imagination with the famous tagline, from a 1980 stump speech to Chicago veterans, in which he posited the "lesson for us all in Vietnam": "We will never again ask young men to fight and possibly die in a war our government is afraid to let them win."[100] This facile promise conflates many complicated issues related to American strategy in Vietnam, including strict rules of engagement for American pilots, civilian micromanagement of bombing targets in North Vietnam, and the decision not to take the ground war to Hanoi. In each case, larger concerns over Soviet and Chinese involvement, not to mention

American and Vietnamese civilian casualties and world opinion, prevented Presidents Kennedy, Johnson, and Nixon from prosecuting the war against North Vietnam more aggressively. Nonetheless, the myth imagines that the United States might have prevailed if more money, bombs, or soldiers had been hurled at the problem.

The we-fought-with-one-hand-behind-our-back trope denies the incredible damage the United States *did* create in Vietnam, and it is hard to imagine what the war would have looked like if no "restraint" had been used. In the war that actually took place there, perhaps 1 million Vietnamese civilians were killed, most of them in the South, and as many were wounded. Because of the disruption to agriculture and the danger of the countryside, about one-third of South Vietnam's population became refugees during the war, resulting in untold deaths from malnutrition and disease. The war also produced over a half million orphans. American firepower, whether directed by U.S. soldiers or their South Vietnamese allies, was responsible for the majority of this suffering because the North Vietnamese and Viet Cong could boast no heavy artillery for much of the war, and the United States held air superiority over South Vietnam 100 percent of the time. Though not a total war—North Vietnam's dikes remained unbombed, concern for civilian casualties tempered air attacks on North Vietnamese population centers, and many South Vietnamese rice paddies were left unsalted with dioxin—the American effort in Vietnam is still remarkable for its severity.

And yet American firepower was ineffective at blunting the insurgency or forestalling North Vietnamese infiltration of South Vietnam, which grew with every passing year. In response to the high-tech warfare that confronted them, Vietnamese people dug in—literally. At Vinh Moc, in the heavily targeted Demilitarized Zone, villagers grew so weary of their homes being destroyed that they relocated the entire community underground, coming out at night only to fish, farm, or shuttle supplies for the Viet Cong. They lived this way for six years. Day to day, American soldiers saw Vietnamese people's grim resignation in the face of adversity, convincing many G.I.'s that there was no way for the United States to win, at least not at an acceptable cost. As the United States waged war with abundance, Vietnamese resistance remained strong, yet American morale faltered. A U.S. Army pamphlet described this phenomenon perfectly, making an unwitting prediction about the outcome of the Vietnam War. "Morale is a weapon," it read. "Other things being equal, victory invariably goes to the army whose morale is high. Indeed history includes many instances in which troops with little to sustain them except excellent morale have out-fought and outlasted forces with superior material." It was the 1953 intro-duction to the Army's Service Club Program.[101]

Fifteen years later, the U.S. military tried to wield the weapon of morale as effectively as the shells and bombs it rained on Vietnam. The result was a bizarre juxtaposition of misery and mirth, with swimming pools and ser-vice clubs cushioning the weight of the combat war for American soldiers. Filmmaker Francis Ford Coppola brought this ironic reality to life in the surreal Playboy Bunny sequence of *Apocalypse Now*. In their trek deep into the wilderness of the war, Willard et al. come upon preparations for a tour-ing show at a remote jungle base. During the performance, the soldiers in the stands go wild when a helicopter delivers three nubile pinups to the garishly lit stage. Two of the women are dressed in naughty costumes that playfully speak to the racialized and distinctly American brand of war being waged in Southeast Asia: an Indian and a cowgirl, who fires her six-shooters in time to the music. Guns factor heavily into the bunnies' hyper-sexual gyrations, with the third woman suggestively straddling a rifle. Cop-pola foregrounds the war's conflation of sex with violence as the crowd menacingly surges onto the stage, the men's arousal no longer contained. The director also casts a knowing glance at the idea of war as entertain-ment, panning across the back of the crowd to show Vietnamese workers watching the soldiers who are watching the show. For just a moment, Cop-pola asks the film audience to consider the war, and the lurid entertain-ments it spawned, from the locals' perspective. "Charlie didn't get much USO," narrator Willard intones at the end of the scene. "He was dug in too deep or moving too fast. His idea of great R&R was cold rice and a little rat meat. He had only two ways home, death or victory."[102]

This fictive narration, written by Vietnam-era journalist Michael Herr, was a fair assessment of living conditions for North Vietnamese and Viet Cong fighters during the war. They lived exposed to the elements or under-ground, often for months at a time. Recreation for them was simply time to rest, which they spent reading poetry, singing songs, or writing letters home. It never involved leaving the battlefield on R&R because the battle-field was the nation. Entertainments were rare, but they did happen occa-sionally. Official touring companies like the Folk Song and Dance Union traveled the war zone, playing remote jungle clearings for North Vietnam-ese soldiers and southern insurgents. Sometimes young people in local vil-lages might sing a song or perform a dance to show their appreciation for fighters as they marched through.

Life was hard for North Vietnamese soldiers and southern insurgents, and their dreams were simple. Recalling his years in the jungle as a combat artist for the NLF, Nguyen Toan Thi wrote, "We stayed two or three days in one place. Each time we moved camp, I built a hut, a chair and a table to feel at home. For life to be beautiful, I wanted my campsite to be beautiful. Our dream was to live in a house on two floors."[103] The sacrifices Vietnamese people made for the revolution were broad and deep. When veteran William Broyles returned to Vietnam in 1983, he noticed that "the word 'sacrifice is used only to mean death, as in 'Many of my comrades sacrificed.' No other hardship is considered worthy of mention. Many Vietnamese saw their own wives and children and mothers and fathers killed, saw their own plans for careers permanently altered, suffered for years, for something larger than themselves." They had no DEROS to look forward to, no individualized point at which the war would end without death or injury, but rather a communal interest in seeing the struggle all the way through, no matter what.[104]

Of course, when it came to the insurgency, the line between fighters and civilians was blurred or nonexistent. The entirety of North Vietnam and much of the South mobilized in a war that was, for them, about independence and social justice. This is not to say that Vietnamese morale never faltered, for Vietnam's authoritarian regimes, during the war and since, did not tolerate the expression of dissatisfaction, resulting in a historical record scrubbed clean of dissent. However, there is evidence that the Vietnamese believed their will would hold indefinitely. One Viet Cong prisoner of war told his interrogators in 1969, "No matter how long it is, we shall fight until the Americans pull out of our country. It could be five years, ten years, or longer. My children and grandchildren would continue to fight until final victory."[105] Five years, or ten, is but the blink of an eye in a country that prides itself on having resisted Chinese occupation for a thousand. Meanwhile, American soldiers struggled to get through one year, marking off the days until they could go home. The war on boredom was supposed to entertain them as they waited, sating the body, nourishing the mind, and indulging the self, while morale-driven programs to provide comfortable living conditions and plentiful consumer goods made life in the war zone more physically tolerable. Thanks to these efforts and the wealth that sustained them, most American soldiers in Vietnam had everything they could possibly need, except a reason to stay in the fight forever.

CHAPTER FOUR

The Things They Bought

G.I. Consumerism in Vietnam

Since its publication in 1990, Tim O'Brien's *The Things They Carried* has emerged as one of the defining works of Vietnam War literature. An exemplar of nonlinear storytelling that blurs the lines between novel and nonfiction, the book is a fixture in high school English classrooms, where students grind through the humor and horror of O'Brien's prose, with visits to the Cliffs Notes version online. The first chapter of the book, "The Things They Carried," introduces the main characters but also the Vietnam War by cataloging the literal and figurative burdens of ground combat. O'Brien describes the weapons and tools of the infantryman's trade at length, that grunts carried "whatever seemed appropriate as a means of killing or staying alive." For each man, the items were determined by necessity, they varied by rank, field specialty, and mission, and O'Brien's persistent mention of their weight, in pounds and ounces, establishes the difficulty of patrol. The story's characters, like real-life foot soldiers, were prepared for terrible contingencies, such as hostile fire and grievous injury, and they had endured them before. They also carried ghosts and memories, a crushing sense of responsibility for their own lives and one another, and an "unweighed fear" that only added to the strain.[1]

O'Brien is a master of pacing, slowly bringing the Vietnam setting into focus with a lilting inventory of the soldiers' liabilities and obligations. The abrupt death, by sniper, of one of the men hits the reader hard, capturing the vaguest essence of what it was like for combat soldiers to witness such a sudden turn of fate. What passes almost unnoticed in O'Brien's story is a description of the American occupation's phenomenal abundance, which allowed soldiers to discard items that got too heavy. "No matter," O'Brien explains, "because by nightfall the resupply choppers would arrive with more of the same, then a day or two later still more, fresh watermelons and crates of ammunition and sunglasses and woolen sweaters—the resources were stunning—sparklers for the Fourth of July, colored eggs for Easter—it was the great American war chest." O'Brien also describes some of the comfort items soldiers carried, like razors, chess sets, and tanning lotion, a humble list that establishes the austerity of combat operations.[2] But he leaves out what his characters, if they were real-life Vietnam-era soldiers, likely had stashed in their duffels and foot lockers back at base camp: electric fans, mini-refrigerators, hi-fi stereos, pinup posters, cameras, and other creature comforts. When entire companies or battalions transferred from one base to another, individual soldiers did not have to carry these things because the U.S. military requisitioned the extra trucks necessary to haul their stuff across the war zone. Combat was infrequent in Vietnam, but consumerism was universal. For many G.I.'s, their war experience was made exceptional not by what they carried but rather by what they bought.

Wars take place in a cultural context, and appreciating that context helps to explain where the consumer goods came from and why the U.S. military facilitated their acquisition. After World War II, Americans went on a consumption bender, releasing pent-up desires to shop and spend from the confines of Depression-era poverty and wartime rationing. Though mid-century Americans consumed fast food, movies, and automobiles at record rates, they directed a great deal of their spending toward the home. Sales of air conditioners, kitchen appliances, televisions, and other home improvements increased dramatically, setting a new standard of comfort for both working- and middle-class families. As a result, much of the postwar generation was raised in cleaner, climate-controlled homes stocked with refrigerators, labor-saving devices, and entertaining gadgets. Even if the affluence could not reach every American household, knowledge of it was pervasive thanks to television, film, and advertising, stimulating desires that might someday be realized. In the context of the Cold War, household amenities even took on symbolic importance as an answer to Soviet critiques of American capitalism. According to historian Karal Ann Marling, appliances "stood for something fundamental to the postwar understanding of national identity: a sense of freedom, of effortless ease, of technical mastery, modernity, and access to conveniences formerly reserved for the very rich."[3] When these children of plenty—or the hope of plenty—grew up and went off to war against communism in Vietnam, they took their standards and desires with them.

Despite all the abundance, consumerism was not without its detractors. As historian Gary Cross points out in *An All-Consuming Century*, reformers had mounted three unsuccessful challenges to the American consuming ethos by the 1970s. Consumer protection advocates targeted the dishonest advertising, misleading product labels, and shoddy safety records that helped corporate capitalists amass their fortunes. And environmentalists cautioned that rampant consumerism was killing the planet by depleting and polluting nonrenewable resources. Both of these critiques tended to embrace pragmatic solutions like government regulation and voluntary behavior modification. They enjoyed limited success with Great Society legislation and the development of a new environmental awareness, but consumer protectionism and environmentalism failed to stimulate Americans to question the fundamental necessity and value of mass consumption. The Sixties counterculture mounted its own attack on consumerism from this direction, but it also proved ephemeral, "the last gasp of an elitist culture embodied briefly in the youthful excess of a pampered generation."[4] By the time the buildup began in Vietnam, consumerism was a fundamental part of American life.

It is no surprise that consumerism, having survived a war on three fronts in the United States, prevailed in the midst of war itself. In the public's imagination, wars are spare in all things except violence and suffering, with life-or-death stakes filtering out trivial concerns like whether or not to buy a new tape deck. Military culture is supposed to flourish in this arena, where the threat of dying and a desire to support one's peers make subordination seem like a good idea. But the Vietnam War failed to provide an experience of urgency for most soldiers who fought it, raising their expectations for what constituted a basic war zone standard of living. American consumer culture thrived in this environment, as soldiers snapped up goods and services to improve their living and working conditions, fill their leisure time, assuage their loneliness, and fulfill social and material aspirations with purchases that were out of reach in civilian life. In Vietnam, consumerism was a force so powerful that military authorities could not excise it from the lives and will of the soldiers they led; they did not even try.

Instead, they used it to advantage, cultivating desires and stimulating consumption to encourage compliant service. Soldier morale was damaged by inequities in the draft and military assignments, not to mention the dubious merits of American intervention in Southeast Asia. As morale within the military fell, consumption seemed a facile way to stop the slide. If soldiers stationed in Vietnam were allowed to purchase goods that ameliorated the discrepancies between life in Vietnam and life in the United

States, military authorities' reasoning went, then spirits might rise and military efficiency might improve. Returning home from war decked out in the trappings of affluence also enhanced the appeal of military service. To these ends, military authorities created a vast network of shopping opportunities for soldiers, using military policies to normalize and encourage consumption and aggressively promoting these programs to the troops. In essence, service in Vietnam might be a bitter pill to swallow, but military authorities hoped that the availability of consumer goods in the war zone would help American soldiers choke it down.

෴

You will find that life in South Vietnam can be frustrating,
tense, and at times full of danger. But, you will also
find that it brings great rewards.
—*A Pocket Guide to Vietnam*, 1966

When military sociologist Charles Moskos did his field research on American soldiers in Vietnam in the mid-1960s, he found that their conception of "homeland" hinged on material things—the objects and opportunities afforded by American consumer culture. Soldiers did associate the United States with democracy and religious freedom, but far more often they described "creature comforts" like cars, leisure activities, and consumer goods as the "overriding feature in the soldier's perceptions of America." Vietnamese poverty seemed to affirm the superiority of American culture, intensifying soldiers' longing for home. Moskos also found that soldiers understood morale primarily in terms of material satisfaction, that their happiness expanded and contracted based on what they had and how they lived.[5] Military authorities understood morale differently, of course, formally conceptualizing it in field manuals and policies in terms of fitness for duty, worker efficiency, and commitment to cause. And yet in other contexts they recognized that if the United States was, in the G.I.'s vernacular, "the Land of the Big P.X.," then soldiers' contentment in the war zone might be influenced by establishing a comparable retail venture in Vietnam.

The post exchange (P.X.)[6] system in Vietnam was the culmination of decades of effort by the military to provide material comfort to American soldiers serving at home and abroad. The system as a whole began in 1895, when the War Department mandated construction of a P.X. on every post to serve soldiers' retail needs. The exchange service grew dramatically in the following decades, providing comfort items like magazines, toiletries, and nonperishable processed foods to soldiers in both the world wars and Korea. As the U.S. military settled into an international garrison posture in the 1950s, the exchange system expanded its merchandise and its reach to provide a broad array of consumer goods to American soldiers and their families stationed throughout the world. A turning point came during the Korean War, when exchange employees launched Operation REINDEER to allow troops in contested areas to do some Christmas shopping. Instead of requiring soldiers to visit a P.X. in the rear while on leave, exchange employees arranged to deliver an array of merchandise into forward areas and then facilitated the shipping of combat soldiers' purchases home to their families. In the process, Operation REINDEER subtly broadened the exchange system's mission in a way that would be fully realized in Vietnam.

No longer were P.X.'s just about selling small comfort items to American soldiers far from home, as the War Department had originally intended. From Korea forward, P.X.'s were increasingly designed to replicate—and eventually surpass—the retail opportunities American civilians enjoyed in the United States. In Vietnam, the P.X. system took yet another leap forward when the military erected the first physical retail stores in an "active war zone." In prior conflicts, stateside or regional exchanges issued inexpensive, portable merchandise directly to individual units for distribution to the troops. But in Vietnam, the officers and civilians running the exchange system took advantage of the stable tactical situation to minimize the difference between stateside and wartime retail opportunities, extending the reach of American consumer culture deep into the war zone. For the first time in history, soldiers at war could take a break from their duties to go shopping in an actual American-run store. Very quickly, the acquisition of goods became a key feature of the Vietnam experience.[7]

The organization and management of the Vietnam post exchanges recast the U.S. military as a department store chain and the officers who ran it as company men. Army and Air Force officers, enlisted personnel, and American civilians managed the P.X.'s, which were mostly staffed by Vietnamese civilian employees. Local managers, in turn, answered to the Vietnam Regional Exchange (VRE), which was supervised in-country by the six-member Joint Vietnam Regional Exchange Council, composed of three officers each from U.S. Army Vietnam and the 7th Air Force. The Pacific Exchange (PACEX), headquartered in Japan and Hawaii, oversaw VRE's operation on behalf of the Army and Air Force Exchange Service (AAFES), a quasi-military retail service at that time headquartered in Hawaii and New York.[8] As this chain of command suggests, every P.X. in Vietnam—

whether housed in a shipping crate or a modern, air-conditioned showroom—was but one outlet in an international, multi-million-dollar retail chain.

Military Assistance Command Vietnam explained the P.X. system and its intended purpose in a pamphlet, "Your Vietnam Regional Exchange: Service in War and Peace," that was directed at the troops. Like P.X.'s in the United States and at other overseas bases, the military's retail facilities in South Vietnam were open only to American military personnel, authorized civilian contract employees, and Free World Military Forces, which included all American allies in South Vietnam, except, ironically, for the South Vietnamese. The P.X.'s also carried most of the same products, "from shoelaces to televisions," as their American and European counterparts. According to the pamphlet, MACV considered P.X.'s in Vietnam "neither a luxury nor a 'nice-to-have' benefit" but rather an operational necessity because of their effect on morale. The officers manning the P.X. system hoped that, despite the war going on around them, or perhaps because of it, American G.I.'s would literally shop to their hearts' content.[9]

In the retail war for the hearts and minds of American soldiers, the opening salvos were issued even before they left for Vietnam. As more and more veterans came home toting expensive stereos, watches, and cameras, soldiers heading off to war could take some measure of consolation in looking forward to making their own purchases. While telling new recruits to expect the worst in Vietnam, the military also began socializing them to regard their service as a consumption opportunity. Pamphlets and booklets designed to orient soldiers to life in the war zone taught them what kinds of products to expect and how to acquire them through the military's post exchange system and its companion mail order catalog. Through these retail outlets, one guide boasted, American military personnel could access a "wide variety of merchandise, e.g. jewelry, watches, dolls, china, silverware, cameras, radios, tape recorders, stereo tuner-amplifiers, speakers, rings, silk, brassware, wood carvings, television sets, and linens," an array of merchandise that often exceeded what was available at stateside P.X.'s. With markups of just 5 to 25 percent and no sales tax, P.X. prices were considerably lower than those in civilian stores. On the retail front, service in Vietnam was a relative bargain.[10]

In terms of amenities, Vietnam P.X.'s varied from base to base, but their ubiquity was remarkable. The smallest P.X.'s might be housed in a spare room or even an abandoned shipping container, selling only "health, welfare, and comfort items" like toiletries, magazines, and small electronics.[11]

For example, the P.X. at Camp Smith near Tam Quan was housed in an abandoned wood-frame building and carried only "foodstuffs and toiletries" and "small control articles such as watches, small cameras, film for cameras, and small radios" selling for less than $30. What the Camp Smith P.X. lacked in variety, it delivered in convenience. The local unit newspaper declared that it would "be a real asset to the men since they will be able to purchase items which they had been going to Cam Ranh [Bay] to obtain. Our P.X. brings a little bit of the world to us here at Camp Smith."[12] Known as "Troop Stores" or "Imprest Funds," these small retail outlets could still do tens of thousands of dollars in business each month. On its first day of operation, for example, the 39th Engineer Battalion's P.X. set a new sales record of $4,500, "leaving some of the shelves looking like 'mother-hubbards' at the end of the day."[13]

At the other end of the spectrum, "Base Stores" and "Main Stores" carried a full range of items and generated over $50,000 in sales each month.[14] The Main Exchange P.X. at Camp Enari in the Central Highlands covered 8,800 square feet and featured six checkout counters "to speed the flow of customers," just like department stores at home. Air-conditioning provided added incentive for soldiers to linger in the store. This deluxe facility replaced a P.X. half its size, creating quite a stir among the men of the 4th Infantry Division. When the new store was dedicated, a crowd of 500 gathered for a ceremony complete with marching band, ribbon cutting, and visiting officials. Shortly thereafter, about $5,000 in merchandise was sold in the first four hours of operation.[15]

As nice as the Camp Enari P.X. was, it was not the largest in South Vietnam. When the Camp Radcliff P.X. was expanded in 1970, it provided a selection of products that, in the pre-Walmart days of American retail, was unlike anything most Americans had ever seen. As an *Ivy Leaf* reporter put it, "There are a lot of shopping centers—in fact, whole towns—back in the world where you couldn't find snuff, anchovies, baby oil, dice, flash bulbs, radios and steak sauce in the same store, or even in the same general area. But at Camp Radcliff you can buy almost anything you want." Variety was not trumped by convenience, however, for soldiers unable to make it to the main exchange could shop for items costing less than $10 at several annexes sprinkled around the base.[16] Likewise, the Preston Park P.X. on Long Binh Post was a sizable facility—10,000 square feet of retail space, following a 1970 renovation—that offered "added conveniences in a more modern atmosphere." In addition to the usual consumer products, the new complex housed a variety of specialty stores, including two foreign gift shops, a leatherwear shop, an optician, and a custom furniture builder. Even though troop withdrawals had been proceeding for over a year, P.X. officials continued to develop the Preston Park P.X., adding a 4,000-square-foot warehouse and a 6,700-square-foot annex to the main store later that year.[17]

The P.X. system in Vietnam was extremely lucrative. During the month of December 1971, for example, the top ten P.X.'s in Vietnam generated over $7 million in net sales, and an additional twenty sold at least $100,000 in consumer goods and services in the month around Christmas.[18] December may have realized greater sales because of the season, but given the length of time it took to mail gifts and keepsakes home, holiday shopping would have peaked a month earlier. The war in 1971 was also on the decline, with a smaller, more sedentary troop presence in Vietnam. The sales figures speak to the acquisitiveness of a camp-bound force with lots of time on its hands. (See Table 1.)

Like entrepreneurs in civilian life, military personnel managing the Vietnam Regional Exchange system focused on maximizing the earnings potential of the operation. The culture of careerism that prevailed in combat also affected staff officers soldiering for VRE. In the retail war for morale, sales figures, not body counts and kill ratios, determined the success of the enterprise and influenced the professional advancement of the individuals managing it. The exchanges also functioned entirely without taxpayer dollars, providing additional incentive to adopt a vigorous, profit-seeking posture. More customers meant higher sales, so exchange managers expanded store hours to accommodate the shift schedules of rearward personnel whose workplaces operated around the clock. More products meant more customers, so items that ran out or were not carried by a particular store could be special-ordered and held for the requesting soldier. Lower prices boosted sales, so VRE sponsored "Extra Savings Programs" to clear out unwanted merchandise (but only if it was made in the United States). One Extra Savings Program even fell on 11 November 1970, an event that would be known stateside as a "Veterans Day Sale."[19]

Advertising also stimulated demand, so VRE aggressively promoted its services in the hundreds of unit newspapers published by and for soldiers throughout Vietnam. Articles like "The P.X. and You: What's for Sale" or regular columns like "Serving You" educated the troops about the retail opportunities awaiting them. These stories listed popular items for sale, "ranging from shoes to potato chips to tape recorders," and informed the reader about exchange policies. Advertisements for the P.X. were sand-

TABLE 1
Sales Figures for Vietnam's Largest Post Exchanges in December 1971

P.X. LOCATION	GROSS SALES
Tan Son Nhut Base P.X., Saigon	$1,273,900
China Beach Main P.X., Danang	965,862
Preston Park P.X., Long Binh Post	860,224
101st Airborne Division P.X., Phu Bai	743,401
Gunfighter Main P.X., Danang	650,205
Army Main P.X., Cam Ranh Bay	645,729
Freedom Hill P.X., Danang	581,386
USARV Main P.X., Long Binh Post	550,739
Camp McDermott P.X., Nha Trang	489,102
Air Force Main P.X., Cam Ranh Bay	465,067

Source: "VRE (PACEX) Retail Facilities w/ over $100,000 Sales as of 13 March 1972," NFD.

wiched between news stories, reminding soldiers about store hours and locations. And the opening of new P.X.'s or the expansion of existing outlets was big news in local unit newspapers. In short, military authorities carefully orchestrated constant coverage of the VRE system to ensure that consumption remained in the forefront of soldiers' minds and to help them spend their Vietnam paychecks as efficiently as possible.[20]

The Vietnam Regional Exchange's mission was not solely profit oriented, however, because the rationale behind the consumption was maintaining soldier morale. When antiwar sentiment surged in the wake of the 1968 Tet Offensive, VRE placed renewed emphasis on delivering the comforts of home to men in the field. Officials eased exchange policies to make popular items like cameras and radios more widely available. VRE also raised price ceilings at forward bases to allow the sale of more expensive items, and it increased the number of items carried at each outlet. Military authorities widely publicized the changes in *Army Reporter*, which had a countrywide circulation in the tens of thousands, to ensure that soldiers knew they "would soon have access to more Exchange goods than ever before."[21] During the enemy offensive, North Vietnamese and Viet Cong fighters gravely tested American resolve, and VRE answered the challenge by inviting the troops to go shopping.

In addition to more liberal exchange policies, VRE met concerns about flagging morale by expanding the number of retail outlets, especially in forward areas. Indeed, fifteen new retail outlets opened in February and March 1968 despite disruptions caused by the Tet Offensive, and several of these served combat troops in contested areas near Quang Tri, Danang, and Qui Nhon.[22] Efforts to improve service up-country continued for the next three years, such as the renovation of the 173rd Airborne Brigade's P.X. at L.Z. English. The story of its reopening made front-page news in *Fire Base 173*, right next to the headline "Hamlet Chief Gives Life—Leads Ambush; Kills V.C." One is an archetypal war story, replete with violence and sacrifice: a Vietnamese man bled to death after saving American soldiers during a grenade attack. The other is a war story for the consumer age. It describes "retailing for the man in the field" and explains that retail managers intentionally stocked lightweight products infantrymen could carry into the bush. Combat troops in Vietnam tried to travel light, but the austerity of patrol did not necessarily carry over into life at base camp. The brigade's exchange officer explained, "Everyone at some time wants to buy a refrigerator or stereo so we are stocking a complete line of goods." And soldiers bought in droves; eventually, their mini-refrigerators placed such a drain on the power supply at L.Z. English that the commanding general banned their use.[23]

The Vietnam Regional Exchange's promise of "Service to the Fighting Man" kept P.X.'s open, even under extreme conditions. If monsoon storms caused power outages, most exchanges could operate by lamplight, recording sales by hand or with hand-cranked cash registers. When an exchange in Phan Chu Trinh was damaged by a rocket attack, its doors were open the following morning.[24] VRE also opened new fronts in its retail war for morale, setting up shop even in contested areas. If soldiers could not make it to a P.X., VRE would bring the P.X. to them by transforming eighteen-wheelers into mobile exchanges that trolled the roads through combat areas. For example, the 169th Engineer Battalion's P.X. ran a two-ton truck twice a week to small base camps in forward areas, stopping along the way to sell goods to men working at their job sites. For marines serving in the Con Thien area, a mobile P.X. ran a twelve-mile gauntlet between Dong Ha and Con Thien once a week, selling merchandise along the way. This mobile exchange was ambushed twice in its first few months of operation, but it continued to make deliveries.[25]

The helicopter made its combat debut in Vietnam, adding a vertical element to the battlefield that enabled the swift introduction and evacuation of troops. The Vietnam Regional Exchange also employed helicopters to press consumer goods into the most remote areas of the war zone. Because roads to most firebases were perilous or nonexistent, helicopters lifted large objects like artillery pieces, jeeps, and latrines to these installations. VRE capitalized on this idea, using helicopters to deliver enormous shipping crates stocked with consumer goods. These flying P.X.'s specialized in sundries like magazines, cigarettes, beer, soda, snack foods, and portable electronics. Military news articles about these operations suggested that soldiers at remote firebases were so desperate to consume that they cared little about *what* they bought, just as long as they could buy *something*. "With a sandbag for a shopping bag the men will buy all there is," *Southern Cross* reported. "And when the day's supplies start to deplete, they will just go big for something else," consuming everything on the shelves. A helicopter would stay only a few hours at a base, but that was usually all it took to clear out $2,000 in merchandise.[26] Even the business of war was not sufficient to distract G.I.'s from their shopping. At a firebase near Dak To in 1969, P.X. merchandise was unloaded while gun crewmen rained artillery fire down on a Viet Cong mortar position. Though the mountain shook from the big guns, soldiers lined up with cash in hand. As *Army Reporter* put it, "Harassment from V.C. mortar, machine gun and small arms fire may slow down, but not stop the men from making purchases."[27]

American consumption was so endemic to the Vietnam experience that the U.S. military also opened new retail fronts overseas, emphasizing shopping as a core feature of the R&R program. Penang, Singapore, and especially Hong Kong were aggressively promoted in R&R brochures as free ports where luxury goods could be purchased at discount prices and without customs duties.[28] Unit newspapers characterized Hong Kong in particular as the "Orient's Bargain Mart," "Paradise for Traveler, Shopper," and the "World's Shopping Capital." Official travelogues described the city's markets as brimming with goods of every variety: paintings, ivory, silk, rugs, luggage, perfume, watches, cameras and electronics, jewels and jewelry, silver, leather goods, rattanware, and clothing. Hong Kong's tailors were especially well known, for their craftsmanship and speed but also for their aggressiveness, sending salesmen to greet American soldiers at the airport or to skulk around their hotels.

The cacophony of the open-air market and the thrill of the haggle were all part of Hong Kong's lure and charm, but when it came time to spend those hard-earned dollars, the U.S. military provided soldiers on R&R with a more familiar retail experience: the American shopping mall. Every G.I.

newspaper article about R&R in Hong Kong emphasized the quality, economy, and convenience of the China Fleet Club, an emporium of civilian retail outlets run by the U.S. Navy Purchasing Department. The China Fleet Club eliminated the need for comparison shopping by putting 65 contract firms and 15,000 items "marked at fair prices" under one roof. Under the Navy's supervision, the Fleet Club guaranteed the authenticity of its products, especially name-brand electronics, and offered high-ticket items for stateside delivery. Shopping there also eliminated the need for certificates of origin for customs purposes, and the Fleet Post Office onsite offered free packing and shipping back to the United States. With all the inconveniences of overseas shopping removed, there was no reason not to buy.[29]

Despite the opportunities presented by Vietnam P.X.'s and R&R shopping destinations, there were still gaps in soldiers' ability to consume. R&R came but once a tour, if it came at all, and Vietnam P.X.'s had limited selections, compared with their counterparts elsewhere in the world. To fill the breach in soldiers' retail options, military authorities extended mail-order P.X. service to the Vietnam war zone in 1969 through the Pacific Exchange Catalog. The PACEX Catalog was a thick, full-color affair that passed on the standard P.X. discount to mail-order customers stationed throughout the Pacific. It carried over 1,500 items, including brand-name electronics, jewelry, and housewares, which soldiers ordered and paid for by mail, usually with money orders or personal checks. Acquiring the catalog could be tricky. With 70,000 copies circulating in Vietnam, soldiers might be able to get one through the mail or borrow one from a buddy, but often they had to go to a brick-and-mortar P.X. (or send a proxy), where copies of the catalog were bolted to a display table with forms and pencils to complete the orders, just like catalog kiosks at Sears or J. C. Penney back home. G.I. consumers usually sent the luxury items they bought directly to the United States for future use or as gifts, but plenty of PACEX products—from appliances to civilian clothes to electronics—were shipped directly to Vietnam to be enjoyed by American soldiers stationed there.[30]

Even though thousands of consumer goods were available for American soldiers to buy in Vietnam, certain purchasing patterns emerged. In "Your Vietnam Regional Exchange: Service in War and Peace," VRE boasted that 120 million pounds of merchandise were required *each month* to service American soldiers' retail needs. Among the top sellers were sundries that spoke to the exchange system's original mission of providing small comfort items to the troops: deodorant (80,000 sticks per month), razor blades (191,800 packages per month), and snack foods like peanuts (260,000 cans per month).[31] As VRE did its part to erase discrepancies between life in Vietnam and life at home, it expanded its stock list by 50 percent over the course of the war. When troop withdrawals caused VRE's sales to decline in 1970, it reduced its stock assortment from 3,000 products to just 1,600 "Must Items" that fell into several essential categories: tobacco and accessories; candy, gum, and nonperishable foods; alcoholic and nonalcoholic beverages; toiletries, "sanitary products" (condoms and feminine hygiene products), and over-the-counter remedies; military clothing and accessories; clocks and watches; stationery, cards, and writing utensils; civilian clothing and shoes; linens, irons, and laundry aids; paper products; flashlights, can openers, and batteries; luggage; cameras and film; and radios and tape recorders. Despite the contraction in available merchandise, American soldiers in Vietnam were still well cared for, assuming they had cash on hand.[32]

Beverage sales in Vietnam were also impressive because they helped soldiers kill time and beat the heat. An ice-cold Coke offered a nice break from work, but ice-cold beer could provide an evening's worth of entertainment. The Vietnam Regional Exchange did not report sales of alcoholic beverages in its promotional materials, focusing instead on the 1.1 million cases of soft drinks it moved each month. Sales reports give some hint as to the rates of alcohol consumption, even though VRE lumped beer and soft drinks together in its statistics. From October 1968 to October 1969, for example, VRE sold on average $9,980,000 in soda and beer each month. If sales information from local exchanges is an accurate guide, beer accounted for about half of all beverage sales.[33]

Though small consumables like food and drink sold more units, expensive items like cameras and electronics were extremely popular among G.I.'s, forcing the U.S. military to adopt decidedly anticapitalist measures to regulate their sale. Ration policies were designed to prevent black marketeering, in particular the resale of imported consumer goods to civilians, whereby a single Vietnamese market could turn over millions of dollars in stolen goods each month.[34] The ration program also worked to preserve morale, by ensuring that all American personnel were able to acquire high-demand items. Each soldier received a P.X. ration card with squares to be punched as he made his purchases. In one year, a soldier in Vietnam was allowed to purchase a great array of merchandise at the P.X. that was worth between $2,000 and $3,000 on the black market, hence the need to limit each soldier's purchases and relieve the temptation to buy and resell. The ration list varied over time, but generally it included two still cameras, two radios under $30, one radio over $30, one television, one movie camera, one slide projector, one record player, one tuner, one amplifier, two speakers, two tape recorders under $75, one tape recorder over $75, one movie projector, one typewriter, one electric fan, one refrigerator, and two non-U.S. watches. This ration did not apply to PACEX merchandise or to "repaired, damaged, used, or discount electronic and offshore merchandise," exceptions that enabled soldiers to purchase even more.[35] (See Table 2.)

The rationed items suggest the myriad ways consumption ameliorated soldiers' discomfort in Vietnam. Healthy sales of fans and half-size refrigerators reflected a desire for cool air and cold drinks in Vietnam's stifling heat, as well as some freedom from the communal mess hall experience. The reel-to-reel tape recorders provided a way to record messages to loved ones and to hear the voices of friends and family since telephone calls from Vietnam to the United States were so rare that most soldiers went a year without making one. And soldiers purchased radios and televisions to fill their leisure time and provide both news from home and news of the war going on around them. By 1971, a study conducted by the U.S.-run military broadcast service in Vietnam found that 99 percent of American military personnel stationed there either owned or had access to a radio, while 15 to 20 percent of them owned their own television set.[36]

Sophisticated stereo systems also improved soldiers' quarters, and their acquisition became one of the hallmarks of the Vietnam experience. So many soldiers purchased hi-fi stereo equipment that music columns became standard in unit newspapers. "Listen Up in Stereo," which alternated in *Army Reporter* with the music-review column "Sounds from the World," advised soldiers how to choose components, assemble a system, and maximize sound quality. An October 1970 column underscored the prevalence of stereos among soldiers' personal possessions and why they bought them: "The majority of us who come to Vietnam will go home with some piece of hi-fi equipment. And at the prices and savings over here, it would be an oversight not to take advantage of the opportunity."[37] Another columnist, "The Idler," parodied the drive to consume simply for the sake of "saving" money. He described a fictional private first class with a "stupendous" stereo system that seemed quite out of his price range:

> I thought someday I might need this receiver. You know, no one can afford to pass up these buys over here, so I bought it for $586 and it costs $1000 in the States. Well, since I had suddenly earned $414 on

TABLE 2

Unit Sales of Rationed Items for 1969, 1970, and January–November 1971

RATIONED ITEM	1969	1970	JAN.–NOV. 1971
Refrigerators	10,946	53,706	2,656
Fans	104,515	153,360	116,977
Cameras	42,103	58,762	133,562
Projectors, slide/movie	14,400	16,834	15,429
Radios	223,800	245,971	86,569
Record players	7,135	6,900	30,757
Reel to reels	91,120	87,219	36,826
Cassette recorders over $50	NA	NA	220,428
Tuners	24,448	26,700	28,928
Amplifiers	1,220	1,200	0
Televisions	22,704	30,152	45,673

Source: "Joint Vietnam Regional Exchange Council Agenda, 1971," NFD.

that deal I figured I might as well spend that extra money on a deck and speakers. Besides, I had already put aside $652 for a camera, but then my brother wrote he had bought me one for my birthday. So there was that much more money I had saved and could put into music. It sounds like a lot of money, but it's really only about half of what I had to spend.[38]

And a 1969 *Esprit* editorial, "A Glimpse at Ourselves," offered a wry look at the epidemic of "Prolific Purchasing" that had swept through Vietnam. Its companion cartoon depicted a grunt in full combat gear struggling under the additional weight of a television, cameras, and several pieces of stereo equipment. Though these representations are exaggerated for comedic effect, they contain a kernel of truth: soldiers had come to regard service in Vietnam as a way to get expensive items that would otherwise be out of reach.[39]

Even more so than televisions and stereos, cameras were a staple in every soldier's footlocker, hooch, or pack, and photography became an obsession for many eight-to-five warriors. Darkrooms were common in craft shops on large bases, enabling serious hobbyists to develop their own film. Photog-

Published in the 4th Infantry Division's magazine *Esprit* in 1969, this cartoon rendering
of the soldier as a consumer accompanied an article about "prolific purchasing," a mock
disease that infected all G.I.'s, including the soldier-journalist who authored the piece.
(Courtesy of the U.S. Army Military History Institute)

raphy columns like "Photo Tips," "Camera Corner," "Saigon Shutterbugs,"
and "Negative Views" appeared in unit newspapers all over South Vietnam. They helped soldiers choose the right camera and advised budding
photographers how to get the most from their equipment or even just how
to work it. Lured by bargain prices, many soldiers purchased ever more
sophisticated cameras as their skills improved. One photo column, "The
Shutterbug," joked about the phenomenon, describing a fictional soldier
who purchased a camera for daytime pictures, a camera for nighttime pictures, and assorted other cameras, including one for total eclipses, plus one
"for taking pictures of all my other cameras."[40]

Even with all the cameras, stereos, and comfort items for sale in the P.X.'s and PACEX catalog, soldiers still needed goods and services that could not be met by the Vietnam Regional Exchange. To fill the void, VRE negotiated contracts with American, local-national (i.e., Vietnamese), and third-country-national firms to operate concessions in or near exchange outlets on American bases. Like the sales figures for rationed goods, the presence of these businesses throughout South Vietnam reveals a lot about how American soldiers' daily life had developed over the course of the war.[41] Some of the concessions reflect the desire of American firms to market their products to a captive audience. In particular, car and encyclopedia dealers encouraged soldiers to direct their paychecks in installments toward expensive items that were markers of middle-class affluence. If they survived their tour, soldiers would enjoy delivery of their cars or volumes on returning home. Other concessions eased the burdens of military life in the here and now. Tailors, laundries, dry cleaners, and barbershops helped soldiers maintain appropriate military attire, especially on rearward bases where Courtesy Patrols might cite them for an unkempt appearance. American women, employed as military personnel, USO and relief volunteers, and Department of the Army civilians, had enough purchasing power to support beauty shops that catered specifically to them, and some of these establishments also offered spa services to men. Chinese restaurants located on American bases gave soldiers a safe, ethnic alternative to mess hall and P.X. snack-bar fare, lending an air of Asian authenticity to otherwise provincial tours of duty. Camera repair, photo processing, and hi-fi stereo concessions reflect intersections between consumption and leisure as soldiers made purchases to record the war and entertain themselves in their off-duty hours. Embroidery outlets and engravers provided military-oriented services like sewing patches onto uniforms or engraving plaques for official ceremonies. They also provided popular extramilitary products such as custom-made patches and engraved souvenirs that proclaimed soldiers' cynicism, disgust, or pride about the war and their role in it.[42] Custom tailors, fur dealers, portrait painters, and gift shops that sold Vietnamese handicrafts enabled soldiers to purchase souvenirs to help them remember their time in Vietnam, to establish their bona fides as Vietnam veterans, and to return to the United States bearing exotic gifts for family and friends. Finally, the ubiquity of storage and shipping services suggests a soldier's need, in excess of what the military could provide, to manage the pile of goods he had already acquired. (See Table 3.)

Some of these concessions were small businesses—laundries or barbershops—run by local Vietnamese firms. Yet many concessions were essen-

TABLE 3

VRE Concessions in South Vietnam, June 1969

CONCESSION	NO. OF OUTLETS	NO. OF CONTRACTS
Laundry	375	201
Barbershop	371	175
Gift shop	236	146
Tailor/alteration	220	36
Custom tailor	201	14
Photofinishing	78	7
Engraving/rubber stamp	75	15
Car sales	71	4
Jewelry	69	2
Tailor/embroidery	67	13
Portrait and Painting	62	14
Florist by air	46	2
Watch/camera repair	41	2
Optical	25	1
Packing and wrapping	23	8
Hi-fi components	18	1
Steam bath and massage	17	22
Fur sales	16	1
Shoe repair	10	6
Ice cream	7	1
Encyclopedia	5	1
Beauty shop	4	6
Custom footlockers	1	1

Source: "Joint Vietnam Regional Exchange Council Agenda, July 1969," NFD.

tially chain stores operated by a few firms or even by a single firm. Thirteen of these firms had the distinction of selling in excess of $1 million per year, including the optical outlets, jewelers, tailors, photo finishers, and car retailers. The last two concessions were among the most profitable. Film processing in Vietnam was a volume business, and VRE estimated it was selling $1.5 million in film each month by early 1970. The Korean firm Saehan International capitalized on the camera craze by building two photo labs in Saigon and Danang at a cost of $500,000 each. Subsequently, all film dropped off at VRE outlets throughout South Vietnam was sent to one of these facilities, and soldiers got their photos of the war back in a few weeks.[43] Cars generated significantly higher sales figures than the other million-dollar concessions because of the high cost of each vehicle, though the dealers still managed to move a lot of product. Chrysler, Ford, and General Motors sold about 2,000 units per month in the late 1960s, generating gross sales of $26 million annually among the three manufacturers. Car sales in Vietnam are even more impressive when the manufacturer's overhead is considered: no showrooms, few salesmen, and no cars. Soldiers made their selections from glossy, full-color brochures, an onsite salesman answered questions and made the pitch, and local dealers in the United States delivered the cars to stateside addresses. With savings of 11 to 18 percent off the stateside sticker price, waiting out the months before slipping behind the wheel was the most difficult part of the transaction.[44]

Late in the war, when retail sales declined as the troops withdrew, VRE looked for other ways to maximize its profits. It actually managed to increase its concession income despite the drop in customers by employing an aggressive "capture" program that targeted unauthorized concessions already operating on or near American bases. For example, Vietnamese civilians with access to Long Binh Post managed to erect an illegal store that offered barber services and Vietnamese souvenirs in two abandoned latrines that had been shoved together. This bizarre little shop says everything about Long Binh's epic sprawl; post commanders had only a vague notion of what went on in many of its 3,500 buildings. For VRE, the concern was that an illegal business generated income for its Vietnamese proprietors but not for the U.S. military. The capture program amended this situation, hundreds of times over, by absorbing unauthorized concession outlets into the VRE system, increasing the number of authorized concessions from 2,000 to 2,234 in one year. The number of concessions began to decline in late 1971, but VRE still held contracts to operate over 400 concessions in the last months of the war.[45]

Overall, the U.S. military's retail operation in Vietnam yielded impressive sales. Concessions alone grossed $43 million in FY 1968, $68 million in FY 1969, and around $90 million in FY 1970. (In the greater PACEX system, the fiscal year ran from 1 February to 31 January. For example, fiscal year 1968 ran from 1 February 1967 to 31 January 1968.) For all concessions except automobiles, the Vietnam Regional Exchange received between 10

A soldier browses through a car catalog in 1970, in the midst of the Cambodian incursion. Cars were sold to G.I.'s in Vietnam at a steep discount, serving as a kind of consolation prize for losing a year of life in service to the state. (Philip Jones Griffiths/Magnum Photos)

and 12 percent of concession sales, which translated into a tidy profit, since its overhead was merely the negotiation and enforcement of the contract itself. For car sales, VRE netted $25 per unit sold, which amounted to up to $600,000 each year.[46] Of course, concession income was just a fraction of what was coming in. The P.X. system grew as the war escalated, accommodating soldiers' needs and expectations as local managers identified them. In early 1967, VRE had about 200 stores and 50 snack bars carrying a total of around 2,000 products. By August 1970, VRE had grown to 310 retail stores and 189 snack bars carrying over 3,000 items.[47] Though most of these outlets were the smaller Troop Stores or Imprest Funds, the Vietnam P.X.'s still managed to generate big sales, exceeding $1.9 billion for fiscal years 1969 through 1972.[48] (See Table 4.)

In fiscal year 1971, sales for the Pacific Exchange as a whole, which included U.S. military retail outlets throughout the Pacific Rim, including Vietnam, peaked at $903 million, effectively making it one of the largest department store chains in the world. But what proportion of the gross originated in Vietnam? The troop concentration in Vietnam was enormous, and, unlike American soldiers stationed elsewhere in Asia, these soldiers had few shopping alternatives to military-run retail stores. As a result, the P.X.'s in Vietnam generated a huge proportion, nearly half, of the Pacific Exchange's total sales—and healthy profits too.[49] In 1967, VRE reported that its net profits averaged 6 to 7 percent each year. For subsequent years, that figure grew considerably to 8 percent ($29.6 million) in FY 1969 and 12 percent ($44.6 million) in FY 1970. A VRE-sponsored study of sales conducted between August 1969 and June 1970 determined that it had realized a net profit of $24.3 million on $173 million in sales, or a robust 14 percent.[50]

The military-run PACEX Catalog also generated impressive sales in Vietnam. Prior to its introduction in the war zone, the catalog sold approximately $1 million in merchandise per year to military personnel and their families stationed throughout the Pacific. When mail-order service was extended to Vietnam, annual PACEX Catalog sales rose precipitously, reaching $95 million in FY 1972. Within a few months of the program's introduction to Vietnam, PACEX was swamped with a backlog of 30,000 orders. And a PACEX study of its mail-order program found that 87 percent of the 220,000 orders processed between April and September 1969 originated in Vietnam. As the war wound down in the early 1970s, P.X. operations in Vietnam also declined, and merchandise selling for more than $50 became harder to find in-country. The Vietnam Regional Exchange mar-

TABLE 4

Gross P.X. Sales in Vietnam, Fiscal Years 1968–1972,
Not Including Concession Income

FISCAL YEAR	GROSS P.X. SALES
1968	$325,150,378
1969	366,131,110
1970	417,582,166
1971	364,194,112

Source: "Joint Vietnam Regional Exchange Council Agenda, 29 April 1969," and
"Joint Vietnam Regional Exchange Council Meeting, May 1971," NFD.

keted the catalog to soldiers as a viable substitute for shopping in person, and sales remained brisk for the duration of the war. In 1971, long after troop withdrawals began, soldiers in Vietnam were still generating 75,000 PACEX catalog orders each month.[51]

As a rule, the profits VRE and PACEX realized from these ventures were first directed toward the P.X. system itself, then toward morale programs for U.S. soldiers. The P.X. system received no direct support from taxpayers, though it did survive and thrive thanks to a great deal of indirect support. The federal government insured the goods sold in the exchanges, and the U.S. military provided the stores and convoys with security, which would have been prohibitively expensive if the retailers had to purchase their security from private contractors. With its profits, VRE then concentrated on improving the shopping experience by adding more staff and making capital improvements like extra checkout counters, air-conditioning, and new construction in underserved areas. As demand grew, whether from bored soldiers spending more or from increases in troop population, local outlets would add on to their retail space, build warehouses to address problems with backorders, or create separate branches elsewhere on a base. The P.X.'s were generating so much money that it made little sense to keep making the retail establishments ever more elaborate. After internal improvements were made, the proceeds went toward nonappropriated fund activities like athletic facilities, libraries, and craft centers that were also designed to enhance troop morale. The VRE proceeds remained largely in-country, supporting morale initiatives in Vietnam itself, while the PACEX proceeds supported morale initiatives around the world. Stocking, staffing, transporting, securing, and insuring P.X. goods as they were brought into and ferried around the war zone surely put a drain on military resources. But as a morale program, consumerism literally paid for itself.

The shopping opportunities made possible by the Vietnam Regional Exchange, with its vast network of stores and mobile P.X.'s, not to mention the PACEX catalog, sent a clear message from military authorities to individual soldiers: we want you to shop. But the retail opportunities themselves were only one facet of the military's attempt to exchange comfort for compliance. While the availability of consumer goods in the war zone underscored the importance of soldiers *buying* things, several military policies recognized the importance of soldiers *having* things to keep them happy. Any boost in mood that accrued from making a purchase would have been nullified if a soldier were denied the right or ability to use it. In fact, having a stereo but no electricity, or a broken camera with no way to fix it, was probably worse than having nothing at all. As mentioned previously, the military normalized soldiers' spending on electronics by providing electricity to run them—at least until the power drain imperiled other, more pressing activities—and by using military transport to haul soldiers' personal effects when units transferred from base to base. Beyond these efforts, military authorities also implemented policies and programs to help soldiers maintain, insure, and ship their belongings. Consumption quickly became an essential part of life in Vietnam, and military authorities felt bound to facilitate it, all in the name of morale.

Vietnam could be a very dangerous place, for people but also for electronics. Breakage and damage were serious threats to American soldiers' belongings, and by extension to their morale. Even if a soldier's finances did not prevent purchase of a replacement, the rationing program might. And mailing a broken radio or tape recorder back to the manufacturer for repair could take ages, leaving lonely and bored men bereft of a principal connection to home. To address this concern, VRE inaugurated the Electronic Repair Program in early 1969. The program established eleven repair shops around South Vietnam to which soldiers could mail broken items, to be returned in working order in a few weeks. Private electronics vendors subsidized the program, which was able to process 6,000 items per month at minimal cost to American servicemen. Thanks to the Electronic Repair Program, one unit newspaper reported, "no serviceman in Vietnam need be without the sound of music to while away his leisure hours."[52]

While Vietnam's challenging environment—water damage, power surges, boredom-induced overuse—caused electronics to break down, the war itself could wreak havoc on soldiers' personal possessions. The

Military Personnel and Civilian Employees' Claims Act of 1964 offered an official remedy: compensation up to $10,000 for personal property lost or damaged incident to military service. The act was based on the premise that the military often places its personnel in situations where "property losses are almost inevitable," such as frequent moves, living areas with minimal police or fire protection, and even combat. Therefore, the legislation sought to "maintain morale by alleviating concern over personal losses attendant to performance of duty and to relieve hardships which arise when United States personnel are exposed to unusual risks of loss." In theory, provisions in the legislation gave military authorities license to deny claims on the grounds that some personal property was not "reasonable, useful, or proper" given the circumstances of the war. But in practice, the military's emphasis on consumption and the variety of merchandise for sale in the P.X.'s suggested that most, if not all, of the goods soldiers could purchase in Vietnam were officially sanctioned.[53] Military authorities frequently promoted the Military Personnel and Civilian Employees' Claims Act to the troops in unit newspapers. For example, *Army Reporter* printed the following query in its policy advice column, "From the Desk of Shortimer Sam," to address the insurance program: "Recently, our basecamp was mortared and my hooch took a direct hit. I had a radio and a camera destroyed. Is there anything I can do to be reimbursed for the loss?" "Sam" helpfully replied, "Sure enough! You can get some coins for destroyed or damaged personal items. Zip over to your unit's staff judge advocate section and ask to see the claims officer. He will help you fill out all of those cute little forms." A settlement would in turn encourage more consumption, so Sam admonished the reader, "Don't spend it all in one place now."[54]

Official publications educating American military personnel about U.S. customs laws also underscored the importance of consumerism in the war zone. Official fact sheets laid out customs policies, which unit newspapers then repeatedly summarized and disseminated to the troops. Under the "Tourist Exemption," soldiers could carry up to $100 in merchandise into the United States duty-free. Beyond that, the "Gift Exemption" allowed a soldier to send home up to $10 in gifts per recipient per day. Finally, the "Combat Zone Exemption" allowed soldiers to send home up to $50 in gifts tax- and duty-free, as long as they were purchased through an authorized agency of the U.S. military. This last provision offered additional incentive to purchase goods from the P.X.'s or their authorized concessionaires, rather than from local civilian businesses.[55] Taken together, the various exemptions allowed soldiers to mail a great deal of merchandise home duty-free. Because there was no way to verify whether the goods were actually gifts or items for personal use mailed to friends and family under that guise, the military in effect educated soldiers about how to avoid paying customs duties, whether they were obligated to or not.

The military also encouraged and legitimized consumption through its baggage policies, which set limits on how much soldiers could bring to and from Vietnam. Each soldier was allowed to carry up to 200 pounds of baggage each way, and G.I.'s often purchased new luggage—a signifier of both affluence and civilian identity—at the P.X.'s to carry their belongings home. In 1967 alone, some 300,000 pieces of luggage flew off the P.X. shelves.[56] But after a year of consuming, soldiers sometimes needed more than a new set of suitcases to haul their purchases. To address this need, the military provided a generous "hold baggage" service, in which military postal workers packed and shipped additional property for free. Hold baggage arrived in the United States in three to five weeks and suffered a damage/loss rate of just 5 percent, making the program a good risk at a bargain price. These policies were helpfully publicized in directives like the USARV Fact Sheet "Returning to CONUS," portions of which were frequently reprinted in unit newspapers.[57] The amount of hold baggage per soldier was determined by rank, from 200 pounds for privates to 1,000 pounds for generals with two or more stars. Essentially, the hold baggage policy suggested that even the lowest-ranking enlisted man could expect to *double* the weight of his personal property while serving in Vietnam.[58]

Consumer goods were everywhere in the war zone, and the U.S. military worked hard to ensure their equal distribution, their good working order, and their transport to the United States. Consumerism was an entrenched part of daily life, but some military authorities still regarded it with ambivalence. The records of the Vietnam Regional Exchange system reflect several concerns from high-placed officers about all the shopping going on. Some objected to the morality of certain forms of consumption, while others questioned the impact of G.I. spending on the local economy and on the war effort itself. Always, when contraction of P.X. services and privileges was discussed, opponents of a change in policy raised the specter of a decline in troop morale, ensuring that consumption in some form would continue throughout the war. Indeed, the last American exchanges in Vietnam opened for business as usual on 28 April 1975, just two days before the fall of Saigon.

In 1971, VRE began scaling back its concession operations, generating a great deal of discussion among commanders about which types of outlets—

that is, which forms of consumption—ought to be retained. The Vietnam Regional Exchange proposed three categories of concessions: Essential, Nonessential, and Highly Desirable for Morale. Some personal services like steam baths and souvenir businesses like engraving, leatherware, wood burning, custom-made Oriental clothing, embroidery, and photo studios for portraiture were declared nonessential, while a range of others made the cut. VRE deemed watch and camera repair, barber and beauty shops, photo processing, packing and wrapping services, Vietnamese gift shops, potable ice, locker storage, tailoring and alterations, laundry and dry cleaning, and ice cream stands as essential concessions. Services that fell in between—nonessential but "highly desirable for morale"—included "Oriental restaurants" (usually Chinese restaurants), non-Vietnamese gift shops, opticians, and custom-built furniture builders.[59] But VRE's designations were not necessarily shared by local commanders or by the troops they led.

In 1972, VRE surveyed twenty-three base commanders about which concessions they felt ought to be retained in order to maintain the morale of their troops. The commanders generally agreed with VRE's assessment that tailors, laundries, dry cleaners, barbers, film processing centers, lockers, and potable ice were necessary for the well-being of their men, granting at least eleven votes to each. But they failed to reach a consensus over the other concessions, with the steam baths generating the most discussion. The Vietnam Regional Exchange dubbed them nonessential, but four base commanders endorsed their retention. One colonel, stationed at Phu Bai, made a special plea on behalf of his men. "It is understood that steam baths have been declared nonessential," he began. "However, the essentialness of a service depends upon the availability of other services for troop utilization." Given the primitive conditions at Phu Bai, he argued, the steam bath was essential to morale, and his argument underscored the workaday nature of combat in Vietnam. "After a hot dirty day on the bunker line, the steam bath is a welcome retreat. The mental and physical exertion and strain of constant vigilance against enemy action adds to the importance of the steam bath as a place to relax." In making his well-reasoned case, the fact that the steam baths were also brothels must have slipped the colonel's mind.[60]

This internal negotiation over the retention of steam baths suggests the first of several ways that the military attempted to channel G.I. consumption in Vietnam. Concern over the moral implications of some forms of consumption periodically surfaced within the military, casting officers in the role of concerned elites wringing their hands over the turpitude of the consuming crowd. The steam baths were extremely popular among the troops for their massage and sauna services. Latin Quarter, the steam bath that Phu Bai's commander argued was so essential, consisted of twenty-six massage rooms for enlisted men and NCOs, plus nine more just for officers, nine steam boxes, and a sauna. All these official services could be had for less than $3 an hour.[61] Latin Quarter's forty-five young female attendants were the main draw, of course, because of the massage and sex services they typically offered, a potent combination crudely dubbed the "steam and cream." The military tacitly acknowledged that the steam baths were actually brothels by checking female employees regularly for venereal disease, and military authorities objected to their presence only when the appearance of propriety was compromised. For example, a brothel flourished on Long Binh Post, employing up to 400 young women at once. But it was threatened with censure only when the Vietnamese madam erected four bronze nude statues outside the establishment, a gesture too brazen for local military authorities, who preferred to maintain the fiction that young men patronized the establishment solely for spa treatments.[62]

Officers also raised moral objections to the proliferation of smut in the P.X.'s, which sold a wide variety of print material. "Reading" was big business in Vietnam because, as a handful of concerned officers complained, the magazines for sale at every P.X. catered to the libidinal appetites of heterosexual men. Known officially to the U.S. military as "girlie magazines,"[63] these publications constituted thirteen of the top twenty titles and 60 percent of P.X. magazine sales. With regard to policy, VRE was conflicted. Its chief of sales pointed out, in April 1969, "Restrictions placed upon the sale of the best selling magazines, girlies or otherwise, would have a serious impact on sales and net profit." Still, there was something unseemly about the U.S. military peddling *Climax*, *Stag*, and *For Men Only* to American boys in the name of fighting communism.[64]

In response to the officers' complaints, VRE launched a lengthy investigation into Star Far East Corporation, the private concern that held the contract to procure all books and magazines for sale in the P.X.'s. The contract yielded Star a profit of about 31 percent on annual sales of $12 million, so millions were at stake. After months of scrutiny, VRE canceled Star's contract on the grounds that it had realized excess profits at the expense of the U.S. government by flooding Vietnam with smut. Instead of reassigning the contract, however, VRE assumed direct responsibility for purchasing periodicals for its retail outlets, a measure that enabled military authorities to control which books and magazines were available in Vietnam and VRE to retain all profits generated by their sale. Under this arrangement, VRE confronted the same set of competing objectives, which pitted morality against morale, not to mention profit. Six months later, girlie magazines were still available in the P.X.'s, but they had declined to just 6 percent of titles and 29 percent of magazine sales. Even so, members of the Joint Vietnam Regional Exchange Council continued to lament that exchanges were still selling "too many trash-type magazines and insufficient good magazines."[65] Clearly, VRE had reached some kind of internal compromise to reconcile the contradictions inherent in maintaining both high morale and high moral standards. As for the troops, they could buy nudie magazines from civilian outlets, and they still had the pinups that appeared in nearly every issue of their command-sanctioned unit newspapers, suggesting more than an element of hypocrisy in military authorities' outrage over the prevalence of smut.

The military's efforts to channel consumption into officially sanctioned venues also applied to sales of alcohol. On large, rearward bases, the war was routinized much like civilian life. Despite all the chaste recreational facilities detailed earlier, many soldiers elected to fill the hours between shifts with heavy drinking. One visitor to Long Binh Post commented, "Directing the war against the enemy . . . seemed to be the easiest job of all for the new commander. The difficulty was in figuring out what to do with a post full of practicing alcoholics who at cocktail time every day turned into lounge lizards."[66] On the surface, the military seemed concerned about the drinking because rations on beer and alcohol were strictly enforced. Yet the restrictions fell well shy of temperance. In addition to five cartons of cigarettes, each soldier was allowed to purchase five bottles of liquor or wine and five cases of beer or soda *every month*. Because soldiers could purchase alcohol in unlimited quantities at local clubs, and given the ubiquity of officially sanctioned unit parties, the ration policies were more inconvenience than deterrent. There may have been a limit on how much alcohol soldiers could purchase, at least by the bottle or by the case, but there was no limit on what they could consume, and stateside drinking ages, which were set by individual states (mostly at twenty-one), were utterly irrelevant.[67]

As with girlie magazines, military authorities tried to strike a balance between profit and propriety with alcohol consumption. To prevent soldiers from hoarding alcohol to resell for profit or to fuel giant parties, MACV regulations forbade possession of more than two times the monthly ration, meaning that soldiers were expected to regularly consume what they purchased. These limits were in effect through July 1969, when MACV reduced the beer/soda ration to three cases per month. Again, the new policy appears to demonstrate concern that soldiers were drinking too much, yet the liquor/wine ration was actually raised to six bottles at the same time.[68] Most G.I.'s were not sipping cognac or mixing gin and tonics in their hooches, however; they drank beer. Reducing the beer ration only channeled soldiers' alcohol consumption into the venue that was most profitable, the open messes, where alcoholic beverages were sold in unlimited quantities on a far more lucrative per-drink basis.[69]

Morality was not the only reason military authorities cited as they channeled soldiers' spending into more wholesome—or profitable—arenas. They also attempted to contain G.I. consumption for security reasons, both military and economic. Inflation was rampant in South Vietnam because Americans stationed there were able to spend more on goods and services than most Vietnamese. In 1966 alone, American military personnel spent over 12 billion piasters on the local economy, "more than the sum spent by all U.S. civilian agencies, including non-military contractors, for both official and personal purchases." As a result, the price of bread rose 179 percent, condensed milk (essential for Vietnamese coffee) went up 75 percent, omnipresent *nước mắm* (fish sauce) increased 80 percent, and the cost of rice doubled—in one year.[70] The attendant Vietnamese poverty was not the United States' sole concern, however. Dollars placed in circulation in Vietnam might find their way into communist coffers, including those of the People's Republic of China and the Democratic Republic of Vietnam (North Vietnam). These dollars contributed to a serious balance-of-payments deficit for the United States and a steady drain on U.S. gold reserves. Last, dollars spent on the local economy also fueled the black market on which Vietnamese insurgents quietly relied for some of their weapons and supplies. As one unit newspaper editorial warned soldiers, "In effect, the money you place on the black market could purchase the weapon used to kill you."[71] So grave was the concern about black market profiteering that Major General Verne Bowers, who was in charge of morale-building programs at the height of the American occupation, suggested "the elimination of luxury items in the post exchanges" altogether. This was an enormously unpopular proposal, which he made only after his tenure in that position had ended.[72]

To reduce Vietnamese inflation, the U.S. military asked its soldiers *not* to consume, at least not from local businesses, a measure seemingly out of step with the spend-spend-spend ethos suggested by other policies. A 1967 poster entitled "Prune Piaster Spending" advised American military personnel to save money, use American facilities, and, "When you buy, buy at the lowest fair price." The companion graphic depicted a tree with multiple branches, each one labeled with goods and personal services that soldiers were likely to purchase: "bars, beer, broads, souvenirs, ice, private rentals, taxis, excess tips, shoe shines, restaurants, car wash, hotels."[73] The incidental and personal nature of these forms of consumption is obvious, with the exception of car washes, which involved improving the appearance of military vehicles. But in Vietnam, even a car wash was an invitation to party. Vietnamese "car washes" were usually drinking establishments and brothels located between bases. While the proprietor threw muddy water over a vehicle, its driver could have sex and/or knock back a few beers. The use of this euphemism gave the poster a knowing quality—wink wink—but it also undermined the sober message about avoiding excess spending. The informal tone and the grouping of "bars, beer, broads" on consecutive branches of the cartoon tree spoke directly to G.I.'s in casual language, acknowledging and legitimizing the way they spent their money in Vietnam. In this case, the very act of telling soldiers *not* to spend their money taught them *how* to spend it—where to go, what to buy, and how much to pay.

Currency controls and other policies also ostensibly discouraged G.I. spending on the local economy in order to reduce Vietnamese inflation and keep American dollars out of international circulation. When regulating consumption in this manner, the military had to tread lightly, for any perceived restriction on spending might prove catastrophic to morale. For example, when *Army Reporter* announced new consumer regulations for soldiers in 1968, the headline was written with defensive reassurance: "Limit Cuts Black Market, Not Your Ability to Spend." The article forcefully explained, "There will be no limit fixed to the amount of money that may be spent in the P.X. or anywhere else in Vietnam. For example, there is nothing to prevent you from buying a $300 tape recorder."[74] Crisis averted; the purchase of high-end electronics was still guaranteed.

When consumption opportunities in Vietnam finally contracted during the drawdown in 1972, some officers criticized the Joint Vietnam Regional Exchange Council for undermining soldier morale. A new P.X. policy attempted to curtail losses due to soldiers writing bad checks by limiting purchases with personal checks to $100, forcing soldiers to pay for high-ticket items like furniture and jewelry with multiple checks over the course of several days. One officer hyperbolized, "The implementation of the proposed policy is the final blow; a mortal wound to personnel serving in [the Republic of Vietnam]." Soldiers might survive mortar attacks or combat, he seemed to say, but impeded access to expensive specialty items was more than they could bear. Thanks to morale-building efforts that had, for years, made consumption readily available to troops throughout South Vietnam, shopping was no longer understood to be a privilege of military service; it had become a right.[75]

The right to acquire expensive consumer goods that were otherwise beyond reach was but one facet of an emerging soldier/veteran identity that was fully realized with the all-volunteer force in the following decades. During the Vietnam War, military service was a tough sell to the American people, and those who performed it were an increasingly slim minority, unlike the millions who answered the call of duty during World War II. Members of the armed forces and their families long fought for expanded benefits within the military, such as day care, job training, educational centers, health benefits, and improved family housing, which were finally, meaningfully realized starting in the 1980s. Taken together, these institutionalized programs set military life apart from the civilian world and helped to elevate military service into an exceptional form of citizenship marked by personal sacrifice but also by special privileges. The right to consume, tax-free and at a discount, was the best part, and the appeal of getting more for less became an essential perk of military service. The temporary soldiers of the Vietnam era recognized this, in part because the military constantly reminded them that it was so. The spending helped them to feel like Americans in a war-torn, Asian context. Then, when they went home, the spending had a transformative effect. High-end goods bought at a discount set soldiers apart from other citizens and from the people they had been before.

Over the course of the 1960s, the expansion of the Vietnam Regional Exchange system and the consumption-friendly drift in policy transformed the U.S. military—ostensibly a nonprofit institution—into a retail conglomerate. In turn, the military maintained morale—of soldiers serving in Vietnam and of would-be soldiers awaiting their fate in the United States—by offering a better life through goods to each soldier who consented to serve. If soldiers were prudent with their spending, service in Vietnam could be a springboard into affluence, or at least a way of acquiring its trappings. This transformation was perhaps less meaningful than the social engineering of the World War II G.I. Bill, which expanded the American middle class by making a college education more widely accessible. But it was certainly more appealing to twenty-year-old kids, who otherwise might never own the fancy cameras and pricey hi-fis they could buy in Vietnam.

Of course, soldiers could only expect to make such transformative purchases if they had discretionary income. On the surface, base pay for military personnel in Vietnam was a token sum based on rank and years of service. In 1968, starting monthly pay for enlisted men was $102.30 to $190.20, noncommissioned officers' pay was $226.20 to $303.90, warrant officers' pay was $336.60 to $507.30, and commissioned officers' pay was $343.20 to $1,607.70. These numbers do not take into account pay raises for cumulative years of service, nor the "basic allowance for quarters," which increased a soldier's pay by $55.20 to $201 per month, depending on his rank and the number of dependents he had.[76] Many soldiers in Vietnam also received a "family separation allowance," and all of them earned overseas pay and an additional $65 per month combat pay, regardless of where and how they served in-country. They paid little or no federal income tax and had few living expenses, because their housing, meals, transportation, medical care, and clothing were provided by the military. Therefore, if he did not have to support a family waiting at home, the typical G.I. in Vietnam was flush come payday. Compounding his windfall, P.X., PACEX, and concession goods were sold tax-free and at a discount over stateside prices, and the dollar was extremely strong against Vietnamese currency, increasing the purchasing power of the G.I.'s paycheck well beyond its stateside value. The widespread availability of credit to American servicemen stretched it even further. In his memoir *Voices from the Rear*, veteran George Watson took the unusual step of describing his finances in Vietnam, reflecting the situation described here: "The promotion [to SP5] brought my pay up over $300 a month: $254 base pay, $65 combat pay, and $13 overseas pay, totaling $332. I would get an additional $105 if I were married plus another $30 if my wife did not live with either parent. . . . I could survive on $40 to $50 per month because there was essentially nothing to spend it on. The books I was reading were free. Beer was 15¢ for a 12-ounce can and cigarettes were 15¢ a pack."[77] Watson's candid description of his monthly balance sheet demonstrates soldiers' awareness of their service's economic potential. It also demonstrates how $600 cameras—the equivalent of several months' rent in the United States—could fall within reach of soldiers who were careful with their money.

The U.S. military seeded the transition from poverty to affluence by encouraging soldiers to save, at least initially. In posters, brochures, and unit newspaper editorials, impulsive purchases made on the local economy were consistently depicted as destructive—to the Vietnamese economy, to U.S. gold reserves, but also to individual soldiers. Tacky souvenirs, pedicab rides, and "Saigon tea" emptied soldiers' wallets and left them with little to show for their time in Vietnam.[78] To shield them from this fate, the military offered a variety of savings programs that maximized the economic benefits of military service. Bank of America and Chase Manhattan Bank offered American servicemen special no-fee checking accounts that paid 5 percent interest per annum on a minimum balance of $100. U.S. savings bonds paid 4.15 percent interest over seven and a half years, while "Freedom Shares" treasury notes paid 4.74 percent interest over four and a half years to those who already held regular savings bonds. The most lucrative program was the Uniformed Services Savings Deposit Program, which paid a whopping 10 percent interest, compounded quarterly, for fifteen months on accounts up to $10,000. To facilitate participation in the program, the military offered direct deposit of up to $65 per month from a soldier's paycheck—coincidentally, the same bonus every soldier in Vietnam received for serving "in combat."[79]

If military authorities wanted soldiers to save their nickels for a rainy day, however, they would not have provided all of the shopping opportunities detailed earlier. Instead, the military embraced the American consumer ethos, which demanded that soldiers spend their money *somewhere*. Rational spending at an official military retail outlet, not thrift, was the ultimate goal. To encourage soldiers to make better choices, the USARV Information Office created a series of brochures and editorials for dissemination in unit newspapers. These publications included cautionary tales that contrasted the story of a fiscally responsible soldier with that of a spendthrift. For example, the 1968 USARV Fact Sheet "The Expeditious Management of Superfluous Currency, or Making Your Pay Work for You" tells the story of SP4 Titus Frugalbean, "the man who never bought a ceramic elephant," a common purchase made by Americans in Vietnam.[80] Frugalbean also resists the six-foot bronze candleholders, "genuine" Viet Cong battle flags, whale bone Buddhas, and elephant hide purses that were standards in Vietnamese souvenir shops. When he gets home to the United States, he has a lot to show for his tour of duty. A before-and-after cartoon illustrates Frugalbean's transformation from slacker to affluent consumer. In Vietnam, he was a stoop-shouldered private performing one of the worst tasks of the war, tending to a burning barrel filled with diesel fuel and excrement from a recently emptied latrine. Back in the United States, the money he saved in Vietnam facilitates a life of spotless luxury. The cartoon depicts him decked out with elitist accoutrements like a martini, golf togs, and a sleek sports car.[81]

The appearance of a car at the end of this cautionary tale is not incidental, for anyone who has watched a game show knows that Americans have long regarded automobiles as the ultimate prize or purchase. In the 1950s, when the Vietnam generation was longing for their driver's licenses, Americans' love affair with the car went from teenage crush to lifelong commitment. Young men bound for Vietnam carried this passion with them, creating a retail niche for U.S. automobile manufacturers and a morale opportunity for the U.S. military. In another brochure, with the frank title "Happy/Sad: The Choice Is Yours," a penny-pinching G.I. dreams of three postwar purchases, all valued equally: a college education, a home, and a new car.[82] Real-life soldiers dreamed too. Veteran Dean Muehlberg admitted after the war that a car catalog had induced months of wishful thinking about an M.G., "having it sent to the west coast, and picking it up on my way home, returning triumphantly, coolly, as world conqueror and hero." At his parents' urging, Muehlberg reconsidered, partly because they said it was unpatriotic to buy a foreign car, and partly because "home" was ice-bound North Dakota.[83] For those who did take the plunge, an automobile purchase powerfully demonstrated the consumption-for-morale equation at work. If soldiers ensnared in an unpopular war—many against their will—were able to forgo temptations like alcohol and prostitutes, they could save up their military pay to buy a car. This purchase, widely recognized as a rite of passage into adulthood and even the middle class, served as a special consolation prize for losing a year of life in service to the state.

Customs policies also acknowledged how young men might be transformed by their time in Vietnam. Late in the war, regulations were amended to protect the interests of soldiers returning to the United States on R&R or for emergency leave. The new exemptions allowed soldiers to bring home an extraordinary amount of stuff duty-free: all clothing and personal effects (very broadly defined); up to 50 cigars, 300 cigarettes, or 3 pounds of smoking tobacco; $100 worth of gifts; and up to 1 quart of alcohol for personal use. Working-class young men could return from Vietnam transformed; they looked affluent and came bearing gifts. As a USARV Command Information Fact Sheet put it, "[N]ow you can wear that $200 watch, your $300 suit, and carry another one with you, and take that new $500 camera home to get those great snapshots."[84] The scene conjured by this description is reminiscent of Norman Rockwell's May 1945 *Saturday*

Evening Post cover, "Homecoming G.I.," in which members of a working-class family crowd their tenement's stoop to greet their crisply uniformed World War II veteran. But the Vietnam version of the painting would put the G.I. in a custom-made suit and a designer watch, toting a hi-fi stereo, a quart of booze, and fifteen packs of cigarettes. There is something unsettling about the fact sheet's facts, perhaps because they suggest a sleight of hand: all those consumer goods tend to divert the family's attention away from what has truly happened to their son.

Soldiers usually return from war transformed: boys with soft faces and pale skin come home tan and lean, and young men with little experience in the world come home hardened to it. The last lines of the Army's own orientation handbook, *A Pocket Guide to Vietnam*, allude to this kind of transformation: "You will find that life in South Vietnam can be frustrating, tense, and at times full of danger. But, you will also find that it brings great rewards." The kinds of rewards envisioned by the guide reflected official rationale for the war: helping the Vietnamese to "maintain their freedom," "sharing the experience of a staunch and dedicated nation in a most critical period of its history," and of course "block[ing] the spread of communism through Southeast Asia."[85] Young soldiers and their families also imagined that military service in Vietnam would impart self-discipline, strength, personal pride, and a sense of proportion about what in life deserves worry or panic. For many it did. But in the process of acquiring these qualities, many veterans endured traumas for which a new car would seem poor compensation indeed.

During the Vietnam War, combat trauma ruined some of the most vulnerable Americans, inflicting psychological distress that made existing economic and social obstacles seem insurmountable. Prior to the war, draftees and volunteers from hardscrabble farms or forsaken urban streets struggled to find their place in the world, and they looked to military service—an ordinary citizen's most profound contribution to the state—for upward mobility. According to historian Christian Appy, these men were poor and powerless in the United States, but in Vietnam, when confronted with developing-world poverty, they were transformed into the "rich Yankee," the "representatives of American national wealth and power."[86] The ability to purchase expensive consumer goods from the local P.X. or the PACEX catalog only enhanced the disparity between American soldiers and Vietnamese peasants. On returning home, the consumer goods had the opposite effect, easing distinctions between working-class soldiers and middle-class civilians, at least superficially. However, when the suits wore through and the tape decks became obsolete, these young men confronted the same problems they had known before Vietnam—a declining economy, an unsympathetic public—but with the bruises and cynicism of uncelebrated war veterans.

Even if the transformation wrought by consumption in Vietnam was fleeting, the *hope* of a better life through goods persisted. Military authorities perpetuated it, bringing consumer goods into every shabby corner of the war and promoting G.I. consumption through numerous policies and informational campaigns. That hope infected new arrivals to Vietnam as they searched for an upside to their service, and it helped to placate disgruntled short-timers who searched for meaning in their sacrifices. It was clear to most soldiers that the war would not be won, so what was it all for? The consumer goods did not provide an answer, but they did ease the sting of there not being any answers. If he finished his tour of duty and spent his paychecks well, a working-class kid could return to the United States decked out in the accoutrements of wealth—a fancy suit, a flashy watch, and gifts to impress those who knew him when. What the uniform itself once related to the folks at home—I am a citizen, and I am a man—was now expressed by the consumer goods. The *Los Angeles Times* reported in 1968 that returning veterans tended to put the uniforms and medals away, "to slip back into civilian life unnoticed, throw off their identities as ex-G.I.s and avoid the difficult questions about Vietnam."[87] Home from the war, the veteran might hide his uniform, but his slick stereo and exotic souvenirs could be prominently displayed. In the final chapter of a retail war story, an unfortunate American son who survived his year in Vietnam could come home to the World a big man.

Of course, 58,000 Americans perished in Vietnam, felled by disease, killed in accidents, and especially cut down during combat. They returned home without their things, leaving piles of belongings in packs and footlockers to be inventoried, crated up, and mailed back to grieving families. A survey of personal effects lists from surviving USARV Mortuary Services records at the National Archives offers a small glimpse into the intimate life of the dead, and they hint at the consumption patterns of the living. Among 314 files from the Pleiku, Saigon, and Danang Graves Registration Points, certain items emerge as being standard equipment for soldiers in Vietnam: 38 of these men owned tape recorders, 53 owned radios, and 106 owned cameras. The figures would be higher still, but at least nineteen of the files (and likely many more) describe only items found on the remains at the time of death. Among the belongings these men had acquired in

Vietnam were pieces of furniture, lamps, televisions and stereos, record albums, refrigerators, art supplies, banjos, harmonicas, guitars, hobby kits, gifts of silk and perfume, tennis rackets, jewelry, Frisbees, board games, calculators, baseball mitts, cooking utensils, blenders and toasters and hot-plates, books, photo albums, a surfboard, a recipe book, stuffed animals, a boomerang, a garden shovel, a tiger head, a pool cue, and diapers. There was also one small Christmas tree, beckoning an exchange of gifts that would never take place.[88]

The names of the men who owned these things are now inscribed on the Vietnam Veterans Memorial in Washington, D.C. There, since 1982, visitors to the Wall have left offerings to the dead that move and confound. What to make of the cans of beer and fruit cocktail, the tapes and records, cups and saucers, tennis balls, baseballs, pieces of jewelry, Vietnam photos and Vietnamese souvenirs, stuffed toys, snacks and smokes, shot glasses, and bottles of Jack and Jim?[89] Some are surely promises fulfilled, like the drink two buddies would share back home. Others are memories of a war, love, or lives left behind. And some are references, intended or not, to a vast retail campaign that encouraged soldiers to ameliorate their discomfort on their own dime as they sought the "great rewards" promised by the state in return for their willing sacrifice.

CHAPTER FIVE

War Zone Wonderland

The Strange World of "the Nam"

In 1969, the Phuoc Vinh Special Services club sponsored a "Cavalry Carnival" to lift the spirits of the 1,000 Skytroopers of the 1st Air Cavalry Division. To encourage participation in the event's planning, service club workers created a contest in which the unit that came up with the best amusement booth would win a new television set for their dayroom. Among standards like darts, the ring toss, and a batting cage, games that simulated violence were the most popular at the carnival. The division newspaper's coverage included a picture of one such booth designed to test marksmanship. In the photograph, an attractive female service club worker with a pixie haircut stands next to a soldier in fatigues at the counter of a shooting gallery mock-up. Both are in a ready stance taking aim with rifles at a target somewhere outside the frame. The article also describes the most popular booth at the carnival, and winner of the television set, a game called "Bombs Away," which enabled carnival goers to call in imaginary air strikes on a tin can.[1]

The Skytroopers' desire to play war during the carnival can be interpreted many ways. Perhaps it was an innocuous extension of the boyhood fascination with war, a grown-up retreat into the past to act out simpler, more benign forms of violence. Perhaps some members of the 1st Cav were not getting their fill of explosions and gunfire in the field, or maybe non-combat personnel in the division were unconsciously seeking to experience the power and thrill of framing a target and raining fire down upon it. Or perhaps the workaday quality of many combat operations, which involved hours or days in the bush followed by a return to simulated normalcy at base camp, and the profound disconnect many soldiers felt between themselves and the South Vietnamese people they had come to "liberate" conspired to turn the war into a deadly game. The Pentagon's emphasis on body counts rendered Vietnamese people's deaths an operational goal, while cultural differences, racism, and a language barrier served to dehumanize them, making it easier for Americans to kill. Certainly, soldiers' allusions to "cowboys and Indians"—contested areas in Vietnam were known as "Indian Country," and "Kit Carsons" were former insurgents who scouted for the marines—and the scorelike reports of body counts in unit newspapers lend credence to this interpretation. Perhaps the Skytroopers just played "Bombs Away" because it was fun.

In the simplest terms, the Cavalry Carnival was a fleeting diversion from the hardships of warfare: loneliness and boredom for some, terror and bloodshed for others. The event's festive tone and playful approximations of combat aptly demonstrate the wonderland of contradictions that defined the Vietnam war zone: abundance in the midst of grinding poverty, laughter amidst violence, revelry juxtaposed with death. But the *idea* of a carnival also suggests a way of thinking about war as a temporary departure from the norms of civil and civilian life. The original carnivals of early modern Europe, so beautifully interpreted by Mikhail Bakhtin in *Rabelais and His World*, represented a time outside time, when peasants threw off behavioral restraints normally imposed by the state or the church and created their own temporary life "subject only to its laws, the laws of its own freedom." The essential themes of these celebrations included fertility, growth, and a "brimming-over abundance," while public performances emphasized the turnabout, "a continual shifting from top to bottom, from front to rear, of numerous parodies and travesties, humiliations, profanations, comic crownings and uncrownings."[2] In this kind of carnival, which survives in contemporary guise as Mardi Gras and *Fasching*, peasants used the break from ordinary life to assault authority with mockery and derision, donning satiric costumes of noblemen and clergy. In Vietnam, privates did not openly mock their colonels, but soldiers did routinely express antiwar and antimilitary sentiments in their graffiti, barracks décor, and souvenirs, especially late in the war. And the war's atmosphere of experimentation allowed them to try on a host of new identities: warriors, killers, lovers, lechers, junkies, gadabouts, grifters, drifters, and finally war veterans, a role laden with assumptions about military service. If the focus is softened around the edges, a snapshot of the Vietnam experience captures something truly carnivalesque: a second life, a time outside time, in which appetites of all kinds—for food and drink, drugs, sex, and violence—were nourished and indulged; a process of transformation through which men became what they could not be in the normal order of things; a space in which weapons made the powerless powerful; and a grotesquerie of Americana in which the capriciousness of fortune was exposed.

American soldiers in the Vietnam War were very far from home, and what they experienced there was strangely wondrous. They were Westerners in the Orient, they were Americans in Vietnam, and many of them—having been coerced into service by the draft—were essentially civilians passing through the military. They arrived in-country with their sense of otherness intact. For those isolated on rearward bases, experiences with combat were mediated by physical distance and by literal media—radio, television, and newspaper reports that told them what was happening in contested areas nearby. With the military's encouragement, soldiers functioned as tourists, literally and figuratively, heading out on exotic R&R excursions, but also documenting the quaintness of Vietnamese life and the breathtaking spectacle of modern warfare. In this place apart—the war zone, but not quite the war; home base, but not quite the home front—soldiers expressed concern that Vietnam was not the kind of defining struggle that had made their fathers men in the crucibles of World War II and Korea a generation before. Anxious over what they were missing, and with a natural curiosity for the curious set of circumstances in which they found themselves, they authenticated their experiences by taking photographs of suffering to document their proximity to it and by acquiring trophies of combat to validate that they too had been touched by violence. Though the draft exploited economic and social vulnerabilities to draw young Americans into military service, many members of the U.S. occupation force did not hesitate to exploit the vulnerabilities of Vietnamese people, especially women, as they pursued the sensual pleasures of the Asian market. All these activities took place in a carnivalesque atmosphere that indulged young, male bodies even as the violence of the war literally tore them apart. Life in "the Nam" was lived close to the bone, and for many Americans who experienced it, nothing else in their lives would prove as memorable.

∽∘∾

Why do I miss it?
—William Broyles, "Why Men Love War"

In his landmark study *The Great War and Modern Memory*, Paul Fussell argues that irony is the "one dominating form of modern understanding," a mechanism by which twentieth-century human beings retrieved, cataloged, and hence understood memories of war. According to Fussell, irony is "hope abridged," the corruption of innocence, and was expressed in World War I by the "ridiculous proximity" of blood-soaked Flanders trenches to the comforts and safety of London. British soldiers could receive packages of goodies from home unspoiled, and the *Daily Mirror* arrived only one or two days late. These constant reminders of home, so close and yet so far away, "constituted a further satire on the misery of the troops in their ironic close exile." In contrast, Fussell writes, soldiers who fought during World War II experienced "dire long-term exile at an unbridgeable distance from 'home.'"[3]

At first glance, the Vietnam War would seem to share these World War II characteristics: the United States was half a world away, mail from home could take weeks to deliver, and live communication across the divide was a rare and precious treat. There was no Internet, no text messaging, no cell phones, and usually no landlines—no way to tell the story to loved ones in real time, unless a soldier won a contest or earned a special reward: an unwieldy telephone call in which the signal was relayed by a network of volunteer ham radio operators stretched across the globe. On the other hand, the military's wide-ranging efforts to provide comfort and recreation helped to bridge the distance, giving Vietnam its own "ridiculous proximity" to the home front. And yet, despite living in or near contested areas, most soldiers in Vietnam never participated in combat, so they also lived in "ironic close exile" from the war.

American military personnel in Vietnam tended to experience the war as spectacle, watching the violence unfold from a distance, and South Vietnam's topography sometimes afforded an excellent view. The Central Highlands, where infantrymen hiked up and down steep, jungle-covered hills and through valleys of lacerating grass, quickly flattened into wide plains where lazy rivers nourished the rice and watchful soldiers could see for miles. The nearness of high to low, of mountain to plain, meant that the war in the countryside could sometimes be witnessed from rearward bases or even the high-rise rooftops of big cities, where its dangerous imperatives rarely penetrated. As a result, support troops stationed well in the rear could be intoxicated by danger's proximity, but it seldom came close enough to kill the buzz.

Veteran William Upton used the metaphor of watching a movie to describe what he witnessed one October afternoon as an off-duty sunbather at Vung Tau. He laid out a blanket and picnic lunch atop a shipping container near the flight line and settled into a book, but soon his attention was drawn by helicopter gunships firing on a target some four miles away. "It was like sitting at a drive-in theater back home. In wrap-a-round panorama vision," he wrote. "The only thing I didn't have was Myra Faye to put my arm around or popcorn to munch. It wouldn't have surprised me to see John Wayne, in full combat gear, crouched, rushing to the side of my CONEX, pulling a grenade pin with his teeth, and throwing it at a nearby VC gun position. Now, I couldn't turn away." He continued to watch as one of the Hueys went down. Then a Chinook rescue team arrived on the scene to lift the Huey back to the airfield near where Upton watched from his picnic perch. "The war was over for the moment and all was well," he concluded. "I wondered what would be playing tomorrow."[4] His curiosity satisfied, Upton was free to resume his book, as though the combat he witnessed—perhaps the most searing moments of the Huey pilot's life—was just a welcome distraction from the boredom of his rearward job.

Upton, like a lot of his peers, was isolated from the war he was ostensibly helping to fight. Life in the rear revolved around shift work, guard duty, following military regulations, and leeching pleasure from off-duty hours, not life-or-death decisions about where to step or when to fire. Arthur Wiknik deeply resented the softer war fellow veterans like Upton lived through, alleging in his memoir that "the danger a REMF experienced was limited to reading about it in newspapers."[5] He was partly right. For most Americans in Vietnam, contact with the war was mediated by physical distance, the miles of road or airspace that separated rearward bases from contested areas and Upton's picnic area from the shooting war he watched so intently. Contact with the war was also mediated by media itself, but unit newspapers were only one part of the steady diet of war information rearward troops consumed.

Whether clerk, corpsman, or grunt in Vietnam, all soldiers had access to military-published newspapers, which played a key role in educating them about the war and service life. Military authorities sanctioned the publication of hundreds of such newssheets over the years and throughout the country. The smallest reached a company of perhaps 140 men, while the largest, *Army Reporter*, had a peak circulation of 95,000 copies weekly. The most sophisticated papers were weeklies like the MACV *Observer*, *Army Reporter*, or even the Pacific edition of *Stars and Stripes*. They deployed soldiers as professional journalists and covered the war in broad strokes, reporting on large-scale operations and intriguing human-interest stories. As a matter of policy, all G.I. newspapers were used to build morale, with editors and journalists giving priority to stories that promoted goodwill between Americans and South Vietnamese, the better to demonstrate the

United States' good intentions.[6] Nearly every issue hailed "civic action" projects like village infrastructure improvements and fund-raisers for Vietnamese orphans, leaving unspoken the terrible irony that American weapons killed many of the children's parents. True to form, the papers seldom acknowledged the brutality of U.S. combat operations, for Americans and Vietnamese alike, providing noncombat soldiers with a perspective on the war that had the cachet of inside information, but without the unsettling details. Smaller unit newspapers, published down to the company level, tended to mirror their mass-circulation counterparts, but with a local flavor. Written by volunteers or amateur soldier-journalists, they reported enemy body counts (but usually not American), soldiers' near misses, and unit statistics like number of rounds fired, acres of jungle cleared, or miles driven without fatalities. Reports about their division's escapades familiarized rearward personnel with the combat effort they were supporting and gave them a stake, however indirect, in the fighting and dying going on nearby.[7]

Like unit newspapers, broadcast media also provided a conduit through which rearward soldiers could experience the war vicariously. AFVN radio was the U.S. military's official mouthpiece in Vietnam, broadcasting news reports on the hour, including updates about the shooting war. Starting in 1966, AFVN-TV produced original programming in-country to educate soldiers about the enemy they faced and to familiarize them with the roles played by their action-oriented peers. For example, the series *This Is Vietnam* aired episodes such as "Viet Cong Atrocities," "Army of Vietnam Units," and "Vietnamese Refugees," while other documentaries profiled the activities of American combat and combat-support personnel. "The Holehunters" followed tunnel rats who searched Vietnamese caves and tunnels; "7th Air Force Story," "Air Rescue North," and "145th Huey Company" addressed the exploits of fixed-wing and helicopter pilots; "Big Guns on the DMZ" depicted life on fire support bases; and "The Men of Khe Sanh" proffered images of the shell-shocked survivors of siege warfare. Through this early version of reality television, cooks and clerks could tune in the war in discrete increments and experience it as spectacle, much like the folks at home—except with better seats.[8]

While military programming on AFVN television and radio provided constant updates about the war, civilian programming broadcast for morale purposes on the same networks provided constant reminders of home, cushioning the loneliness and isolation of overseas deployment and creating a set of ironic contrasts that was nothing short of bizarre. Vietnam is often called "the first television war," an expression typically understood to reference uncensored footage beamed directly from the battlefield into American living rooms. Adventurous journalists in Vietnam usually had unfettered access to combat operations, and trans-Pacific flights enabled media outlets to broadcast moving pictures in the United States within forty-eight hours. (Media satellite hookups were nonexistent, so none of the coverage was live.) In its common usage, the phrase "the first television war" conjures images of the average American family watching the war in their wood-paneled den. The scene is infused with irony: the comforts of a middle-class home juxtaposed against the suffering of Vietnamese peasants, the tidy order of suburbia colliding with the chaos of air strikes and search-and-destroy operations. Yet, while television enabled the Vietnam War to reach into American living rooms, so too did the medium allow the home front to reach into the war. The resulting image is less familiar: American soldiers dressed in fatigues relaxing in front of a television set while the war booms in the distance.

Vietnam was indeed the first television war; it was the first war in which the soldiers fighting it watched television. Statistics about the extent of viewership are rare, but by 1971, 25 percent of G.I.'s with access to TV watched two to three hours per day.[9] Unit newspapers regularly printed local television listings, which read like a stateside copy of *TV Guide*. By watching civilian programs, soldiers in the war zone could still be privy to the jokes of the late-1960s zeitgeist, they could track the shortening of actresses' hemlines, and they could be transported back to the familiar settings of their youth: the stage of the Ed Sullivan Theater, Perry Mason's courtroom, *Gunsmoke's* black-and-white Dodge City, or *Bonanza's* Ponderosa Ranch. TV forced the war to recede into abstraction, making the prospect of a year in Vietnam seem less isolating and more manageable.

The widespread availability of popular music, by way of soldiers' personal stereos but, more consistently, through radio, served a similar function. Hollywood movies make it seem like there was music all the time in Vietnam, and there was, because military authorities made sure of it in order to boost morale. By 1969, one-third of American soldiers listened to the radio more than five hours per day, a figure that rose to 50 percent for soldiers aged seventeen to twenty. Most of the listening audience consisted of young men aged eighteen to twenty-five, so AFVN radio adopted a format calculated to please them by "emulat[ing] the best facets of Stateside commercial radio."[10] The AM band had a wider reach, so AFVN infused it with modern programming that was dominated by psychedelic rock and disc jockeys trying to be cool. In a bid for legitimacy, their on-air antics and playlists mimicked those of underground soldier-D.J.'s who broadcast clandestinely on open bands.[11] While covering life in the war zone, journalist Mark Jury transcribed a snippet of AFVN banter, which brought a touch of 1960s counterculture to military life:

> I can't think of anything else to say, so let's play some more. (Military commercial on keeping shot record up-to-date) Wow . . . that wasn't really in keeping with what we've been playing. Uh, well now . . . (laughter). Edit! Speak, my friend. I was just wondering whether the sky was falling in, or if we're falling into the sky with this music. I don't know, but here's Vanilla Fudge . . . (music). Sgt. Pepper until 8:00 . . . you can taste it—"Make Love Free . . ." Look . . . (mumble) you jump out and shoot back . . . we don't know what we're doing here, folks (laughter). This is Sgt. Pepper . . . and Pistol Pete is eating crackers. And it's time to move on.[12]

Time to move on, indeed. While they ticked off the days until they could go home, American soldiers relied on rock-n-roll music to help pass the time, but also to express the civilian identities they had been forced to surrender upon entering the service.

Irony was one of the defining features of life in Vietnam, for no one expected to find so much revelry in a war zone. Contemporary music— a product of creativity and collaboration—often accompanied destructive activities as the ubiquity of radio brought stateside culture right into combat. During his 1969–70 sojourn in Vietnam, Jury witnessed tanks invading Cambodia with the Beatles singing "Let It Be" in the background; artillerymen pumping out a deadly barrage to Steppenwolf's "Monster;" and grunts listening to Kenny Roger's "Ruby, Don't Take Your Love to Town"—about a wounded veteran confined to a wheelchair after serving in an Asian war— while stringing claymore mines near the DMZ.[13] Music could be a balm, an inspiration, and an ironic commentary, sometimes all at once. Most of all, it offered reassurance to American soldiers far, far from home that they were still a part of the world they remembered before they left for Vietnam.

Between the music and the TV shows, not to mention the nightly movies screened on rearward bases, soldiers were awash in mass media. The airwaves beamed American pop culture into the farthest reaches of the war zone, asserting the power and permanence of the U.S. occupation even as other signs pointed to its decline. Intentionally or not, the U.S. military normalized and domesticated the war's violent eccentricities by broadcasting the familiar sights and sounds of home. At the same time, the abundance disseminated through military-run mess halls, clubs, entertainment venues, and shopping centers worked to absorb soldiers' discontent over the indiscriminate and sometimes pointless violence they were charged, directly or indirectly, with creating. For soldiers desperately in need of a pick-me-up, American pop culture became an instrument of war that shielded them from its demoralizing effects. When the thud of a howitzer synched with the thunder of the bass, the effect was empowering yet disorienting, like the rush of a new drug.

Amid the sensory confusion, American soldiers in Vietnam had to reconcile a complex set of mixed messages from military authorities. On the one hand, documentaries and news stories about combat worked with military propaganda and the regimentation of service life to affirm their identities as warriors defending democracy's frontier. On the other, civilian mass media broadcast through military outlets, as well as the physical distance between contested areas and rearward bases, worked with all the stateside amenities discussed previously to insulate American military personnel from the exigencies of war. Given the temporary nature of their tenure in the military and their ambivalence about the American cause in Vietnam, the buffer of abundance virtually guaranteed that those most isolated from combat would never really see themselves as soldiers. Indeed, draftees and draft-motivated volunteers routinely derided "lifers"—career soldiers—for their conformity, rigidity, and conservatism. The term itself contemptuously suggests the permanence of military identity—it lasted for life—as though it were a congenital defect, in contrast to the temporary nature of the condition for most G.I.'s. Noncombat personnel knew they would be departing Vietnam one day, most likely on a big, air-conditioned jet—alive, with their bodies intact—and leaving the military soon after. For many citizen-soldiers, the war was something to ride out, not to win, mitigating individuals' willingness to take risks and encouraging them to direct their energies not toward the mission but toward the self. Once new arrivals got their footing in Vietnam and realized the possibilities, many approached the experience more like tourists than soldiers—temporary visitors to a strange, vaguely threatening, yet fantastically indulgent land. Military authorities helped to sustain this adventurer identity by encouraging soldiers to think about their time in Vietnam as an exotic excursion, a recruiting and morale strategy they had employed at least since the early twentieth century.

Military service has long afforded young men an opportunity to see the world. Before air travel made the planet seem smaller, American soldiers and sailors answered their country's calls to arms in part to satisfy a personal lust for adventure. In the twentieth century, young men who had never traveled beyond the counties of their birth suddenly found themselves in Manila or Paris or Tokyo. The U.S. military's recruitment strategies appealed to this desire, promising in World War I, for example, that men who joined the Navy could "go somewhere, see something, learn something." This particular recruiting poster's companion graphic showed sailors riding atop an elephant, strolling through an exotic port of call, and taking photographs of the strangely clad natives.[14] With the advent of the All-Volunteer Force in 1973, the U.S. Army continued to promote "fun, travel, and adventure," characterized by the unfortunate acronym FTA,[15] as key features of military life. In the 1970s, print advertisements designed to encourage enlistment in the Army's combat arms featured images of soldiers in civilian attire touring picturesque Europe, where they might be stationed to blunt a potential Soviet offensive. And more recently, the Marine Corps' recruiting Web site enticed those who "thirst for adventure" with a photograph of a rock climber hanging by one arm from a cliff, while the Air Force paired an image of whitewater rafters with a knowing appeal: "Be honest—travel is one of the main reasons you're considering the Air Force." And for years, the Navy lured new recruits by promising, "It's not just a job, it's an adventure."[16]

Like the military's recruiting Web sites of today, the U.S. military of the Vietnam era also emphasized "Fun, Travel, and Adventure," not just to potential recruits but to soldiers headed for Vietnam, the better to assuage lingering feelings of resentment over the draft or the war itself. Official orientation materials cast G.I.'s as intrepid travelers and framed military service in Vietnam as an exotic excursion. In particular, the Army's *Pocket Guide to Vietnam* offered soldiers idealized travelogues of South Vietnam's unique attractions: the "hustle and bustle" of Saigon, sampans drifting on the Perfume River, the royal tombs outside Hue, and the "sightseeing area of mountains, lakes, and waterfalls" near Dalat. The *Pocket Guide* describes these and other locales as destinations of choice, a literary conceit that belied the map of bases, barbed wire, and checkpoints the occupation force had imposed on Vietnam's geography.[17]

Opportunities for soldiers in Vietnam to behave like tourists were limited, but the chance for sightseeing did present itself if they were stationed in the right places. For those serving in the greater Saigon area, tourist stops like the Saigon Zoo, the Truong Dua Phu Tho Racetrack, and the city's many markets were described at length in unit newspapers, always as though the reader might one day retrace the author's footsteps. Special Services sometimes helped American soldiers encounter Vietnamese culture directly by sponsoring bus tours of local attractions. Military personnel in the Danang area, for example, could take a "Culture Tour" that visited a Cao Dai temple, the Sacred Heart Catholic Church, the Cham Museum, the scenic overlook atop Monkey Mountain, and the China Beach Orphanage. If not for the war's intrusion at this last stop, where abandoned children searched for comfort in the laps of their visitors, a tour of duty in Vietnam might momentarily seem like just a tour.[18]

More often, though, American military personnel got to experience a Vietnam defined not by its cultural attractions but by its sensuous landscape and the laborious efforts of its people to eke out a living. They regarded it with wonder. Airmen saw Vietnam from high above as a patchwork of paddies, waterways, hills, and impenetrable masses of vegetation. On the ground, foot soldiers humped a variety of terrains or rode in trucks and jeeps down a thousand dirt roads and the occasional paved highway. Along the way, they saw villages isolated in paddies and surrounded by hedges or trees, each one its own little world of thatch-roofed homes organized around rice cultivation and perhaps a handicraft, like pottery or basketry. Solitary water buffalo grazed in the fields, and enormous haystacks dotted the roads, representing a family's hard work and collective hope for the coming season. Vietnamese towns tended to radiate from a main drag of concrete structures eaten away by the damp, while the remnants of French colonialism—graceful administrative buildings, but also intimidating guard towers—spoke to Vietnam's previous experience with foreign occupation. Mopeds and bikes were parked right outside shop doors, where live-in proprietors sold an array of products and services; tire repair, detergent, and shoes would not be an unusual combination. On the streets, old men sipped coffee or beer at outdoor cafés, which might be just a scattering of chairs, and old women tended kettles of *phở* over open fires. Everyone napped in the heat of the day, on mats in their stores or market stalls, dogs and children wandered about, and comely girls in flowing *áo dài's* glided past on bicycles. On the best days, it was lovely, and different, like nothing American soldiers had ever seen, not even in a movie. On the worst, it was frustrating and horrifying, as poverty and disease trespassed on the quaint tableaux: inadequate food and water, raw sewage in the streets, and ringworm-infested babies dying for want of a bar of soap. Slipping momentarily into tourist mode, soldiers snapped pictures—aerial shots from helicopters, blurry stills from moving trucks, and close-up studies taken during idle moments on the ground—that captured a million variations of these scenes.

Superimposed on South Vietnam's organic landscape was the world of the war, an American creation that blended material comfort and military necessity to varying degrees, with the intensity of the comfort and necessity inversely proportionate to one another. At one extreme were remote camps and firebases, where sandbags and C rations ordered the day. At the other were overstocked bases and military-run recreation centers, where American soldiers' Vietnam tourism became explicit. There, they could enjoy Vietnam's edenic scenery in distinctly Americanized environments, shifting from soldiers to sunbathers and back again with a simple change of clothes. Logmen's Beach near Qui Nhon offers a prime example. This facility was not just the most developed stand-down R&R center in South Vietnam; it was also the most popular. In 1970, Logmen's Beach averaged about 600 visitors daily on weekdays and 4,500 daily on weekends, suggesting a predictable schedule for the work of the war. On one Sunday in August 1970, the center saw an astonishing 8,246 visitors.[19] Most were not from combat units on stand-down but rather were day visitors permanently billeted in the Qui Nhon area. For them, Logmen's Beach was not so much a departure from the war as it was a departure from life in the States, a tropical pleasure ground that aided the U.S. mission by insulating the local American community from the war's harmful effects. It was one part, the most fun part, of the world the U.S. military made for its soldiers in Vietnam. The rest of that world was composed of airfields, revetments, barracks, bunkers, and fences, but also a network of retail outlets, movie theaters, and recreational facilities designed to narrow the divide between civilian life and military service. Casually known as "the Nam," it was a place set apart from civilian life that was demarcated not just by its Americanized, militarized landscape but also by the raucous behavior of the young men who inhabited it.

Veterans' memoirs are peppered with references to stepping "through the looking glass" or dropping "down the rabbit hole" when they set out for Vietnam. These nods to Lewis Carroll's vivid, surreal creation frame the war as Wonderland and cast American soldiers as Alice, the wide-eyed innocent who observed Wonderland's amazing phenomena while searching for a way out of the chaos. To be sure, the U.S. military's replication of stateside amenities in a combat zone created vivid, ironic contrasts that soldiers marveled at daily. But many of them abandoned the passivity of mere visitors, tourists, to participate fully in the war's self-directed excess. Like revelers in carnival, they indulged their appetites and tried on new personas, safe in the knowledge that their behavior would likely go unchecked. The Nam was governed by its own laws, as Bakhtin put it, the laws of its own freedom. Cultural inhibitions collapsed under the weight of combat's urgency, a process common in any war. But in Vietnam, most Americans did not experience combat, except as the abstract rationale for their presence in the war zone. They were a garrison force, an occupation army, charged with standing watch on freedom's frontier. Safe in the embrace of the U.S. military's barbed wire and artillery defenses, they celebrated that freedom by pushing the boundaries of propriety, temporarily stepping out of their ordinary lives and into a war zone wonderland.

The term "the Nam" or simply "Nam" is obviously a shortened version of "Vietnam" that referenced, in its most literal form, the setting of the war. But soldiers also used it to refer to the war itself and to the conflict's strange internal culture. Its use reflects a common practice among soldiers of every war, the naming and renaming of places to impose order and control over strange and hostile territory. During the buildup, Americans reorganized Vietnam's interior by building new roads and bridges, reclaiming land from waterways, and erecting military encampments the size of small cities. In accordance with military policy, American bases were routinely named to honor the fallen, enshrining their memory in the geography of the war. Place names like the Arizona Territory and Dodge City—areas of heavy enemy activity in northern South Vietnam—invoked the American West, as though the Nam lay at the edge of civilization. Landing zones and fire bases like Cantigny, Berchtesgaden, and Bastogne linked Vietnam-era soldiers with their World War I and II forebears. And L.Z.'s named for American women—Jane, Sharon, Betty, Becky, and Sally, just to name a few—were chaste reminders of home in a setting thick with crude sexuality and unrestrained violence.

The Nam occupied the same physical space as the country the United States had come to liberate, except in a militarized, Americanized form. It was as if an Oriental silkscreen had come to life only to be invaded by the machinery of modern warfare and inundated with Western consumer goods and mass media. The result was sensory overload, like nothing its inhabitants had seen before. The observing eye fell on undulating lines of men in uniform, fantastically large pieces of equipment, and menacing weapons that conducted the brutal business of war against a paradisal backdrop. The Nam's palette was an earthy mix of greens, reds, and browns: rural Vietnam's verdant foliage, the distinctive red soil of the Central Highlands, the muddy browns of the Mekong Delta, faded fatigues and olive drab paint, the desiccated tans of cantonment roads, sandbag beige, and too often, bloody crimson drying to black in open, untreated wounds. The war's rhythm was a blend of rumbling engines, whirring chopper blades, and the deceptively benign pops and thuds of distant combat. The air on American bases was heavy with the smell of diesel fuel, sweat, and excrement that might be cut, every once in a while, by fresh bread wafting from a field bakery, the perfume of a dancer in a visiting floorshow, or spilled beer and cigarettes lingering from last night's bender. Everything was shrouded in the fetor of tropical decay. And through it all, AFVN radio and soldiers' personal stereos blasted an epic rock-n-roll soundtrack, which films from *Apocalypse Now* to *Forrest Gump* have exploited to establish the driving urgency and essential coolness of the war. Set against images of the American occupation, the music instantly evokes soldiers' frustration (The Animals' "We Gotta Get Out of This Place"), their loneliness and pathos (The Box Tops' "The Letter"), and the otherworldly trippiness (Jefferson Airplane's "White Rabbit") of life in the Nam.

As a place apart, the Nam had its own language, a pungent blend of English, Vietnamese, a little pidgin French, and a lot of military slang, all liberally punctuated with profanity. Like all languages, the Nam's vernacular helped to order life therein, separating draftees from lifers, enlisted men (E.M.'s, G.I.'s, pennies) from officers (butter bars, di wees, L.T.'s, the Old Man), newcomers (newbies, FNGs, cherries) from veterans (short-timers), and infantry (grunts, Snuffy) from support personnel (REMFs, pencil pushers, base camp commandos). There were also terms to demarcate "us" from "them." American women were roundeyes, and American allies were friendlies, while the Vietnamese were described with a slew of racialized pejoratives: slope, gook, dink, as well as patronizing terms like Ruff Puffs (Regional Forces/Popular Forces, or local militias) and white mice (South Vietnam's national police). Meanwhile, the enemy was described neutrally (Viet Cong, Victor Charles, V.C., Charlie) or even with grudging respect (Mr. Charles). The language served to demarcate those who served in Vietnam from those who did not; the ability to deploy the Nam's slang convincingly was a means of establishing one's bona fides as a veteran back in the States. But speaking the language of the Nam beyond its borders had consequences, too. In memoirs and oral histories, many veterans remarked at how difficult it was to stop swearing once they returned to civilian life.

Common expressions that reflect the language's blend of origins include *boo koo* for "many" (a bastardization of *beaucoup*), *ville* for "village," *di di mau* for "go, quickly" (from đi đi mau), *dinky dau* for "crazy" (a bastardization of *điên kái đầu*), and *sin loy* for "sorry 'bout that" or "tough shit," from *xin lỗi*, the Vietnamese term for "I'm sorry." A thicket of military acronyms and colloquialisms expanded the Nam's vocabulary, from AAA (antiaircraft artillery) to ZULU (a casualty report or the signal code for the letter Z), from Agent Orange (the infamous, dioxin-based defoliant) to Zippo Track (an armored personnel carrier converted into a mechanized flamethrower). Soldiers' fixation on consumerism was reflected in their term for the United States (the Land of the Big P.X.) and the afterlife (the Big P.X. in the Sky), a dark conflation suggesting that much of what they thought was good about their lives in Vietnam could be bought and sold. Their resentment of the U.S. military and the war it made there was evident in their term, the Freedom Bird, for the plane that ferried them back to the World, as everywhere but Vietnam was known. More than anything, the term "the World" suggested the Nam's status as a fringe existence set apart from all things familiar, ordered, and civilized. This binary construction forgave the excesses that took place there, as though the Nam was a safety zone in which the sins of the World could not be punished.[20]

Like the vocabularies of other wars, the Nam's language relied heavily on euphemism to liberate soldiers from the violence they endured and created. "We didn't burn houses and shoot people," veteran William Broyles recalled. "We burned hooches and shot gooks."[21] Items that would have been addressed with gravity in another time and place were given innocuous names that reflected the impassive, workaday quality of combat that emerges after soldiers have done it for a while. On the trail, soldiers encountered Bouncing Betties, antipersonnel mines that popped up to explode at waist height, eviscerating the G.I. who stepped on one. Nape was the obfuscating diminutive of napalm, an incendiary composed of jellied gasoline that American forces dropped to burn vegetation, dwellings, and people. Willie Pete was a friendlier version of white phosphorous, another incendiary Americans ostensibly used as a target marker that surpassed napalm's effectiveness as an antipersonnel weapon by burning, unless underwater, all the way to the bone. And Puff the Magic Dragon was the Air Force's A.C.-47 gunship, which could orbit a target for hours, laying down sheets of fire that chopped everything below into mulch. Veteran W. D. Ehrhart described the plane's handiwork this way: "I've seen places where Puff's left his calling card. Unbelievable. Looks like a freshly plowed field ready for planting. I saw a body once, got chopped up by Puff. You wouldn't have known it had ever been a human being. Just a pile of pulp stuck to little pieces of cement and straw that used to be the guy's hootch. . . . It was so gross, it wasn't even sickening. It was just there, like litter or something."[22]

Just as it spawned its own language, the Nam also fostered its own aesthetic, in which the use of such weapons was a thing of terrible beauty. Soldiers called it "eye-fucking," the act of staring with pornographic fascination as great plumes of flame engulfed a forest or a .50-caliber machine gun cut a man in half. For troops who had been in-country a while, such scenes lacked a moral or emotional component; they simply happened. American military technology was designed to maximize devastation at minimal cost, so it created visuals that simply did not exist in any other context. The spectacle elevated routinized warfare above simple routine by feeding the lust of the eye, and the violence was spectacular, in the most literal sense of the word. On returning home, soldiers might be nostalgic for it, as though they knew they would never see anything like it again. Years later, William Broyles fondly remembered "the mechanical elegance of an M-60 machine gun" as it etched red tracers into the night sky, and the "fulsome elegance" of a white phosphorous explosion "wreathing its target in intense and billowing white smoke, throwing out glowing red comets trailing brilliant white plumes."[23] In *Dispatches*, journalist Michael Herr described the beauty of the war with more than a hint of longing.

> I remembered the way a Phantom pilot had talked about how beautiful the surface-to-air missiles looked as they drifted up toward his plane to kill him, and remembered myself how lovely .50-caliber tracers could be, coming at you as you flew at night in a helicopter, how slow and graceful, arching up easily, a dream, so remote from anything that could harm you. It could make you feel a total serenity, an elevation that put you above death, but that never lasted very long.[24]

For warriors and journalists who came under fire, the reverie ended when the adrenaline dump wore off and the body reminded them, with nausea and grim awareness, of how close they had come to death. For the people trapped by the curtains of fire far below, the violence produced not reverie but terror and the helpless longing for it to stop.

The fetishization of violence is timeless in the history of warfare, of course; Civil War soldiers called combat "seeing the elephant," in reference to the most exotic thing their provincial minds could conjure. But the Nam was also striated with touches of home—music and amenities, consumer goods, entertainment and entertainers—that did not appear, at least not with comparable intensity, in earlier conflicts. American G.I.'s were selective in what they extracted from the home front to insert into the Nam. The resulting aesthetic in open messes, hooches, and Vietnamese establishments that catered to soldiers' appetites borrowed more from the garish self-indulgence of the Vegas strip than from the chaste community orientation of the average American Main Street. The Nam was like a frontier boomtown, where the imperatives of basic survival—whether real or imagined—allowed Americans to rationalize discarding civilization's quaint notions about modesty, adultery, brutality, and due process.

Mark Jury instinctively knew where he was when he got off the plane at Danang. "An armored personnel carrier roared past the soft ice cream stand. In the forward hatch was a gorgeous blond, her long hair blowing. 'This isn't a war,' I thought, 'it's a happening.'"[25] He had arrived in the Nam, where the introduction of civilization (the presence of the ice cream stand and the blond) to warfare (represented by the military hardware baking on the tarmac, as well as the base itself) served not as a moderating influence on excessive behavior but rather as a legitimizing signifier of U.S. superiority. The go-anywhere, do-anything prowess of American military technology was evident throughout South Vietnam. Its promise of endless construction and destruction—especially in contrast to Vietnamese poverty—granted American soldiers the swagger to behave in ways that would have made their mothers blush. What emerged was a moral wonderland in which stateside checks on taboo behavior simply did not exist.

Military authorities acknowledged the freewheeling nature of life in the Nam not by eliminating behaviors like drug use, drunkenness, and sexual solicitation but by moderating and channeling them. Prosecution of every violator was impossible, so although the infamous Long Binh Jail swelled literally to bursting with inmates, they represented but a tiny fraction of violators. To cope with, not stem, the tide of unwanted behavior, the military authorized nonpunitive measures like amnesty programs and rap groups to deal with drugs, while the ration program attempted to limit drinking or at least confine it to establishments that allowed the military to capture the profits. Educational programs on venereal disease and the military medical care given to prostitutes tempered the most painful effects—for the G.I.'s, at least—of Vietnam's sex trade, but nothing was done to eliminate it. Still, soldiers who had been civilians just months before arriving in the Nam bristled at the strictures of military life. A military newspaper editorial,

"Your Civilian Soldier," urged noncommissioned officers to ease the new recruit's transition to service life by communicating the rationale behind the regimentation. On the other hand, the 1st Sergeant acknowledged, "the new soldier may find in military life a personal freedom greater than he was allowed in a civilian environment." Writing specifically about the Vietnam context, he explained, "The restrictions formerly imposed by his parents, teachers, church, and community are remote to him. This sudden release may lead to thoughtless and uninhibited behavior."[26] The sergeant almost certainly meant drinking and carousing, activities in which many soldiers enthusiastically indulged. But successful prosecution of the combat war actually *required* soldiers to engage in automatic responses and uninhibited behavior, in order to perform under hostile fire and overcome taboos against killing. The irony of the contradictions—do this, but not that—was not lost on the young men who navigated them.

The most obvious example of the Nam's unrestraint was the business of war itself, which required young men to violate moral, ethical, and religious prohibitions on killing. Many of them struggled with it, if not during the war then long after, as they tried to reconcile what was asked of them in Vietnam with what they had been taught by parents and pastors in the United States.[27] Poet and veteran Frank Cross poured his own memories into his work, sculpting a narrative of violence and regret in the spare poem "Rice Will Grow Again." In the poem, an American infantryman named Mitch kills a Vietnamese farmer in his rice paddy, mistakenly thinking he is reaching into the muck for a hidden weapon. Long after the war, he cannot not shake the memory. "Sometimes, / On dark nights in Indiana / The farmer comes to Mitch's bed / And plants rice shoots all around."[28] American soldiers would always wrestle, the poem seemed to say, with the killings they committed in the grip of fear.

Likewise, Dwight "Skip" Johnson returned from Vietnam without the lightness in his step suggested by his nickname. In January 1968, a North Vietnamese battalion ambushed Johnson's tank company near Dak To, instantly killing several of Johnson's friends and fellow soldiers. In the ensuing skirmish, he exposed himself to enemy fire for thirty minutes, emptying first his .45-caliber pistol, and then a submachine gun, then the main gun on his platoon sergeant's tank, and finally the .50-caliber machine gun on the roof of his own disabled tank. At one point, out of ammunition and with the enemy closing in, he beat a North Vietnamese soldier to death with the butt of a gun. After the war, Johnson struggled with psychological problems that stemmed from an acute case of survivors' guilt over the loss of his friends and from an inability to reconcile the killings he committed with the values of his family and church. He asked his psychiatrist, "What would happen if I lost control of myself in Detroit and behaved like I did in Vietnam?" In the spring of 1971, he died holding up a grocery store, shot five times by the manager. His mother viewed the robbery, his first brush with the law, as a sort of suicide. She told a reporter, "Sometimes I wonder if Skip tired of this life and needed someone else to pull the trigger."[29]

Back home, without the context provided by enemy soldiers closing in, Johnson's actions near Dak To would have been those of a spree killer, but in Vietnam, they earned him the Medal of Honor. His actions were justified, heroic even, but Johnson still marveled at the absurdity of an environment that encouraged him to behave that way. But that was the Nam, where the taking of Vietnamese life by Americans was usually met with reward or indifference, even when civilians lay among the dead. The United States fought a war of attrition in Vietnam, and the resulting body counts read like box scores in the pages of unit newspapers. "Reds Smashed," "Polar Bears Score Well," and "Hornets Rout V.C. and NVA" all referred to violent engagements in which enemy body counts exceeded those of the home team. If the headlines were celebratory, their explanations were downright gruesome. "Sharks Down Reds," from a combat aviation group's newsletter, was clarified by its subtitle, "At Quang Ngai City, 238 Killed in a Day." However, the headline "11th BN Bombs 48th GRP" merely referred to a five-to-four win in the Saigon Support Command's fast pitch softball tournament.[30] The celebration of death served to trivialize it, a phenomenon that helped to police the borders of the Nam: anywhere else, and all that killing would be illegal.

Rearward personnel, whose support duties placed them on the periphery of the action, were often ambivalent about their role in the war. Reflecting on their time in the Nam, these veterans expressed an awareness that, while their tours of duty were real, they sometimes only played at being soldiers. After the war, many of them struggled, too, as they tried to reconcile what they did in Vietnam with what their family and friends thought they had done. In REMF "War Stories," Dean Muehlberg recalls his year as a clerk-typist in Nha Trang in 1968–69. Toward the end of his tour, the Army required the men in his unit to renew their rifle qualifications—the only time they had an opportunity to fire their weapons during the war. Off they went to a rifle range away from the city, giving these chairborne warriors a small taste of the adventure they had been missing. "We were nervous, but happy and excited at the same time, that old adolescent, playground, tough guy heroism and valor tickling our fancy as we trudged through the knee deep mud holes and brush. Pictures were taken so that we could send them back to our girls and wives, and kid them about how we really were in the war." While shooting at targets and trees (they took turns trying to knock down a sapling with a grenade launcher), Muehlberg fantasized about what it would be like to be in the boonies for real, under fire with no means of escape. Instead, the clerks gathered up their spent shell casings and hiked back to the waiting trucks, "leaving the make-believe world behind on the scarred hill."[31]

Lifeguard Pete Whalon was also cognizant of his wartime relationship to soldiering, that it was something to play at from time to time. His memoir *The Saigon Zoo* includes several photographs taken during his years in the Nam, including two in which he poses with weapons. In one picture, he and another man stand between their bunks with rifles in hand and an assortment of pin-ups on the wall behind. The caption reads, "Dave Schrunk (left) and I playing 'soldier.' Don't panic," he reassures the reader, "we didn't have bullets." In another picture, Whalon sits alone at the base of a sandbag wall cradling a serious-looking weapon in his lap. "Here I pretend to be a 'grunt'—the picture was taken to impress chicks back home." Whalon further complicates the joke by adding, "I know it looks like a Thompson submachine gun, but it's actually a 'bong.'" It is hard to know whether the joke within a joke is true; soldiers in Vietnam did successfully use shotguns to smoke marijuana through the barrel, and Whalon describes his own rampant drug use at length in the book. Even if the Tommy gun was real, though, and not just an assortment of parts cleverly assembled to get high, Whalon was still a lifeguard in a war zone pretending to be a grunt, and having a laugh at how ridiculous it all was.[32]

Other soldiers sought to acquire souvenirs that established their warrior credentials, whether real or imagined, like props to establish a character's identity in a play. The officer corps in the U.S. military maintained the tradition of using calling cards for social purposes long after civilians had abandoned it. In Vietnam, the gentility of the practice was ripe for parody.[33] Combat units often commissioned cards that reflected their collective handiwork, such as this one from the 4th Special Operations Squadron based at Pleiku:

RVN's #1 Fly By Night Outfit

We Defend: Outposts, Hamlets, Special Forces Camps, Ambush
    Patrols and Any Other TIC

Our 7.62 Devastates: Rubber Trees, Monkeys, Sampans, Ground
    Markers, Campfires, Water Buffalo

The slogan at the bottom of the card slyly references ground troops' dependence on tactical air support to get them out of trouble, framing the infantry as potential clients: "When You Hurt Enough to Want the Very Best." An artillery unit attached to the 101st Airborne Division boasted similar services with a card promising "Death on Call." The men of this unit claimed to "Love by Nature, Live by Luck, [and] Kill by Profession." Individuals further extended the joke by ordering their own personal cards, which listed skill sets like "International Playboy, War Monger, Renowned Booze Hound, Social Lion, Ladies Man" or "Experienced World Traveler, Adventurer, Casual Hero, Soldier of Fortune specializing in insurgencies and counterterrorism." One helicopter pilot described his occupation simply as "Mercinary [*sic*]."[34] For combat veterans, these cards wryly expressed general truths about their deployments. But in the pockets of rearward personnel, they project both laughter and anxiety, suggesting a need for tangible props to sustain fantasies about the war they were missing.

Whether soldiers played at war or made it for real, they were experiencing another key feature of the Nam: the ability to experiment with a variety of roles, from liberator to libertine, that were unavailable to them in the United States. When W. D. Ehrhart first arrived in Vietnam in 1967, he assumed the mantle of liberator, modeling his behavior on "American soldiers rolling through newly liberated French villages, gathering bouquets and kisses from fresh young maidens in skirts and puffy white blouses." As he rode in a jeep toward his first duty station in I Corps, he "smiled and nodded at the alien faces, waving stiffly from the elbow." The short-timer riding with him offered a stiff rebuke: "Who do you think you are? Douglas MacArthur?" And then, an admonishment that offered a potent lesson in how Vietnam differed from the European theater in World War II, that American G.I.'s were not regarded as liberators by most of the Vietnamese people. "Better pay attention, kid. We get sniped at along this road all the time. Half the people you're waving to are probably V.C. Couple of weeks ago, some gook tossed a grenade into a truck right here in this marketplace. Messed up a few guys real good." Not long after, Ehrhart shot an unarmed woman running along a paddy dike from 300 meters away. Her body "went flying like a piece of paper in a gust of wind," and one American teenager's transition from liberator to executioner was complete.[35]

The Nam's unrestraint also helped to create an illegal economy in which otherwise honest soldiers experimented with criminality, engaging in larcenous behavior they might never have attempted back home. The United States was peddling capitalism, if not democracy, in South Vietnam, through programs designed to raise the Vietnamese standard of living and demonstrate the free market's appeal. But pervasive Vietnamese corruption and the combat war itself tended to undermine the economic programs and exacerbate an already poor distribution of wealth. Ironically, the black market provided hands-on proof of capitalism's ability to create fortunes, though not general prosperity, as enterprising soldiers and civilians on all sides sought to make a quick buck. American policymakers and military officials tried to regulate the war's economy, but there were so many people, so much paperwork, so much urgency, and so many official and unofficial channels through which money flowed, that corruption flourished nonetheless.

Examples of bribes, kickbacks, profiteering, and currency manipulation abounded at all levels of the military hierarchy, with the majority of cases linked to P.X.'s, open mess clubs, and the military's entertainment program. At the top of the chain of command, several high-profile offenders embraced the anything-goes ethos of the Nam, setting a poor example for legions of subordinates. For example, the Army's provost marshal general allegedly tried to quash an investigation into a cabal of NCOs linked to massive fraud and theft in Vietnam's service clubs. Another general on active duty in South Vietnam lived in a villa owned by an unscrupulous businessman accused of making $40 million in illicit deals in the combat zone. And an active-duty Navy captain, known as "the mayor of Saigon," had $23 million in U.S. bills, likely the result of buying and selling currency at black market rates, stashed in his office freezer. A subordinate claimed on his behalf that it was due to a lack of storage space.[36]

At lower levels, noncommissioned officers ran the profusion of military clubs, entertainment venues, and P.X.'s for years with little oversight, yielding an array of allegations. The unscrupulous among them charged kickbacks for booking certain acts or purchasing certain products, sometimes in absurd quantities that suggest intent to distribute on the black market. For example, the manager of a Saigon P.X. was found to be in possession of 142,000 cans of hairspray, despite the fact that only 750 women had P.X. privileges in the city at the time. And a club sergeant ordered $400,000 in snacks for the 25th Infantry Division in return for a $4,000 kickback. His scheme unraveled when the contraband inadvertently arrived all at once, engulfing the club. An Australian booking agent familiar with the sergeant's corrupt practices testified before a Senate subcommittee that "the first thing that anybody knew of it was when the general looked out the window and saw a convoy of peanuts coming down the road." She also testified that she overheard a sergeant in charge of an open mess on Long Binh Post brag that being a club custodian in Vietnam was "worth $150,000."[37]

Not everyone was willing or able to make small (or large) fortunes through double-dealing, but the prevalence of the activity—civilian newspapers and the *Stars and Stripes* published many reports on the matter—only enhanced the Nam's endless possibilities. Ordinary soldiers could make small choices to participate in the fringe economy. Just trying to get legitimate supplies for a unit required an entrepreneurial spirit, as scroungers engaged in cumshaw, a Navy term referring to the barter system that tends to emerge among occupation forces; skimming a little extra here and there was a tempting proposition. Soldiers also knew there was extra money to be made selling the rights to their P.X. ration cards, funneling consumer goods to the black market, playing legal and illegal slots in clubs and other forms of gambling, exchanging currency at unofficial rates, or just procuring scarce supplies for needy units. In his memoir of the war, veteran Steve Wilken fondly recalls his introduction to the drug trade, when a friend showed him where in Saigon to buy packs of Park Lane cigarettes rerolled with marijuana. They bought several packs for $5 each, then resold them to G.I.'s at Long Binh for $10. "I had been in 'Nam for over six months," Wilken writes, "but that was the day I really understood what the war was really all about. There was money to be made for anyone willing to take the risk."[38] Military authorities policed these activities, but with little success; the Nam's economy was just too big. The odds of getting caught favored the enterprising, risk-taking soldier, who could easily rationalize the grift because so many people around him were doing it too.[39]

Even if a soldier did not pad his income with black market activity, and most did not, the steady pay and low expenses enabled discretionary spending that far exceeded the typical Vietnamese peasant's. In the Nam, the wealth disparity between Americans and Vietnamese cast U.S. soldiers as benefactors, a role that middle-income and disadvantaged young men had never before experienced. As American citizens, they could bask in the reflected generosity of economic and military aid distributed by U.S. military, governmental, and charitable organizations. And as individuals, they could spend money liberally, on all the retail goods described previously, on the alcohol they were too young to drink back in the States, on cheap narcotics of unrivaled purity, on legal and illegal gambling, on Vietnamese souvenirs, and on Vietnamese bodies. Boys barely out of adolescence and at the bottom of the American social and military hierarchy found themselves able to hire maids, drivers, and prostitutes to service their every need.

Their sense of entitlement is a striking part of life in the war zone, as some American soldiers came to expect the service and deference of Vietnamese people. When new regulations limited soldiers' access to hooch maids at Cu Chi, for example, a local G.I. journalist explained the policy change with scathing contempt for the women who cleaned up after the soldiers on the base. "The mama-sans are going. Jerkmouth and Ugga and Wah aren't coming back to the hootches anymore. The horde of babbling midgets that unloads from the deuce and a half [two-and-a-half-ton truck] every morning will begin to shrink next month." He went on to explain the economic and political reasons behind the new regulations, but concluded, "This really can't satisfy the G.I. who has to do the housecleaning for himself again."[40] Cultural and racial bigotry were surely factors in soldiers' expectations that Vietnamese people serve them, and the feeling that local people did not appreciate the sacrifices American soldiers made on their behalf only compounded their anger. Vietnamese people also looked down on Americans, who, by Vietnamese standards, did not bathe as frequently, were childlike and rude in their directness, and were easily misled. The contempt was often mutual, even if the ability to exploit was not.

To be sure, not all Americans regarded the Vietnamese with contempt, and many meaningful and equitable relationships were forged between soldiers and the people they had come to help. For example, in *Once a Warrior King*, David Donovan recounts his 1969–70 tour of duty as an adviser to South Vietnamese units in the Mekong Delta. As a young officer, he took great pride in the operations he led, and he worked hard to create bonds with local people, lamenting at the abrupt end of his tour that he was unable to say goodbye to the woman who cleaned his quarters or the elderly district chief who called him "my American son." He even demurred, sheepishly but graciously, when a local girl offered herself as a "bed girl" to the five-man advisory team for $40 a month. Donovan's memoir is laden with anger and regret that his team was not equipped to do more to help the Vietnamese. They had the weight of American firepower behind them, but when the Viet Cong booby-trapped a school in reprisal for local villagers' cooperation with the Americans, Donovan had only bandages and two I.V. bottles to treat a room full of wounded children. He expressed particular frustration with other American troops in the region, who harassed and embarrassed Vietnamese civilians at every turn. "Far too many . . . were harsh in their judgments, obvious in their contempt, and expressive of their dissatisfaction," he wrote. "Their attitudes were corrosive and terribly chilling to the ever-sputtering sense of cooperation between the natives and the American soldiery. As a result, I was often grateful later on that there were no American units in my district. . . . The effects of the G.I.s on the local population would have wrecked my own efforts at bringing some sort of peace and calm to my villages."[41]

The Nam was an American construct, but as Donovan suggests, its anarchic norms deeply affected its Vietnamese inhabitants, not just through the indiscriminate violence created by American weapons but also through interactions between American soldiers and Vietnamese civilians. Many G.I.'s spent generously to ease the destitution they witnessed, by raising funds for orphaned children, by volunteering to help with local civic action programs in their off-duty hours, and through gifts to hooch maids or even the extended families of Vietnamese girlfriends. But the largesse was not enough to alleviate the crushing poverty, especially since soldiers' own indulgent behavior served to exploit it. American spending on the local economy profoundly altered the Vietnamese way of life, and not just by exacerbating inflation. People displaced by the war quickly found that catering to the baser needs of American servicemen was their best hope of survival, and occasionally the illicit activities even generated wealth. In her memoir of the war, Duong Van Mai Elliott recalls how some South Vietnamese lamented "that the American presence had turned society upside-down."

> In the old days, the social order was expressed in the saying "scholars first, peasants second, artisans third, and merchants fourth."
> But now, according to these disillusioned traditionalists, this saying should be changed to "prostitutes first, cyclo drivers second, taxi drivers third, and maids fourth." Money, not intellectual achievements or social usefulness, had become the yardstick of success.[42]

The shift was dramatic; the Nam's freewheeling culture deepened a process begun by French colonialism, upending a centuries-old social philosophy that prized education, chastity, and filial piety in just a few years' time.

If the Nam turned Vietnamese society upside down, it turned American sexual mores inside out. In the close quarters of barracks and bunkers, what was private became collective, and the illicit became routine. Veteran Dean Muehlberg recalls that "Nha Trang (and many other cities with concentrations of American G.I.s) was like a sexual fantasyland, a wet dream from which many young and inexperienced soldiers never woke up for a year. The alcohol and drugs made it a psychedelic orgy, a trip into a land of no restraints and no regrets."[43] At euphemistic massage parlors and steam baths all over South Vietnam, soldiers could get fellatio or intercourse for as little as $2. Military authorities dismissed brothels on American bases with a nod and a wink, providing medical care to prostitutes and Johns alike, which sent a strong signal to American soldiers that their exploitation of Vietnamese women was not only excused but also sanctioned as a bonus for a year's worth of service.

As an Air Force officer flying in and out of Tan Son Nhut in the early 1970s, John Adams expressed this very sentiment. One day, he stumbled onto a makeshift brothel in an empty building on the base. An infantry unit stationed up-country had converted it into their own clandestine R&R center, complete with furniture and beds, a cook stove, a full bath, and permanent "hostesses" recruited from Saigon. Adams figured that the combat situation at the unit's home base was "untenable," so the men deserved their naughty playhouse. He declined to report it and later learned that there were several similar operations on Tan Son Nhut. His rationale, published in a memoir some thirty-two years later, reflected his superiors' thinking at the time: "These were beneficial activities since they kept a lot of people away from downtown Saigon, where they were subject to being robbed or mugged if they had too many drinks or were otherwise careless." Military authorities' concern was entirely for the American soldiers in their charge, with little consideration given to the Vietnamese mothers and daughters they had come to save from communism.[44]

Though sexual mores were changing in the United States, the progressive attitudes encouraged by the 1960s counterculture were modest compared with the rapacious and flagrant sexuality of the Nam. Pin-ups appeared in every unit newspaper, even if G.I. editors had to draw them by hand, pornography passed for reading material in the P.X.'s, and a ticket for R&R was widely regarded as a license to copulate; "Rape & Run" and "I&I" ("Intoxication & Intercourse") were common euphemisms for the excursion. Military newspapers sometimes augmented commandwide travelogues about overseas R&R destinations with graphic narratives of soldiers' escapades, providing directions to specific venues and skating the line between propriety and prurience. In 1969, *The Professional* published this description of a G.I.'s encounter on the dance floor of a Hong Kong nightclub: "Music sets one's musculature quivering, jolting, throbbing and contracting. Within moments, one is flooded with delicate distaff. Long, soft hair brushes like a gentle breeze against one's temple. Every nerve is strained, every vein and artery is pulsating and every sense of proportion and balance is lost. The Ultimate Thing is being done." If soldiers were unsure of where to go or how much to pay to have the Ultimate Thing done, they could buy travel guides that listed promising bars in R&R destinations and explained the finer points of hiring prostitutes. For example, the underground paper *The Grunt Free Press* ran an article in March 1970 that offered "The Straight Scoop on Where IT'S At and How Much IT Costs" in Hong Kong, the capital letters providing sophomoric assurance that the article was indeed about sex.[45]

Considering the small towns and conservative homes in which so many G.I.'s were reared, it is hard to imagine them being so lewd back in the United States. They were strikingly uninhibited, and two features of the Nam helped them to overcome their shyness. First, the temporary nature of R&R or even deployment itself empowered soldiers to seize the day. Combat troops rationalized that, with all the shooting going on, tomorrow might never come, while support personnel knew that the carnival would end in twelve or thirteen months. Why not get while the getting was good? Second, American soldiers were empowered by their anonymity. As members of a massive and constantly shifting occupation force, they all dressed similarly, had similar haircuts, and were sequestered behind barbed wire. Even if a Vietnamese woman did come forward with a paternity complaint or an accusation of rape, just locating the man responsible was nearly impossible. With nothing but their own consciences to hold them accountable, many American soldiers became libertines who consumed the Asian other without giving a moment's thought to the diseases they spread or the babies they fathered.[46]

On R&R, it was not uncommon for G.I.'s to blow large sums of money on alcohol, prostitutes, and souvenirs in a once-in-a-lifetime orgy of self-indulgence. In his memoir of the war, Arthur Wiknik recalls a debauched trip to Bangkok, where he spent $200 to keep a prostitute on retainer for five days and his remaining $300 on food, drink, and custom suits. Broke and desperate halfway through his trip, he went to the Red Cross, where the staff helped him get $100 wired from his parents in the States; he told them it was for "food and shelter."[47] For boys fresh from the cornfields of Iowa or

A G.I. exits the Little Country Inn, a Can Tho bar that catered to soldiers' appetites, in 1970. The women hanging around outside, waiting to service American men, are evidence of a sad fact of the war, that Vietnamese bodies—whether those of prostitutes or laborers—were just another commodity for many in the occupation force to consume. (Philip Jones Griffiths/Magnum Photos)

the sandlots of Brooklyn, the ability to throw money away on drinks and entertainment with a guarantee of sex at the end of the night was wondrous and liberating indeed—and nothing the folks at home needed to know about.

On a more regular basis, soldiers kept Vietnamese girlfriends who made their bodies available for sex in return for American companionship but also spending money, evenings out, consumer goods, or even apartments where their American boyfriends would meet them for trysts. Lonely soldiers convinced themselves that these relationships were not transactional, that the women chose to be with them solely for their charms and sexual prowess, and not for their money or the promise of a life in the United States. There was cachet in not having to pay for sex, causing more than one soldier to boast, rather disingenuously, that the relationship "costs me nothing more than the price of cab fare." An American contractor living in civilian quarters in Vietnam explained the benefits of the arrangement to the underground newssheet *The Grunt Free Press* in an instructive article called "How to Meet a Girl." His girlfriend "costs far less than any bar girl, and I don't feel as though I'm keeping a whore." An earlier issue of *The Grunt Free Press* included a side-by-side comparison of "Oriental Girls vs. American Girls" that emphasized Asian women's exotic beauty but also the submissiveness of Asian prostitutes and the convenience of a temporary arrangement. The contractor agreed, describing his concubine as "a living doll"—that is, an object to be played with, then discarded when the fun is over.[48]

The arrangements described in "How to Meet a Girl" were positively chaste compared with the aggressive lechery of South Vietnam's brothels. On American bases, the intimacy of group showers and open barracks easily translated into shared and unembarrassed sexual encounters, as soldiers passed around women like *Playboys* or joints. Dean Muehlberg straightforwardly recalls a trip to a brothel made memorable by the spirit of competition among friends. "I and two others bought three girls simultaneously, each paying for three tricks apiece, to make a bad pun. The plan was to exchange girls after each time, to see if we could last." The facilities in the brothel afforded no privacy, just cots in a large common room separated by thin curtains through which the young men laughed and talked with one another, essentially ignoring the women except as inanimate receptacles. "We exchanged a third time and exhausted ourselves thoroughly, the nonsmoker coming to sit on my bed as I finished, he frantically working on himself [masturbating] so that he could still get his third in." The lack of privacy scarcely warrants a mention in Muehlberg's memoir, for intercourse had been reduced to satiation and idle curiosity.[49]

Nice boys who bargained for sex in the United States with dinner and a movie, if not an engagement ring, haggled over pittances as they negotiated with desperate Vietnamese women. Even with decades to reflect, some Vietnam veterans failed to see in their behavior the exploitation of suffering, articulating instead a lingering bitterness that Vietnamese women had taken advantage of *them*. Arthur Wiknik hired a prostitute while on in-country R&R at Vung Tau, then seethed with resentment thirty-five years later that she only pretended to like him in order to get him to buy her cocktails and trinkets. In *Voices from the Rear*, George Watson recalls group sex in the barracks set up by a fellow soldier. A "mamma [sic] san" would have sex with three men for $10, a transaction that Watson describes as "yet another benefit for the available Vietnamese women." He then proceeds to complain that the sex was not very good, "but you get what you pay for." Watson suggests that the woman, who was "around forty," should have been grateful for the experience, because "all she had to do was lie on her back for twenty minutes with her pants off. She most likely added 25 percent to her week's pay." He concludes the story with a little historical analysis, wondering if "perhaps these local Vietnamese felt that like the French and others before them, we would soon be gone and they had better make their profit quickly."[50] The reality, though, was that millions of Vietnamese were barely breaking even.

In his memoir *Vietnam-Perkasie*, W. D. Ehrhart describes how he once engaged in a similar act, but with the gnawing awareness of its vulgarity. In the midst of heavy fighting to retake Hue following the 1968 Tet Offensive, when much of the city had been destroyed, one of Ehrhart's buddies found "a whore" willing to provide sex for a box of C rations. "A case?" his friends asked. "No. One box. One meal per fuck." Wary but undeterred, Ehrhart joined five other men in a rain-soaked gun emplacement.

> When my turn came, I jumped down into the pit. The woman was sitting up on some cardboard, protecting her body from the mud. She was naked from the waist down. I didn't know what to do or where to begin. "Chow co," I said. "Hello." She just grunted softly, and fumbled for my belt buckle. Her hands were cold. I undid the buckle myself, and dropped my trousers. Cold air and rain bit at my buttocks and tightened my thighs. I hadn't had much experience at this sort of thing—but even I knew that the woman's awkwardness and stiff body suggested either inexperience or deep hatred. "Probably both," I thought. My stomach felt sick. I finished quickly, pulled up my trousers, and climbed out of the pit.[51]

She was not a whore, Ehrhart realized, just a woman with a family and no options left. Afterward, Ehrhart felt guilty about what he had done, so much so that the image of "the woman in the gun pit at Hue" is one of two war memories that haunt him in the final pages of the book.[52] He probably felt guilty going into the pit as well, hence the hesitation and upset stomach. But he went, and he did his business, and he finished, his orgasm providing testament to the body's vulgar triumph over morals and the mind.

For many G.I.'s, the war was really about the struggle between excess and restraint, and excess seemed to win out time and time again. Feasting, drinking, fucking, killing—it was all okay there. The Nam was a wonderland of possibilities, and service therein was a once-in-a-lifetime chance to break taboos and indulge the flesh. In 2002, Dan McKegney, an Air Force radio operator stationed far in the rear, offered an honest assessment of his time in the Nam on a war-related blog. "There was booze, drugs, rock 'n roll, and whores, all on the cheap. God, for a 20-year-old kid, Saigon appeared to be like heaven. . . . It was a great scene, and war was nothing more than a carnival to me." McKegney went on to report his recent diagnosis with "'service-connected' prostate cancer because of Agent Orange," a public projection of private suffering that helped to balance the ledger of his trespasses. Cancer at any age is a devastating diagnosis, and patients always wonder why it happened to them. In McKegney's case, he framed his illness as "payback time for the carnival they made me attend when I was a kid," a description suggesting that both his presence in Vietnam *and* his indulgence there lay beyond his control.[53] In this construction, the veteran's Agent Orange–related cancer makes him a victim of the war, regardless of the role he played—or the fun he had—in fighting it. From unrepentant reveler to stoic survivor—this transformation was the Nam's final bit of alchemy.[54]

There is a great difference between Ehrhart's and McKegney's tours of duty, of course, in that one young man slogged through thirteen months of fear and violence while the other weathered a year of tedium and restlessness. On the other hand, the crux of their actions in the sex trade—detailed in one narrative, casually referenced in another—is essentially the same. American soldiers had not stumbled upon a nation full of petite, Asian women who loved having sex so much that they did it for next to nothing, as some men probably told themselves. Rather, it was the Americans' power—the dollar and the gun—that prescribed the terms of the transaction, whether the soldiers were aware of it or not. And yet, it is easier to forgive the excesses of a frightened, rain-soaked infantryman who was confronted with the near impossible task of retaining his humanity while serving as a professional killer, especially when—at least in Ehrhart's case—he had so much trouble forgiving himself. The context matters, and American soldiers knew it. As a result, some Vietnam veterans placed a premium on being able to demonstrate not just that they had served in Vietnam, but that they had suffered for it too.

This imperative caused some support personnel to co-opt the experiences of combat soldiers, the better to align their Vietnam stories with what family and friends back home expected. Enough soldiers took literary license when writing home that their exaggerations were a running joke in G.I. publications. The "PFC REMF" cartoon, in which a clerk flirts with attractive Vietnamese women in his office while a letter to his girlfriend describing combat and its deprivation sits in his typewriter, is but one example.

Another is a series of fictional letters published in *The Grunt Free Press* that mocked soldiers' tendency to embellish. To his parents, "Harry" had a safe assignment in Saigon, was eager in his work, and was saving money for school. To his girlfriend, he was under constant mortar attack and conducting clandestine missions in the bush, all while remaining faithful to her. To his buddy, he had an easy job in the motor pool and a regular Vietnamese girlfriend whom he did not have to pay for sex. And to his creditors, whom he owed for an electric guitar and amplifier, he would not be able to meet his financial obligations, because his paychecks were "the last thing that's holding a local orphanage together."[55] Which identity was real? The letters are a humorous rumination on a common wartime meme, but even if they were true, it would be impossible to tell. In the carnival of the Nam, soldiers could be whatever they wanted in the identities they projected to the folks at home.

With the World so far away and communication so tenuous across the divide, it was easy to maintain the fiction while still in-country. Returning home was another matter, and challenging stateside expectations about wartime service exacted a toll. When self-described REMF Dean Muehlberg was heading home, he reveled in his newfound distinction as a war veteran while wandering around the Seattle-Tacoma Airport in uniform. "I felt kind of cocky too, a real 'Nam' veteran. I knew I wasn't much of a veteran, but it was fun playing the part for awhile and I was too tired to fight it."[56] In his self-published memoir *Nik Boldrini's Sitting Duck: Adventures of a Saigon Warrior*, Nik Boldrini captures the frustration and inadequacy returning veterans felt when they glimpsed disappointment in their loved ones' faces:

> A party was given in honor of my safe return from Vietnam. I was repeatedly asked to share my war stories with the guests and I sensed they were disappointed because I couldn't replay those dramatic television news scenes they had all watched in the comfort of their living-room battlefields. I couldn't shock or enthrall them with tales of hand-to-hand jungle fighting. No hair-raising rescues from a downed helicopter in the delta. No bail-out over North Vietnam. No tales of a Purple Heart.[57]

The list stops there, as though brushes with death were the sum total of the war, a calculus that deletes the vast majority of soldiers from the story. After the war, most veterans who served in the rear were not interested in publicizing or celebrating the banal reality of their tours, plus the market for noncombat memoirs was and remains nonexistent, hence the paucity of these stories in print. Anticipating this problem, some soldiers preemptively sought out keepsakes to authenticate their identities as combat veterans and to document what they had done—or what the American public assumed they had done—while serving in the war.

Journalist Mark Jury deemed the 1970 invasion of Cambodia "the Great Souvenir Hunt" because soldiers were so fixated on acquiring tangible proof of their participation, in the form of Cambodian artifacts or North Vietnamese war matériel. The term could also describe the war as a whole because noncombat soldiers constantly sought ways to authenticate not just time spent in the war zone but also participation in the war. Asian handicrafts that proved deployment to Vietnam were easy to acquire; they could be purchased in local markets, at vendors' counters inside post exchanges, or somewhere on R&R. Harder, for noncombat troops, were trophies to document time in or near combat operations. An informal economy filled the demand, as rearward personnel with access to supplies and consumer goods traded with members of deprived combat units who had access to items suggestive of battle. In the spring of 1970, the soldiers Mark Jury followed into Cambodia traded their booty of captured North Vietnamese weapons and scavenged Cambodian pottery to support troops for electronics, beer, and soda.[58] And in his memoir *In Pharaoh's Army*, Tobias Wolff recalls the trades he made with support troops at Dong Tam during his 1967–68 tour.

> They never saw any action, nor for that matter did most of the soldiers who did go into the field. The letters they wrote home didn't always make this clear. In their boredom they sometimes allowed themselves to say things that weren't strictly true, and in time, as they approached the end of their tours, a fever came upon them to find some enemy artifacts to back up the stories they'd been telling their friends and girlfriends and little brothers.

Wolff and his peers in an advisory team supplied the support troops with combat souvenirs they purchased from South Vietnamese soldiers. The most desired commodities were Viet Cong battle flags, "all convincingly worn and shredded," bloodstained V.C. identity cards, belt buckles and bayonets embossed with communist symbols, and especially Chicom rifles. This Chinese-manufactured gun was "a very mean-looking weapon, and indisputably a communist weapon," as Wolff describes it, a trophy so perfect that "some of the guys at Dong Tam even had them chromed, like baby shoes."[59]

Of course, the authenticity of all but the Chicoms was questionable because enterprising South Vietnamese seamstresses, printers, and tinkers could easily fake the other items. Wolff claims he never knew which souvenirs were real and which were forgeries, but he acknowledges that potentially counterfeit items were priced at a discount. Some Americans knowingly trafficked in fake war trophies, such as a group of Green Berets who were busted for selling fake Viet Cong battle flags. They paid a Vietnamese woman to sew the flags, then distressed them with mud and chicken blood to lend an air of authenticity. The buyer assumed the details, presumably that the flag had been plucked off the body of a dead insurgent. The Green Berets used their credibility as battle hardened infantrymen to sell the resulting product—by the hundreds—to unsuspecting helicopter pilots for $25 apiece.[60]

An antique pot or a Viet Cong battle flag could be interesting conversation pieces at home, but photographic evidence of participation in combat—or at least of being nearby when the shooting started—spoke for itself. There was no need for context with a photograph's violent narrative, which stated explicitly, "I was there." And a vivid snapshot of lifeless Asian bodies was a far more exotic keepsake than a jade Buddha. Thanks to the P.X. system, cameras were ubiquitous in Vietnam, enabling soldiers to snap away on their tours of duty, as middle-class excursionists had done since the early twentieth century. In her landmark collection of essays *On Photography*, Susan Sontag describes the importance of photo taking to tourism: "As photographs give people an imaginary possession of a past that is unreal, they also help people take possession of a space in which they are insecure."[61] Picture taking soothed support troops' anxieties twice over, empowering them as they navigated a strange environment, and arming them with proof that they really had served in a war.

Wartime military service, however benign, certainly fits Sontag's definition of an insecure space, as do the uncomfortable encounters between American servicemen and the Asian inhabitants of South Vietnam and the R&R destinations. Soldiers on leave used cameras to document their exploits, at the beach or in exotic ports of call, to provide, in her words, "indisputable evidence that the trip was made, that the program was carried out, that fun was had."[62] They also used them to document daily life in Vietnam—from posed shots of their buddies, to informative glimpses of their barracks or duty stations, to grisly exposés of combat's aftermath. Above all, picture taking in Vietnam or on R&R placed soldiers at a critical distance from the object under scrutiny. The peasant farmer in black pajamas, the wrinkled Vietnamese laundress with betel-stained teeth, the grasping children on every Asian street—all were cut down to size by the camera, objectified by its tiny window, and rendered impotent by this symbolic act of possession. In the photograph, the farmer does not decry his crop's destruction, the laundress does not steal cardboard boxes to shelter her family, and the children cease ravaging soldiers' pockets in search of food.

Military service afforded soldiers the opportunity to experience something exotic that most Americans had only heard of: life in South Vietnam and, through the R&R program, travel to select Asian cities. But the most exotic experience of all was the seductive violence of modern warfare, which soldiers who did not engage in combat on a regular basis—if ever—tended to regard with fascination. Taking pictures of Vietnamese bodies was a reflexive activity, one that speaks both to the Nam's disordered values and to noncombat soldiers' anxieties about what they were missing.[63] When self-described "desk warrior" Joe Dunn inadvertently witnessed a firefight, he pulled out his Kodak Instamatic when it was over to take snapshots of the Vietnamese dead, thereby authenticating his proximity to danger. Veteran Tom O'Hara also remembers the enthusiasm that would grip men stationed at Phu Cat Air Force Base near Qui Nhon when the perimeter guard realized a body count. Enemy body counts were a rarity at this relatively secure installation, so word that Viet Cong sappers had been killed on the base resulted in "guys running down to the Military Police compound because they heard the bodies were out front. They all took their new Nikon cameras that they bought at the P.X. and ran down to take pictures of these poor bastards who had broken through the perimeter, thrown a couple of hand grenades on the flight line, and got mowed down." Arthur Wiknik's "low opinion" of REMFs was confirmed when three of them came out to a chopper pad to ogle the bodies of dead insurgents. They climbed atop the pile of corpses to pose for photos. William Upton admitted his own instincts in this regard, as he set out to photograph the burning wreckage of what he presumed to be a fatal plane crash. (Under the Nam's strange logic, it was inappropriate to photograph American bodies, but not the debris that entombed them.) "When I saw the smoke, I snatched up my Instamatic and ran as fast as I could towards the fire. By the time I got there the tail of the Caribou lay smoldering, detached from the rest of the plane, and the fire, for all practical purposes, had gone out. I snapped two photos." With evidence in hand, Upton was then free to make up whatever stories he liked to go with the images. And why should he be honest, if the Army wasn't? Though forensic evidence suggested that the fire was caused by a maintenance error, Upton writes, the officers in charge chalked it up as Viet Cong sabotage.[64]

When noncombat soldiers took pictures of corpses, they were, in Susan Sontag's words, "lay[ing] claim to another reality" and satisfying a cultural curiosity about death. She argues that the American fascination with photographing calamities like plane crashes and war is rooted in contemporary Americans' expectation that deprivation and tragedy are reserved for others.[65] That was certainly the case for rearward personnel who could take possession of the dead in photographs without having to identify with the struggle for survival that took place in the last moments of life. Indeed, Arthur Wiknik was incensed that the men he observed posing atop a heap of Vietnamese corpses "probably gave no thought to how many G.I.s lost their lives for these and other body counts."[66] His ire concerned the cooptation of other soldiers' triumph: REMFs laying claim to grunts' reality, authenticating their own war experiences by celebrating the strange fruits of someone else's struggle. Wiknik seemed unconcerned that the anonymous piling and counting of Vietnamese bodies was, in itself, an act of dehumanization; presumably, the mugging for the camera would have sat better with him if the men standing atop the pile had been the ones responsible for it. Regardless of who did the killing, though, the photographs fashioned soldiers into revelers celebrating their own vitality and superiority by objectifying the lifeless bodies at their feet. They were also sightseers chasing an authentic war experience, or at least evidence of one, as they passed their time in boredom and routine. The pictures proved—to paraphrase Sontag—that the trip was made, the program was carried out, and danger was had, even if it was had by someone else.

The search for tangible souvenirs of a year in the Nam did not end when soldiers climbed aboard their Freedom Bird. Years later, when being a Vietnam veteran started to have some cultural cachet, soldiers who were dissatisfied with prosaic deployments could burnish their war stories with a host of mementos purchased in the United States. Commemorative license plates declaring the driver a recipient of the Purple Heart or a former prisoner of war could be obtained for years from several states' Departments of Motor Vehicles with no proof of entitlement, only an additional fee for the special plate. Medals, campaign ribbons, uniforms, weapons, and equipment were also easily acquired—even before the advent of the Internet and eBay—from pawnshops near military bases, military surplus stores, ads in the back of *Soldier of Fortune* or *Vietnam* magazine, flea markets and garage sales, and even the sidewalk vendors who set up shop within spitting distance of the Wall in Washington, D.C. At the right age and with the right souvenirs, any man could "become" a Vietnam veteran.

For Vietnam veterans who bore no tangible signs of their service, the makeshift kiosks at the Wall once sold an iron-on patch with a potent Vietnam-related slogan: "Not All Wounds Are Visible." The text wraps around a primitive, embroidered rendering of a man with silver hair wearing a camouflage jacket and a boonie hat, accoutrements which gesture to the iconic image of the troubled Vietnam vet. His hand covers his eyes, signaling internal distress.[67] By donning such a patch, or displaying other symbols associated with the war, a Vietnam veteran could make the invisible wound visible, contributing to a special logic that has long prevailed where war veterans are concerned. If "not all wounds are visible," then presumably any veteran who served in Vietnam might be traumatized by his war experience. Certainly, the war left terrible marks on the psyches of thousands of Americans, but to an extent we will never know, veterans who never served in combat—and in some cases, poseurs who did not even serve in the war zone—have claimed emotional wounds they did not incur. American society offers considerable incentive to do so: the sympathy of families, communities, and society at large; a legitimizing explanation for social problems like unemployment, homelessness, substance abuse, and violent behavior; and, when a diagnosis of post-traumatic stress disorder can be tied to a particular event in Vietnam, significant financial compensation from the Veterans Administration.[68]

But really, an outward signifier like the "Not All Wounds Are Visible" patch is unnecessary, for just the *knowledge* that a man of a certain age is a veteran prompts all manner of assumptions. Vietnam veterans do not have to announce their internal trauma to the world—and most do not—in order to claim whatever societal benefits the identification of that trauma might confer. Silence can speak volumes, for it is axiomatic of warfare that people who have done and seen terrible things do not like to talk about it: the fewer the words, the greater the mystique. Tracy Kidder understood this calculus when he was a young lieutenant just home from Vietnam, and he was brave enough to write about it in his 2006 memoir, *My Detachment*. Kidder spent his tour of duty commanding a small communications intelligence detachment that never left its base. After the war, he describes meeting another veteran in a bar who spins an elaborate Vietnam tale of violence and bloodshed, then later admits privately that most of it was a lie. "When one considers the suffering of actual combatants and the much more numerous sufferings of Vietnamese civilians," Kidder writes, "it seems like sheer perversity for a rear-echelon soldier to come home wishing his experiences were more dreadful than they were. But Bill was not alone. . . ."[69]

Kidder goes on to recount his own tall tale, which "wasn't exactly a story, just a freighted suggestion." After getting drunk at a Christmas party in the mid-1970s, he started crying, "imagining that I'd been insulted by the various people I'd insulted there." His friend asked what was wrong, and Kidder played the Vietnam card: "I felt the need for a better explanation than the real one, whatever the real one was. My friend knew I'd been in Vietnam. 'Did you ever kill anyone, buddy?' I said. 'No,' he said. 'Did you?' 'I don't want to talk about it.'"[70] Kidder's silence made its point, but only because his friend filled in the gaps, selecting details from the graphic buffet of violent images and stories on which the American public had gorged itself since the war began. The archetypal Vietnam vet must have been in danger, he must have killed someone, he must have seen the gruesome aftermath, he must be wracked by guilt. The mystique Kidder sought would have disappeared—and with it whatever dispensation his friend was willing to provide—if he had spoken the words of a typical tour of duty: boredom, comfort, safety. The desire to authenticate an otherwise conventional war experience in this way suggests that, short of dying, the worst fate a veteran could endure would be to return home from war entirely unscathed.

As veterans like Kidder perpetuated the myth of universal participation in combat, they kept quiet the war's festive possibilities. Inclusion of the entertainments, consumer goods, and access to alcohol and prostitutes would have lightened the burden of sacrifice in the stories veterans told out loud, and these forgotten elements would have undermined justifications for the undisciplined and exploitative behavior featured in the stories they kept to themselves. There is much about the conflict as a whole that remains unknown, but the Vietnam War's lingering secret is not a hidden massacre, nor a forsaken opportunity to win the war, revelations to which scholars and journalists have long tried to stake a claim. Rather, the great secret of the Vietnam War is the Nam's own noisy misrule, which is whispered in the bits of ephemera gathered for this book. The Nam's anarchic norms, sanctioned by the U.S. military's inability or unwillingness to exert control over its forces, encouraged American soldiers to indulge their appetites for fun, sex, and violence in a ribald celebration of power, youth, and life. No wonder Vietnam veterans look back on those days with longing.

"Why do I miss it?" William Broyles asked in his thoughtful 1984 essay "Why Men Love War." In a passing reference, he suggests that even men who did not go to Vietnam yearned for it too. Years later, they felt "a sort of nostalgic longing for something they missed, some classic male experience, the way some women who didn't have children worry they missed something basic about being a woman, something they didn't value when they could have done it."[71] In an interview published in 2003, novelist Tim O'Brien also commented on this phenomenon:

> Almost everybody I know who got out of the war somehow and
> stayed in the country says the same thing, almost to a man. They
> say, "Oh my God, I missed the great experience of my generation."
> . . . I always say, "Well, you missed out on having your legs blown
> off and you missed out on having nightmares the rest of your life.
> You missed out on horror." They nod, but I can see they're thinking
> something else to themselves.[72]

In the construct suggested by O'Brien's acquaintances, war is brutal, elemental, and necessary, if for no other reason than so men can prove their manhood to themselves and one another.

As gender analyses, Broyles's and O'Brien's observations are flawed; women are certainly capable of the same bloodlust and wanderlust as men. While both writers are veterans of combat in Vietnam, their remarks also tend to obscure the reality of the war as most of their comrades in arms experienced it—that the typical tour of duty in Vietnam did not place American soldiers in situations where limbs might be lost or nightmares spawned. Instead, they slogged through a year of hot, sticky days, trying out roles they could never play back home, and yearning for experiences that would set them apart from those who did not go to war and from the boys they had been before they left. Soldiers played tourist on R&R and within Vietnam itself, taking snapshots to document and remember the peculiar scenes their presence helped to create. Men who were essentially civilians ensnared by the draft played soldier when required, acquiring trophies of combat to sustain the fiction. The war was home to so much beauty, in the landscape, in the music, in the intoxicant-fueled reveries, in the pretty, painted girls, and even in the terrible violence of high-tech warfare—and American soldiers devoured it all with relish. If they chose to, they could luxuriate in excess, and only their return to the World provided a bottom to the Nam's well of desire.

William Broyles succinctly answers his own question: "I missed it because I loved it, loved it in strange and troubling ways." He treats that love as a dirty secret, assuming a confessional tone as he illuminates the darkened corners of its nature. War is a game, "the best there is." War is exotic, providing, with its spectacular violence, "enough 'I couldn't fucking believe it!'s to last a lifetime." War is beauty, "divorced from all civilized values, but beauty still." War is a turn-on that "heightens all appetites," for sex, food, and dominance. And, most poetically, war is the ugliness that allows all human beings to know love and redemption. For the Vietnam War in particular, the explanation for why Broyles missed life in the Nam is much simpler. It resides in his essay, though the words do not belong to him. "What people can't understand," a fellow veteran told him years later, "is how much fun Vietnam was."[73] At the end of it all, the Nam was a wonderland, and, though unsavory to admit, much of what American soldiers experienced there felt wonderful.

From Vietnam to Iraq

Reimagining the American Way of War

During his 2004–5 deployment to Iraq, Alex Barnes struggled with the same kinds of questions that plagued rearward soldiers in Vietnam decades earlier: What is my role here? What does my contribution mean? How does my war experience compare with those of my fellow soldiers and those of soldiers in wars past? As a member of a National Guard signal unit, Barnes's assigned duties were sedentary and never required him to leave the safety of the base where he was stationed. Writing under the name Delobius on his blog, "Blog Machine City," he recorded his activities on 1 December 2004 as "a typical day in the life of one Signal soldier on the day shift."

0600: Attempt to wake up.
0630: Actually wake up; brush teeth, shave.
0650: Equip M249 and backpack (and body armor + Kevlar if
    necessary) and commence to walk to site.
0700: Arrive at site and commence . . . sitting.
0700–1200: Try to stave off insanity by playing video games, watch-
    ing movies, listening to music or reading. Even reading an
    Army Technical Manual is preferable to doing nothing.

The body armor and weapon were the only items in his routine suggestive of a hostile environment, but he shed them on arriving at work, as if taking off a winter coat in a warm room. Like Phil Kiver, whose perspectives on an Iraq War dining facility began this book, Barnes compared his routine with what he expected the war would be and with what he knew of soldiering in earlier conflicts. In many ways, life in Iraq was good, but that did not make it satisfying.

The monotony of Barnes's day was broken up by mealtimes, when the abundance of choices at the base's DFAC momentarily assuaged soldiers' boredom and frustration and gave them a sense of freedom and control in an otherwise authoritarian environment. "1200–1245: Lunchtime—a major milestone in my day. Typical food includes Philly cheese steak sandwich, onion rings, apple pie a la mode. The lasagna is good (MWF only) as is the pizza (brought to you by Freschetta™)." The afternoon was a return to tedium in which Barnes reported doing nothing for five hours straight, a repeat of the morning: "1245–1800: See 0700–1200. On a good day, something will break and I'll have work to do." But after a month on the job, that "only happened once." In the evening, a meal at the DFAC provided another highlight to the day. "1800–1845: Dinner. Yeah! There's a friendly guy of Arab descent who dishes out the ice cream and whatever toppings you want, and another who hands out pieces of various fresh cakes." For readers wondering at the incongruity of these features in a war zone, Barnes clarified, "Yes, each DFAC does have a 'head pastry chef,' as well as a 'head salad chef.'" His shift ended at 7:00 P.M., and the next five or six hours were spent in the base's "internet shack" online or in a friend's room playing video games. Sleep came at midnight or 1:00 A.M. on a new mattress that was "quite comfortable." He concluded, with a note of wonder, "I can't believe they pay me for this!"[1]

Barnes's war story is pretty typical, not just of Iraq but of all major overseas deployments since Vietnam. The U.S. military of the twenty-first century is the most lethal instrument in the history of warfare, but only a small fraction of its personnel actually engage the enemy directly. As American warfare becomes increasingly mechanized, "combat" consists of a broad range of activities. The foot patrol by "door kickers," who walk contested areas and enter the homes of suspected insurgents, remains the most intimate, traditional form, but air strikes by remote-controlled drones over Iraq and especially Afghanistan suggest the battlefield's high-tech, impersonal future.

The Vietnam War marked one stage of the U.S. military's long progression toward computerized, routinized warfare, in which the vast majority of soldiers work to support combat operations, sometimes directly but usually indirectly, without ever themselves experiencing battle or the deprivations associated with it. What was new in Vietnam was all the *stuff*. Military authorities' comfort-for-morale formula established a pattern of material abundance amid war that became enmeshed in U.S. military doctrine just as surely as it has been omitted from the American public's perceptions of military service. To save lives and enhance efficiency, the U.S. military prepared its soldiers for the worst in Vietnam, creating expectations of discomfort and danger that matched war's portrayal in film, television, personal narratives, and other combat-oriented treatments of the American soldiery. But once soldiers deployed to Vietnam, the U.S. military maintained their morale by providing every conceivable amenity allowed by the tactical situation. Given the United States' wealth and technological superiority, especially in the developing world, the tactical situation was usually good and always getting better. Many facets of this process would be repeated decades later in Iraq.

The irony of plenty displacing the deprivations of war speaks to two contradictory facets of American culture. On the one hand, Americans privilege war narratives that emphasize shared sacrifice, a historical phenomenon dating from the Revolution. On the other, post–World War II prosperity allowed Americans to enjoy an extraordinary standard of living that made the normal deprivations of war seem intolerable. Since Vietnam, indulgent military policies and incomplete public discourses about the war have allowed Americans to split the difference. The U.S. military works hard to provide material comfort to insulate both soldiers and citizens from war's deleterious effects, and private military contractors are only too happy to facilitate this, yet Americans conveniently omit that abundance from most depictions of the nation at war. At the same time, popular representations of the Vietnam War have consistently touted U.S. soldiers' material sacrifices and emphasized their suffering during the war and after, elements of the Vietnam narrative that work to legitimize the disproportionate violence meted out on the nation's behalf. What gets put into a war story and what gets left out are instructive, not just of the American military art but also of American culture at large. Somehow, when Americans imagine themselves at war, the notion of unlimited bullets and bombs is less disconcerting than the notion of unlimited ice cream, and the prospect of endless suffering is more affirming than the promise of endless time and plenty. Ultimately, the erasure of abundance from old war stories helps the United States to create new ones because it allows the American public to revel in the *idea* of wartime hardship without actually having to experience it.

Imagine all the bullshit stories Vietnam inspired.
—Tracy Kidder, *My Detachment*

Many of the features of daily life in Vietnam illuminated by this book were also evident in the Iraq War, as the bloom of consumer culture once again drifted far into a war zone. To be sure, American soldiers did endure hardships in Iraq. Oppressive heat, water and food shortages, and hostile acts plagued troops actually engaged in combat, and every soldier suffered the loneliness, stress, and isolation of deploying far from home. But material deprivation and physical trauma were hardly the norm, since most military personnel lived on well-stocked, heavily fortified bases. In fact, just as in Vietnam, living conditions in Iraq were surprisingly comfortable, and consumer goods even more prevalent, prompting contemporary American soldiers to experience the same gee-whiz surprise at their good fortune, the same tensions between combat and noncombat personnel, and the same existential crises as their fathers or grandfathers forty years before. Indeed, every major overseas incursion by U.S. forces since Vietnam has been marked by morale efforts that blended comfort with combat, suggesting the need to reimagine not only daily life in Vietnam but also the American way of war.

Reflexive expressions of support for American soldiers were everywhere during the Iraq War, and, just as with Vietnam, they tended to conflate wartime service with service in combat. Starting in 2001, the yellow ribbon motif, an expression of longing since the Iran hostage crisis, merged with images of American flags, weeping eagles, the burning Twin Towers, and Osama bin Laden or Saddam Hussein in the crosshairs of a rifle. These images appeared on a host of products, such as posters, T-shirts, bumper stickers, shot glasses, teddy bears, and tattoos, in a branding of war that conflated patriotism with vengeful militarism. Soldiers in uniform received free drinks and words of thanks from total strangers, and brash declarations of adoration for "the troops" sprang up all over the Internet. On Facebook, the community bulletin board of the early twenty-first century, dozens and perhaps hundreds of groups emerged from the digital ether, some with millions of adherents, to pledge their prayers and thanks to the United States armed forces. Embedded in the adulation were weighty assumptions about modern warfare, that universal suffering and sacrifice accompany soldiers into battle and that battle itself is an essential part of wartime experience.

The Facebook group "Don't Support Our Troops? Think About This" is a prime example. Though the group is relatively small (it drew its first 100,000 members between May 2007 and October 2008), its founding text reads like a primer of Americans' assumptions about daily life in the Iraq war zone. The group's creator scolds visitors, "It may take you two minutes to read this. If you do not take the time to read this, you are probably one of the people this post is talking about." A litany of comparisons follows, juxtaposing stateside quality-of-life concerns against the "real" complaints of American servicemen and -women at war. The guilt nonmilitary group members are supposed to feel is palpable.

> You walk down the beach, staring at all the pretty girls/guys. They patrol the streets, searching for insurgents and terrorists. You complain about how hot it is. They wear their heavy gear, not daring to take off their helmet to wipe their brow. You go out to lunch, and complain because the restaurant got your order wrong. They may not get to eat today. . . . You hear the jokes about war, and make fun of men/women like him/her. They hear the gunfire, bombs and screams of the wounded. You see only what the media wants you to see. They see the broken bodies lying around them. . . . You crawl into your soft bed, with down pillows, and get comfortable. They try to sleep but get woken up by mortars and helicopters all night long.[2]

The comparisons go on for pages. In this version of the Iraq War, "our troops" go without adequate food and water while patrolling dangerous streets in full combat gear, dodging hostile fire, witnessing scenes of carnage on a regular basis, and every night falling exhausted into a fitful sleep that might be broken by violent attack. Yet, while some soldiers in Iraq endured all the hardships enumerated on the Facebook list at one time or another, those hardships were far from the norm, especially a few years into the occupation.

Living conditions for military personnel in Iraq varied by time and place, but, just as in Vietnam, the longer American bases stood, the more elaborate they became. And it did not take long. Units at the tip of the invading spear in March 2003 had nothing for comfort but what they carried with them; they slept in freshly dug foxholes every night, and they ate prepackaged food at every meal, a life of austerity that paralleled the shared sufferings of foot soldiers throughout American history. Two months later, a *Washington Post* reporter found, troops were still living without electricity or running water, "subsisting on barely palatable food and sweltering unhappily under the stunning Mesopotamian summer sun." An Army unit garrisoned at Baghdad International Airport dubbed its quarters "The Crack House" because, the soldiers said, "it looks like one. The dust blows through the broken windows. The pigeons fly in and crap on your stuff." The acrid stench of burn-out latrines (with burnable waste bags, an improvement over the Vietnam-era barrels of excrement and diesel fuel) periodically filled the air, and computers and other electronic equipment gave out after a few hours of operating in the stifling heat.[3]

Just a few months later, however, conditions were dramatically improved. Troops still stationed at Baghdad International Airport could dine under an air-conditioned, circus-sized tent for three hot meals each day or patronize Iraq's first Burger King, which flame-broiled over 5,000 burgers daily, making it one of the most successful franchises in the worldwide chain. A large P.X. offered creature comforts like junk food, portable DVD players, and baby wipes, which were essential for keeping bodies and equipment free of Iraqi dust. Nearby, Iraqi civilians ran several gift shops for troops looking to document their overseas adventures with souvenirs of the region. Early efforts to provide recreational activities included dayrooms with televisions and video games, computer labs with Internet access, phone centers for calling home, and state-of-the-art fitness equipment.[4] By the time Taysha Deaton arrived in Iraq with her Louisiana National Guard unit in 2005, air-conditioned trailers were the norm for soldiers' quarters. During her deployment at Camp Liberty in western Baghdad, she slept in a king-sized bed "beneath imported sheets and a fluffy down comforter" and enjoyed the conveniences of the "refrigerator, television, cell phone, microwave oven, boom box and DVD player" she had purchased from the P.X. or from departing soldiers. "We had no idea conditions were going to be this great!" she exclaimed to a visiting journalist. "My first thought was, Oh my God! This is good!"[5]

Deaton's experience was pretty common, but that is not to say that some troops did not still live in awful conditions in Iraq, even years into the war. In 2007, "the surge" strategy inserted combat units into violent Baghdad neighborhoods, the better to forge ties with the locals while suppressing the insurgency. Army soldier Owen Powell, blogging under the screen name "Roy Batty," termed his unit's quarters in the spring of 2007 "the Termite Mound," in reference to the way soldiers were piled on top of one another in the bombed-out, multilevel shopping mall they called home. Six hundred soldiers shared just four shower stalls, and they had no access to laundry, despite the 125-degree heat. When they moved in, one entire floor was filled with excrement, courtesy of an Iraqi unit that had previously occupied the darkened, shell-pocked hulk. After several weeks, electricity, wireless Internet access, and plywood partitions between units' sleeping areas ameliorated some of the discomfort, but each soldier's private world was confined to his cot and the few inches between it and his neighbor's. It was, Powell wrote, like "living in a coal mine, a bunker, and a ruined city, in one convenient package."[6]

Despite the austerity, Powell was glad for the change of pace. "But really it's not that bad," he wrote. "Part of me has wanted a rougher experience." He went on to describe life at his previous Iraq duty station, a rearward base where support troops served on the same side as foot soldiers like Powell, but in a very different war. "The surrealism of eating Alaskan King Crab every single day for three months at [Forward Operating Base] Shield was not exactly what I had in mind when I first envisioned coming to this war torn city." The austerity of the Termite Mound and foot patrols in a volatile Baghdad neighborhood provided Powell with a chance to prove himself as a soldier and a man and to be a part of history. "This is more of a 'real' experience, as if we are getting a little taste of what it was like back in OIF I during the invasion [Operation Iraqi Freedom I, a reference to the first year of the war], when food was scarce but America was winning, and who cared if you only got one MRE a day when you were allowed to actually shoot back at the bad guys?" For Powell, a professional soldier, combat was its own reward, because it allowed him to fulfill years of training and to experience the strange thrill of violating taboos against killing in a morally, culturally, and legally sanctioned way. Shooting "bad guys" who had shot at you also provided indisputable proof, on an individual level, that a soldier's sacrifices—living in dumps like the Termite Mound, being separated from loved ones, and, for National Guard troops and reservists, disrupting their professional lives—had meaning, that the war really was for something, after all.[7]

Just as in Vietnam, soldiers' morale in Iraq was a precarious thing. Though the factors undermining it were different, the remedy—abundance—was the same. Powell's longing for combat in Iraq was a by-product of American military restraint, because U.S. forces worked hard to avoid civilian casualties while rooting out insurgents. Strict rules of engagement were, in part, the realization of one of the Vietnam War's many lessons, that the shooting war had undermined the effort to "win hearts and minds." But restraint in Iraq was also a by-product of a support-heavy style of warfare that allocated only a small percentage of troops to combat operations— also a lesson of Vietnam, that American public support for war is inversely proportionate to American casualties. The admirable desire to limit casualties on both sides had an unintended side effect, however; thousands of professionally trained soldiers longed for action and wondered why they were far from home, if they were not going to be allowed to shoot anybody.

In Iraq, the collapse of Bush administration arguments about the necessity of the war—the never found "weapons of mass destruction" and the debunked link between Saddam Hussein and Al Qaeda—also undermined soldiers' enthusiasm for the mission. As in Vietnam, military authorities tried to maintain troop morale by closing the gap between stateside and war zone living conditions. Absent a compelling justification for war, abundance would once again absorb discontent and help substitute for a clear sense of purpose.

Powell's reference to Alaskan king crab is a perfect example of the comfort-for-morale equation at work in Iraq. The food provided to U.S. soldiers deployed there was almost beyond comprehension, with menu options that not only met stateside standards but often exceeded them. Military contractor KBR (formerly Kellogg, Brown, and Root), which, as construction firm Brown and Root prior to its 1998 merger with M. W. Kellogg, had built so much for the American occupation in Vietnam, once more heeded its country's call to arms. With $12 billion in Iraq War contracts by 2005, KBR provided spectacular meal service to the troops at taxpayers' expense.[8] At DFAC buffets throughout Iraq, American soldiers could consume unlimited quantities of free food, all of which was imported from the United States. For example, the largest dining facility at Al Asad Airbase, "Warrior Hall," was not so much a hall as it was a cavern, covering an area the size of two football fields. It offered "main line" and "short order" food counters, plus a pasta bar, a taco bar, a health food bar, and a dessert bar. The menu at Warrior Hall was bleak compared with the DFAC at the Balad superbase, where a *Washington Post* journalist recorded a typical evening's menu options in January 2006: "baked salmon, roast turkey, grilled pork chops, fried crab bites, breaded scallops, and fried rice," plus two salad bars, a deli counter, a short-order counter for hot dogs and hamburgers, two soups of the day, and a dessert bar with "chocolate mint and vanilla ice cream, banana pudding, pumpkin pie, cherry pie, and yellow cake." If soldiers tired of the free options in the DFACs, most bases also had for-profit eateries where they could pay cash for a meal. These included snack bars run by the local P.X., ice cream parlors, fast food concessions (eventually including Subway, Pizza Hut, Taco Bell, and Popeye's, in addition to the aforementioned Burger King), some of which had drive-throughs or were open twenty-four hours a day. There was also a full-service coffee chain called Green Beans (slogan: "Honor First, Coffee Second"), a soldier's Starbucks that cranked out lattes made to order. According to the U.S. Army dietician stationed at Joint Base Balad, the average American soldier lost ten pounds while deployed to Iraq for a year in 2003. But, given the menu options, she reported in 2006, "Now they gain that much." Rich fare, air-conditioning, sedentary duty, and stress-related eating combined to reverse the weight-loss trend because the Iraq War was—for Americans, at least—the best all-you-can-eat buffet the world has ever seen.[9]

The shopping was pretty good, too. True to its slogan, "We Go Where You Go," the Army and Air Force Exchange Service (AAFES) provided retail opportunities to facilitate comfort and enhance the fighting spirit of soldiers stationed throughout Iraq. Before the March 2003 war began, AAFES organized twenty-three stores in invasion staging areas throughout the Middle East, and the first P.X. opened at Tallil Air Base (later known as Ali Air Base) in Iraq even before the fall of Baghdad. By 2008, the military-run retail system in Iraq had grown to fifty-six P.X.'s run by AAFES, plus nineteen more run by individual units.[10] In the opening months of the war, soldiers stocked up on sundries like flashlights, Ziploc bags, bandanas, baby wipes, sleeping mats, lip balm, toilet paper, and water pouches to ease the discomfort of combat operations. Once the tactical situation stabilized and living conditions improved, purchases tended to emphasize comfort and leisure: snack foods, cases of soda, household appliances, bed linens, beauty products, Middle Eastern souvenirs, and sophisticated electronics. The gadgets ranged from the portable (MP3 players, cell phones, and laptops) to the entrenched (forty-two-inch plasma screen televisions, satellite dishes, and video game setups that could connect a dozen players in separate quarters at one time). Soldiers also accumulated epic DVD collections, sometimes numbering over a thousand. A lot of these consumer goods were bought at below-market prices in the P.X.'s, others were ordered from private vendors online (the U.S. Postal Service charged domestic rates for goods shipped to Iraq), and many changed hands in a yard-sale economy whereby departing soldiers tried to unload their stuff on incoming troops so that they would not have to pay to ship it home.[11]

In Vietnam, elaborate bases arose from the need to keep soldiers both confined to camp and entertained, though local commanders often acceded to soldiers' demands that they be allowed off-post after work. In Iraq, concerns about American soldiers violating Muslim sensibilities during off-duty excursions, plus the threat of snipers, car bombs, and improvised explosive devices on civilian streets, led to a no-fraternization policy that kept the vast majority of personnel confined to their bases. U.S. military installations in Iraq quickly developed into small, Americanized cities replete with recreational facilities that replicated many features of civilian life. In addition to the usual day rooms, gyms, retail outlets, call centers, and computer labs, all but the smallest bases acquired some combination of the following: libraries, educational centers (once again, with college courses offered by the University of Maryland), miniature golf, movie theaters, coffee shops, community rooms that offered classes in yoga, martial arts, and salsa dancing, and salons that offered standard barber services but also manicures, pedicures, and therapeutic massage. In 2009, a *Washington Post* reporter found that the effect of a manicure in a war zone could be transporting. "It makes you go into a different world," explained soldier Billy Scott, as a civilian beautician from Krygyzstan rubbed his hands with lotion at the salon on Forward Operating Base Marez. "You get here, and your mind goes blank. You have a pretty lady doing your nails." The manicure, the consumer goods, and the all-you-can-eat crab legs worked together to assuage the boredom and discomfort of American soldiers who were not only far from home but also isolated from the very country they had come to liberate.[12]

The escapism suggested by a manicurist's touch was realized in a literal way when soldiers took their leave. As in Vietnam, R&R was a critical part of the Iraq experience because military authorities still regarded taking breaks from the mission as essential to good morale.[13] For units living in austerity, or for individuals seeking a quick getaway from their work environment, the Army created in-country MWR (morale, welfare, and recreation) centers designed to accommodate individual soldiers or units on stand-down for four-day stays. The Army did not have to build these facilities from scratch, because Ba'athist elites' profligate spending left several palatial estates perfect for adapting into military resorts with names like Freedom Rest, the Iron Horse Inn, or Q-West (pronounced "Key West"). Built by Saddam Hussein or his inner circle, many of these manses sat on the Tigris River, offering scenic views and slightly cooler breezes. Their marbled halls opened onto grand patios, swimming pools, and elaborate but poorly tended gardens newly amended by volleyball nets and horseshoe pits. Inside, MWR personnel—the Special Services troops of the twenty-first century—carved gift shops, eateries, weight rooms, screening rooms, game rooms, computer labs, phone centers, saunas, and sleeping quarters out of ornate salons and bedroom suites. The scenes conjured by T-bone steaks, crystal chandeliers, and uniformed Iraqi or TCN attendants were more Gatsby than grunt, making Iraq a strange war indeed.[14]

Of course, there were many facets of the soldier's life in Iraq that did not accord with the Vietnam experience, in particular the Nam's unrestraint.

In deference to Iraqi social mores, the U.S. military banned soldiers in the war zone from consuming alcohol, which, as an inhibition-lifting depressant, tends to have a negative effect on military decorum and productivity. On the other hand, clever soldiers still managed to party with alcohol and drugs hidden in packages sent from home, smuggled in by NATO troops or private military contractors or purchased clandestinely from Iraqi purveyors outside American bases.[15] The military also strongly discouraged fraternization between American servicemen and local women, causing male soldiers to direct their sexual energies elsewhere. Rumors abounded about Americans purchasing sex from TCN contract workers in Iraq, especially in Baghdad's fortified Green Zone, while the presence of servicewomen on American bases created a new set of romantic opportunities. Though policies dictated that no American military personnel were supposed to be having sex in Iraq (with the exception of a few married service couples that the Army allowed to cohabit), the condoms and pregnancy tests available for purchase in the P.X.'s spoke to the futility and hypocrisy of the ban. Even so, the military's tight rein on troop behavior prevented the Iraq war zone from devolving into a moral wonderland like the Nam, though the fullest extent of the American occupation's effects on Iraqis and TCN contract employees has yet to be determined.

Despite the chaste professionalism of U.S. forces, there was still a surreal, otherworldly quality to the Iraq war zone. It was perhaps not as distinct as the Nam, but the world Americans inhabited there was nonetheless a strange place quite apart from U.S. and Iraqi civilian life. Within months of the invasion, the Iraqi map was overlaid with the geographic features of American militarism. When an Iraqi man living in Texas was hired to go to Iraq as an interpreter, he learned he would be living in a place called Bucca. "I said, 'There is no city called Bucca,'" he told a reporter. "They showed me it on the map and I said, 'I am from Iraq and there is no city called Bucca." But there was. It was an American base that had been built from scratch and named in honor of a New York soldier and fire marshal killed on 9/11. Eventually, the U.S. presence grew to some 300 bases surrounded by new roads, off-limits security perimeters, and checkpoints that all of Iraq's inhabitants had to navigate.[16]

At the same time, Iraq's own architectural flourishes dotted the landscape, providing exotic backdrops to American soldiers' photographs of deployment. The remnants of Saddam Hussein's authoritarian narcissism decorated intersections and public squares all over the country. U.S. soldiers throughout the war reveled in having their pictures made in front of

Saddam statues and portraits or seated on luxurious furniture in one of his many palaces. Their uniforms and brandished weapons expressed the indisputable fact of American technical mastery over Hussein, his armed forces, and the Iraqi people. In prioritizing security over cultural sensitivity, the American map of Iraq also cordoned off large swaths of territory around U.S. bases. Ancient ruins lay within some of these areas, such as the Sumerian city of Ur, one of the world's oldest city-states and the biblical birthplace of Abraham. Until its transfer to Iraqi forces in 2009, this archaeological treasure lay entirely within the security perimeter of Tallil Air Base, where the U.S. Air Force's sophisticated machines and 350,000 square feet of new buildings bore witness to American civilization's expansive reach. With the great Ziggurat of Ur looming in the distance, unmanned Predator drones flew in and out of Tallil, and the technicians who used them to smite insurgents from miles away took their lunch breaks at two Burger Kings and a Pizza Hut. Tallil mixed the sacred with the profane and the permanent with the ephemeral, for it is hard to imagine the Pizza Hut outlasting the 4,000-year-old Ziggurat. Temporary though they were, U.S. military bases in Iraq nonetheless stood as monuments to American values: order, consumption, military prowess, and enough wealth to discard all that was built when the American people called their soldiers home.[17]

Consumption, in particular, was an essential part of the American experience in Iraq, as fast food, espresso drinks, digital media, and of course consumer goods themselves cushioned the discomforts of occupying a hostile, poorly developed land. Even more so than in Vietnam, soldiers ordered their off-duty lives around their purchases, especially electronic devices that provided temporary escape from the boredom and stressors of modern warfare. Video games proved extremely popular, creating online and real-life communities centered around competition, betting, and ribald heckling. MP3 players were also a major diversion, as soldiers labored over "war mixes," song collections they assembled to reflect and enhance tours of duty. In 2006, *Rolling Stone* magazine conducted an informal poll to determine the most popular songs among American soldiers in Iraq, compiling a list dominated by aggressive bands like Drowning Pool, Linkin Park, and Hatebreed, plus AC/DC's classic "Highway to Hell." As marine Brandon Welsh explained, "You can't put a Dashboard Confessional song on and expect to go out there and kill somebody."[18] Of course, listening to heavy metal or metalcore bands was also a way for support personnel to identify with the trigger pullers who did get to leave the wire. Some soldiers went so far as to produce original music in Iraq, outfitting their quarters with the electric keyboards, drum machines, sequencers, samplers, and mixers one would expect to find in a stateside recording studio. Photo and video editing were also major pastimes, as the troops uploaded still and moving images to their laptops and then to the Internet for sharing with other soldiers, with friends and family back in the States, and with members of a global public.[19]

Soldiers' use of digital media ordered the war, assuaged boredom, and commemorated what was, for many, the most intense and formative experience of their adult lives. Vietnam-era soldiers had to wait for Hollywood to set their war experiences to music on film, but twenty-first-century soldiers could do it themselves. Digital cameras and video recorders were the Iraq war zone's all-seeing eye, as military personnel used these ubiquitous devices to document every facet of the occupation. They captured images of combat's aftermath and memorials for fallen comrades, but also the banal interiors, dusty vistas, menacing equipment, inside jokes, and fast friends that constituted a typical deployment. Soldiers photographed Iraq's desolate landscape on convoys and from the air or even from inside the wire on American bases situated in rural areas. They also captured scenes of Iraqi people's daily activities as best they could, but they usually did so from a distance. The restraint was due to a greater cultural sensitivity than had prevailed in Vietnam, where American gawking was overt and unapologetic, but in Iraq security prohibitions against local-national employees working on American bases were also a factor. Many Americans spent a year in-country without ever meeting an Iraqi person, which tended to reduce the locals to off-screen abstractions in soldiers' visual diaries.[20] Given the isolation of American bases in Iraq, the sights and sounds of a typical deployment were pretty tame, so footage of training exercises with lethal weapons or the billowing sands of Iraqi dust storms helped to infuse soldiers' photo montages with the air of the unfamiliar.

Like their Vietnam War counterparts, American soldiers in Iraq regarded some form of combat as the quintessential war experience, even if most of them never came close to seeing it. Visual evidence of one's proximity to danger—explosions, fires, dead bodies—factored heavily into soldiers' photo and video narratives of deployment. When the images were set to music, the effect was disturbing, bellicose, and strangely nostalgic—but also profoundly misleading about the nature of the war. The combat images in a soldier's personal slideshow might suggest a war environment thick with danger, but the slideshow itself was evidence of a modern war zone culture defined by safety, abundance, and satiety. The slideshows were usu-

U.S. military personnel wait in line at the P.X. on Al-Asad Air Base in Iraq in 2006. Consumption was an enormous part of Americans' Iraq War experience, as the U.S. military facilitated the troops' purchase of nearly every product imaginable and the Internet provided access to everything else. (Charles J. Hanley/A.P. Photo)

ally edited and set to music *in* Iraq, not stateside, in air-conditioned computer labs or on personal laptops in quarters replete with modern amenities. The editing process itself speaks to American bases' isolation from the exigencies of war and to the workaday nature of combat operations, which took only a slim minority of the occupation force outside the wire, usually to return "home" when the day was done. Digital images are also infinitely replicable, and soldiers shared them with a variety of publics, including the Internet as a whole. So a soldier's slideshow of an Iraq deployment might include personal photos of the filmmaker's own war experiences, but there was nothing to prevent him or her from borrowing, without attribution, photographs or film clips that had been circulated privately among service members or from pulling media directly off the Internet. Burning tanker trucks, charred corpses, impassive Iraqi prisoners—images of all of these hallmark Iraq War encounters were within reach of support personnel seeking to embellish and authenticate the otherwise banal narratives of their deployments. As a result, the Iraq War videos found online are extremely problematic texts for scholars and journalists seeking to document American life in the war zone. The events a slideshow depicts surely happened to someone, somewhere, but they may not have happened all to the same individual, and the individual responsible for assembling the images may not have taken any of them at all.

The provenance of soldiers' violent war stories troubled combat veterans, who resented that rearward soldiers could take credit for their struggles without having to endure them. In Vietnam, support personnel were derided as REMFs, but that term disappeared in the years after the war. In Iraq, the pejorative du jour was "Fobbits," a dehumanizing term that simultaneously referenced the troll-like inhabitants of J. R. R. Tolkein's Middle Earth and the forward operating bases (FOBs) on which support personnel lived.[21] Expressions of soldiers' contempt for Fobbits abound on the Internet, such as the song "FOB Life," which became a minor YouTube sensation. When Mikel Fagan and Juan Cotto returned to Camp Falcon after six weeks of conducting mortar missions in the field, they went to the P.X. and were angered to find the shelves picked over by residents of the base who never had to go outside the wire. They then poured their resentment into a song—Fagan and Cotto had been recording hip-hop tracks together for a year—which became a hit among U.S. forces stationed overseas.[22] In one of the music videos that the song "FOB Life" spawned on the Internet, the filmmaker promised, "If you have a five-day work week, shut your shop at 5 P.M., eat B.K. [Burger King] or Dairy Queen once a week, visit the P.X. daily, have cable in your private room, and never spend a night outside your FOB, then this video's for you." What follows is a photo montage that juxtaposes images of combat soldiers conducting the "real" work of the war, combat operations, against images of life on the FOB: orderly streets, sterile offices, fast food counters, P.X. aisles, and out-of-shape military personnel roaming among them.[23]

In fact, the song's angry tone and vicious accusations really appealed to combat veterans wanting to deride the contributions and masculinity of support personnel, a generalized assault that masked a subtle misogyny, since women tended to serve in those roles. Fagan and Cotto took issue with the lack of danger on rearward bases, mocking the duties of the FOB inhabitants: "So what up, dope? Oh, you just got off guard? Man, you protecting a gym? That must be hard." A few stanzas later, they focused their ire on soldiers who succumbed to the temptation to embellish. "You fucking liar / Coming home and saying you go out the wire / And on top

M.Sgt. Steve Opet's 2007 cartoon, "The Evolution of a FOBbit," in which a gung-ho G.I. slowly morphs into a portly, subhuman creature "who seldom, if ever, goes outside the wire." Opet's depiction of the P.X. shopping bag, made-to-order coffee, dining facility carryout containers, and souvenir pipe speaks to the important role consumption played in providing American soldiers in Iraq with a comfortable war experience. (Courtesy of M.Sgt. Steve Opet)

of that your weapon's never been fired / Bitch ass." They then leveled a critique about the uneven distribution of danger in Iraq, demonstrating combat troops' belief, given the voluntary nature of American military service, that support personnel *could* request combat duty if they wanted to. "You've never had bodies in your site / You be sleeping while the mortars do the missions at night / You ain't even in the fight / If your job is in the TOC [tactical operations center] / On behalf of all the mortars . . ." The line concludes with an invitation to perform what would be, for heterosexual men, a degrading sex act. Hundreds of comments on YouTube endorsed the song's message of contempt, but they also contained a spirited disagreement over which MOS—the Infantryman (11B) or the Cavalry Scout (19D), which was Fagan and Cotto's specialty—was "cooler," meaning more technically difficult and authentically warlike. As in Vietnam, everything was relative; infantrymen looked down on mortar men, and everyone who ventured beyond the wire looked down on the Fobbits.[24]

Meanwhile, support personnel in Iraq wrestled with the chasm that lay between their own expectations of war, to say nothing of the public's expectations, and the dull reality of most deployments. The co-optation by support personnel of combat soldiers' experiences was not just an issue of self-indulgence but rather suggests the deep ambivalence with which they regarded their duties. Alex Barnes, whose tedious daily routine opened this chapter, explored this issue on his blog. Yes, he enjoyed the material comfort afforded by the military's morale-building initiatives, and yet he felt his wartime service lacked a sense of purpose. Two weeks after the "Day in the Life" post, Barnes found himself envying a group of soldiers in full combat gear headed out for a mission. At first, he chastised himself: "Don't be a retard—you've got it great, chilling out inside the wire with nary a care but what's on the menu." And then the wondering began. "All the same, though, I'm struck by a certain sense of . . . guilt? Insanity? Boredom? Obligation?" It was all of those. He compared his duty to combat soldiers on patrol in Iraq's ragged urban neighborhoods. "If you go out on a patrol, at the end of the day someone can say, 'Good job, you bagged X bad guys / handed out Y soccer balls / traded Z frozen chickens for W RPGs [rocket propelled grenades].' At the end of my day, what can someone say to me? 'Good job, your antenna didn't fall over today?'" Though the communications equipment he maintained was essential to the war effort, Barnes did not feel his service measured up because it did not place him in danger, nor did it afford him contact with the Iraqi people and, hence, with the war itself.[25]

Barnes continued to question his contribution, framing his concerns— like so many soldiers before him—in reference to the famous World War I British recruiting poster that tied a man's masculinity and reputation to wartime military service. "Maybe it has to do with contemplating the answer to the proverbial 'Daddy, what did you do in the war?' question. Truth is, no one's going to believe you if you say you went to Iraq for a year and *nothing happened*." Like soldiers headed for Vietnam with *The Sands of Iwo Jima* and Robert Capa's D-Day photographs flashing in their heads, twenty-first-century Americans held their own ideas about what a war should be, and so did Alex Barnes. He wrote, "Given the news reports, the popular image is that Iraq is like Iwo Jima + Tet Offensive, with a little bit of south-central L.A. thrown in for good measure." A year's worth of days made memorable only by the appearance of lasagna or lobster on the DFAC menu simply were not what anyone had in mind.[26]

Barnes's confusion and alienation were common to soldiers in both Iraq and Vietnam and probably every major American deployment in between.

As American warfare became increasingly high-tech, American soldiers functioned less as warriors and more as technicians, who tended, literally, to the war machine. Without the urgency of combat to infuse their deployments with meaning, support personnel's morale tended to flag. A *Stars and Stripes* survey conducted five months into the occupation found that nearly half of U.S. troops considered their unit's morale "low" or "very low," and one-third claimed the war had not, thus far, been worthwhile. The Army's own study, conducted around the same time, found similar levels of discontent, and reports of low morale gained traction in the media when the Army revealed disturbingly high rates of suicide among the occupation force, at least compared with rates from earlier wars.[27]

Around the same time, an internal Army study also revealed that support troops regarded themselves as such, rather than as soldiers. "They'll tell you, 'I'm a mechanic,' not 'I'm a soldier,'" explained a concerned commanding general. Recognizing the morale problem inherent in soldiers' tendency to see themselves as supporters rather than fighters, he pledged, "We've got to change that." To remedy the problem, the Army's chief of staff ordered the service to embrace the "warrior ethos," a contemporary version of the Vietnam-era MOS profiles that propagandized about the necessity and difficulty of supporting roles like entertainment specialist or lifeguard. Like the Marines, the Army wanted every soldier to regard him- or herself as "a rifleman first," so it intensified combat training for noncombat troops and codified use of the term "warrior" in lieu of other descriptors, including "soldier." The adoption of the warrior ethos paralleled uniform modifications that allowed all Army personnel to adopt facets of dress once reserved for deployed troops or elite units.[28] But in Iraq, staggering differentials between the experiences of combat and noncombat troops laid bare the lie of a shared uniform. What's more, life on the FOB simply did not accord with traditional war stories, which tend to cast every soldier as a fighter and every fight as a very near thing. Instead, the wealth and power of the United States in the twenty-first century spawned an armed force of such high-tech lethality that most of its "warriors" were not even armed.

It is not surprising that comfort would accompany an affluent nation's soldiers to war. What is culturally significant is that the abundance is so often ignored in tellings of the Iraq and Vietnam war stories. The presence of comfort in a war story tends to complicate the benevolence and nobility Americans project onto their soldiers, undermining values that are rooted in the nation's foundation myth. Writer and veteran W. D. Ehrhart stumbled onto this concern as a teenage marine serving in Vietnam. "In grade school," he recalled, "we learned about the redcoats, the nasty British soldiers that tried to stifle our freedom." Ehrhart's characterization of the British army in North America owed more to an entrenched collective memory of the American Revolution than to its history, in which most colonists had scant direct experience with British soldiers. But it was the memory of their oppression that survived and found its way to Ehrhart as a boy growing up in Perkasie, Pennsylvania, in the mid-twentieth century. The redcoats were "nasty" because they were foreign, they were better trained and equipped than the ragtag Continentals, and they imposed themselves so gratuitously on unhappy colonists in Boston, New York, and Philadelphia that the founding fathers dedicated an entire constitutional amendment (the third) to preventing such excess from happening again.

Of course, there are holes in these facts as wide as the Mekong River, but the essence of the story lies at the heart of the American foundation myth, and the essence is what counts. In their mythology, Americans tend to cast indomitable, foreign occupiers as the bad guys, while they root for the plucky, overmatched defenders of home and hearth. As a grunt who fought in the famed battle for Hue in 1968, Ehrhart was ostensibly fighting to protect American and South Vietnamese freedom, but in the process he witnessed terrible things, did terrible things. "Subconsciously, but not very subconsciously," he explained, "I began increasingly to have the feeling that I was a redcoat. I think it was one of the most staggering realizations of my life."[29]

For Ehrhart and other true believers, Vietnam represented a disturbing role reversal and an undoing of character, both collective and personal, that took place when national security interests diverged from American ideals like justice and freedom. That is, the Cold War imperative to contain communism abroad was a questionable end realized through dubious means: the contraction of some American citizens' freedoms when they were forced to serve in a war that they opposed; U.S. support of despotic, anticommunist regimes throughout the world; and American soldiers imposing their will on Vietnamese people who did not want them in their country.[30] In an interview conducted a few years after the war, Ehrhart described one of the incidents that made him feel like an oppressor in Vietnam. An old Vietnamese woman was afraid he would shoot her, so she ran from him. And he shot her because she ran from him.[31] The self-fulfilling logic of that moment was exquisitely simple, and yet it told the whole story of the Vietnam War. For fear of communism spreading to the United States, the U.S. government deployed its armed forces to a fiercely nationalistic country and then authorized its combat troops to kill anyone who shot at them for being there. If American soldiers were redcoats in Vietnam, then the abundance that loomed behind the bayonets only exacerbated the sense of oppression.

Comfortable living conditions on U.S. bases were nourishing and affirming for the American servicemen who lived therein, but they created problems for the war effort in Vietnam and, later, in Iraq. American bases in Vietnam were isolated worlds set apart from Vietnamese civilians, and the material comfort that existed on them did not go unnoticed by Vietnamese workers who performed much of the unskilled labor that was required to keep American soldiers clean, fed, and happy. Millions of South Vietnamese people's lives during the war were marked by desperate efforts to find food, haul water, and improvise shelter for their families, who had been displaced from their homes by U.S. forces' indiscriminate use of heavy firepower in rural areas, if not by direct relocation orders from the U.S. military. In addition to the black market activities discussed earlier, Vietnamese people scavenged, begged, and stole from Americans in order to survive. Small children worked civilian streets as beggars and pickpockets, using their adorable faces and nimble fingers to relieve G.I.'s of their cash, and Vietnamese employees on U.S. bases tried to salvage discarded materials like cardboard and food scraps from their job sites. American military police thoroughly searched local workers everyday as they left the bases in order to stop this pilferage. Many Vietnamese people also made their living by picking through the massive garbage heaps that lay outside U.S. bases, but the military sought ways to prevent even that by burning or booby-trapping some of the dumps. The policy stemmed from concern that Viet Cong artisans could turn scavenged American supplies into weapons, and they did, transforming unexploded shells into mortars and mines and pounding old canteens into lamps, grenades, and other improvised explosive devices. American lives might be saved by the policy, but impoverished Vietnamese civilians bore the cost of this security.[32]

American television broadcasts that delivered the comforting sights of home to American soldiers were also viewed by South Vietnamese people, who surely marveled at the luxury of life in the United States. Vietnamese civilians also saw firsthand the consumer goods that tumbled out of American ships, crammed P.X. shelves, and decorated American soldiers' bunks. The United States dangled abundance before them, but it floated just out of reach, leading to resentments that fueled the underground economy. The resentment also undercut counterinsurgency efforts to win hearts and minds, as Vietnamese people increasingly directed their sympathies to the Viet Cong. In contrast to Americans' ostentatious displays of wealth and power, communist propaganda emphasized sacrifice and humility. One pamphlet "used as a handbook by the Party militants" described the ideal cadre as someone who "will not hesitate to be the first to endure hardship and the last to enjoy happiness."[33] The Viet Cong understood their culture in a way that Americans did not; in Vietnam, austerity did not project helplessness, the meaning Americans ascribed to Vietnamese poverty. Rather, austerity signaled virtue and the righteousness of a cause, values Americans claimed to share but declined to express through austerity of their own.

Military histories of the Vietnam War have touched on abundance in their examinations of why the United States failed to meet its objectives in South Vietnam, but they have done so only in the context of "lessons learned" for the U.S. military's efficiency. Generally, these studies concur that the American war machine had too much tail and not enough tooth.[34] The U.S. Army commissioned its own examination of the logistical effort and arrived at a similar conclusion: that "possibly Army base development was too elaborate" because it strained the logistics pipeline and because it raised the morale of some military personnel at the expense of others. With no explicit, official construction standards in place at the start of the buildup in Vietnam, the Army's study concluded, "the true line between 'necessary' and 'nice to have' was often difficult to define." Local commanders were free to interpret their orders as generously as budgets would allow, yielding great inequities in living conditions between bases and between branches of the service (Army and Marine Corps personnel resented Air Force and Navy personnel, who generally enjoyed higher standards of living). For the U.S. Army, then, the logistics lessons of the Vietnam War were that P.X. supplies overtaxed the system and that elaborate bases fostered resentment of one another among American soldiers. The fact that Vietnamese people, whose support or antipathy would ultimately determine the success or failure of the United States' endeavor, held resentments of their own did not draw comment.[35]

The Army's lessons of Vietnam, as far as logistics go, barely affected the Iraq War, which was fought with what seemed like unlimited resources. Critics were aware of the problems elaborate U.S. bases posed for the counterinsurgency effort there, and one of them even drew a parallel with Vietnam in order to make the point. In an interview with *Frontline* about the use of private military contractors in Iraq, retired Marine colonel Thomas

Hammes, an authority on fourth-generation warfare, commented on the impact of abundance on the war effort. "Some [bases in Iraq] were better, some were more austere, but all were quite, quite comfortable." Stocking them to American standards placed heavy demands on transportation, as private trucking firms hauled goods across hostile territory, with American troops providing convoy security and dodging insurgent attacks along the way. "Somebody's risking their life to deliver that luxury," Hammes pointed out. "Maybe you could tone down the luxury, put fewer vehicles on the road. Again, fewer vehicles on the road creates less tension with the locals, because they get tired of these high-speed convoys running them off the road." Semi-trucks blasting through intersections filled with cars and pedestrians irritated and endangered Iraqi citizens. The fact that the trucks carried food, fuel, and consumer goods that were beyond most civilians' reach only made it worse. "We did it in Vietnam, too," he added. "We created these huge base isolations in Vietnam where we set ourselves aside from the population to create a great luxury for the forces that live[d] there, and that doesn't really get you anything in the counterinsurgency. It creates a lot of problems." "And resentments?" the interviewer asked. "Yes."[36]

Like the Vietnamese before them, Iraqi people resented the abundance American soldiers enjoyed because their own lives were filled with so much struggle. The "shock and awe" bombing of 2003 dismantled Iraq's infrastructure, but years later the United States still had not fulfilled its promise to rebuild. On the eve of American combat troops' withdrawal in 2010, the *New York Times* reported, Iraq's city streets were still "littered with trash, drinking water is polluted, hospitals are bleak and often unsafe, and buildings bombed by the Americans in 2003 or by insurgents since remain ruined shells." News reports about staggering levels of corruption, including $8.7 billion in missing Iraqi oil and gas money entrusted to the U.S. Department of Defense for reconstruction, verified what the Iraqi people already knew: their basic needs were not being met. In Baghdad, residents could count on electrical power for only five hours each day, resulting in a rash of electricity "thefts" as merchants jury-rigged cables to siphon what little juice the grid could give. "Democracy didn't bring us anything," a shop owner told a reporter when his power went down. "Then he corrected himself. 'Democracy brought us a can of Coke and a beer.'"[37] In the absence of health care, security, and a decent standard of living, the consumer goods would have to do. Meanwhile, Iraqis living in darkened homes without running water could look out into the desert night and see isolated American bases lit up like Christmas, where sewage treatment plants made clean water flow from the tap, where power stations allowed the lights to glitter until dawn, and where most Iraqi people were forbidden to go.

The war zone abundance on U.S. military bases abroad has had many effects. Within the context of military occupation, consumerism worked alongside heavy firepower to demonstrate American mastery over the hungry and homeless of the developing world. Perhaps the best that could be said of American prosperity, beyond the comfort it afforded scared, lonely kids in military service far from home, is that it seeded material desires in poor, local people, teaching them more about capitalism and Western values than any propaganda leaflet ever could. Indeed, those seeds finally germinated in the Socialist Republic of Vietnam during the economic reforms of the 1990s, which brought foreign investment and relative prosperity to the embattled country. But freedom to choose between brands of cameras or imported clothes did not result in actual freedom, such as civil liberties or democratically elected leaders, for the Vietnamese people. As for the effects of G.I. consumerism on the Iraqi people, time will tell.

For the United States, the high standard of living on American bases has made the project of war very expensive, but Congress and the public have so far been willing to do whatever is necessary to support troops already in the field. The greatest effect of war zone abundance seems to be that it has made it easier for the United States to go to war. The bounty on American bases eases life for the troops, and by extension, for the communities at home that love and support them. Meanwhile, that bounty's absence in war narratives ensures that the American people continue to think of their country not as a superpower capable of fielding a massive army of professional killers anywhere in the world, but rather as an exemplar nation that deploys its citizen soldiers only when absolutely necessary.

As the previous chapters demonstrate, it is difficult to reconcile the routinized, media-saturated, recreation-filled, product-encrusted warscape of the U.S. occupation in Vietnam with popular ideas about the Vietnam War. The U.S. military's morale efforts there were a celebration of American ingenuity, technological superiority, and phenomenal wealth. But the Americanized worlds the U.S. military built in Vietnam were not just the product of an institution's desire to keep its charges happy. They were also evidence of an imperial power nearing the apogee of its strength. There was nothing American forces could not do in Vietnam—no natural resource they could not exploit, no hill they could not take, no target they could not destroy—except win the loyalty of a majority of the Vietnamese people. Yet American suffering displaces American strength in most of the war's stories, as though all the support troops and amenities described in this book—not to mention atrocities visited on Vietnamese people that are described elsewhere—never really existed.

When veteran Tracy Kidder asked the readers of his Vietnam memoir to "imagine all the bullshit stories Vietnam inspired," he was thinking specifically of the tendency of noncombat troops, himself among them, to embellish their war stories, the better to extract sympathy from loved ones and to accord with public expectations of what a war should be.[38] But in a broader sense, misapprehensions about American soldiers' universal suffering in Vietnam inspired tall tales all their own, facilitating the march to war in subsequent conflicts like Iraq. The imagined deprivations of war, which for Americans are increasingly rare, work to establish hostilities as a matter of urgent necessity. "We would not live this way unless we *had* to," the deprived soldiers in a typical war story seem to say. Because their wartime deprivation is self-imposed—all present-day American soldiers are volunteers—the sacrifice is particularly ennobling, which helps to affirm the good intentions of the people who send them off to war. Finally, the supposed deprivations of war enable the American citizenry to play a direct role in the fighting by providing sustenance to their troops in the form of care packages, gift cards, and other donations meant to assuage the hardships of military service.

In the twenty-first century, this kind of civic engagement is particularly necessary for rallying public support because the proportion of citizens actually in the fight has declined dramatically, from 12 percent during World War II to 4 percent in Vietnam to less than 1 percent in the global war on terror.[39] During the Vietnam War, church ladies, elementary school classes, and other civic groups sent care packages to American soldiers in droves, with some units receiving so many goodies that a relentless tide of chocolate chip cookies becomes a running joke in W. D. Ehrhart's memoir *Vietnam-Perkasie*. During the Iraq War, private citizens sent care packages by the thousands to loved ones overseas, but they also gifted them to anonymous service members through the website AnySoldier.com or one of many organizations gathered under the Pentagon's community relations umbrella organization America Supports You. In 2008, a Chicago pizzeria even started an annual fundraising drive called "Pizza 4 Patriots" to send thousands of frozen pizzas to soldiers in Iraq for the Fourth of July.[40] All of these efforts were infused with patriotism and genuine kindness, but also with tremendous naïveté about life in the Iraq war zone. There, soldiers could buy at the local P.X. or online almost anything that might be sent in a care package (organizations like AnySoldier.com actually discouraged sending homemade baked goods because the Pentagon advised troops not to eat anything homemade unless it came from someone they knew). And the elaborate menu options at the DFAC made pizza—even Chicago-style pizza—seem mundane. Folding abundance into a war story exposes these home front contributions as unnecessary, casting foreign occupation as an elective policy, rather than a life-or-death necessity, and warfare itself as the sober business of professionals.

Even in the 1960s, the U.S. military was a terribly efficient destroying machine, designed to maximize devastation while protecting American servicemen from harm. It has only grown stronger since then. Abundance—rich food, more than adequate shelter, frequent entertainments, and plentiful consumer goods—projected the war machine's power, which was more profoundly expressed by the military's production of ice cream and musical theater in a tropical war zone than by any weapon the Defense Department could commission. Abundance was also the war machine's armor, insulating American soldiers—and, by extension, the folks at home—from the war's harmful effects. It helped to absorb soldiers' discontent, and, long after the war, it inspired malformed ideas about American power and responsibility in a global community defined largely by suffering. Old war stories inform new ones, and the continuities between them tell us a lot about what Americans claim to value: hard work, thrift, and selflessness. The missing pieces are instructive, too. As acts of heroism (the Battle of the Ia Drang Valley, for example) or ignominy (the My Lai massacre) came to define the myth and memory of Vietnam, they pushed to the margins the banal realities of military occupation. By emphasizing only the struggles, just or not, that their soldiers endured, Americans declined to take ownership of their unprecedented wealth and strength. But the lingering presence of poisonous defoliants in Vietnam's watersheds, the shocking differential between American and Vietnamese war casualties, and the occupation's corrosive effect on Vietnamese society expose the lie of American victimhood and reflect poorly on the ethics of the American military art; the suffering was so lopsided. American soldiers did suffer in Vietnam and long after, as casualty figures and the rates of Agent Orange–related illnesses and post-traumatic stress disorder in veterans attest. But more often, their traumas consisted of the loneliness and alienation of military life, stressors which were mitigated by the Nam's boisterous atmosphere and somatic gratification. In the conflicts following Vietnam—Kuwait, Bosnia, Kosovo,

Afghanistan, and especially Iraq—the war zone wonderlands the United States built abroad made it easier to go to war, again and again and again.

Traditional war stories foreground suffering, not satisfaction, enabling readers or moviegoers to indulge their appetites for sentimentality, and to romanticize—and cheapen—the sufferings of soldiers and civilians at war. The Vietnam War I have reimagined in these pages instead foregrounds satisfaction, pressing suffering into the background, like a shadow cast by something ominous and far away. In this new telling of the Vietnam war story, soldiers arrived in-country with expectations of storming the beaches but found instead a vast network of heavily fortified and elaborately adorned American bases. Cold beer and clean sheets, not foxholes and firefights, were often the norm, and most of the meals were served hot, except, of course, for the ice cream. At work, they settled into wearisome routines, shuffling paper and equipment from one side of South Vietnam to the other, and at night, they looked for ways to while away the hot, sticky hours until dawn. Just like the folks at home, they relaxed to music or in front of the TV, and time off was given to sports and home improvements, though many also found satisfaction in the seedy bars and brothels that sprang up all around them. For most, R&R was a reprieve not from danger but from hard work and boredom, and some lucky G.I.'s stationed near the beach got to have it all the time. Everywhere, in this version of the Vietnam War, there were things to buy: silks, statues, house wares, electronics, war trophies, and especially the camera to document it all. Through its lens, American soldiers recorded the quaintness of Vietnamese village life, the verdant beauty of the countryside, and the carnage wrought by high-tech warfare. Returning home, once provincial boys were transformed into men of the world, and they had the goods—custom suits, flashy watches, and war trophies—to prove it. They had the stories, too. These conquering warriors could boast of all that they had seen of war, even if they saw it on the nightly news or read it in their unit's newspaper. No one doubted their John Wayne claims because the burnished tales fit so well with what a war was supposed to be. And yet, for all the abundance pervading them, American war zones would seldom ever be that way again.

At the opening of this book, I quoted the last lines of Michael Herr's *Dispatches*, one of the seminal works of journalism to emerge from the Vietnam War. Reflecting on the fall of South Vietnam to communism in 1975, Herr concludes, "And no moves left for me at all but to write down some few last words and make the dispersion, Vietnam Vietnam Vietnam, we've all been there."[41] The passage is cryptic, suggesting with its determinism and finality that there exists some shared understanding of the war. For combat veterans and cowboy reporters like Herr, that might be true: Vietnam was, for them, a wilderness of such violence and erratic cruelty that the war forever undermined their ability to believe in an orderly universe. For everyone else, including the majority of Vietnam veterans, the war zone was a liminal space between wilderness and the World, where abundance served to amplify violence produced in the name of freedom. It was a strange place and, despite Herr's dispersion, nowhere Americans had ever been before. It would also prove to be the destination, going forward, every time they marched to war.

NOTES

ABBREVIATIONS

MHI   U.S. Army Military History Institute, Carlisle, Pa.

NARA   National Archives and Records Administration, College Park, Md.

The following sources are all in Record Group 472, National Archives and Records Administration, College Park, Md.

EB	Entertainment Branch, U.S. Army Vietnam Special Services Agency
MACV IG	Military Assistance Command Vietnam Inspector General
MACV IO	Military Assistance Command Vietnam Information Office
MPPD	Military Personnel Policy Division, U.S. Army Vietnam Deputy Chief of Staff for Personnel and Administration
MWB	Morale and Welfare Branch, Military Personnel Policy Division, U.S. Army Vietnam Deputy Chief of Staff for Personnel and Administration
NFD	Non-appropriated Funds Division, U.S. Army Vietnam Deputy Chief of Staff for Personnel and Administration
ORLLS	Operational Reports—Lessons Learned, U.S. Army Vietnam Command Historian
USARV AG	U.S. Army Vietnam Adjutant General
USARV CH	U.S. Army Vietnam Command Historian
USARV IG	U.S. Army Vietnam Inspector General
USARV IO	U.S. Army Vietnam Information Office
USARV PMS	U.S. Army Vietnam Provost Marshall Section

INTRODUCTION

1. Kiver, *182 Days in Iraq*, 103.

2. Ibid.

3. Neither the U.S. military nor historians have settled on a uniform set of statistics indicating what percentage of U.S. military personnel in Vietnam experienced combat. John J. McGrath's "The Other End of the Spear: The Tooth-to-Tail Ratio (T3) in Modern Military Operations" is an outlier with its argument that the U.S. Army fielded a force with 35 percent combat troops in Vietnam. McGrath acknowledges that most scholars agree that only 10 to 25 percent of U.S. forces were combat troops, and his figures exclude other branches of the service, especially the Navy, Air Force, and Coast Guard,

which had much higher proportions of support personnel. McGrath, "The Other End of the Spear," 28–32. See also Appy, *Working-Class War*, 167.

4. "Headquarters and Headquarters Company 34th General Support Group Briefing Book for Newly-Assigned Personnel," USARV IO (ellipsis in caption in the original).

5. Andrews, Elliott, and Levin, *Vietnam*, 61.

6. See, for example, Herring, *America's Longest War*, 182.

7. An eighth woman died as a result of combat, from shrapnel wounds incurred during a rocket attack on her base. The other seven women died as a result of disease or air accidents not caused by combat.

8. Dunn, *Desk Warrior*, xi.

9. For discussions of postwar consumer culture and abundance, see Cohen, *Consumer's Republic*; Hine, *Populuxe*; Potter, *People of Plenty*; and Yarrow, "Visions of Abundance."

10. Baritz, *Backfire*, 288–89, 299–300; Kinnard, *War Managers*, 110–11; McMaster, *Dereliction of Duty*, 327–28, 332–33.

11. Baritz, *Backfire*, 288–89.

12. The all-volunteer force is not a true mercenary army, like those of early modern Europe, because the U.S. military affords its members civil liberties and due process (though not to the same extent as their civilian counterparts) and because patriotism and a sense of duty still motivate individuals to join. And yet twenty-first-century military personnel with Special Forces training—U.S. Navy SEALs and Green Berets, for example—have also found that they can sell their service at a much higher rate to private military contractors, which then send them to war alongside professional soldiers hired from other countries. This current iteration of the mercenary casts the individual soldier as a worker who, with the right set of skills, may contract his or her labor to the highest bidder.

13. For a sample of these antiprofiteering cartoons and of underground G.I. newspapers in general, see the companion Web site to the 2005 documentary *Sir! No Sir!*, which contains a gallery of cartoons titled "Corporate Interests and the Power Elite," http://www.sirnosir.com/archives_and_resources/galleries/cartoon_pages/corporation.html (1 April 2009).

14. Ronald Reagan, first inaugural address, 20 January 1981; Appy, *Working-Class War*, 9.

15. For a narrative of the My Lai incident, see Bilton and Sim, *Four Hours in My Lai*. For a discussion of the Winter Soldier Hearings, see Nicosia, *Home to War*, 73–97, and Hunt, *The Turning*, 68–76.

16. For a critique of the Winter Soldier hearings that reflects this point of view, see Burkett and Whitley, *Stolen Valor*, 130–38.

17. Quoted in Broyles, *Brothers in Arms*, 95.

18. "U.S. Soldiers in Vietnam an Army of Noncombatants," *New York Times*, 1 July 1972, 3. For a discussion of escalation and withdrawal, see Clodfelter, *Vietnam in Military Statistics*, 248–59.

19. See, for example, Marshall, *In the Combat Zone*; Walker, *Piece of My Heart*; and Vuic, *Officer, Nurse, Woman*.

20. This thesis has long been a staple of the Vietnam War's discourse, but it is

not without its critics. For discussions of Vietnam as a working-class war, see Appy, *Working-Class War*; Baskir and Strauss, *Chance and Circumstance*; and Fallows, "What Did You Do in the Class War, Daddy?" In 1992, Arnold Barnett, Timothy Stanley, and Michael Shore published a statistical study that argued that poor and working-class Americans were not overrepresented in the ranks sent to Vietnam, a thesis that James Fallows then persuasively rebutted. See Barnett, Stanley, and Shore, "America's Vietnam Casualties," and Fallows, "Low-Class Conclusions."

21. Kiver, *182 Days in Iraq*, 103.

CHAPTER 1

1. Jury, *Vietnam Photo Book*, 47.

2. "Two Americans Dead in Saigon Bombing," *New York Times*, 10 February 1964, 1; "Many Are Injured; Bomb in Vietnam Rips U.S. Embassy," *New York Times*, 30 March 1965, 1.

3. Willson, *REMF Diary*, 41.

4. "Officials in U.S. Irked by Report of Low Ratio of Combat Troops," *New York Times*, 13 July 1967, 16; "Pentagon Rebuts Assertions of $10.8 Billion in 'Fat,'" *Congressional Quarterly*, 20 September 1968, 2483.

5. "Officials in U.S. Irked by Report of Low Ratio of Combat Troops."

6. "U.S. Soldiers in Vietnam an Army of Noncombatants," *New York Times*, 1 July 1972, 3.

7. Dunn, *Desk Warrior*, 41; Yarborough, *Da Nang Diary*, 9.

8. Watson, *Voices from the Rear*, 118.

9. "Social Worker, Dog Doctor, News Editor, Canvasman," *Rendezvous with Destiny*, Summer 1969, 30–31.

10. "The Paper War . . . and the Battle of Boredom," *First Team*, Fall 1969, 25–28; "MOS Close-up: Clerks Are 'Typed' Cast," *Army Reporter*, 28 June 1971, 11.

11. Jury, *Vietnam Photo Book*, 58–60.

12. Dunn took his Ph.D. in history. Dunn, *Desk Warrior*, 109; "Unit Party Is Smashing Success," *Short-Timers Gazette*, 21 May 1969.

13. "U.S. Acts to Ease Saigon Overcrowding," *New York Times*, 7 October 1966, 15.

14. Ibid.; "Private Firm Builds Warehouse," *Informer*, 30 March 1969, 10; "Just Like Home: In Vietnam the Place to Be As War Rages On Is Luxurious Long Binh," *Wall Street Journal*, 1 May 1972, 1; untitled routing and transmittal slip, 3 May 1972; "Adequacy of After-Duty Hours Bus Service on LBP"; "Long Binh Post Bus Service," 9 November 1971. The last three documents are in the General Records of MWB.

15. Dunn, *Desk Warrior*, 43.

16. "Operational Report for Quarterly Period Ending 31 July 1967," ORLLS.

17. "Recreational Facility Status as of 1 JAN, 1 APR, and 1 JUL 71," MWB.

18. "Sandlot Sebring Roars into Long Binh," *Hi-Lite* (newspaper), January 1972, 4–5; "Go-Karts," *Hi-Lite Magazine*, Winter–Spring 1972, 20–21; "Go Cart Races" and "Rules and Standards for Go-Cart and Motorcycle Races," MWB. Go-cart tracks were also present on a U.S. Marine base near Danang and at Camp Eagle, home to the 101st Airborne Division. See "Wermter Takes Prize in Second Annual Memorial Day 'Da

Nang 500,'" *Sea Tiger*, 8 June 1967, 6–7, and "Karts Get Green Light," *Army Reporter*, 7 December 1970, 8.

19. Long Binh was not even the largest open mess system in Vietnam; the one at Qui Nhon included fifty-four separate annexes. "IG Investigation of the USARV Open Mess System," 7 August 1969, "Report of Investigation of the USARV Open Mess System," 17 August 1969, and "IG Investigation of the Qui Nhon Officer and NCO Open Mess Associations," 9 July 1969, all in files of the USARV IG.

20. Dunn, *Desk Warrior*, 43; "Just Like Home"; Larry Green, "Pullout Won't Halt Cash for G.I. Play Sites," article in unidentified periodical, General Administrative Records, 1968, EB.

21. "Major Recreation Projects," June 1970, MWB.

22. "Pullout Won't Halt Cash for G.I. Play Sites"; "Recreational Facility Status as of 1 JAN, 1 APR, 1 JUL 71."

23. USARV Memorandum No. 210-4, "Installations: Nature of War Museum," 29 August 1969, USARV CH; "V.C. Village 'Discovered' at USARV HQ," *Army Reporter*, 11 October 1971, 10.

24. "Maintenance of the Nature of the War Museum," Memo from Capt. D. Meyerson, 16th Military History Detachment, HQUSARV, to HQ Commandant, Long Binh Post, 13 September 1971, USARV CH.

25. Anderson, *Vietnam*, 7; Upton, *Pizza and Mortars*, 242; Wiknik, *Nam Sense*, 184; Sgt. Tom Fitzharris to Peter Widulski, 21 May 1970, in Edelman, *Dear America*, 157–58.

26. *Long Binh Post*, 3 August 1971, 9 November 1971.

27. Willson, *REMF Diary*, 5; Dunn, *Desk Warrior*, 43; "Long Bing [sic], USA.???????????" *Guardians & Enforcers*, September 1969, 2.

28. USARV Supplement No. 1, "Courtesy Patrols," to MACV Directive No. 10-4, "Transportation and Security for E.X. Merchandise," NFD.

29. Jury, *Vietnam Photo Book*, 58.

30. "Cooks and Clerks Learn the Infantrymen's Trade First Hand," *Southern Cross*, 3 September 1969, 4–5.

31. "Grunts, Remfs Give Each Other Some Joy," *Army Reporter*, 11 January 1971, 10.

32. Dunn, *Desk Warrior*, 90–92.

33. "Clerk Wanders Right into Action," *Observer*, 9 August 1971, 1.

34. Back cover to Leninger, *Time Heals No Wounds*.

35. Muehlberg, *REMF "War Stories,"* 149, 259; Upton, *Pizza and Mortars*, 173–74; Watson, *Voices from the Rear*, 111.

36. Whalon, *Saigon Zoo*, 195.

37. Willson, *REMF Returns*, 44.

38. Anderson, *Vietnam*, 33.

39. Whalon, *Saigon Zoo*, 105, 117, 126, 213, 227–40.

40. Willson, *REMF Diary*, 82.

41. "The Grunt—It Was His War," *Army Reporter*, 24 April 1970, 10.

42. "Our Sky Pilot," *Professional*, 3 December 1969, 10.

43. Victor David Westphall III to Doug Westphall, n.d. but between October 1967 and May 1968, in Edelman, *Dear America*, 84–85.

44. Muehlberg, *REMF "War Stories,"* 200–202.

45. Heiser, *Vietnam Studies*, vi.

46. "Dear Nguyen," *Octagon*, June 1969, 9.

47. Members of Delta Company, 3/21, 196th Light Infantry Brigade, American Division, to President Nixon, 20 April 1969, in Edelman, *Dear America*, 139.

48. Lt. Col. (Ret.) John H. Funston, "Extra Pay for Riflemen," letter to the editor, *New York Times*, 16 December 1970, 46.

49. "U.S. Cuts Allowance for Vietnam G.I.'s; Deems It Justified," *New York Times*, 9 March 1967, 5.

50. "Troop Recreation," memo from Commanding General, II Field Force Vietnam, to Commanding General, USARV, 3 February 1971, MWB.

51. Broyles, *Brothers in Arms*, 131–32.

52. Appy, *Working-Class War*, 26. Appy cites the Veterans' Administration study *Myths and Realities: A Study of Attitudes toward Vietnam Era Veterans*.

53. I have not located any official records that acknowledge the existence of the watch list. However, Mark Jury addresses the phenomenon in *The Vietnam Photo Book*, 49.

54. "MOS Close-up: Dog's No Problem in 'Nam," *Army Reporter*, 27 September 1971, 11; "MOS Close-up: All the World's a Stage," *Army Reporter*, 4 October 1971, 11; "MOS Close-up: Clerks Are 'Typed' Cast," 11.

55. "Corps Special Services Office Busy Place: Provides Off-Time Activities, Facilities," *Delta Advisor*, September 1968, 2; "A Different War in Here," *Sea Tiger*, 4 December 1970, 4–5; "Barrels, Bolts, Bread 'n Butter," *First Team*, Winter 1970, 19–21.

56. "Paper War . . . and the Battle of Boredom"; "Lifeguard's Job Not an Easy One," *Southern Cross*, 4 June 1971, 8. This last article reported that two U.S. Army lifeguards at Chu Lai had saved ten swimmers in six months.

57. Broyles, *Brothers in Arms*, 131–32.

58. Savile Lumley, "Daddy, What Did YOU Do in the Great War?" The poster is reprinted in *What Did You Do in the War, Daddy? A Visual History of Propaganda Posters*, 44–45.

59. "What Did You Do in the War, Daddy?" *Kysu*, Summer 1970, inside back cover.

60. "And the Rockets Red Glare," *Traffic Lite*, 15 March 1969, 1, 6.

61. "PFC Remf," drawn by William Coulter, *Hi-Lite Magazine*, Winter–Spring 1970, inside back cover.

62. "Silver Paper Clip: Combat Clerk Cops Citation," *Army Reporter*, 24 August 1970, 8.

63. Muehlberg, *REMF "War Stories,"* 39; Dunn, *Desk Warrior*, ix.

64. Department of the Army Poster 360-119, "The Soldier in Vietnam"; a copy of the modified version is in the personal files of the author.

65. SP4 Rob Riggan to his father, 17 June 1969, in Edelman, *Dear America*, 165–67 (brackets in the original published text).

66. Muehlberg, *REMF "War Stories,"* 244; Watson, *Voices from the Rear*, 124–26.

67. "It Only Takes One," *Professionals*, 4 October 1969, 3.

68. "R&R Spent 'Eating Jungle,'" *Castle Courier*, 23 March 1970, 6.

69. SP4 Rob Riggan to his father, 17 June 1969.

70. Thomas Giltner, quoted in Bergerud, *Red Thunder, Tropic Lightning*, 279.

71. Members of Delta Company to President Nixon, 29 April 1969.

72. Moskos, "American Combat Soldier in Vietnam."

73. "McKissic's Corner," *Syke's Regulars Reporter*, 28 January 1970, 1.

74. "A Rear Job for the Grunt?" *Southern Cross*, 23 July 1971, 2.

75. "Fact or Wish??" *Professional*, 3 December 1969, 1.

76. See Dunnigan and Nofi, "The Enduring Myths of the Vietnam War," in *Dirty Little Secrets of the Vietnam War*, 1–24; Burkett and Whitley, *Stolen Valor*; and Lembcke, *Spitting Image*. In July 2010, a federal judge found the Stolen Valor Act to be unconstitutional.

77. Nicosia, *Home to War*, 17 (emphasis in the original).

78. Leed, *No Man's Land*, 204.

79. For discussions of these efforts, see Nicosia, *Home to War*; Severo and Milford, *Wages of War*, 345–426; and Bonior, Champlin, and Kolly, *Vietnam Veteran*.

80. For discussions of the development of the G.I. Movement, see Moser, *New Winter Soldiers*; Nicosia, *Home to War*; Cortright and Watts, *Left Face*; and Lewes, *Protest and Survive*, 51–80.

81. Moser, *New Winter Soldiers*, 88.

82. Nicosia, *Home to War*, 18, 24.

83. Ibid., 19–22.

84. Wiknik, *Nam Sense*, 133.

85. Hoffman, "Grunt's Dream."

86. Wheatley, "Hello, and Welcome! . . . Who Am I?" and "What Motivated Me to Establish Viet-REMF?"

87. Billy Ray Cyrus and Cindy Cyrus, "Some Gave All," 1992.

CHAPTER 2

1. Lair, "Tour of Duty."

2. "Vietnam War Museum Shifts Focus to Soldiers," *New York Times*, 10 December 1997, B7; "After Fighting Its Own Battles, a Museum Opens," *New York Times*, 27 September 1998, 14NJ.

3. For a discussion of the mythology surrounding Valley Forge, see Bodle, *Valley Forge Winter*, especially "The Myth and the Map." For discussions of the Revolutionary War's role in the American foundation myth, see Purcell, *Sealed with Blood*, and Kammen, *Season of Youth*. For a discussion of Valley Forge's role in developing a separate American identity, see Lair, "Redcoat Theater."

4. Carter, *Inventing Vietnam*, 5–19, 155.

5. J. A. Jones Construction emerged from the Vietnam War as the largest construction firm in the United States, while Brown and Root eventually became Kellogg, Brown, and Root (later shortened to KBR), which fulfilled military construction contracts in Kosovo, Afghanistan, and Iraq. "South Viet Nam toward Negotiation," *Time*, June 1966, http://www.time.com/time/magazine/article/0,9171,899256,00.html (9 August 2010); "GAO Unable to Trace Vast Supplies for War," *Washington Post*, 5 June 1971, A18; "Epic Era Ends: Another Viet Pullout—Now, the Hard Hats," *Los Angeles Times*, 4 July 1972, A1.

6. Joint Logistics Review Board, *Logistic Support in the Vietnam Era*, 4; *Logistics Review*, 14; Dunn, *Vietnam Studies*, 113.

7. *Logistics Review*, 19.

8. During World War II, 325,000 Seabees (combat engineers) erected more than 400 advance bases, 111 major airstrips, 441 piers, hospitals with 70,000 beds, and housing for 1.5 million men in the Pacific theater alone. See Tregaskis, *Building the Bases*, 53.

9. Melbourne, *Advance Base Construction by Civilian Contractors in War Zones*, 356; Heiser, *Vietnam Studies*, 17.

10. "Civilian in the Combat Zone," *Kysu*, Spring 1969, 16–18. About 300 private contractors operated in South Vietnam during the war. The vast majority of them were U.S. firms, and a handful of those fulfilled a majority of the contracts. In addition to construction consortium RMK-BRJ, the largest firms included facilities engineering and maintenance firm PA&E (Pacific Architects and Engineers), which helped to design and maintain those properties; Vinnel Corporation, which erected power plants; refrigerated cargo shipper Sea Land Corporation; and electronics manufacturer Philco Ford, which provided technical assistance for electronics to units in the war zone.

11. *Logistics Review*, 8:2.

12. "Plywood Joining Vietnam War," *New York Times*, 19 April 1966, 55; *Logistics Review*, 18–9.

13. "Camp Enari: A City Born of Necessity," *Esprit*, Summer 1970, 18–21.

14. "Dong Tam," *Octofoil*, Summer 1968, 36; "Building Boom Hits Dong Tam," *Octofoil*, Fall 1968, 15–19; "Largest Base in Delta Nears Completion," *Delta Developer*, 21 April 1969, 3; "93rd Inherits Ghost Town," *Delta Developer*, 6 October 1969, 3.

15. 2nd Lt. Frederick Downs Jr. to Linda Downs, 5 November 1967, and 1st Lt. Alan Bourne to Christina Haskin, 30 January 1968, in Edelman, *Dear America*, 10, 34–36.

16. "Nui Ba Den—Lonely Outpost," *Blackjack Flier*, 1 May 1968, 3.

17. MACV Directive 30-2, "Food Program: Mess Operations," 24 May 1969, Investigation Division Reports, MACV IG; "Food for the Fighting Man Is Log's Business," *Vietnam Review*, November 1967, 9, 12.

18. "Nothing Is Too Good for the Troops," *1st Logistical Command Magazine*, April 1968, 20; "Food for the Fighting Man Is Log's Business," 9, 12.

19. "Culinary Art It's Not, but Best in the Boonies," *First Team*, Winter 1970, 27–29. See also Heiser, *Vietnam Studies*, 203.

20. "1st Log Provides Many Services," *1st Logistical Command Magazine*, April 1968, 24; "Real Fresh Bread!" *Vietnam Review*, June 1968, 9; "Lots o' Dough," *Cavalair*, 8 December 1970, 4–5.

21. "FLC Bakery School Students Turn Out Delectable Pastries," *Sea Tiger*, 17 April 1970, 4.

22. "Nothing Is Too Good for the Troops," 21.

23. "Ice Plant Revamps, Ups Production," *PA&E News*, 15 February 1971, 3.

24. "Cool It, the Depot Way!" *Hi-Lite Magazine*, Winter 1970, 20–21; "84th Completes Warehouse—Largest U.S. Built Structure in Vietnam," *Frontier Courier*, 29 July 1969, 1.

25. "Nothing Is Too Good for the Troops," 20.

26. "Milk and Ice Cream . . . Real Morale Boosters," *1st Logistical Command Mag-*

azine, 25; "Getting (Real) Milk to the Field," *Vietnam Review*, November 1968, 1, 3; "Filled Milk—with What?" *Brigadier*, 1 April 1969, 2.

27. *Cà phê sữa đá* (milk coffee with ice) is practically Vietnam's national beverage. Both the coffee and the key ingredient, sweetened condensed milk, were introduced by the French during the colonial period. "Foremost Dairies Opens Product Plant in Saigon," *New York Times*, 9 September 1965, 61; "Business in Saigon Is Red Tape, Frustration—and Profit," *New York Times*, 18 January 1971, 54.

28. "Long Binh Depot 'Cools It' for Soldiers in the Field," *Hi-Lite Magazine*, Autumn 1968, 10–11; "Plant Provides Lickin' Good Ice Cream," *Northern Log*, 12 April 1969, 5; "Ice Cream Made in a Motor Pool?" *Qui Nhon Logman*, April 1970, 3; "Log Floats Ice Cream in the Delta," *Vietnam Review*, September 1968, 2.

29. "SUPCOM Gets Donut Shop," *Northern Log*, 15 January 1972, 7.

30. "Nothing Is Too Good for the Troops," 20; "Food for the Fighting Man Is Log's Business," 9, 12.

31. Adams, *Noise That Never Dies*, 26; Broyles, *Brothers in Arms*, 132.

32. Watson, *Voices from the Rear*, 130.

33. "Your Health: Physical Fitness," *Griffin Gab*, 25 April 1969, 3; "You and Your Waistline," *Griffin Gab*, 25 May 1969, 5, 11.

34. Heiser, *Vietnam Studies*, 17; *Logistics Review*, 8:17.

35. Edwin Simmons, quoted in Broyles, *Brothers in Arms*, 172.

36. Heiser, *Vietnam Studies*, 189; Dunn, *Vietnam Studies*, 46.

37. MACV Directive No. 210-3, "Installations: Billeting Policy (RCS: MACJ1-48)," 28 July 1970, Investigation Division Reports, MACV IG.

38. Watson, *Voices from the Rear*, 106–7; Muehlberg, *REMF "War Stories,"* 43.

39. *Logistics Review*, 7:5, 23.

40. Ibid., 7:17.

41. "Installations: Billeting Policy," 17 June 1969, Inspection and Complaint Division, USARV IG.

42. Anderson, *Vietnam*, 31–32.

43. "Vietnamese Modern: Five Build DMZ Mansion," *Eliminators*, 1 August 1969, 3.

44. "At Pump Station: Bunker Is a 'Manhattan Townhouse,'" *Qui Nhon Logman*, October 1969, 3; "Bunker Décor: What the Bon Vivant of the Boondocks Has Done with Sandbags and Ingenuity," *Esprit*, Spring 1970, 14–15.

45. Ellis, *Eye-Deep in Hell*, 19–20; Pyle, *Here Is Your War*, 133–35.

46. Heiser, *Vietnam Studies*, 45.

47. Schurr et al., *Electricity in the American Economy*, 251, 256, 259, 262. See also Wattenberg, *Statistical History of the United States from Colonial Times to the Present*, 827.

48. Heiser, *Vietnam Studies*, 45.

49. Summary of Investigation/Inquiry/Inspection: Headquarters, 101st Airborne Division, 8–11 January 1968, Inspection and Complaints Division, USARV IG.

50. "Electrical Hazards," 17 May 1972, MWB.

51. The 1960 field manual defined morale as "the attitude of individuals toward military life and everything associated with it," while the 1968 and 1972 field manuals declined to define morale at all. Their discussions of morale focused solely on the fac-

tors that influenced it. Department of the Army Field Manual FM 101–01, *Staff Officers Field Manual*, 82; Department of the Army Field Manual FM 101-5, *Staff Officers Field Manual: Staff Organization and Procedure*, 88.

52. Jack S. Swender to his family, 20 September 1965, in Edelman, *Dear America*, 213.

53. Volunteers were given more discretion over what branch of service they entered, what kind of job they would be assigned, and sometimes their duty station. "Army Is Shaken by Crisis in Morale and Discipline," *New York Times*, 5 September 1971, 1, 36; Foley, *Confronting the War Machine*, 309. See also Baskir and Strauss, *Chance and Circumstance*, 3–13.

54. Baskir and Strauss, *Chance and Circumstance*, 8–10; Broyles, *Brothers in Arms*, 135; *Gallup Poll*, 2017.

55. Lewes, *Protest and Survive*, 4.

56. "Void for Servicemen," in "G.I. Rights and the Constitution," *Sir! No Sir!* companion Web site http://www.sirnosir.com/archives_and_resources/galleries/cartoon_pages/constitution.html (10 August 2010); Lisa Lyons, "The Evolution of a Lifer," *Gigline*, April 1970, 12; "Eat Shit for Four Years," artist unknown, *Duck Power*, 4 October 1969, 3. The last two cartoons are reprinted in Lewes, *Protest and Survive*, 113–14.

57. Broyles, *Brothers in Arms*, 174 (italics mine).

58. *Staff Officers Field Manual*, 83.

59. See Kuzmarov, *Myth of the Addicted Army*. Kuzmarov privileges internal military studies of the drug problem conducted during the war, which suggest usage rates of 40 percent or less, over subsequent civilian reports that, Kuzmarov argues, inflated usage rates to 90 percent for a variety of social and political purposes.

60. Cortright, *Soldiers in Revolt*, 28–49, 267.

61. For example, Project 100,000 resulted in 240,000 soldiers being inducted into the military, but only 6 percent of them received the additional training that was supposed to render them equivalent to troops admitted under normal guidelines. The program netted 400,000 troops overall, almost half of whom were sent to Vietnam. Appy, *Working-Class War*, 32–33.

62. "Army Is Shaken by Crisis In Morale and Discipline," 1.

63. Bailey, *America's Army*, 1–33.

64. General William Westmoreland, "Presentation to Officers and NCOs," MWB.

65. "Promoting the Volunteer Army," MWB.

66. "The Mickey Mouse War," *Newsweek*, 14 December 1970.

67. "Military Discipline: Ebbing Morale of Men at War," *Congressional Quarterly*, 19 February 1972, 393.

68. Baritz, *Backfire*, 299–300. To be fair, junior officers suffered some of the highest casualty rates in Vietnam, so Baritz would do well to single out general officers and perhaps colonels who made command decisions from the vantage point of helicopters hovering over a battle or from offices far in the rear.

69. Pfc. Armand R. Heroux Jr. to President Nixon, 9 August 1969, in "Report of Inquiry Concerning Alleged Irregularities within B Company, 2d Battalion, 14th Infantry, 28 August–6 September 1969," USARV IG.

70. "Inspector General Action Requests: Edelburg, William, December 1970–July 1971," USARV IG.

71. "List of Complaints and Requests for Assistance from Personnel of U.S. Army Depot, Cam Ranh Bay, 15–16 December 1969," in "Summary of Investigation/Inquiry/ Inspection: U.S. Army Depot, Cam Ranh Bay, 15–17 December 1969," USARV IG.

72. "Report of Inquiry Concerning the Circumstances Surrounding the Apparent Discrepancy Which Existed between the Issue and Receipt of Fresh Meats in the 9th Infantry Division, 1 November 1968–12 June 1969," USARV IG.

73. "The Men of Battery A, 7th Battalion, 8th Field Artillery" to President Nixon, in "I.G. Investigation/Inquiry/Summary: Report of Investigation of Conditions within Battery A, 7th Battalion, 8th Artillery, 19 February–31 March 1970," USARV IG.

74. "Summary of Investigation/Inquiry/Inspection: 384th Quartermaster Detachment, 1st Logistical Command, Da Nang, 1 September 1968," USARV IG.

75. Mrs. Alan Robertson to General Stanley A. Resor, Secretary of the Army, 27 January 1970, in "Report of Inquiry Related to Alleged Food Shortage at Fire Base Tuffy"; Mrs. George L. Anderson to Senator Mark O. Hatfield, in "White House Inquiry: Team 67 Rations," both in Investigation Reports, MACV IG.

76. "Report of Inquiry Related to Alleged Food Shortage at Fire Base Tuffy"; "White House Inquiry."

77. Broyles, *Brothers in Arms*, 144.

78. "Dear Hugh," *Fireball Express*, May 1970, 8.

79. These generalizations are the result of extensive research into the following records: General Records, 1968–1972, MWB; General Records, Plans and Operations Division, USARV PMS; and Complaints Files—Administrative, Investigations and Complaints Division Reports, MACV IG.

80. These descriptions are based on actual complaints from the Case Files, Inspection and Complaint Division, USARV IG, and the Investigation Division Reports and the Investigations and Complaints Division Reports of MACV IG.

81. "List of Complaints and Requests for Assistance from Personnel of U.S. Army Depot, Cam Ranh Bay, 15–16 December 1969."

82. For a discussion of Wayne's meaning in American culture, see Wills, *John Wayne's America*.

83. Veterans' allusions to John Wayne have been noted by many scholars. See Kinney, "Indian Country Revisited: The Persistence of John Wayne," in *Friendly Fire*, 11–42; Moser, *New Winter Soldiers*, 30; Appy, *Working-Class War*, 60–62, 75, 125; and Longley, *Grunts*, 24–26.

84. Appy, *Working-Class War*, 119.

85. Dunn, *Desk Warrior*, 39.

86. "G.I.s Arriving in Vietnam Find War Begins with Punch Cards," *New York Times*, 28 June 1969, 3.

87. "Remember When?" *Scars and Gripes*, August 1969, 4; "Impressions of an FNG," *Cavalair*, 6 May 1970, 6; Muehlberg, *REMF "War Stories,"* 15.

88. Mosse, *Nationalism and Sexuality*, 114.

89. Watson, *When Soldiers Quit*, 19.

90. For a discussion of Vietnam as a locus of gender negotiation in American culture, see Jeffords, *Remasculinization of America*.

91. Herr, *Dispatches*, 98; Kevin Macaulay to his parents, 29 January 1968, in Edelman, *Dear America*, 60.

92. O'Brien, *Things They Carried*, 84. See also Taylor, "Cacciato's Grassy Hill"; Meyers, "Fragmentary Mosaics"; and Zinman, "Search and Destroy."

CHAPTER 3

1. Ho Chi Minh to French scholar and journalist Paul Mus, on the eve of the Franco-Vietminh War, in Halberstam, *Ho*, 84.

2. North Vietnam did derive material support and military advice from China during the latter years of the Franco-Vietminh War, and both China and the Soviet Union provided material support during the American War. Despite the aid, North Vietnamese soldiers still had to forage for food on the march in South Vietnam, and only a small proportion of foreign aid ever reached the NLF. "MACV J-2 Logistics Fact Book," 1 June 1967, 13, 16, 19–20, MHI; Heiser, *Vietnam Studies*, 263.

3. Page, *Another Vietnam*, 138–39, 176–77; "No More Picnics: V.C. R&R Site Is Shut Down," *Ivy Leaf*, 4 October 1970, 8.

4. "Homecoming for Viet Veterans: Apathy, Hostility," *Los Angeles Times*, 20 October 1968, A1.

5. "Troop Recreation," 3 February 1971, memo from the Commanding General, II Field Force Vietnam, to the Commanding General, USARV, Vung Tau Recreational Facility (1971), MWB.

6. MACV Directive No. 28-3, "Welfare, Recreation, and Morale: R&R Activities Out-of-Country," 20 July 1969, Investigation Division Reports, MACV IG.

7. USARV Command Information Fact Sheet No. 7-66, "Your R&R Program," 7 June 1966; MACV Command Information Pamphlet No. 13-67, "Your R&R Program," April 1967, both in MHI.

8. Guam was also available for American military personnel of Guamanian descent, and soldiers with immediate family residing on Okinawa could travel there. "Welfare, Recreation, and Morale: R&R Activities Out-of-Country;" Fact Sheet: "R&R Programs," 13 June 1972, in "G1 Conference Fact Sheets," General Records, Administrative Services Division, USARV AG.

9. "Estimate of R&R Airfare," *Tropic Lightning News*, 26 October 1970, 3; "The Commander Speaks," *Triumvirate*, 28 February 1970, 3.

10. USARV Command Information Fact Sheet No. 7-66, "Your R&R Program"; "Your Bag Is Packed, You're Ready to Go," *Army Reporter*, 18 October 1971, 10–11.

11. Numbers were available only for July 1970 through December 1971, with a gap for May and June 1971. "USARV Morale Indicators," MWB.

12. "China Beach: In-Country R&R," *Thunder*, Fall–Winter 1970, 34–36; "China Beach Open," *Red Devil Brigade*, 17 August 1970, 3; "China Beach Success Story Involves Sun, Sand, Surf," *Army Reporter*, 21 September 1970, 6–7.

13. "Vung Tau, Center of Sun and Surf," *Army Reporter*, 6 January 1969, 12.

14. "China Beach R&R Site to Open," *Northern Log*, 15 May 1970, 1, 8.

15. "China Beach R&R Site to Open"; "China Beach Open"; "China Beach Success

Story Involves Sun, Sand, and Surf"; "A Little Bit of Heaven," *Uptight*, Fall 1970, 45–47; "Vung Tau, Center of Sun and Surf"; "Surf's Up at Vung Tau!" *Hi-Lite Magazine*, August 1969, 16–17; "New Vung Tau R&R Center Awaits You," *Army Reporter*, 17 April 1971, 6–7; "Trip Report—Staff Liaison Visit to Da Nang Area R&R and Recreation Facilities," November 1971, MWB.

16. "Surf's Up at Vung Tau!"; "Vung Tau, Center of Sun and Surf."

17. "Bien Hoa VIP Center Great Morale Builder," *Cavalair*, 8 April 1970, 4–5.

18. "'Popsmoke' Means Stand-Down," *Uptight*, Winter 1969, 46–47.

19. "A Place in the Sun," *Thunder*, Fall 1969, 2–5.

20. "Trip Report—Staff Liaison Visit to Da Nang Area R&R and Recreation Facilities."

21. "Eagle Beach Is All-Right," *Colt 45 News*, 15 August 1969, 6; "Eagle Beach," *Rendezvous with Destiny*, Winter–Spring 1971, 26–27; "Sky Soldier Beach—The Fighting Man's Resort," *Firebase 173*, 20 July 1970, 4–5.

22. "R&R for a Day in Qui Nhon," *Qui Nhon Logman*, September 1970, 4–5.

23. War Department Film Bulletin No. 155, "Special Services in Action," 1944, Army Pictorial Service/Signal Corps, Record Group 111, Records of the Office of the Chief Signal Officer, NARA.

24. "High Morale: Aim of Special Services," *Sea Tiger*, 27 February 1970, 8; "Beer, Barbells, Baseball: Vietnam MPs Fill Off-Duty Hours," *Roundup*, July 1970, 8.

25. MACV Directive No. 28-5, "Welfare, Recreation, and Morale—Special Service Activities," NFD.

26. "Historical Resume, Entertainment Activities," in "Organization and Functions Manual: United States Army in Vietnam Special Services Agency (Provisional)," March 1970, History Files, 1970–1972, EB.

27. The fiscal year ran from 1 February to 31 January, so there is a gap in available budget figures for the period August 1967 to January 1968. "Headquarters 1st Logistical Command; Debriefing Report," Senior Officer Debriefing Reports, USARV CH; Fact Sheet: "Special Services Funds," 20 April 1969, MWB; "Special Services Expenditures by Source of Funds and by Command," Second 6 Months FY71, MWB.

28. MACV Directive No. 28-5, "Welfare, Recreation, and Morale—Special Services Activities."

29. "Senior Officer Debriefing of Colonel Gilbert P. Levy, 27 July 1966 to 1 July 1967," Senior Officer Debriefing Reports, USARV CH; Facilities Review Board, 2 June 1972, NFD; "Distribution of Special Services Facilities," 30 June 1971, MPPD; "Morale and Welfare Activities," 31 May 1971, MPPD; "Special Services Available in Pleiku Area," 11 February 1971, MPPD.

30. "Golf Shop Run by Cpl," *Sea Tiger*, 3 April 1970, 7; "Fore!!!!," *Castle Courier*, 30 November 1970, 6–7; "Golf Anyone?" *Long Binh Post*, 9 November 1971, 8; "Special Services," 9 July 1971, MPPD.

31. The existence of this bowling alley is denied in documents reacting to negative publicity in the American press, but it is clearly depicted on maps of the base. Map of Long Binh Post, MPPD.

32. "Special SVCs Aids the Bowler," *USAHAC Command Newsletter*, May 1969, 7;

"USAHAC Special Services SOP: Bowling Center," Investigation Division Reports, MACV IG.

33. "When It Comes to Recreation Try Chu Lai Special Services," *Sea Tiger*, 8 March 1967; "War Zone Recreation Provides Spare Time Entertainment," *Steadfast and Loyal*, 3 August 1969, 4–5; "Headquarters and Headquarters Company 34th General Support Group Briefing Book for Newly-Assigned Personnel," USARV IO; "Morale and Welfare Activities," 31 May 1971, MPPD.

34. "USAHAC Special Services SOP: Swimming Pool," Investigation Division Reports, MACV IG.

35. "Operational Report for Quarterly Period Ending 31 July 1967, USASUPCOM, Saigon," ORLLS; "Memorandum: Special Services Budget," 9 May 1969, NFD.

36. "Special Services Available in Pleiku Area."

37. "USAHAC Opens New Swimming Pool," *USAHAC Command Newsletter*, November 1969, 8; "Recreational Facility Status as of 1 JAN, 1 APR, and 1 JUL 71," MPPD.

38. Department of the Army Pamphlet No. 28-5, *Facility Management Guide: The Army Crafts Program*.

39. "Dong Tam Craft Shop Offers Woodworking and Oil Painting," *Old Reliable*, 4 October 1967, 7; "Craft Shop Opens for Shutterbug," *Army Reporter*, 17 February 1969, 11; "Craft Shop—Something for Everyone," *Southern Cross*, 11 June 1971, 4; "Fact Sheet: USARV Crafts Program Photography Capabilities," MPPD; "Arts and Crafts Contest," *USAHAC Command Newsletter*, December 1969, 8.

40. "Special Services Agency Conference," 14 July 1970, General Administrative Records, EB; "'Crafty' Idea for Isolated G.I.'s," *Castle Courier*, 15 June 1970, 2.

41. "Summary of Special Service Facilities," NFD; "Special Services Facilities," NFD; "Organization and Functions Manual: United States Army Vietnam Special Services Agency (Provisional)"; "Distribution of Special Services Facilities"; "Fact Sheet: USARV Crafts Program Photography Capabilities."

42. "Special Services: Have Library, Will Travel," *44th Brigadier*, December 1969, 1; "A Touch of Home in 'Nam," *Hi-Lite Magazine*, Winter 1970, 11–12; "Library Features 19 Miles of Tape," *Army Reporter*, 15 June 1970, 11; "Libraries Offer Troop Pastime," *Castle Courier*, 13 July 1970, 2; "Special Services Agency Conference."

43. "Special Services: Have Library, Will Travel"; "Libraries Offer Troop Pastime."

44. "Libraries Offer Troop Pastime"; "Special Services: Have Library, Will Travel"; "A Touch of Home in 'Nam."

45. "Special Services Agency Conference"; "Distribution of Special Services Facilities."

46. "A Touch of Home in 'Nam"; "Libraries Offer Troop Pastime."

47. "Special Services Agency Conference"; "Distribution of Special Services Facilities."

48. "War Zone Campus," *Uptight*, Summer 1969, 9–11. The education centers were located on bases at Danang, Chu Lai, An Khe, Qui Nhon, Pleiku, Nha Trang, Cam Ranh Bay, Phuoc Vinh, Long Binh, Saigon, Can Tho, and Cu Chi.

49. "General Education Development FY72," in "The Command Progress Report—DCS P&A," MPPD.

50. "Operational Report—Lessons Learned, Headquarters Long Binh Subarea Command," 1 February to 30 April 1967, ORLLS; "War Zone Campus."

51. "6,000 Study Topics by Bearcat Education Center," *Old Reliable*, 20 September 1967, 8; "War Zone Campus."

52. "Editorial: The Battle of Boredom," *Hawk*, Fall 1970, 7; "Operational Reports—Lessons Learned, U.S. Army Headquarters Area Command," 1967–1971, ORLLS; "Operational Report-Lessons Learned, U.S. Army Headquarters Area Command," April 1971, General Records, Administrative Office, USARV PMS.

53. Department of the Army Pamphlet No. 28-8, *Army Entertainment Program Operational Guide*; "DA Conference for Major Command Chiefs of PSD and SSO," 19 June 1969, NFD.

54. "Administrative History," Finding Aid, U.S. Army Vietnam Special Services Agency, Record Group 472, NARA; "Distribution of Special Services Facilities"; USARV Regulation No. 28-13, "Welfare, Recreation, and Morale: Military Show and Military Music Program, Vietnam," 15 September 1969, General Administrative Records, 1966–1972, EB.

55. Plays were certainly conducted at Qui Nhon, home to the 55th Medical Group, and Special Services records suggest but do not name other theater companies at bases in South Vietnam. "Playhouse '55 Gives First Performance," *Double Nickel*, 25 December 1968; "Special Services Agency Conference."

56. "'The Fantasticks': Cause for Some Memories," *Hi-Lite* (newspaper), March 1971, 4; "Long Binh Players Play for Rain," *Hi-Lite* (newspaper), May 1971, 2. See also "Army Actors Like Their Vietnam Duty," *New York Times*, 15 March 1970, 3.

57. "Can You Act?" *Triumvirate*, 30 September 1969, 4; "Armed Forces Theatre Long Binh Casting for 'Guys & Dolls,'" *Triumvirate*, 30 November 1969, 10.

58. "Administrative History"; "Headquarters 1st Logistical Command: Debriefing Report," Senior Officer Debriefing Reports, USARV CH.

59. "Organization and Functions Manual: United States Army Vietnam Special Services Agency (Provisional)"; "Information of Special Importance to USO Shows Personnel Touring in South Vietnam," General Administrative Records, 1966–1972, EB; MACV Directive No. 28-6, "Welfare, Recreation, and Morale: Entertainment Program," 30 June 1970, General Administrative Records, 1966–1972, EB.

60. "Organization and Functions Manual: United States Army Vietnam Special Services Agency (Provisional)"; "Revised Orientation Information for Armed Forces Professional Entertainment Units Touring the Republic of Vietnam," June 1970, General Administrative Records, 1966–1972, EB.

61. "Special Services Stays Busy," *Long Binh Post*, 28 December 1971, 1, 6.

62. "After-Action Report: Troy Donahue, 28 February 1969," General Administrative Records, EB.

63. "Approved Commercial Entertainment," 17 July 1972, NFD; "Vietnam's Talent Scouts," *Uptight*, Spring 1970, 12–14.

64. "Welfare, Recreation, and Morale: Entertainment Program"; "Approved Commercial Entertainment"; "Vietnam's Talent Scouts."

65. "MR4 Military Touring Shows Evaluation Report," 20 March 1971, and "After-

Action Report: Mr. Daniel and Friends Show, 15 February 1969," both in General Administrative Records, EB.

66. "Minutes of the Professional Entertainment Conference," General Administrative Records, EB. For a wry portrait of the celebrity "invasion," see Jury, *Vietnam Photo Book*, 74–75.

67. "Revised Orientation Information for Armed Forces Professional Entertainment Units Touring the Republic of Vietnam."

68. "Synopsis of Subjects Addressed in the Special Services Area," NFD.

69. "Something for Everyone," *Hi-Lite Magazine*, Spring 1969, 26.

70. Untitled document, General Administrative Records 1966–1972, EB.

71. "Special Services," General Administrative Records, 1968, EB; "Welfare, Recreation, and Morale: Entertainment Program"; "Star Search," General Administrative Records, 1966–1972, EB; "Servicemen Compete in Area Talent Show," *Delta Advisor*, October 1969, 8; ad in the "White Market," *Long Binh Post*, 28 December 1971, 6.

72. "Dayroom," *Dollars & Sense*, 28 March 1969, 1; "Hog Heaven," *Semper Primus*, 19 May 1969, 7.

73. "AFVN Signals Inform, Entertain Vietnam Servicemen," *Army Reporter*, 16 March 1968; "Vietnam Network Moves on Automation," *Broadcast Engineering*, February 1970, 44–45; "Upgrading the Armed Forces Radio Network," memo from Col. Rodger R. Bankson, GS Chief of Information, to Chief of Staff HQ MACV, 3 March 1967, AFVN Organizational History Files, MACV IO; "American Forces Vietnam Network Fact Sheet," AFVN Organizational History Files, MACV IO.

74. "The American Forces Vietnam Network: An Extra Dimension for the IO," Drug Suppression (June 1971), General Records, Administrative Office, USARV PMS.

75. "American Forces Vietnam Network Fact Sheet."

76. "Television on the Wing," *TV Guide*, 11 February 1967.

77. "American Forces Vietnam Network Fact Sheet"; "The American Forces Vietnam Network: An Extra Dimension for the IO."

78. "Requirement for Addition to AFRT Vietnam Key Station in Saigon," 13 April 1967, AFVN Organizational History Files, MACV IO.

79. "Vietnam Network Moves on Automation."

80. "American Forces Vietnam Network," 1970, AFVN Organizational History Files, MACV IO.

81. "AFVN Historical Summary, Fourth Quarter CY68," 18 January 1969, AFVN Organizational History Files, MACV IO; "TV Happenings," *Army Reporter*, 2 June 1969; "Television on the Wing."

82. "Summary of Special Services Facilities" and "Special Services Budget," 9 May 1969, both in NFD.

83. "Service Club Opens," *USAHAC Command Newsletter*, July 1969, 11; "Service Club Initiates 'Outside the Walls' Program," *USAHAC Command Newsletter*, August 1970, 7–8; "Organization and Functions Manual: United States Army Vietnam Special Services Agency (Provisional)"; "Special Services Agency Conference."

84. "Party on the Saigon River," *Long Binh Post*, 21 December 1971; "Luau: Hawaii Comes to Long Binh," *Hi-Lite Magazine*, Winter–Spring 1971, 10–11.

85. "March Psychedelia, Copter Corner Service Club," *Guardian*, March 1969, 2–3.

86. Stur, "Perfume and Lipstick in the Boonies: Red Cross SRAO and the Vietnam War," *The Sixties* 1 (December 2008): 151–65.

87. Command Circular No. 230-1, "Non-appropriated Funds and Related Activities: Operation and Administration of Messes and Other Sundry Funds," 6 December 1962, Administrative Services Division, USARV AG; MACV Directive No. 230-3, "Non-appropriated Funds and Related Activities: Open Messes and Other Sundry Funds, 8 February 1970, Investigation Division Reports, MACV IG.

88. "EM Open New Club at 2/503d," *Fire Base 173*, 25 December 1968; "The Show Must Go On," *Drumfire Blaze*, 9 June 1969, 4; "Build Club-Theater," *Lion's Roar*, 2 August 1969, 1; "EM Club Gets Face-Lifting," *This Week with the 39th*, 15 March 1970, 3.

89. "Non-appropriated Fund and Related Activities: Operation and Administration of Messes and Other Sundry Funds"; MACV Directive No. 230-3, "Non-appropriated Funds and Related Activities: Open Messes and Other Sundry Funds"; "Open Mess Briefing," NFD.

90. "Open Mess Briefing."

91. Wilken, *Why Didn't You Have to Go to Vietnam, Daddy?*, 105.

92. For recent analysis of drug use in Vietnam, see Kuzmarov, *Myth of the Addicted Army*. "Getting at Getting Down in 185th Coffee House," *Hi-Lite* (newspaper), September 1971, 1; "'Firebase Bastogne,' FB Coffee Shack," *Screaming Eagle*, 13 September 1971, 8; "Coffee/Safe House: A New Concept," *Hi-Lite* (newspaper), n.d.

93. "Joint Service Non-appropriated Welfare Fund (JSNAWF) Board Minutes," 20 December 1970, NFD.

94. "Sand, Sea, and Sanctuary," *Army Reporter*, 22 November 1971, 6–7.

95. See, for example, ORLLS; General Records, 1968–1972, MWB; and General Administrative Records, EB.

96. Whalon, *Saigon Zoo*, 227.

97. For a localized example of this circular phenomenon, see the U.S. Army Staff Study, *Improvement of U.S. Logistic Systems in Republic of Vietnam—Logistical Situation in RVN, October 26, 1964*, 1–4, MHI.

98. This figure does not include the shows Special Services contracted directly or the military's own productions, which accounted for thousands more performances, albeit with less stringent security measures. "Letter of Instruction: Project Denton Beauty," Administrative Records, EB. See also "History of the USO."

99. "Major Recreation Projects," June 1970, MWB.

100. Ronald Reagan, "Peace: Restoring the Margin of Safety", Chicago, 18 August 1980. Reagan used a slightly less robust version of the line again in a 1988 Veterans Day speech at the Vietnam Veterans Memorial, "that young Americans must never again be sent to fight and die unless we are prepared to let them win."

101. Department of the Army Pamphlet No. 21-59, *Introduction to the Army Service Club Program.*

102. John Milius, Francis Ford Coppola, and Michael Herr, *Apocalypse Now*, 1979. Milius and Coppola wrote the screenplay, while Herr wrote the voice-over narration.

103. Quoted in Buchanan, *Mekong Diaries*, 99.

104. Broyles, *Brothers in Arms*, 121–22.

105. This study concluded, "Neither our military actions nor our political or psywar efforts seem to have made an appreciable dent on the enemy's overall motivation and morale structure." Quoted in Kellen, *Conversations with Enemy Soldiers in Late 1968/ Early 1969*, 100.

CHAPTER 4

1. O'Brien, "The Things They Carried," in *Things They Carried*, 3–25, esp. 7–9.

2. Ibid., 14–16.

3. Marling, *As Seen on TV*, 255. See also Cross, "Promises of More," in *All-Consuming Century*, 67–109; May, "Commodity Trap"; and Hine, *Populuxe*.

4. Cross, *All-Consuming Century*, 145–55.

5. Moskos, "Why Men Fight," 21–22.

6. Each branch of service had its own term for the exchanges, but for simplicity's sake, I am using the term "P.X." to describe all military exchanges.

7. Army and Air Force Exchange Service, "AAFES History"; MACV Command Information Pamphlet No. 6-67, "Your Vietnam Regional Exchange: Service in War and Peace," February 1967, Command Information Division Files, MACV IO.

8. "Your Vietnam Regional Exchange: Service in War and Peace."

9. Ibid.

10. Department of the Army Pamphlet No. 608-16, *Helpful Hints for Personnel Ordered to the Republic of Vietnam*, August 1970; "Your Vietnam Regional Exchange: Service in War and Peace."

11. USARV Regulation No. 60-5, "Exchange Service Responsibilities and Relationships," 29 September 1968, General Records, Administrative Office, USARV PMS.

12. "P.X. Opens," *Seahorse News*, 30 April 1970, 3.

13. Ibid.; "New P.X. Opens," *This Month with the 39th*, 31 August 1970, 4.

14. "Exchange Service Responsibilities and Relationships."

15. "P.X. Has Grand Reopening," *Steadfast and Loyal*, 18 May 1969, 1, 6.

16. "P.X. Grows," *Ivy Leaf*, 2 August 1970, 6.

17. "New LBP P.X.," *Laterite Lantern*, 16 December 1969, 1; "Delta Company Completes P.X.," *Laterite Lantern*, 17 May 1970, 3; "P.X. Additions Are Planned," *Laterite Lantern*, 30 September 1970, 1; "Preston Park P.X.," *Dirtmover*, November 1970, 6.

18. "VRE (PACEX) Retail Facilities w/over $100,000 Sales as of 13 March 72," NFD.

19. "Your Vietnam Regional Exchange: Service in War and Peace"; Unit Press Bulletin No. 23: "VRE Extra Savings Program (ESP)," 29 October 1970, Command Information Division Files, MACV IO.

20. "The P.X. and You: What's for Sale," *Americal News Sheet*, 23 April 1969, 2; "Serving You," *This Month with the 39th,* November 1970, 2.

21. "P.X. Goods Moving to Forward Areas," *Army Reporter*, 4 November 1968, 15.

22. "New P.X. Facilities," *Eagle Talons*, 9 March 1968, 1.

23. "Hamlet Chief Gives Life—Leads Ambush; Kills VC" and "Business Is Flourishing: New Improved P.X. Opens at English," *Fire Base 173*, 16 February 1970, 1.

24. "VRE Is Handy for Field Troops," *Army Reporter*, 9 December 1968, 15.

25. Ibid.

26. "Up in the Sky! A Flying P.X.," *Army Reporter*, 19 May 1969, 12; "Hits L.Z.s: Fourth's Flying P.X.," *Ivy Leaf*, 12 July 1970, 8; "Flying P.X. Takes Items to FSB's, L.Z.'s," *Southern Cross*, 23 July 1971, 2.

27. "Troops Buy atop Mountain: P.X. Is Where the Action Is," *Army Reporter*, 18 August 1969, 11; "Flying 'Grocery Store' a Booming Business," *Trac III*, September 1971, 2.

28. USARV Command Information Fact Sheet No. 7-66, "Your R&R Program," 7 June 1966, MHI.

29. "Hong Kong R&R Is for Shopping—and Swimming and Relaxing," *Cavalair*, 25 March 1967, 7; "Hong Kong—Paradise for Traveler, Shopper," *Dimension*, November 1968, 16; "Hong Kong: The Jewel of the Orient," *Professional*, 11 October 1969, 3–5; "R and R to Hong Kong," *Hell Fire Herald*, 11 October 1969, 3; "Hong Kong: Orient's Bargain Mart," *Uptight*, Summer 1970, 40–44; "Hong Kong—World's Shopping Capitol," *Messenger*, 31 July 1970.

30. Goods could be shipped to soldiers in Vietnam until early 1972, when the drawdown required that PACEX merchandise be shipped directly to the United States. "PACEX to Distribute '71 Mail Order Catalog," *Sky Master*, October 1970, 7; "Minutes of Meeting, 15 March 1972," Joint Vietnam Regional Exchange Council, NFD.

31. "Your Vietnam Regional Exchange: Service in War and Peace."

32. "VRE Inventory, Stock Assortment and 'Must Items,' 25 April 1972," NFD.

33. "Your Vietnam Regional Exchange: Service in War and Peace;" "Joint Vietnam Regional Exchange Council Agenda, 29 April 1969," NFD; "Average Monthly Sales—Camp Horn Troop Store, October 1972," NFD.

34. Hamilton-Paterson, *Greedy War*, 62. Paterson's protagonist, Cornelius Hawkridge, who investigated black market corruption in Vietnam as a private citizen and eventually testified before a Senate subcommittee on the matter, offered this figure in reference to the market in Qui Nhon.

35. Free World Military Forces and civilian contract employees were also allowed to shop at the P.X.'s, making it impossible to determine what percentage of the sales was generated by American soldiers alone. However, American soldiers constituted the largest group with access to the P.X.'s, and they had the most discretionary income. There is also no way to know how many of these controlled items ended up for sale on the black market, either from authorized P.X. shoppers selling them directly or from American soldiers and civilians gifting them to Vietnamese friends and acquaintances. MACV Directive No. 60-7, "Exchange Service: MACV Ration Cards," 14 July 1969, and MACV Directive No. 60-6, "Exchange Service: Exchange Privileges," 10 October 1971, both in MHI; "PACEX Catalog System," *Sea Tiger*, 24 October 1969, 2.

36. "The American Forces Vietnam Network: An Extra Dimension for the IO," Drug Suppression (June 1971), General Records, Administrative Office, USARV PMS; "Television on the Wing," *TV Guide*, 11 February 1967.

37. "Listen Up in Stereo: Choose Components Carefully," *Army Reporter*, 26 October 1970, 8.

38. "The Idler: PFC Jon Clarke on the Hi-Fi," *Diamond Dust*, 22 August 1969, 4.

39. "A Glimpse at Ourselves," *Esprit*, Fall 1969, 16–17.

40. "The Shutterbug," *Headshed*, 26 April 1969, 5.

41. "Joint Vietnam Regional Exchange Council Agenda, July 1969," NFD.

42. A prime example is the souvenir Zippo lighter, engraved with maps of South Vietnam, the dates of a soldier's tour, and popular epigrams like "Yea, though I walk through the valley of the shadow of death, I shall fear no evil for I am the meanest motherfucker in the valley" or "We are the unknown sent by the unwise to do the unnecessary for the ungrateful." See Buchanan, *Vietnam Zippos*.

43. "Cameras Are Big Business for Vietnam P.X. System," *Roger That*, 7 March 1970, 9.

44. In FY1969, Chrysler grossed $7.5 million in annual sales, Ford $7.7 million, and General Motors $11.5 million. "Joint Vietnam Regional Exchange Council Agenda, July 1969"; "Car Sales in Vietnam," *Eagle Talons*, 9 March 1968, 3; "P.X. Talk: Car Sales and Refunds," *Sin Loi Times*, 7 March 1969, 1.

45. "Joint Vietnam Regional Exchange Council Agenda, July 1969"; "Joint Vietnam Regional Exchange Council Agenda, August 1970"; "Joint Vietnam Regional Exchange Council Agenda, 15 June 1972"; "Capture of Unauthorized Concessions," 15 May 1969, all in NFD.

46. "Joint Vietnam Regional Exchange Council Agenda, July 1969"; "Joint Vietnam Regional Exchange Council Agenda, August 1970"; "Joint Vietnam Regional Exchange Council Agenda, 15 June 1972."

47. "Your Vietnam Regional Exchange: Service in War and Peace"; "Joint Vietnam Regional Exchange Council Agenda, August 1970."

48. "Joint Vietnam Regional Exchange Council Agenda, 29 April 1969," "Joint Vietnam Regional Exchange Council Agenda, August 1970," "Joint Vietnam Regional Exchange Council Agenda, May 1971," and "Joint Vietnam Regional Exchange Council Agenda, 15 March 1972," all in NFD.

49. "Pacific Exchange System by Mr. Brian Connors," in "Report of the USARPAC Provost Marshall Conference, 3–5 October 1972," Plans and Operations Division, USARV PMS.

50. "Your Vietnam Regional Exchange: Service in War and Peace"; "Minutes of the Joint Vietnam Regional Exchange Council, 20 February 1970," NFD; "Joint Vietnam Regional Exchange Council Agenda, August 1970."

51. "Delay in PACEX Orders," *Delta Advisor*, May 1969, 6; "Joint Vietnam Regional Exchange Council Agenda, November 1969," NFD; "PACEX to Distribute 71 Mail Order Catalog," *Sky Master*, October 1970, 7; "Joint Vietnam Regional Exchange Council Meeting, May 1971," NFD; "Minutes of Meeting, 15 March 1972"; "Pacific Exchange System by Mr. Brian Connors."

52. "P.X. Talk," *Sin Loi Times*, 18 April 1969, 10, 11; "Vietnam Exchange Establishes Electronic Repair Shops," *Hi-Lite* (newspaper), 1 May 1969, 5.

53. Department of the Army Pamphlet No. 27-162, *Claims*, 13–15, 17, 21–22.

54. "From the Desk of Shortimer Sam," *Army Reporter*, 4 November 1968, 5.

55. USARV Fact Sheet No. 3-70, "Customs Laws and You," 20 July 1969, MHI.

56. "Your Vietnam Regional Exchange: Service in War and Peace."

57. Department of the Army Pamphlet No. 608-16, *Helpful Hints for Personnel Ordered to Vietnam* (March 1968); Department of the Army Pamphlet No. 608-16, *Helpful Hints for Personnel Ordered to the Republic of Vietnam*" (August 1970); USARV Fact Sheet No. 15-68, "Returning to CONUS," 22 February 1968, MHI.

58. "Returning to CONUS"; "Hold Baggage," *Black Baron Release*, 15 December 1970, 3, 6; "Hold Baggage," *Long Binh Post*, 26 October 1971, 1, 8.

59. "Disposition Form: Vietnam Regional Exchange Concessions, April 1972," in "Joint Vietnam Regional Exchange Council Agenda, August 1970."

60. Col. Louis W. Powers to VRE Commander, "Steambath Contract Extension, 27 June 1972," NFD.

61. "Phu Bai 'Steamed-Up' over Opening Latin Quarter," *XXIV Corps Courier*, 24 December 1969, 4.

62. "We Need Your Help!! B Med," *Scars & Gripes*, June 1969, 2; "Ex-Colonel Relates How He Prevented a Brothel on Base," *New York Times*, 5 March 1971, 70; Noel and Noel, *Saigon for a Song*, 151, 250.

63. Like everything else, "girlie magazines" had an official Army definition. They were "publications predominantly devoted to portraying females in various stages of undress and in provocative poses." "Report of Investigation Concerning Star Far East Corporation," Investigation Division Reports, MACV IG.

64. Ibid. *Playboy* topped the list, followed by *Newsweek*, *Time*, and *Cavalier*. *Girl Illustrated*, *Climax*, *All Man*, *Mr.*, *Stag*, and *Escapade* rounded out the top ten, followed by *Sir*, *For Men Only*, *Swank*, *Men*, *Male*, and *Man's Magazine*. In 1969, VRE sold about 329,500 magazines per month, of which 196,700 were girlies.

65. "Joint Vietnam Regional Exchange Council Agenda, November 1970"; "Joint Vietnam Regional Exchange Council Agenda, 15 March 1972," both in NFD.

66. Noel and Noel, *Saigon for a Song*, 151.

67. "Exchange Service: MACV Ration Cards."

68. Ibid.

69. MACV Directive No. 60-8, "Exchange Service Alcoholic Beverage Control," 4 March 1969, MHI. This document clearly states, "Alcoholic beverages will be sold primarily on a drink basis through authorized clubs and messes."

70. Inflation in Vietnam continued to rise throughout the war, with the cost of rice ballooning 385 percent between 1965 and 1970. MACV Command Information Pamphlet No. 16-67, "Piaster Control: Fighting Inflation in Vietnam," May 1967, MACV IO; "Careless Spending and Black Marketing Only Your Funeral," *Sunday Punch*, 22 February 1970, 2.

71. "Piaster Control: Fighting Inflation in Vietnam"; USARV Fact Sheet No. 13-70, "The Black Market and You," November 1969, USARV IO; Herring, *America's Longest War*, 222–223; "Careless Spending and Black Marketing Only Your Funeral."

72. Major General Verne L. Bowers, USARV Deputy Chief of Staff for Personnel and Administration, "Final Report," 10 September 1970, MHI.

73. "Prune Piaster Spending" (poster), Public Information Division, USARV AG.

74. "Limit Cuts Black Market, Not Your Ability to Spend," *Army Reporter*, 30 March 1968, 4.

75. "Dishonored Check Problem in the Vietnam Regional Exchange System," 9 October 1972, NFD.

76. Defense Finance and Accounting Service, "Monthly Basic Pay and Allowances."

77. Watson, *Voices from the Rear*, 205.

78. "Saigon tea" involved soldiers buying drinks for themselves and a bargirl. The

soldier had to pay for the girl's time and affection, making it a very expensive way to get drunk, though soldiers often did not know the terms of the arrangement until they were told to pay up.

79. "Piaster Control: Fighting Inflation in Vietnam"; "Savings Program," *Black Baron Release*, 17 August 1969, 5, 7; "Editorial: Save It for the Good Stuff," *Hawk*, Spring 1972, 25.

80. Affectionately known by the acronym "BUFE" (Big Ugly Fucking Elephant, pronounced "buffy"), these statues were large enough to be converted into end tables. In 1971, Vietnam produced 30,000 ceramic elephants. According to the *New York Times*, 50 percent were sent to the United States as exports, where they sold for $40 to $150, and 50 percent were sent to the United States as gifts purchased by servicemen for just $5 to $15. This "authentic" souvenir of the region was thus purchased by approximately 0 percent of Vietnamese natives. "Hit Souvenir of Vietnam—Ceramic Elephants," *New York Times*, 18 March 1972, 20.

81. USARV Fact Sheet No. 10-69, "The Expeditious Management of Superfluous Currency, or Making Your Pay Work For You," 15 November 1968, MHI.

82. USARV Command Information Pamphlet No. 1-67, "Happy/Sad: The Choice Is Yours," February 1967, USARV IO.

83. Muehlberg, *REMF "War Stories,"* 51.

84. Except for consumables and items declared as gifts, everything else had to return with the soldier to Vietnam. USARV Command Information Fact Sheet No. 5-72, "Changes in U.S. Customs Law," 30 June 1972, and USARV Command Information Fact Sheet No. 6-72, "U.S. Customs Information," 30 June 1972, MPPD.

85. Department of the Army Pamphlet No. 360-411, *A Pocket Guide to Vietnam*, 72. The distribution of these guides was extensive, with the Army trying to put some kind of orientation guide in the hands of every soldier bound for Vietnam.

86. Appy, *Working-Class War*, 286–97.

87. "Homecoming for Viet Veterans: Apathy, Hostility," *Los Angeles Times*, 20 October 1968, A1.

88. "Records of Personal Property Received, 1969–1970," U.S. Army Mortuary, Saigon; "Can Tho Graves Registration Point, 1970," U.S. Army Mortuary, Saigon; "Duc Pho Graves Registration Point, May 1967–June 1969," U.S. Army Mortuary, Danang; "Records of Personal Effects, 1971," Pleiku Graves Registration Point.

89. Hass, *Carried to the Wall*.

CHAPTER 5

1. "Cavalry-Carnival Sponsored by PV Service Club," *Cavalair*, 5 March 1969, 4–5.

2. Bakhtin, *Rabelais and His World*, 7–11, 19.

3. Fussell, *Great War and Modern Memory*, 35, 64–69.

4. Upton, *Pizza and Mortars*, 222–25.

5. Wiknik, *Nam Sense*, 133.

6. For a statement of the policy, see a memo from Maj. Fletcher L. Jones, USARV Command Information Officer, to the Information Officer for the 173rd Airborne Brigade, 11 August 1967, USARV IO.

7. These generalizations are based on the examination of the Military History Institute's extensive collection of unit newspapers. A complete list of the publications consulted is included in the bibliography.

8. "AFVN Historical Summary, Second Quarter FY67," 11 January 1967, and "AFVN Historical Summary, Third Quarter FY68," 17 April 1968, in AFVN Organizational History Files, MACV IO.

9. "The American Forces Vietnam Network: An Extra Dimension for the IO," Drug Suppression (June 1971), General Records, Administrative Office, USARV PMS.

10. Ibid.; "AFVN Historical Summary, Second Quarter, FY68," 15 January 1968, AFVN Organizational History Files, MACV IO.

11. For a discussion of rock music's role in creating a sense of community in Vietnam, see Kramer, "Civics of Rock," 270–336.

12. Jury, *Vietnam Photo Book*, 23 (ellipses in the original).

13. Ibid., 22.

14. "Shove Off," World War I U.S. Navy recruitment poster, reproduced in postcard form, n.d., National Archives and Records Administration, Washington, D.C.

15. The antiwar movement co-opted "FTA," translating it to "Fuck the Army," with the abbreviation appearing in graffiti on U.S. military installations throughout the world, including South Vietnam.

16. For a discussion of the consumer-driven nature of military recruitment for the All-Volunteer Force, including the Cold War ad described here, see Bailey, "Army in the Marketplace."

17. Department of the Army Pamphlet No. 360-411, *A Pocket Guide to Vietnam*, 66–72.

18. "Zoo Saigon Style," *Hawk*, June 1970, 22–23; "Race Track—Saigon," *Hawk*, Winter 1971, 29–31; "Saigon: The Paris of the East," *Uptight*, Summer 1971, 20–25; "'Tourists' Record Da Nang Sights on Film, Learn Vietnamese Ways," *Sea Tiger*, 16 October 1970, 4.

19. "R&R for a Day in Qui Nhon," *Qui Nhon Logman*, September 1970, 4–5.

20. For more examples of the Nam's language, see Clark, *Words of the Vietnam War*, and Reinberg, *In the Field*.

21. Broyles, "Why Men Love War," 58.

22. Ehrhart, *Vietnam Perkasie*, 101–2.

23. Broyles, "Why Men Love War," 62.

24. Herr, *Dispatches*, 132.

25. Jury, *Vietnam Photo Book*, 28.

26. "Your Civilian Soldier," *Warrior*, 28 February 1969, 2.

27. For a social science perspective on killing in war, see Grossman, *On Killing*. Grossman reports a staggering rate of combat trauma, not just for Vietnam veterans but for veterans of all wars, with psychiatric casualties generally exceeding deaths in combat.

28. Cross, "Rice Will Grow Again." Other published versions cite Kansas instead of Indiana in the final stanza.

29. "From Dakto to Detroit: Death of a Troubled Hero," *New York Times*, 26 May

1971, 1. Johnson's story was fictionalized in Tom Cole's play *Medal of Honor Rag*, first produced in 1975.

30. "Reds Smashed," *Firebase 173*, 8 June 1970; "Polar Bears Score Well," *Charger*, 11 November 1966; "Hornets Rout V.C. and NVA," *Black Baron Release*, 1 April 1969; "Sharks Down Reds," *Falcon*, 16 February 1969; "11th BN 'Bombs' 48th GRP," *Ship 'n Shore*, 15 May 1969.

31. Muehlberg, *REMF "War Stories,"* 288–90.

32. Whalon, *Saigon Zoo*, 181, 196.

33. Calling cards are not to be confused with death cards or trail cards, which took the size and shape of playing cards, usually the ace of spades. These cards were placed on the bodies of dead or wounded enemy combatants in order to strike fear and to identify the unit responsible, sometimes in Vietnamese. The intended audience was presumably other Vietnamese combatants, but when American units evacuated enemy wounded, only American medical personnel received the message. Jury, *Vietnam Photo Book*, 21.

34. Personal files of the author. The cards were ubiquitous, available for custom design and purchase by mail order, on R&R, or from Vietnamese vendors operating in or near post exchanges.

35. Ehrhart, *Vietnam Perkasie*, 42–43, 130.

36. "Investigator Says General Hid Abuses in Army Clubs," *New York Times*, 3 October 1969, 1, 28; "Captain's Trial Hears of Funds," *New York Times*, 5 November 1966, 3.

37. "Too Much Hair Spray Trips Saigon P.X. Chief," *New York Times*, 12 May 1966, 15; "Blonde: Club Sgts. Demanded Favors," *Pacific Stars and Stripes*, 11 October, 1969, 1.

38. Wilken, *Why Didn't You Have to Go to Vietnam, Daddy?*, 102–4.

39. For a general discussion of economic corruption in Vietnam, see Allison, "War for Sale."

40. "Goodbye, Ugga," *Varsity Newsletter*, 25 February 1970, 3.

41. Donovan, *Once a Warrior King*, 32–33. "David Donovan" is the pen name of Terry T. Turner, who uses his own name for his scientific publications.

42. Elliott, *Sacred Willow*, 313–14.

43. Muehlberg, *REMF "War Stories,"* 143.

44. Adams, *Noise That Never Dies*, 36–37.

45. "Hong Kong—The Jewel of the Orient," *Professional*, 11 October 1969, 3–5; "Good Time in Hong Kong: The Straight Scoop on Where IT'S At and How Much IT Costs," *Grunt Free Press*, March 1970, 11. The *Grunt Free Press* (formerly *The Vietnam Grunt* and *Grunt*) was published from 1968 to 1971 by current or former G.I.'s in Vietnam for other American servicemen. Ten issues of the magazine are now available online at http://www.craigsams.com/pages/grunt.html. The main difference between the *Grunt Free Press* and the military-sanctioned G.I. newspapers is not that the former was especially antiwar but just that it was especially lewd.

46. It is not clear how many Amerasian children were sired by American soldiers and born to Vietnamese mothers. Estimates reach as high as 100,000, and all but a handful were abandoned by their fathers. Some 30,000 Amerasians immigrated to the United States as a result of the Amerasian Homecoming Act of 1988, which per-

mitted them to claim a biracial identity based on appearance alone. U.S. support for the program declined sharply in the early 1990s as a result of widespread abuse. An estimated 3,000–15,000 Amerasian Vietnamese still survived in Vietnam by the late 1990s, where they continued to suffer racial prejudice and economic hardship. Yarborough, *Surviving Twice*.

47. Wiknik, *Nam Sense*, 235. For another typical description of an overseas R&R, see Nik Boldrini, *Sitting Duck*.

48. "How to Meet a Girl," *Grunt Free Press*, July 1970, 13; "Oriental Girls vs. American Girls," *Grunt Free Press*, April 1970, 2.

49. Muehlberg, *REMF "War Stories,"* 160–61.

50. Wiknik, *Nam Sense*, 117–43; Watson, *Voices from the Rear*, 128–29.

51. Ehrhart, *Vietnam-Perkasie*, 364–65.

52. Ibid., 423. The other memory that haunted Ehrhart is of the old woman he shot from 300 meters away.

53. McKegney, "Carnival of Vietnam, a REMF View."

54. There is no way to know whether exposure to Agent Orange caused McKegney's prostate cancer. With the Agent Orange Act of 1991, Congress granted the Veterans Administration the power to declare illnesses, including prostate cancer, "presumptive to Agent Orange exposure" for any veteran, regardless of when, where, and in what capacity he served in South Vietnam, so long as he could document having the illness and being at least 10 percent disabled because of it. As a result, both a veteran's exposure to Agent Orange and the cause of his illness are assumed by law, if not by science. A man's likelihood of contracting prostate cancer increases with age, exceeding 50 percent by age eighty, whether he was exposed to Agent Orange or not. See "'Presumptive' Disability Benefits for Certain Groups of Veterans."

55. Untitled (four letters by a soldier named "Harry"), *Grunt Free Press*, April 1970, 18.

56. Muehlberg, *REMF "War Stories,"* 314.

57. Boldrini, *Nik Boldrini's Sitting Duck*, 56.

58. Jury, *Vietnam Photo Book*, 44–45.

59. Wolff, *In Pharaoh's Army*, 15–18.

60. "Battle-Flag Hoax of Green Berets Has Met Its Fate," *New York Times*, 8 April 1966, 3.

61. Sontag, *On Photography*, 9.

62. Ibid.

63. American soldiers seldom photographed American bodies because they did not objectify them as they did the Vietnamese; moreover, it was regarded as bad form by other soldiers. Professional journalists did photograph the American dead, with mixed reactions from soldiers. Soldiers who supported the war tended to regard such images as ghoulish and exploitative, while soldiers who questioned the war tended to see the practice as necessary in order to raise awareness of the war's brutality at home.

64. Dunn, *Desk Warrior*, 90–92; Tom O'Hara, interviewed in Appy, *Patriots*, 326; Wiknik, *Nam Sense*, 133; Upton, *Pizza and Mortars*, 135.

65. Sontag, *On Photography*, 16, 167.

66. Wiknik, *Nam Sense*, 133.

67. "Not All Wounds Are Visible," iron-on patch acquired in 2002, personal files of the author.

68. An estimated 94 percent of Vietnam veterans diagnosed with PTSD seek compensation, which may yield tens of thousands of dollars annually, tax free, if a veteran is deemed completely disabled. For discussions critical of the prevalence of PTSD among Vietnam veterans, see McNally, "Progress and Controversy in the Study of Post-traumatic Stress Disorder"; Burkett and Whitley, *Stolen Valor*, 139-161; and Lembcke, *Spitting Image*, 101–26.

69. Kidder, *My Detachment*, 7–8.

70. Ibid., 8.

71. Broyles, "Why Men Love War," 56.

72. O'Brien quoted in Appy, *Patriots*, 544.

73. Broyles, "Why Men Love War," 56.

EPILOGUE

1. Delobius [Alex Barnes], "Day in the Life Of."

2. The group purports to support all NATO troops engaged in fighting terrorism around the world, but all of its administrators are American. "Don't Support the Troops? Think about This."

3. "Comfort Rare in Iraq, Even for U.S. Troops; Soldiers Swelter in 'Primitive' Quarters," *Washington Post*, 26 May 2003, A1. See also "Fort Stewart-Based Soldiers Fight Heat, Boredom in Iraq," *Atlanta Journal-Constitution*, 20 July 2003, A1.

4. "U.S. Troops Order Comfort, with Fries on the Side; Soldiers Looking for a Taste of Home Make for a Booming Business at Iraq's First Burger King," *Washington Post*, 19 October 2003, A25; "In the Center of Baghdad, an Escape to America," *New York Times*, 12 January 2004, A10; "Iraq: A Respite from War," *Soldiers*, 59 (February 2004): 10–19.

5. "G.I.s Deployed in Iraq Desert with Lots of American Stuff," *New York Times*, 13 August 2005, 1.

6. Batty [Owen Powell], "The Keep"; Batty [Owen Powell], "The Termite Mound."

7. Batty, "The Keep." Powell did subsequently experience combat, in an intense firefight that led to his evacuation from Baghdad to Germany for treatment of post-traumatic stress disorder. See Batty [Owen Powell], "Bonkers."

8. Frontline, "Private Warriors."

9. "FOBs the Closest Thing to Home in Iraq; at Forward Operating Bases, U.S. Forces Find Respite and Recreation," *Washington Times*, 26 March 2008, A15; "Biggest Base in Iraq Has Small-Town Feel; Most Troops at Balad Never Meet Iraqis," *Washington Post*, 4 February 2006, A14.

10. Army and Air Force Exchange Service, "Milestones."

11. "G.I.s Deployed in Iraq Desert with Lots of American Stuff."

12. Ibid.; "On a Base in Iraq, the Pedi-Cure; Salon in Still-Volatile Area Refreshes Hands, Feet and Exhausted Spirits," *Washington Post*, 8 February 2009, A16.

13. Most soldiers elected to take their R&R leave by returning to the United States, which the military facilitated by paying for airfare to the commercial airport near-

est the authorized leave destination and by allowing soldiers fifteen days, excluding travel time, for the trip.

14. "In the Center of Baghdad, an Escape to America"; "Iraq: A Respite from War"; "Holiday in a Hussein Palace, Troops' New Recreation Center Offers Respite Amid Opulence," *Washington Post*, 5 July 2003, A1.

15. "For U.S. Troops at War, Liquor Is Spur to Crime," *New York Times*, March 13, 2007, A1.

16. "Big U.S. Bases, Part of Iraqi Landscape, Are a World Apart," *New York Times*, 9 September 2009, A4.

17. "Army Engineers Taste History, Humility As They Explore the Ziggurat of Ur," *Washington Post*, 11 August 2006, A16; "Tallil Air Base."

18. "Soundtrack to the War," *Rolling Stone*, 24 August 2006, 20, 22.

19. "G.I.s Deployed in Iraq Desert with Lots of American Stuff."

20. "Biggest Base in Iraq Has Small-Town Feel; Most Troops at Balad Never Meet Iraqis."

21. "Pogue," possibly a reference to the acronym POG, or "Person Other Than Grunt," was also popular, particularly among marines.

22. Fagan and Cotto describe the genesis of the song and the attention it garnered on their shared MySpace page. Fagan and Cotto, MySpace profile created 1 October 2006, http://www.myspace.com/fagancotto (15 August 2010).

23. Parrottrooper, "FOBbit!!!". Though the soldiers responsible for the song "FOB Life" that accompanies Parrottrooper's video were stationed in Iraq, Parrottrooper was stationed in Afghanistan, where large rearward bases had most of the same amenities as those in Iraq. There are at least two other video montages on YouTube inspired by "FOB Life," both of which consist of photographs and film taken in Iraq.

24. Mikel Fagan and Juan Cotto, "FOB Life," as played in the music video "FOBbit!!!" See also Ccimsiko9, "Fob Life SONG FOBBIT Iraq," and Tianoterrorist, "Fobbit Music Video." All together, the three videos had about 150,000 hits on YouTube and nearly 600 comments as of December 2010.

25. Delobius [Alex Barnes], "Guilt of a REMF."

26. Ibid. (emphasis in the original).

27. The suicide rate among U.S. Army troops in Iraq in 2003 was 15.6 per 100,000, higher than the Army's recent average of 11.9, but still lower than the rate for men of comparable age in general. "Many Troops Dissatisfied, Iraq Poll Finds," *Washington Post*, 16 October 2003, A1; "In Army Survey, Troops in Iraq Report Low Morale," *Washington Post*, 26 March 2004, A18.

28. For example, the Army replaced its caps with berets, which were once reserved for Rangers and the Special Forces, and it required all soldiers, everywhere in the world, to wear the army combat uniform. "Army Plans Steps to Heighten 'Warrior Ethos'; Leaders View Many Soldiers as Too Specialized," *Washington Post*, 8 September 2003, A19; "U.S. Army's Kill-Kill Ethos under Fire," *Sunday Times* (London), 24 September 2006, 27.

29. W. D. Ehrhart, quoted in Moser, *New Winter Soldiers*, 41.

30. David Levy discusses the fracturing of the post–World War II consensus over U.S. foreign policy at length in *The Debate over Vietnam*.

31. See "Vietnam: A Television History."

32. Griffiths, *Vietnam Inc.*, 174–77.

33. "Let's Change Our Methods of Work," quoted in Nguyen Khac Vien, *Tradition and Revolution in Vietnam*, 48.

34. See, for example, Sharp, *Strategy for Defeat*; Summers, *On Strategy*; Krepinevich, *The Army and Vietnam*; and Walton, *The Myth of Inevitable U.S. Defeat in Vietnam*.

35. *Logistics Review*, 8:17; Heiser, *Vietnam Studies*, 259–60.

36. "Interview with Marine Col. Thomas X. Hammes (Ret.)," in Frontline, *Private Warriors*.

37. "What Is Left Behind: A Benchmark of Progress, Electrical Grid Fails Iraqis," *New York Times*, 2 August 2010, A1; "Audit: U.S. Can't Account for Billions In Iraqi Funds."

38. Kidder, *My Detachment*, 8.

39. "Their War," *Washington Post*, 22 July 2007, W10.

40. "The View from over There"; "Stuffing Battlefield Stockings; Churches and Schools Send Items, from Tuna to Toothpaste," *Washington Post*, 14 December 2007, B03; Pizza4Patriots Web site, http://www.pizzas4patriots.com (18 August 2010).

41. Herr, *Dispatches*, 260.

BIBLIOGRAPHY

ARCHIVES

Military History Institute, Carlisle, Pa.

   Bowers, Verne L. Deputy Chief of Staff for Personnel and Administration, Head-
      quarters, U.S. Army Vietnam. "Final Report." 10 September
      1970.

   "Improvement of U.S. Logistic Support in RVN, October 26, 1964."

   MACV Command Information Pamphlet No. 13-67, "Your R&R Program."
      April 1967.

   MACV Directive No. 60-6, "Exchange Service: Exchange Privileges." 10 October
      1971.

   MACV Directive No. 60-7, "Exchange Service: MACV Ration Cards." 14 July 1969.

   MACV Directive No. 60-8, "Exchange Service Alcoholic Beverage Control."
      4 March 1969.

   "MACV J-2 Logistics Fact Book." 1 June 1967.

   U.S. Army Staff Study. *Improvement of U.S. Logistic Systems in Republic of
      Vietnam—Logistic Situation in RVN, October 26, 1964.*

   USARV Command Information Fact Sheet No. 7-66, "Your R&R Program."
      7 June 1966.

   USARV Fact Sheet No. 3-70, "Customs Laws and You." 20 July 1969.

   USARV Fact Sheet No. 10-69, "The Expeditious Management of Superfluous
      Currency, or Making Your Pay Work for You." 15 November
      1968.

   USARV Fact Sheet No. 15-68, "Returning to CONUS." 22 February 1968.

National Archives and Records Administration, College Park, Md.

   Record Group 111. Records of the Office of the Chief Signal Officer
      Army Pictorial Service/Signal Corps

   Record Group 472. United States Forces in Southeast Asia, 1950–1975
      Military Assistance Command Vietnam Information Office
         AFVN Organizational History Files
         Command Information Division Files
            Command Fact Sheets and Instructions, 1968–1971
               Unit Press Bulletins, 1970
      Military Assistance Command Vietnam Inspector General
         Investigation Division Reports
         Investigations and Complaints Division Reports
            Complaints Files—Administrative

Personal Property Division
    U.S. Army Mortuary, Saigon
Records of Personal Effects
    Mortuary Services Division
        U.S. Army Mortuary, Danang
Records of the Pleiku Graves Registration Point
U.S. Army Vietnam Adjutant General
    Administrative Services Division
        Circulars
            United States Army Support Group Vietnam
    Public Information Division
        General Records
            USARV Posters, 1967
        Office Administration, 1972
U.S. Army Vietnam Command Historian
    History Source File
        HQUSARV War Museum, 1969
    Operational Reports—Lessons Learned (ORLLS)
    Senior Officer Debriefing Reports
U.S. Army Vietnam Deputy Chief of Staff for Personnel and
        Administration
    Military Personnel and Policy Division
        Morale and Welfare Branch
            General Records, 1968–1972
                Misc. Correspondence, 1972
    Non-appropriated Funds Division
        General Records, 1969–1972
            AFVN File, 1969
                Joint Services NAF Minutes (Pt. 1 of 2), 1971
U.S. Army Vietnam Information Office
    Command Information Division
        General Records, 1965–1971
U.S. Army Vietnam Inspector General
    Inspection and Complaint Division
        Case Files
U.S. Army Vietnam Provost Marshall Section
    Administrative Office
        General Records
            Criminal Investigation Instruction File, 1969
    Plans and Operations Division
        General Records
U.S. Army Vietnam Special Services Agency
    "Administrative History" (Finding Aid)
    Entertainment Branch
        Administrative Records

General Administrative Records
General Administrative Records, 1966–1972
General Administrative Records, 1968
History Files, 1970–1972

GOVERNMENT PUBLICATIONS

Army and Air Force Exchange Service. "AAFES History." N.d. http://www.aafes.com/pa/history/milestones.asp. 28 May 2009.
———. "Milestones." N.d. http://www.aafes.com/pa/history/milestones.asp#2000s. 14 August 2009.
Defense Finance and Accounting Service. "Monthly Basic Pay and Allowances," 1 July 1968. *http://www.dfas.mil/militarypay/militarypaytables/militarypaypriorrates/1968.pdf*. 8 June 2009.
Department of the Army Field Manual FM 101-01, *Staff Officers Field Manual: The G.1. Manual*. Washington: Department of the Army, 1955.
Department of the Army Field Manual FM 101-5, *Staff Officers Field Manual: Staff Organization and Procedure*. Washington: Department of the Army, 1960.
Department of the Army Field Manual FM 101-5, *Staff Officers Field Manual: Staff Organization and Procedure*. Washington: Department of the Army, 1968.
Department of the Army Field Manual FM 101-5, *Staff Officers Field Manual: Staff Organization and Procedure*. Washington: Department of the Army, 1972.
Department of the Army Pamphlet No. 21-59, *An Introduction to the Army Service Club Program*. Washington: Department of the Army, 1953.
Department of the Army Pamphlet No. 27-162, *Claims*. Washington: Department of the Army, January 1968.
Department of the Army Pamphlet No. 28-5, *Facility Management Guide: The Army Crafts Program*. Washington: Department of the Army, 1965.
Department of the Army Pamphlet No. 28-8, *Army Entertainment Program Operational Guide*. Washington: Department of the Army, September 1966.
Department of the Army Pamphlet No. 360-411, *A Pocket Guide to Vietnam*. Washington: Department of the Army, 1966.
Department of the Army Pamphlet No. 360-608, *Shopping in the Far East*. Washington: Department of the Army, 1968.
Department of the Army Pamphlet No. 608-16, *Helpful Hints for Personnel Ordered to Vietnam*. Washington: Department of the Army, March 1968.
Department of the Army Pamphlet No. 608-16, *Helpful Hints for Personnel Ordered to the Republic of Vietnam*. Washington: Department of the Army, August 1970.
Department of the Army Poster 360-119, "The Soldier in Vietnam." Washington: USGPO, June 1969.
Department of Veterans Affairs. "'Presumptive' Disability Benefits for Certain Groups of Veterans," December 2008. http://www.vba.va.gov/VBA/benefits/factsheets/serviceconnected/presumptive.doc. 30 June 2009.
Dunn, Carroll H. *Vietnam Studies: Base Development in South Vietnam, 1965–1970*. Washington: USGPO, 1973.

Heiser, Joseph M., Jr. *Vietnam Studies: Logistic Support.* Washington: Department of the Army, 1974.

Joint Logistics Review Board. *Logistic Support in the Vietnam Era.* Vol. 2, *A Summary Assessment with Major Findings and Recommendations.* Washington: Department of the Army, n.d.

Kellen, Konrad. *Conversations with Enemy Soldiers in Late 1968/Early 1969: A Study of Motivation and Morale.* Prepared for the Office of the Assistant Secretary of Defense/International Security Affairs and the Advanced Research Projects Agency. Santa Monica, Calif.: Rand, 1970.

The Logistics Review: U.S. Army in Vietnam, 1965–1969. Vol. 1, *System Overview.* San Francisco: Headquarters, U.S. Army Vietnam, [ca. 1970].

McGrath, John J. "The Other End of the Spear: The Tooth-to-Tail Ratio (T3R) in Modern Military Operations." The Long War Series Occasional Paper 23. Fort Leavenworth, Kans.: Combat Studies Institute Press, 2007.

Termination and Closeout of Southeast Asia Contracts. Fort Shafter, Hawaii: U.S. Army, Western Command, 1979.

Tregaskis, Richard. *Building the Bases: The History of Construction in Southeast Asia.* Washington: USGPO, 1973.

Veterans Administration. *Myths and Realities: A Study of Attitudes toward Vietnam Era Veterans.* Washington: USGPO, 1980.

UNIT NEWSPAPERS

These officially sanctioned newspapers were published by and for American soldiers in Vietnam. All the titles are housed at the U.S. Army Military History Institute (MHI) in Carlisle, Pa., except those marked with †, which were examined in the Command Information Division Files of the MACV Command Information Office at the National Archives and Records Administration in College Park, Md. I read the available issues in their entirety. Titles marked with * are quoted directly in the text.

Americal
*Americal News Sheet**
American Traveler
*Army Reporter**
Artillery Review
Automatic Eighth
Avian 34
Aviator
Battle-Ax Banner
*Black Baron Release**
Black Horse
Black Lightning Newsletter
*Blackjack Flier†**
Black Spade

Blades of Destiny
Blazer
Brigade By-Line
*Brigadier**
Bronco Tribune
Bulldozer Bugle
Cannon Ears
Cannoneer
*Castle Courier**
Castle Horizon
*Cavalair**
*Charger**
Charlie Chatter
CMAC Harpoon
*Colt 45 News**

Command Communications Communicator
Constructioneer
Credibilis
Crusader
Culvert
Cyclo-Media
Daily News Brief
Danger Forward
Dateline-29
*Delta Advisor**
*Delta Developer**
*Delta Dragon**
Delta Provider
Dental Newsletter

Diamond Dust*
Diehard Digest
Dimension*
Dirtmover*
Dollars & Sense*
Double Nickel*
Dragon Chatter
Dragonfire
Drumfire Blaze*
Dynamo
Dynamo Dispatch
Eagle Talons*
815th Times
Eliminators*
Esprit*
Express
Falcon*
Feedback
Fireball Express*
Fire Base 173*
1st Logistical Command
    Magazine*
1st Signal Team
First Team*
Five-O-Duce
5-Star Review
Flight Watcher
44th Brigadier†*
Frontier Courier*
Geronimo Weekly
Gimlet
Gimlet News
Go Devil
Green Beret*
Griffin Gab*
Guardian*
Guardians & Enforcers*
Hawk*
Hawk Talk
Head Shed*
Head Shed Happenings
Hellcat
Hell Fire Herald*
Hi-Lite (newsletter)
Hi-Lite (newspaper)*

Hi-Lite Magazine*
Hipshoot
Hook & Star
Horizon
Hurricane
Informer*
Innkeeper
Ivy Leaf*
·Jackstaff News
Kysu*
Laterite Lantern*
Legionnaire's Ledger
Link
Lion's Roar*
Long Binh Post†*
Messenger*
Monthly News Bulletin
Morning News
Morning News Highlights
Nighthawk
Northern Log*
Northernmost
Observer†*
Octagon*
Octofoil*
Old Guard Mountainmen
Old Reliable*
128th Signal Reporter
PA&E News*
Pacific Paraglide
Pacific Stars and Stripes
Pan-Tel, 1st Battalion*
Peace Builders Progress
Poolside Parable
Practice Alert
Professional*
Professionals*
Qui Nhon Logman*
Redcatcher
Red Devil Brigade*
Redhorse Review
Redleg Special
Reflector
Rendezvous with Destiny*
Roadrunner

Roger That*
Roundup*
Sandbagger
Scars & Gripes*
Scars & Scrapes
Screaming Eagle†*
Seahorse Gazette
Seahorse News*
Sea Lion
Sea Tiger*
Semper Primus*
79th Pioneer
Ship 'n Shore*
Short-Timers Gazette*
Signal Sounds
Sin Loi Times*
Sky Beaver Blurb
Sky Builder
Sky Master*
Sky Soldier Magazine
Southern Cross*
Spearheader
Spirit of the 87th
Spurs and Lightning
Steadfast and Loyal*
Steady Humper
Sunday Punch*
Super Group Poop
Swampy Sentinel
Syke's Regulars Reporter*
This Month with the 39th*
This Week with the 39th
Thong Com
Thunder*
Tiger Tales
Tour 365
Trac III*
Traffic Lite*
Triumvirate, 5th Battalion*
Tropic Lightning News*
XXIV Corps Courier*
299th Engineer Battalion
    Newsletter
Typhoon
Unicorn

Up Against the Wall
Uptight*
USAHAC Command
   Newsletter*
Vagabond Voice

Validus Videre
Varsity Newsletter*
Vietnam Builders
Vietnam Review*
Voice of the Delta

Voice of the Viking
Volcano
Warrior*
Wavy Arrow
West of the West

CIVILIAN NEWSPAPERS AND MAGAZINES

Atlanta Journal-
   Constitution
Broadcast Engineering
Congressional Quarterly
Grunt Free Press

Los Angeles Times
Newsweek
New York Times
Rolling Stone
Sunday Times (London)

Time
T.V. Guide
Wall Street Journal
Washington Post
Washington Times

OTHER PUBLISHED SOURCES

Adams, John A. *The Noise That Never Dies: Tan Son Nhut, 1970–1971*. College Station, Tex.: Intaglio Press, 2003.

Allison, William. "War for Sale: The Black Market, Currency Manipulation and Corruption in the American War in Vietnam." *War & Society* 21 (October 2003): 135–64.

Anderson, Charles R. *Vietnam: The Other War*. Novato, Calif.: Presidio Press, 1982.

Andrews, Owen, C., Douglass Elliott, and Laurence L. Levin, eds. *Vietnam: Images from Combat Photographers*. Washington: Starwood Publishing, 1991.

Appy, Christian G., ed. *Patriots: The Vietnam War Remembered from All Sides*. New York: Viking, 2003.

———. *Working-Class War: American Combat Soldiers and Vietnam*. Chapel Hill: University of North Carolina Press, 1993.

"Audit: U.S. Can't Account for Billions In Iraqi Funds." *NPR*, 27 July 2010. http://www.npr.org/templates/story/story.php?storyId=128793151. 16 August 2010.

Bailey, Beth. *America's Army: Making the All-Volunteer Force*. Cambridge: Harvard University Press, Belknap Press, 2009.

———. "The Army in the Marketplace: Recruiting an All-Volunteer Force." *Journal of American History* 94 (June 2007): 47–74.

Bakhtin, Mikhail. *Rabelais and His World*. Translated by Helene Iswolsky. Bloomington: Indiana University Press, 1984.

Baritz, Loren. *Backfire: A History of How American Culture Led Us into Vietnam and Made Us Fight the Way We Did*. New York: William Morrow and Co., 1985.

Barnett, Arnold, Timothy Stanley, and Michael Shore. "America's Vietnam Casualties: Victims of a Class War?" *Operations Research* 40 (September–October 1992): 856–66.

Baskir, Lawrence M., and William A. Strauss. *Chance and Circumstance: The Draft, the War, and the Vietnam Generation*. New York: Knopf, 1978.

Batty, Roy [Owen Powell]. "Bonkers." 26 July 2007. http://gocomics.typepad.com/the_sandbox/2007/07/bonkers---batty.html. 15 August 2010.

————. "The Keep." 8 March 2007. http://gocomics.typepad.com/the_sandbox/ 2007/03/the_keep.html. 1 September 2009.

————. "The Termite Mound." 23 April 2007. http://gocomics.typepad.com/the_ sandbox/2007/04/the_termite_mou.html. 1 September 2009.

Bergerud, Eric M. *Red Thunder, Tropic Lightning: The World of a Combat Division in Vietnam.* Boulder, Colo.: Westview Press, 1993.

Bilton, Michael, and Kevin Sim. *Four Hours in My Lai.* New York: Penguin Books, 1993.

Bodle, Wayne. *The Valley Forge Winter: Civilians and Soldiers in War.* University Park: Pennsylvania State University Press, 2002.

Boldrini, Nik. *Nik Boldrini's Sitting Duck: Adventures of a Saigon Warrior.* Seattle, Wash.: OBS Publishing, 1996.

Bonior, David E., Steven M. Champlin, and Timothy S. Kolly. *The Vietnam Veteran: A History of Neglect.* New York: Praeger, 1984.

Broyles, William, Jr. *Brothers in Arms: A Journey from War to Peace.* New York: Knopf, 1986.

————. "Why Men Love War." *Esquire*, November 1984, 55–58, 61–62, 65.

Buchanan, Sherry, ed. *Mekong Diaries: Viet Cong Drawings and Stories, 1964–1975.* Chicago: University of Chicago Press, 2008.

————, ed. *Vietnam Zippos: American Soldiers' Engravings and Stories, 1965–1973.* Chicago: University of Chicago Press, 2007.

Burkett, B. G., and Glenna Whitley. *Stolen Valor: How the Vietnam Generation Was Robbed of Its Heroes and Its History.* Dallas: Verity Press, 1998.

Carter, James M. *Inventing Vietnam: The United States and State Building, 1954–1968.* New York: Cambridge University Press, 2008.

Ccimsik09. "Fob Life SONG FOBBIT Iraq." YouTube video. 28 January 2009. http:// www.youtube.com/watch?v=p_ZS_UxF6Bw&feature=related. 1 August 2009.

Clark, Gregory C., ed. *Words of the Vietnam War: The Slang, Jargon, Abbreviations, Acronyms, Nomenclature, Nicknames, Pseudonyms, Slogans, Specs, Euphemisms, Double-talk, Chants, and Names and Places of the Era of United States Involvement in Vietnam.* Jefferson, N.C.: McFarland, 1990.

Clodfelter, Michael. *Vietnam in Military Statistics: A History of the Indochina Wars, 1772–1991.* Jefferson, N.C.: McFarland, 1995.

Cohen, Lizabeth. *A Consumer's Republic: The Politics of Mass Consumption in Postwar America.* New York: Knopf, 2003.

Cortright, David. *Soldiers in Revolt: G.I. Resistance during the Vietnam War.* Chicago: Haymarket Books, 2005.

Cortright, David, and Max Watts. *Left Face: Soldier Unions and Resistance Movements in Modern Armies.* Westport, Conn.: Greenwood Press, 1991.

Cross, Frank A., Jr. "Rice Will Grow Again." In *Made in America, Sold in the Nam: A Continuing Legacy of Pain*, edited by Rick Ritter and Paul Richards, 76. Ann Arbor, Mich.: Loving Healing Press, 2006.

Cross, Gary. *An All-Consuming Century: Why Commercialism Won in Modern America.* New York: Columbia University Press, 2000.

Delobius [Alex Barnes]. "A Day in the Life Of." *Blog Machine City*, 1 December 2004. http://blog.delobi.us/2004/12/01/a-day-in-the-life-of/. 5 August 2009.

———. "Guilt of a REMF." *Blog Machine City*, 14 December 2004. http://blog.delobi.us/2004/12/14/guilt-of-a-remf/. 5 August 2009.

Donovan, David. *Once a Warrior King: Memories of an Officer in Vietnam*. New York: McGraw-Hill, 1985.

"Don't Support the Troops? Think about This." Facebook Group, May 2007. http://www.facebook.com/group.php?gid=2546176744&ref=search&sid=767757914.3792284816..1. 14 August 2009.

Dunn, Joe P. *Desk Warrior: Memoirs of a Combat REMF*. Needham Heights, Mass.: Pearson Custom Publishing, 1999.

Dunnigan, James F., and Albert A. Nofi. *Dirty Little Secrets of the Vietnam War*. New York: St. Martin's Griffin, 2000.

Edelman, Bernard, ed. *Dear America: Letters Home from Vietnam*. New York: Pocket Books, 1985.

Ehrhart, W. D. *Vietnam Perkasie: A Combat Marine's Memoir*. New York: Zebra Books, 1983.

Elliott, Duong Van Mai. *The Sacred Willow: Four Generations in the Life of a Vietnamese Family*. New York: Oxford University Press, 1999.

Ellis, John. *Eye-Deep in Hell: Trench Warfare in World War I*. Baltimore: Johns Hopkins University Press, 1976.

Evans, Daniel E., Jr., and Charles W. Sasser. *Doc: Platoon Medic*. New York: Writer's Club Press, 2002.

Fallows, James. "Low-Class Conclusions." *Atlantic Monthly*, April 1993, 38–42.

———. "What Did You Do in the Class War, Daddy?" *Washington Monthly*, October 1975, 5–19.

Foley, Michael S. *Confronting the War Machine: Draft Resistance during the Vietnam War*. Chapel Hill: University of North Carolina Press, 2007.

Frontline. "Private Warriors." Companion Web site to PBS broadcast, 21 June 2005. http://www.pbs.org/wgbh/pages/frontline/shows/warriors/. 15 August 2010.

Fussell, Paul. *The Great War and Modern Memory*. Oxford: Oxford University Press, 1975.

The Gallup Poll: Public Opinion, 1935–1971. Vol. 3. New York: Random House, 1972.

Griffiths, Philip Jones. *Vietnam Inc*. New York: Phaidon Press, 2001.

Grossman, Dave. *On Killing: The Psychological Cost of Learning to Kill in War and Society*. New York: Back Bay Books, 1996.

Halberstam, David. *Ho*. New York: McGraw-Hill, 1987.

Hamilton-Paterson, James. *The Greedy War (A Very Personal War)*. New York: David McKay Co., 1971.

Hass, Kristin Ann. *Carried to the Wall: American Memory and the Vietnam Veterans Memorial*. Berkeley: University of California Press, 1998.

Herr, Michael. *Dispatches*. New York: Avon Books, 1978.

Herring, George C. *America's Longest War: The United States and Vietnam, 1950–1975*. Boston: McGraw-Hill, 2002.

Hine, Thomas. *Populuxe*. New York: Knopf, 1986.

"History of the USO." United Service Organizations official Web site. http://www.uso.org/whoweare/ourproudhistory/historyoftheuso/. 9 June 2009.

Hoffman, George. "Grunt's Dream." 1994. http://www.vietvet.org/gdream.htm.
9 August 2010.

Hunt, Andrew E. *The Turning: A History of Vietnam Veterans against the War.* New
York: New York University Press, 1999.

"Iraq: A Respite from War." *Soldiers*, February 2004, 10–19.

Jeffords, Susan. *The Remasculinization of America: Gender and the Vietnam War.*
Bloomington: Indiana University Press, 1989.

Jury, Mark. *The Vietnam Photo Book.* New York: Grossman Publishers, 1971.

Kammen, Michael. *A Season of Youth: The American Revolution and the Historical
Imagination.* New York: Knopf, 1978.

Kidder, Tracy. *My Detachment: A Memoir.* New York: Random House, 2006.

Kinnard, Douglas. *The War Managers.* Hanover, Vt.: University Press of New England,
1977.

Kinney, Katherine. *Friendly Fire: American Images of the Vietnam War.* New York:
Oxford University Press, 2000.

Kiver, Phil. *182 Days in Iraq.* Tarentum, Pa.: Word Association Publishers, 2006.

Kovic, Ron. *Born on the Fourth of July.* New York: McGraw-Hill, 1976.

Kramer, Michael Jacob. "The Civics of Rock: Sixties Countercultural Music and the
Transformation of the Public Sphere." Ph.D. diss., University of North Carolina,
2006.

Krepinevich, Andrew. *The Army and Vietnam.* Baltimore: Johns Hopkins University
Press, 1986.

Kuzmarov, Jeremy. *The Myth of the Addicted Army: Vietnam and the Modern War on
Drugs.* Amherst: University of Massachusetts Press, 2009.

Lair, Meredith H. "Redcoat Theater: Negotiating Identity in Occupied Philadelphia,
1777–78." In *Pennsylvania's Revolution*, edited by William Pencak, 192–210.
University Park: Pennsylvania State University Press, 2009.

———. "Tour of Duty." Exhibit script for the Vietnam Era Educational Center. New
Jersey Vietnam Veterans Memorial Foundation. Holmdel, N.J., 1998.

Leed, Eric J. *No Man's Land: Combat and Identity in World War I.* Cambridge:
Cambridge University Press, 1979.

Lembcke, Jerry. *The Spitting Image: Myth, Memory, and the Legacy of Vietnam.* New
York: New York University Press, 1998.

Leninger, Jack. *Time Heals No Wounds.* New York: Ballantine Books, 1993.

Levy, David. *The Debate over Vietnam.* Baltimore: Johns Hopkins University Press,
1995.

Lewes, James. *Protest and Survive: Underground G.I. Newspapers during the Vietnam
War.* Westport, Conn.: Praeger, 2003.

Longley, Kyle. *Grunts: The American Combat Soldier in Vietnam.* Armonk, N.Y.: M. E.
Sharpe, 2008.

Marling, Karal Ann. *As Seen on TV: The Visual Culture of Everyday Life in the 1950s.*
Cambridge: Harvard University Press, 1994.

Marshall, Kathryn. *In the Combat Zone: An Oral History of American Women in Vietnam, 1966–1975.* Boston: Little, Brown, 1987.

May, Elaine Tyler. "The Commodity Trap: Consumerism and the Modern Home." In

Homeward Bound: American Families in the Cold War Era, 143–62. New York: Basic Books, 1999.

McKegney, Dan. "The Carnival of Vietnam, a REMF View." http://www.viet-remf.net/ HomePage.htm. 14 September 2008.

McMaster, H. R. *Dereliction of Duty: Lyndon Johnson, Robert McNamara, the Joint Chiefs of Staff, and the Lies That Led to Vietnam.* New York: HarperCollins, 1997.

McNally, Robert J. "Progress and Controversy in the Study of Posttraumatic Stress Disorder." *Annual Review of Psychology* 54 (2003): 229–52.

Melbourne, Robert E. *Advance Base Construction by Civilian Contactors in War Zones.* Ph.D. diss., University of Southern California, 1996.

Meyers, Kate Beaird. "Fragmentary Mosaics: Vietnam War 'Histories' and Postmodern Epistemology." *Genre* 21 (Winter 1988): 535–52.

Moser, Richard R. *The New Winter Soldiers: G.I. and Veteran Dissent during the Vietnam Era.* New Brunswick, N.J.: Rutgers University Press, 1996.

Moskos, Charles C., Jr. "The American Combat Soldier in Vietnam." *Journal of Social Issues* 31 (Fall 1975): 25–37.

———. "Why Men Fight: American Combat Soldiers in Vietnam." *Trans-Action: Social Science and Modern Society* 7, no. 1 (1969): 13–23.

Mosse, George L. *Nationalism and Sexuality: Middle-Class Morality and Sexual Norms in Modern Europe.* Madison: University of Wisconsin Press, 1985.

Muehlberg, Dean O. *REMF "War Stories": 17th CAG—Nha Trang, Vietnam—1969.* Lulu.com, 2005.

Nguyen Khac Vien. *Tradition and Revolution in Vietnam.* Translated by Linda Yarr, Jayne Werner, and Tran Tuong Nhu. Berkeley: Indochina Resource Center, 1974.

Nicosia, Gerald. *Home to War: A History of the Vietnam Veterans' Movement.* New York: Three Rivers Press, 2001.

Noel, Reuben, and Nancy Noel. *Saigon for a Song: The True Story of a Gig to Remember.* Phoenix, Ariz.: UCS Press, 1987.

O'Brien, Tim. *The Things They Carried.* Boston: Houghton Mifflin, 1990.

Page, Tim. *Another Vietnam: Pictures of the War from the Other Side.* Edited by Doug Niven and Chris Riley. New York: National Geographic, 2002.

Parrottrooper. "FOBbit!!!" YouTube video. 12 June 2007. http://www.youtube.com/ watch?v=ufCL38cVOkg. 1 August 2009.

Potter, David. *People of Plenty: Economic Abundance and the American Character.* Chicago: University of Chicago Press, 1973.

Purcell, Sarah J. *Sealed with Blood: War, Sacrifice, and Memory in Revolutionary America.* Philadelphia: University of Pennsylvania Press, 2002.

Pyle, Ernie. *Here Is Your War.* New York: Henry Holt and Co., 1943.

Reinberg, Linda, ed. *In the Field: The Language of the Vietnam War.* New York: Facts on File, 1991.

Schurr, Sam H., et al. *Electricity in the American Economy: Agent of Technological Progress.* New York: Greenwood Press, 1990.

Severo, Richard, and Lewis Milford. *The Wages of War: When America's Soldiers Came Home—From Valley Forge to Vietnam.* New York: Simon and Schuster, 1989.

Sharp, U. S. Grant. *Strategy for Defeat: Vietnam in Retrospect*. Novato, Calif.: Presidio Press, 1986.

Sontag, Susan. *On Photography*. New York: Farrar, Straus, and Giroux, 1977.

Stur, Heather. "Perfume and Lipstick in the Boonies: Red Cross SRAO and the Vietnam War." *The Sixties* 1 (December 2008): 151–65.

Summers, Harry G., Jr. *On Strategy: A Critical Analysis of the Vietnam War*. Novato, Calif.: Presidio Press, 1982.

"Tallil Air Base." GlobalSecurity.org. http://www.globalsecurity.org/military/world/iraq/tallil.htm. 18 September 2009.

Taylor, Gordon O. "Cacciato's Grassy Hill." *Genre* 21 (Winter 1988): 393–407.

Tianoterrorist. "Fobbit Music Video." YouTube video. 16 December 2006. http://www.youtube.com/watch?v=6Hqv5yBaXaI. 1 August 2009.

Upton, William R. *Pizza and Mortars: Ba-Muoi-Ba and Body Bags*. Bloomington, Ind.: Xlibris, 2003.

"Vietnam: A Television History." Pt. 5, "America Takes Charge, 1965–1967." Video. 60 minutes. Produced by WGBH Boston, 1982.

"The View from over There." *Newsweek* Web Exclusive, 14 December 2005. http://www.anysoldier.com/Stuff/Articles/2005/MSNBC-Newsweek2-14Dec05.pdf. 18 August 2010.

Vuic, Kara Dixon. *Officer, Nurse, Woman: The U.S. Army Nurse Corps in the Vietnam War*. Baltimore: Johns Hopkins University Press, 2010.

Walker, Keith. *A Piece of My Heart: The Stories of Twenty-Six American Women Who Served in Vietnam*. New York: Ballantine Books, 1985.

Walton, C. Dale. *The Myth of Inevitable U.S. Defeat in Vietnam*. London: Frank Cass, 2002.

Watson, Bruce Allen. *When Soldiers Quit: Studies in Military Disintegration*. Westport, Conn.: Praeger, 1997.

Watson, George M., Jr. *Voices from the Rear: Vietnam, 1969–1970*. Bloomington, Ind.: Xlibris, 2001.

Wattenberg, Ben J., ed. *The Statistical History of the United States from Colonial Times to the Present*. New York: Basic Books, 1976.

Whalon, Pete. *The Saigon Zoo: Vietnam's Other War: Sex, Drugs, and Rock 'n Roll: A Very Different Vietnam Memoir*. West Conshohocken, Pa.: Infinity Publishing, 2004.

What Did You Do in the War, Daddy? A Visual History of Propaganda Posters. Introduction by Peter Stanley. Oxford: Oxford University Press, 1983.

Wheatley, Bob. "Hello, and Welcome! . . . Who Am I?" and "What Motivated Me to Establish Viet-REMF?" http://www.viet-remf.net. 9 August 2010.

Wiknik, Arthur, Jr. *Nam Sense: Surviving Vietnam with the 101st Airborne Division*. Havertown, Pa.: Casemate, 2005.

Wilken, Steve. *Why Didn't You Have to Go to Vietnam, Daddy?* Dallas: Truesource Publishing/Starving Writers, 2009.

Wills, Garry. *John Wayne's America: The Politics of Celebrity*. New York: Simon and Schuster, 1997.

Willson, David A. *REMF Diary: A Novel of the Vietnam War Zone*. Seattle: Black Heron Press, 1988.

———. *The REMF Returns*. Seattle: Black Heron Press, 1992.

Wolff, Tobias. *In Pharaoh's Army: Memories of the Lost War*. New York: Knopf, 1994.

Yarborough, Tom. *Da Nang Diary: A Forward Air Controller's Year of Combat over Vietnam*. New York: St. Martin's, 1990.

Yarborough, Trin. *Surviving Twice: Amerasian Children of the Vietnam War*. Dulles, Va.: Potomac Books, 2005.

Yarrow, Andrew. "Visions of Abundance: The Rise of Economic Thinking and Changing Views of American Identity, 1945–65." Ph.D. diss., George Mason University, 2006.

Zinman, Toby Silverman. "Search and Destroy: The Drama of the Vietnam War." *Theatre Journal* 42 (March 1990): 5–26.

INDEX

Abundance, 8; in American collective memories of war, 20–21, 239; effects of, 22, 70, 91, 241–42, 244; influence on U.S. foreign policy, 246–47; Iraqi perspectives on, 243–44; Vietnamese perspectives on, 241–42

A.C.-47 gunship, 196–97

AFVN radio, 133–34, 187, 188, 195

AFVN-TV, 131–34, 187, 188

Agent Orange, 212, 246

Agent Orange Act of 1991, 272 (n. 54)

Alcohol, 135–37, 172–73. *See also* Open messes

All-volunteer force, 11, 92–95, 250 (n. 12)

Amerasian children, 271–72 (n. 46)

American foundation myth, 68, 239–40

American imperialism, 244

American Revolution, 68, 240

Antiwar movement, 12–14, 88–89

Apocalypse Now, 143, 195

Area Military Shows, 131

Armed Forces Theatre Vietnam, 127

Army and Air Force Exchange Service, 148–49, 230

Army Crafts Program, 121–22

Aspin, Les, 95

Athletics, 117, 118–21

Baggage policies, 169

Bakeries, 76

Bakhtin, Mikhail, 183, 194

Barracks: construction of, 81–82; décor, 83–85

Base development, 72–73

Bataan Death March, 99–100

Battle of Khe Sanh, 105–6

Battle of the Bulge, 68

Beaches, 114–16, 120, 193

Beverage sales, 157, 172–73

Billeting policy, 80–81

Black market, 173

Blue Eagle broadcasts, 133

Body counts, 182–83, 200

Boredom: social consequences of, 49, 108, 132; success in combating, 138–39, 141–42

Bowling, 119–20, 260 (n. 31)

Brothels, 34, 171, 207, 210

Broyles, William, 49, 52, 79, 89, 90–91, 99, 196, 220–21

Calling cards, 201–2, 271 (nn. 33, 34)

Cameras, 159–60, 180, 234–36, 247

Camp Alpha, 111–12

Camp Enari, 72–73

Cam Ranh Bay, 93–95, 118; soldier complaints at, 97–99, 100

Capa, Robert, 102, 238

Careerism, 10–11, 139, 152

Carnival, 182–83, 212

Car sales, 163

Car shopping, 164, 178

Casualties: Iraq War, 22; Persian Gulf War, 22; rates by service branch, 16–17; Vietnamese, 21, 142; Vietnam War, military, 9, 246, 250 (n. 7), 257 (n. 68)

China Beach, 112–13

China Fleet Club, 156

Civic action programs, 187

Civic engagement, 245–46

Civil-military relations, 32–32, 206–7

Class, 18–19, 49–50, 250–51 (n. 20)

Clerks, 28–30, 50–51

Clubs. *See* Open Messes

Coffee houses, 137–38

Cold storage, 76–77

Cold War, 240–41

Combat: definition of, 57, 223; euphemisms for, 197, 200; influence of class on participation in, 49–50; in Iraq War, 234; Vietnam War memoirs of, 40

Combat troops: desire to become non-combat troops, 58–59; ratio to support troops, 25–26, 249 (n. 3); resentment of noncombat troops, 47–50, 59–60, 63–64

Command Military Touring Shows, 131

Commercial Entertainment Units, 128–30

Complaints, 96–100

Concessions, 161–63; necessity of, 169–71; sales figures, 163–65

Construction, 69–70, 71–72, 118–19

Consumer goods, 145; available in Vietnam 150, 151; conflation with American culture, 148; as personal effects, 180–81

Consumerism, 247; challenges to, 146–47; Cold War political dimensions of, 146; definition of, 10; history of, 9, 69, 146; and Iraq War, 230; as key feature of Vietnam military service, 149, 223–24; as morale-building initiative, 153; in slang, 196; and Vietnamese civilians, 178

Consumption: of alcohol, 135–37, 172–73; as corrective for low morale, 91–92, 147–48; in Iraq, 229, 230, 233; limits on, 157–58, 169–75; military policies supporting, 167–69; in prescriptive literature, 177–78; purchasing patterns, 156–57; on R&R, 155–56; in recreation, 116–17; as reward of military service, 150, 178–79; as right of military service, 175; transformative effect of, 148, 175–76, 177–79

Contractors. See Military contractors

Coppola, Francis Ford, 143

Corruption, 203–4, 214–15

Counterinsurgency, 241–42

Courtesy Patrols, 38

Craft shops, 121–22

Currency controls, 174

Customs policies, 168–69, 178–79

Dayrooms, 132–33, 134, 231

D-Day landings, 102, 238

DEROS, 109–10, 116, 144

Dispatches, 247–48

Dollars for Lives policy, 70

Donahue, Troy, 128

Dong Tam, 73, 214–15

Draft system, 89–91, 257 (n. 53)

Drugs, 44, 91, 137, 201, 204; combating abuse of, 137–38

Eagle Beach, 114

Education centers, 124–25, 231

Ehrhart, W. D., 196, 211–12, 239–40, 245

Electricity consumption, 85–86

Electronic Repair Program, 167

Electronics, 158–60, 180, 230, 233–34

Enlistment, motives for, 104, 190–91

Entertainment, 125–31

Entertainment centers, 126–27

Facebook, 225–26

Factors limiting scope of this study, 17–18

Fast food chains, 229, 233

Fetishization of violence, 197–98, 200

5th Infantry Division, 114

1st Air Cavalry Division, 39, 182

1st Logistical Command, 32, 114, 131

Floorshows, 128–29

Fobbits, 236–37

Food: cake, 3, 22; doughnuts, 78; ice cream, 78, 224; in Iraq, 222–23, 229–30; in Vietnam, 74–80. *See also* Fast food chains

Forrest Gump, 195

Fort DeRussey, 137

4th Infantry Division, 72, 108

Fragging, 96

Freedom Hill Recreation Center, 114

"Fun, Travel, Adventure," 191, 270 (n. 15)

Fussell, Paul, 184–85

Gender, 18, 103–5, 135, 220

G.I. Movement, 61–63, 90; critique of war profiteering, 12

G.I. newspapers, 186–87, 207

G.I. resistance, 90

"Girlie magazines," 171, 268 (n. 63)

Go-carts, 33, 250 (n. 18)

Golf, 119

111–12; in-country, 112–13; and Iraq War, 231, 273–74 (n. 13); overseas, 110–12, 259 (n. 8); and prostitution, 207–8; stand-down, 113–14, 116, 193

R&R program, 109–16, 220, 247; rationale for, 109–10; usage rates, 111–12

Ration program, 157–58, 172–73; abuse of, 204

Reading, 122–24, 171–72, 207, 268 (n. 64)

Reagan, Ronald, 13, 141, 264 (n. 100)

Rearward posts, as incentive for reenlistment, 59

Recreation: facilities on Long Binh Post, 33–34; in Iraq War, 230–31; programs as consumption, 116; programs as targets of NLF, 139. *See also* Radio; Special Services; Television

Red Cross clubs, 134

Religious Retreat Center, 138

REMFs, 26–27, 236; postwar self-reflections of, 64–65; postwar transformation into grunts, 59–60, 212–19; wartime self-reflections of, 52–55

RMK-BRJ, 70, 121, 229, 254 (n. 5), 255 (n. 10)

Saigon Library Center, 123

Saigon tea, 177, 268–69 (n. 78)

The Sands of Iwo Jima, 101, 238

Saving Private Ryan, 102

Savings programs, 176–78

Service clubs, 134–35, 143, 182

Sex trade, 34, 171, 198, 207–11, 212

Sexuality, 135, 207–11, 232

Shelter, 80–82

Short timer's stick, 109

Shopping. *See* Consumption; P.X.'s

Showers, 82

Sky Soldier Beach, 114, 116

Slang, 80–81, 148, 190, 195–97

Socialist Republic of Vietnam, 244

"Some Gave All," 64–65

Sontag, Susan, 215–17

South Vietnam: effect of war on, 31–32, 206–7; inflation, 173, 268 (n. 70); insurgency, 142–43; landscape, 192; tourism, 191–93; U.S. nation building in, 69

Souvenirs, 119, 177, 178–79, 201, 214–15, 217–18, 267 (n. 42), 269 (n. 80); in Iraq War, 230. *See also* Photography

Special Services, 117–27, 231; athletics, 117, 118–21; beaches, 114–16, 120, 193; bowling, 119–20; clubs, 134–35; craft shops, 121–22; education centers, 124–25; Entertainment Branch, 125–31; evaluation of entertainment, 129–30; funding, 117–18; golf, 119; history of, 117; Library Branch, 122–24; musical touring shows, 127–31, 264 (n. 98); self-improvement programs, 121–25; swimming, 120–21

Stand-down R&R centers, 113–14

Star Far East Corporation, 171–72

Steam baths, 170–71

Stereos, 158–59

Stolen Valor Act of 2005, 60

Suffering: as essential component of Vietnam service, 212; role in American mythology, 68

Swimming pools, 120–21

Tallil Air Base, 230, 233

Tay Ninh Holiday Inn, 114

Television, 132–34, 187–89

Tet Offensive, 23–24, 153

Theater, 126–27, 262 (n. 55)

The Things They Carried, 106, 145–46

13th Aviation Battalion, 135

Tourism, 190–93, 215–17, 220; as military recruitment strategy, 190–91

Uniformed Services Savings Deposit Program, 177

United States Armed Forces Institute, 124–25

U.S. Army Vietnam, 17

U.S. Civil War, 197

U.S. military in Vietnam: base development, 71, 72–73, 242; civic action programs, 187; construction, 71; culture of, 10–11; euphemisms, 80–81, 195–97, 200; force structure, 25–26; interservice rivalry, 242; lessons learned, 242–43; logistics, 69, 70, 74–80; manpower shortage, 92, 257 (n. 61);

morale crisis, 50, 87–92; policies supporting consumption, 167–69; shift to all-volunteer force, 92–93

U.S. soldiers

—in Iraq: co-optation of combat stories, 236–37, 238; digital photography, 234–36; expectations of, 227, 228, 238; living conditions, 223, 226–28; morale, 228–29, 237–39, 274 (n. 27); music, 233–34; sexuality, 232; support troops' self-reflection, 237–38; weight gain, 229–30; working conditions, 222–23

—in Vietnam: as Alice in Wonderland, 193; arrival of, 103; and barracks décor, 83–84; as benefactors, 204–6; complaints of, 96–100; and corruption, 203–5, 214–15; drug use, 44, 201, 204; education, 124–25; electricity consumption, 85; as executioners, 202–3; expectations of, 10, 101–2, 106, 223–24; exploitation of Vietnamese civilians, 83, 204–11; individual experience, 6–8, 15–17; isolation from home, 185; isolation from war, 35, 37, 43–44, 182, 185–86, 190; as laborers, 11; and laundry, 82; as liberators, 202; living conditions, 31, 37–38, 73–74, 80–82; military pay, 176; morale of, 95–96, 141, 144; negative behaviors, 49, 108, 132, 198–200; noncombat roles, 27–29; oversupply of, 107; personal effects, 180–81; perspectives on food service, 79; and prostitution, 198, 207–11, 212, 271–72 (n. 46); public perceptions of, 14, 15; purchases, 156–57, 158, 161–63; radio, 188–89, 195; ratio of combat troops to support troops, 5, 6, 25; as redcoats, 239–41; respect for Vietnamese civilians, 205–6; role-playing, 200–203, 212–13; sexuality, 135, 207–11; and showers, 82; slang, 148, 190, 195–97; television, 132–34, 188–89; as tourists, 190–93, 194, 216–17, 220; as victims, 212, 219, 246; weight gain, 79–80; working conditions, 30–31, 41–44

University of Maryland, 125, 231

USO: clubs, 134; handshake tours, 127–28; shows, 125–26, 127, 140–41

Valley Forge, 68

Vann, John Paul, 15

Viet Cong. See National Liberation Front

Vietnam Combat Cycle, 58–59

Vietnamese civilians: casualties, 142; and consumerism, 178; contempt for Americans, 205; as open mess employees, 136; and refugee crisis, 83, 241; U.S. soldiers' exploitation of, 83, 204–11

Vietnam Open Mess Agency, 137

The Vietnam Photo Book, 29–30

Vietnam Regional Exchange, 149–50, 175; concern about smut in, 171–72; concessions, 161–63, 165; sales figures, 163, 165–66, 171–72. See also P.X.'s

—system of

Vietnam veterans, 59–64; homecoming, 178–79, 180, 213–14, 219; iconic, 60–61; media representations of, 60, 61; post-traumatic stress disorder among, 218, 273 (n. 68); postwar readjustment, 108; public perceptions of, 4–5; public's conflation of, with combat troops, 61, 62–63, 65; resentment of Vietnamese prostitutes, 210–11

Vietnam Veterans Against the War, 62–63

Vietnam Veterans Memorial, 9, 181

Vietnam War: and allusions to the Old West, 183, 194, 198; American casualties in, 9, 16–17; and American character, 240–41; and antiwar movement, 12–14, 88–89; atrocities, 13–14, 245; as carnival, 183–84; combat memoirs of, 40; commemoration of, 9; consumerism in, 147–48, 149, 223–24; corruption in, 203–4; distribution of danger in, 24, 26; effect on Vietnamese society, 31–32, 206–7; fetishization of violence in, 197–98; as first television war, 187–88; grunts as iconic soldiers in, 43–46; historical representations of, 8; influence on Iraq War, 242–43, 245; landscape, 16, 193–94; media coverage, 187–88; music in, 189, 195; as noble

struggle, 13, 19; noncombat memoirs of, 40–44; noncombat roles in, 27–29; in political rhetoric, 13; popular representations of, 8; purported lessons of, 141; refugee crisis, 83, 241; and U.S. military base development, 71, 72–73; U.S. military construction in, 71; U.S. military force structure in, 25–26; U.S. military logistics in, 69, 70, 74–80; U.S. policy in, 141–42; as wonderland, 193, 221
Vietnam Women's Memorial, 9
Vinh Moc, 142
VIP Center at Bien Hoa, 114
Vung Tau, 112–13

Waikiki East, 114
Warrior Ethos, 239, 274 (n. 28)

War trophies, 214–15, 220
Wayne, John, 100–102
Westmoreland, William, 71, 93–95
Winter Soldier Hearings, 14
Women: among American military casualties, 9, 250 (n. 7); in Iraq, 232; service club workers, 135; in Vietnam, 18
Working conditions of U.S. soldiers in Vietnam, 30–31, 41–44
World War I, 52, 84–85, 185, 191
World War II, 68, 70, 71, 85, 255 (n. 8)
Wunder Beach, 114

Ziggurat of Ur, 233
Zumwalt, Elmo, 95